UNIVERSITY
of
LEARNING

John Bowden and Ference Marton

RoutledgeFalmer
Taylor & Francis Group

LONDON AND NEW YORK

About the cover

The artwork is a unicolour reproduction of a tapestry, 150 × 120 cm, by Nina Kollind, Göteborg, 1986. Dedicated to Kjell Härnqvist, Vice-Chancellor for Göteborg University 1982–86. Photo by Mr Göran Olofsson.

Central University Building, Vasaparken, Göteborg, Sweden

First published in 1998 by Kogan Page Ltd

First published in paperback in 2004 by RoutledgeFalmer
11 New Fetter Lane, London EC4P 4EE

Simultaneously published in the USA and Canada
by RoutledgeFalmer
29 West 35th Street, New York, NY 10001

RoutledgeFalmer is an imprint of the Taylor & Francis Group

© 1998 John Bowden and Ference Marton

Typeset in Great Britain by Saxon Graphics Ltd, Derby
Printed and bound in Great Britain by TJ International Ltd, Padstow, Cornwall

British Library Cataloguing in Publication Data
A catalogue record for this book is available from the British Library

Library of Congress Cataloging in Publication Data
Available on Request

ISBN 0-7494-2292-0 (hardback)
ISBN 0-415-33491-8 (paperback)

Contents

Acknowledgements

This book appears just over a year after another related book appeared.[1] There are several connected ideas and there are quite a few examples that are included in both books, although in different versions. The former book clarifies much of the research foundations on which the present book builds. We believe it is a strength to have two books which genuinely complement each other. The same sentiment was expressed by Naomi Silverman, commissioning editor at Lawrence Erlbaum. We want to thank her for her supportive, generous and scholarly attitude.

We are also grateful to the TEND 97 conference organizers, especially Anthony Billingsley, at the Higher Colleges of Technology in the United Arab Emirates, for their generous agreement for material presented by John Bowden at TEND 97, which is included in this book.

The Department of Employment, Education, Training and Youth Affairs (DEETYA) in Australia, through Michael Gallagher, similarly agreed that material from their publication *Implications for Higher Education of a Competency-based Approach to Education and Training* (Bowden and Masters, 1993) could be included in this book. Our thanks to Michael and DEETYA.

As should be obvious from a reading of the book we have been heavily dependent on friendly colleagues from other disciplines, supplying us with rich examples. Our deeply felt gratitude to Norm Eizenberg, Colleen Johnson, Robyn Lines, Mats Martinsson, Airi Rovio-Johansson and Gerlese Åkerlind.

When writing a book you are also dependent on people with whom you can discuss all the difficulties you are struggling with. For their time, friendship, generosity and interest we would like to thank Berit Askling, Tom Angelo, Marianne Bauer, John Biggs, Li Bennich-Björkman, Shirley Booth, Margareta Boström, Gloria Dall'Alba, Ruth Dunkin, Noel Entwistle, Peter Fensham, Elaine Martin, Susan Marton, Lars-Erik Olsson, Michael Prosser, Bo Samuelsson,

---

1   Marton, F and Booth, S (1997) *Learning and Awareness* Mahwah, NJ, Lawrence Erlbaum

Jörgen Sandberg, Roger Säljö, Lee Shulman, Linda Thomas and Keith Trigwell.

The artwork reproduced on the cover of this book has been dedicated to Kjell Härnqvist, formerly Vice-Chancellor of Göteborg University (1981–86). Much of the original research in Göteborg carried out by Ference Marton and his research group came into being thanks to his support as the founding professor of the Department of Education and Educational Research. Jan Ling, who was Vice-Chancellor at the same University 1992–97, developed together with Marianne Dahlqvist and Ference Marton a vision statement for Göteborg University in which the concept of 'The University of Learning' was first formulated. The current Vice-Chancellor, Bo Samuelsson, is engaged in developing several of the ideas in the vision document.

John Bowden's experience with the development and implementation at RMIT University of its educational quality assurance system, its teaching and learning strategy and its vision for the future have had profound, formative influences on the writing of this book. It has been of immense value to have shared those experiences with a large number of inspiring, dedicated and talented colleagues, not least of whom is the RMIT Deputy Vice-Chancellor, Ruth Dunkin. A special thanks must go to Ruth Dunkin who, within a week and despite an already heavy workload, provided helpful, constructive comments on every chapter of the draft manuscript.

The work reported here was carried out with financial support from the Bank of Sweden Tercentenary Foundation through a grant to Ference Marton and from the Research on Higher Education Programme through a grant to Marianne Bauer and another grant to Ference Marton. Much of the writing was undertaken during a six-month study leave by John Bowden during 1997; the provision of that opportunity by RMIT is greatly appreciated, as was the willingness of Carmen Heliotis and the other staff of the Educational Programme Improvement Group at RMIT to carry extra load during that period.

Agneta Österlund had the courage, the skills and friendly spirit of mind to turn piles of scattered notes into parts of a book. Jane Schnittler provided central support, managed the production process and gave editorial comment on the whole manuscript, always with a quiet and reassuring calm, despite constantly disrupted timetables. This book would never have been completed without their heroic contributions. Thanks also to Josie Ryan and Sally Woollett for their graphic design and editorial support respectively.

Birgitta Marton shared the pain it takes to write a book. She should share the honour as well. Thanks Gittan! Mary Bowden also had to cope with the unpredictable and intrusive work and travel schedules of a husband-author. Her patience and resilience are always appreciated.

Throughout this project we have received helpful and friendly support from Kogan Page, especially Pat Lomax and Nicola Stephens. Our thanks go to them.

Preface

If this book has captured your attention enough for you to turn the cover, you might have reflected on the main title – *The University of Learning* – and it might have struck you as slightly odd. Of course, what else? Universities are about learning, aren't they? Well we would argue that this is not as self-evident as it may sound. If you ask people what a university is, most of them (at least most of those within a university) would say something like: 'It is a place for teaching and research' (or, perhaps, for 'teaching, research and community service'). We offer in this book an alternative, an apparently innocent, answer to that question: the university is a place for learning. This does not imply that the university is only a place for learning or that the university is the only place for learning (obviously we cannot argue that).

It is difficult to object to the statement above; that is why we refer to it as 'innocent'. In consequence it may appear to be a weak statement, but we do not think it is. We believe that, taken seriously, this statement has dramatic potential. We want to take this statement as our point of departure and ask questions such as: A place for what kind of learning? What kind of place for learning? What is learning, by the way? What should it be like? How is it brought about? Why should we learn?

Even if the statement we take as our point of departure is itself very much self-evident, taking it as a point of departure in dealing with the university is far from being so. The point we are making is this: the university does not have three aims, it has one. Teaching, research and service are all supposed to yield learning: for the individuals (through knowledge being formed which is new to a particular person), for humanity (through knowledge being formed which is new in an absolute sense) and for communities (through knowledge being formed for specific purposes). Hence the title *The University of Learning*.

When reading this book you will encounter discussions about bodies in uniform motion, computer languages, clinical decision making, the theory of evolution, planetary motion around the Sun, DNA, supply and demand, solving equations, Anne Frank's diary, acoustic design, and force and acceleration. This may seem curious. Isn't the book about learning and about the

University? Well, this is exactly what it is. Our central thesis is that learning is always the learning of something. Finding out about learning is for us to find out how what we learn is seen, experienced, understood, handled. When a new discovery is made in research, when students come across something important in their studies, when the community is served by developing knowledge profoundly relevant to its needs – in all these cases certain critical aspects of the phenomena dealt with are discerned and focused on simultaneously. Acts of discernment and focusing are common to forms of learning that are different in other respects: knowledge formation by means of studying, by means of research or by means of serving the community.

Most readers of this book will probably be university teachers, interested in learning, teaching and research. Let us assume that you belong to this group. Some of the most interesting questions about learning, teaching and research are likely to be about the historical and social evolution of the phenomena in your own field of knowledge – how the major breakthroughs have come about, and how these are understood and made sense of by your students and by your colleagues. Such questions are about the formation of knowledge in your own field; they represent the epistemological aspects of that field – in the widest sense. In the course of history the epistemological aspects have been separated from the fields of which they are aspects. The acts and processes of knowing have become separated from knowledge itself. We argue for their reunion. Learning, in the sense of formation of knowledge, should be a specialization within every domain of knowledge. In accordance with this, throughout the book we try to communicate a few powerful ideas (well, we think that they are powerful) using some considerably detailed examples. In each case, in each example, we describe how the particular content, the particular object of learning is seen, made sense of, handled, and what critical aspects are discerned and focused on simultaneously. In our view, this is what learning is about.

During the last decade or so universities around the world have been subject to increasing pressure to become accountable, more efficient – well, simply better. As an approach towards that end there have been attempts to define clearly the expected outcomes of learning, the competence, or the *competencies*, the university is supposed to develop in graduates. As another approach, there have been attempts to establish systems for quality development and *quality assurance*. While we share some basic principles with them, our fundamental objection to those two movements is that they represent attempts to improve learning without adequate, if any, inquiry into the nature of learning. Such an inquiry into learning and the implications of its results for universities is very much what this book is about. In this sense, we want to go beyond 'quality' and 'competence'.

It has been our ambition to link different levels in our inquiry. The first chapter examines the university as a societal organization for learning and provides a framework linking the various aspects of the book. Chapters 2, 3 and 4 raise basic questions about the different forms of learning (including research). The next three chapters (5, 6 and 7) deal with what we might call the pedagogy of higher education, while the last four chapters focus on the inner structure of the university, from the point of view of how its potential can be more fully realized.

There are different parts, different chapters, different topics, different examples – quite a lot in fact – in this book. But there is one idea running through it all. Learning – in the sense of knowledge formation – can be considerably facilitated by paying attention to how knowledge is formed within different fields, how new ways of seeing different phenomena are brought about, how critical aspects are discerned and focused on simultaneously.

Even more importantly, the university has a moral obligation. The collective cultural heritage of ideas, insights and memories, which it is expected to embrace and contribute to, is as essential to our existence as human beings as is the collective gene pool of the human race. All of us can claim ownership to our collective heritage – the cultural as well as the biological. But none more than another.

John Bowden and Ference Marton
March 1998

Note on the paperback edition

When the hardback edition of *The University of Learning* became out of stock, we seriously considered revising the manuscript for the new paperback edition and decided against doing so. We think the issues raised and the way they have been treated in the book are even more relevant today than they were in 1998.

We could have made some small additions in parts. For instance we could have included the more recent work on capabilities-driven curriculum design (Bowden, in press) and on variation theory (Marton, Tsui *et al*, 2003). However those recent publications are entirely consistent with, and build upon, the themes of the book and so we recommend that readers of the paperback edition access them directly.

John Bowden and Ference Marton
March 2003

Bowden, John A (forthcoming, April 2004) Capabilities-driven curriculum, in C Baillie and I Moore (eds) *Effective Learning and Teaching in Engineering*, Kogan Page, London

Marton, Ference, Tsui, Amy B M *et al* (2003) *Classroom discourse and the space of learning*, Lawrence Erlbaum, Mahwah, N J

Part One

A Place for Learning

Chapter 1

The idea of the university

The University of Teaching and the University of Research

In the late nineteenth century, well before the celebration was supposed to take place, a committee in Bologna chaired by the famous poet Giosué Carducci suggested 1888 as the eight-hundredth anniversary of the foundation of the University in Bologna. In fact no university had actually been founded in Bologna in 1088. The argument the committee put forward instead was that there was evidence for arrangements existing that year for teaching law independently of the religious schools of Bologna.

That still would not have made Bologna the first university because physicians were already being taught in a medical school in Salerno in the tenth century.[1] However, if the existence of a corporate body were taken as the sole criterion then Bologna would be the oldest university because, towards the end of the twelfth century, foreign students of law grouped themselves in nations, thereby forming the first organizational framework for a university. A short time later, in 1208, students and teachers of various disciplines formed a single corporate body in Paris. In the thirteenth century, associations of students in Bologna and associations of teachers and students in Paris were granted special liberties and privileges for the form of higher education called *studium generale*, which subsequently became the university (Rüegg, 1992).

There is a theme running through these examples. The medieval university was in fact the *University of Teaching*. It was not until the nineteenth century, with the foundation of the new university in Berlin in 1809, that Wilhelm von Humboldt introduced the concept of the *University of Research*, characterized by the interrelatedness of teaching and research, the independent status of staff (*Lehrfreiheit*) and students' free choice of subjects to study (*Lernfreiheit*).

In his inaugural lecture as the first elected rector of the new university in Berlin, Johan Gottlieb Fichte defined the university, in the elevated manner so characteristic for German idealism of his time, as '... the visible representation of humankind's immortality: the university is the institutional appearance of truth, the place where each age consciously and methodically hands down its highest intellectual formation to the coming ages' (Papastephanou, in press).

The University of Teaching and Research or the University of Learning

So universities at different times prior to the twentieth century can be characterized as Universities of Teaching or Universities of Research. During the twentieth century, the conjunction of teaching and research has become the most distinctive aspect of the university and today's university could be styled as the *University of Teaching and Research*. We argue in this book that, as we move into the twenty-first century, the university should be characterized as the *University of Learning*.

Teaching contributes to students' learning, to their developing knowledge, which is new to them but not necessarily new to others. On the other hand, research is about developing knowledge that is new in an absolute sense: nobody has developed it previously. We can therefore talk about two forms of *knowledge formation* – learning on the individual and learning on the collective level – and can then try to find the nature of the relationship between them, instead of looking for the relationship between teaching and research.

Student learning is not only, and probably not even mainly, a function of teaching; students develop knowledge by various means and teaching is simply one of those. Of course, developing entirely new knowledge is also a learning experience for those involved in its development. However, in research, human knowledge in its entirety is also widened and humanity learns, so that we can see research as resulting in learning on the collective level as compared to what students are doing, where the focus is on widening their own knowledge or learning on the individual level. If we accept the thesis that knowledge formation is the main task of the university and that knowledge formation comprises two forms of learning, the statement in the preface, 'the university is a place for learning' appears very reasonable.

The most passionate statement made about the idea of the university was formulated in 1873 by John Henry Newman, often referred to as 'Cardinal Newman'. In *The Idea of a University* he declares that a university is 'a place of teaching universal knowledge', thereby thoroughly challenging the Humboldtian notion of the research university. '[If the university is primarily about] scientific and philosophical discovery, I do not see why a University should have students' (Newman, 1873).

Much more recently Sheldon Rothblatt challenged the very idea that the university has an idea, that is, an essential kernel. He argues that at least the American university is no university at all. It is a *multiversity*, attempting to combine all the different ideas of the university. Highly sensitive to whatever might be imposed upon it '... from above by a central administrative system and a board of trustees, or outside in the form of public opinion or legislative pressure, it is carrying out... on a single campus the functions of the polytechnic, a normal school, a college of arts and crafts, a technological college, law and medical schools, a business school, research institutes and departments, College of Letters and Science (or College of Arts and Sciences) ...' (Rothblatt, 1997). The American university is not so much '... a city on the hill, an outpost of dedication and devotions [but more like] a city of the plain, culturally and ethnically heterogeneous, full of milling crowds, jugglers and tumblers... with suburbs and sub-cultures, separate neighbourhoods, galleries, concert halls and museums' (Rothblatt, 1997).[2]

In response to Rothblatt's formidable assault on the idea of 'the idea of the university' we would argue that learning is the defining element of the university. We cannot conceive the university without the element of learning. But in order to distinguish it from other institutions dealing with learning, such as the school, we would add that it combines learning on the collective and individual level, that is, it comprises both research and studying, or at least it is an interface between the two, by making knowledge developed by the few available to the many.

Conceptualized in this way the university is not primarily about the reproduction of the collective mind (ie the complex of all the different ways in which we are capable of thinking about the world), but it is about expanding, widening and transforming the collective mind. The Humboldtian concept of *Bildung* refers to the process of self-formation, that is how individuals form and transform themselves. In analogy with this, the university is the most vital instrument in the process by which the collective mind is formed and transformed through its diverse ways of grasping the world.

The collective mind is universal in the sense that it cuts across and comprises cultural differences distributed in space as well as in time. The collective mind is the home of everyone: we all contribute to it, we live it, we are it. The different ways of thinking about the world are all linked together. We can grow into them and we can embody them but they always transcend the individual bearers. In this sense none is greater, none is lesser.

The university is frequently said to have three main functions: teaching, research and community service. The third of these tasks has been appropriately labelled by the current Swedish Minister of Education, Carl Tham, as 'the third task'. This refers to being oriented to, co-operating with and serving the society of which the university is a part. In our view, this is also achieved by bringing about learning on the collective and individual level. The third task is not so much about doing something different, but more about doing what the university does anyway, except doing it for and with particular individuals or groups in the community (Tydén, 1997 made this very point recently). It is about serving more immediate community interests, therefore we might refer to it as *learning at the local level*.

We have therefore chosen learning – learning with certain characteristics – as the critical feature of the university. Although informed by past and present practices, it is a definition that we are asserting. This is what we think the university should be like.

If we accept this definition, which this book is here to develop, we may find that no existing institutions of higher education are entirely about learning and that none are entirely without it. So, in spite of what we said about distinguishing universities from schools, our definition cannot be used for sorting current institutions of higher education into those which are universities and those which are not. But we can use the definition for sorting out components of institutions of higher education which are university-like and those which are not. Accordingly, we would like to contribute to making all institutions of higher education more like 'universities of learning'.

Defining the university in terms of the conjunction between teaching and research goes back to the traditional European university with a professor, surrounded by a fairly small group of disciples, engaged in lectures, discussions, sitting in the sun, and drinking beer perhaps. The professors were keen on talking about their own research, and the traditional professor was the conjunction of teaching and research.

But the traditional professor is not around any more. During this century the number of students has increased exponentially, while the size of the staff has not grown in proportion. Moreover, we are at the dawn of a more electronically distributed and internationalized higher education. So the relationship between different levels of learning (collective and individual) cannot rest on face-to-face contact. Rather, this relationship has to be maintained in the space of ideas: with students learning new ways of seeing, including recent additions to collective learning, through any of a range of means, from human to electronic.

Learning

The most important thing about institutional forms of learning, such as studying at university, is that they are supposed to prepare students for handling situations in the future, situations which are often very much unlike the situations in which students are being prepared. These future situations are more or less unknown. The more rapidly the world changes, the less can be said about them and the more unknown they become. And the world is changing more and more rapidly, many would say. The instrument we have for preparing students for an increasingly unknown future is our current knowledge. We have to prepare them for the unknown, by means of the known and we have to work out how that can be done.

We are trying to enable students to engage in effective action in relation to purposes and criteria which they have accepted as their own. This action takes place in various situations, and each situation can be viewed in different ways. We act and react to a situation as we see it and the way we see it decides how we act. Effective action requires an effective way of seeing. The central point of this book is that the most important form of learning is that which enables us to see something in the world in a different way. We see effectively when we discern the aspects of the situation critical to our acts and take them into consideration, often all of them at the same time. This is further explained in the remainder of this chapter, but more completely in Chapter 2.

We can prepare our students for effective action by enabling them to see certain situations in certain ways. By developing their seeing, by developing the eyes through which they see things: the photographer's eyes, the physician's eyes, the forester's eyes. New ways of seeing might occasionally replace old ways of seeing. Once we have seen a pattern in an ambiguous picture it may be difficult to 'unsee' it. This is nicely illustrated by a student talking about an experience of understanding:

> Understanding is the interconnection of lots of disparate things – the way it all hangs together. The feeling that you understand how the whole thing is connected up – you can make sense of it internally... It is as though one's mind has finally 'locked in' to the pattern... If you *really* understand something, why it works, and what the idea is behind it, you cannot *not* understand it afterwards – you cannot *'de-understand'* it!(Entwistle and Entwistle, 1992)

Mostly however, by learning, we widen the range of possibilities of seeing the same thing. Our world grows richer and we have more options for our actions. Not all learning is of this kind of qualitative shift. But it is the kind of learning we are dealing with in this book and throughout the chapters we argue why it is important and discuss how it can be brought about.

We need to consider what it means to see something in a certain way. An effective way of seeing a situation means that all the aspects of the situation which are necessary for handling it effectively are discerned and are taken into consideration. In general, a way of seeing can be characterized in terms of aspects discerned and taken into consideration. Or, even more simply, in terms of a particular pattern of aspects.

Whether or not some particular aspects of a situation are discerned makes the difference between one way of seeing the situation and another, a qualitatively different way of seeing it. Why is it then that a particular aspect is discerned by some, but not by others? Answering this question amounts to answering (at least partially) the question of why we see things differently and why we act differently.

To discern an aspect is to differentiate among the various aspects and focus on the one most relevant to the situation. Without variation there is no discernment. We do not think in a conscious way about breathing until we get a virus or walk into a smoke-filled room. Learning in terms of changes in or widening of our ways of seeing the world can be understood in terms of discernment, simultaneity and variation. Thanks to the variation, we experience and discern critical aspects of the situations or phenomena we have to handle and, to the extent that these critical aspects are focused on simultaneously, a pattern emerges. Thanks to having experienced a varying past we become capable of handling a varying future.

Approaches to learning

Students do not react to the learning environment as such, they react to the learning environment as it is experienced by them. They experience the learning environment in accordance with their way of handling it – or the other way around: they handle the learning environment in accordance with their experience of it. This is just another example of the dialectical relationship between ways of seeing (in this case, experiencing the learning situation) and ways of acting (in this case, handling the learning situation). Approaches to learning comprise both. Differences between approaches to learning are differences in what the learners are focusing on, what they are trying to achieve and how they are going about it.

When adopting a *surface approach* to learning, the learners are focusing on surface characteristics of the situation, on the very wording of a text being read, of the argument put forward, on figures in a problem, on formulas to be used for solving the problem. They want to be able to answer the questions they are anticipating and they will probably fail even though they are trying so hard (they would also fail, of course, if they did not try at all). They will fail because they are not focusing on the meaning of the text.

When adopting a *deep approach* to learning the learners are focusing on the object of learning, they are trying to get hold of the phenomenon dealt with in the text they are reading or in the presentation they are listening to. In problem solving they are initially trying to grasp the problem. And, paradoxically enough, because they do not immediately aim at being able to recall a text or to come up with an answer to the problem given, they will probably be better off when it comes to recalling the text or solving the problem.

The approaches students adopt to different situations relate to the nature of their *project* at university – on the one hand, what kind of meaning studying there carries for them, what their conception of learning is and, on the other hand, their understanding of what the institution wants them to do and what view of learning its way of acting reflects. The nature of student approaches to learning is the focus of Chapter 3.

The quality of the outcomes of learning is functionally related to the approaches adopted by the learners. As we pointed out above, those who are trying to get hold of the object of learning are much more likely to succeed than those who are not trying at all to do so. Approaches to learning are related, in turn, to the perceived demand characteristics of the situation, what students feel is required of them by the institution. Further, the views of learning embodied in and explicitly or implicitly expressed by the institution are affected by, and at the same time affect, the views of learning among those being associated with it: politicians, staff, administrators and students. Achieving our goals and bringing about the quality of learning intended therefore requires considerable consistency in the views of learning held by those involved.

Research

Through the learning of the kind we have discussed so far, the individual student's horizon is widened. This kind of learning changes the borders between knowledge and ignorance, between what the student knows and does not know.

Some research – but far from all – has a similar effect on the collective landscape. It changes the borderline between what is known (by some at least) and what is not. For those who bring such a change about this is a change on the individual level as well: they have learned something and this learning has certain characteristics in common with the learning discussed above. A pattern of critical features of some phenomenon is discovered; it is seen in a new way.

A main element, or the main element, in all great discoveries is the discernment of critical aspects of the problem, a strong sense of the significance of certain observations or certain features, long before the rational reasons of the significance are obvious. There are always 'taken-for-granteds' in the research community which are not taken for granted by the discoverer. There are new dimensions opened up, there is always a pattern arrived at eventually: there are meaningful relations between the parts and features. What was not seen before is now able to be seen and what was seen before is now seen differently. Kuhn (1970) has written about scientific research in this way.

Learning, research, scholarship

There are important similarities between what we describe as essential forms of learning and common forms of research, which is, after all – as was pointed out above – a particular kind of learning.

The difference between learning in the context of studies and learning in the context of path-breaking research is not just that the latter yields knowledge which is new in an absolute sense, while the former yields knowledge which is new for the learner. Nor are these differences only in the level of sophistication. There are, above all else, differences in time scale, differences in what happens over time and differences in what one is trying to do. Major breakthroughs in research are fruits of what has taken place not only during some years, but often during decades. In research, one is frequently moving in much wider circles in much narrower fields. The object of learning is more constrained in research, the acts of learning are less so. Trying to find out something that nobody has found previously is different from trying to find out what somebody else has found out earlier.

Once again, the similarity lies in the fact that by discerning certain related aspects of a phenomenon, seeing them at the same time, by discovering the pattern they form, we see the phenomenon – in an important sense – in the same way as someone else who had discerned and focused on the same pattern of aspects. The University of Learning is about widening our ways of viewing the world, both individually and collectively.

Research is not the only way in which we can expand the frontiers of knowledge. There are other ways, even within the university. Boyer (1990) talks about the original sense of *scholarship* as creative engagement in producing knowledge, in bringing learning about. In addition to scholarship in the sense of engaging in original research, the scholarship of *discovery*, there are three other forms of scholarship. The scholarship of *integration* involves stepping back from one's investigation, looking for connections; interpreting, fitting one's own research, or the research of others, into larger intellectual patterns. The scholarship of *application* comes close to the third task of the university – service to society: 'How can knowledge be responsibly applied to consequential problems? How can it be helpful to individuals as well as institutions? And further: Can social problems *themselves* define an agenda for scholarly investigation?' (Boyer, 1990).

Just like Boyer, we too prefer using the term 'application' in a wider sense than is usually the case. In addition to asking 'how can our knowledge be used to solve problems outside the university?', we ask: 'how can we develop knowledge for dealing with questions formulated outside the university?' Serving the interests of 'the larger community' can bring about learning not only in the individual, but also in the collective sense: genuinely new and fundamentally important knowledge might be produced.

Boyer talks also about the scholarship of *teaching* and he quotes Aristotle: 'Teaching is the highest form of understanding'. As a scholarly enterprise, teaching involves the development of new knowledge through the building of bridges between the teacher's understanding and the students' learning and through teachers learning from the students about their learning. Teaching at its best means not only – and not even primarily – transmitting knowledge, but enabling it to be transformed and extended as well.

All four forms of scholarship can bring about learning, both on the individual and on the collective level. This gives further support to our suggestion that we define the mission of the university in terms of the learning it brings about, in the three different senses mentioned previously – individual, collective and local – instead of defining it in terms of teaching, research and service. The linkages between learning on these three levels are discussed further in Chapter 4.

Competence and competencies

In accordance with the line of reasoning above, there has been an increased pressure on universities in recent years to live up to demands coming from outside the university. Some of the demands concern the kind of outcomes that universities are producing, in terms of student learning. Universities are expected to develop capabilities which enable graduates to function efficiently in the workplace, for instance. Accordingly, outcomes are being defined in relation to the needs of working life within different professions, independently of the specific educational arrangements that might produce these outcomes. This is the idea of the competency movement: for each profession a number of necessary competencies should be identified and it is argued that educational institutions should then be judged in terms of the extent to which they develop these competencies in their graduates.

We, too, believe that what universities are supposed to achieve, and what they are achieving, should be expressed in terms of the learning that they are expected to bring about and the learning that they actually bring about. Such a description is an alternative to describing the kinds of course the students have to take, how many contact hours they will have, what books they have to read and how the teaching is arranged. In common with the competency movement, we have the idea of defining learning in terms of expected and achieved outcomes, rather than in terms of educational inputs. But we argue that outcomes described in terms of narrowly defined units of professional behaviour, derived from what professionals currently are believed to be capable of doing, is not appropriate. Education is about the future, not the present.

Graduates are going to face a great variety of situations in their professional lives. We cannot grasp this variation in advance, nor do we have to. What is effective action varies from situation to situation. We cannot therefore specify competence just in terms of what a person can do. Effective action springs from the way the situation is seen, as we mentioned previously and ways of seeing can be understood in terms of aspects of the situation discerned and attended to simultaneously. So what the student should learn, above all, is to focus on critical aspects of professional situations. Now, while the set of the different things one may need to do is practically unlimited, the set of critical aspects to pay attention to is not. The capability of discerning and focusing on critical aspects of situations and seeing the patterns characterizing those situations is a far more holistic capability than those commonly defined in competency-based approaches. Moreover, such holistic capabilities represent the links between disciplinary knowledge and professional skills. They are results of the transformation of the eyes through which the professional world is seen, brought about in, and by, the scholarly world. We deal with these ideas in considerable detail in Chapter 5 and provide a lengthy illustration of how the curriculum can be designed to meet these needs.

Designing learning environments

For centuries the focus in universities has been on teaching rather than on learning. Accordingly, discussions about optimal learning environments have been phrased in terms of the pros and cons of different teaching methods, such as lectures, seminars, working in groups, problem-based learning or project-directed learning, among others. But face-to-face teaching is only one of the means by which learning is brought about and is decreasing in importance with the rise of more flexible, more electronically distributed, more open, more learner-controlled forms of learning.

We argued above that the capability of seeing certain things in certain ways amounts to the capability of discerning certain aspects and attending to them all at the same time. Discernment in its turn is a function of the variation experienced by the learner. So the capability of discerning certain aspects and patterns of certain aspects derives from having encountered variation in those aspects and in the combination of those aspects. Again, as we will argue in Chapter 2, the only way of mastering variation in the yet unknown future is by having met variation in the now known past. Regardless of the teaching method or educational arrangement used, variation must be present in the learning environment in dimensions corresponding to the aspects students have to become capable of discerning.

Differences of importance in this particular respect are not so much to be found between different teaching methods, but between patterns of dimensions of variation that characterize different learning environments. Such patterns cannot be derived from any general principles or theories of learning and instruction (the idea of focusing on such patterns is of course derived from our own general conjectures about learning), as they are specific for the specific object or aim of learning. So when it comes to teaching, for instance, the question of how the specific object or aim of learning is dealt with is more important than what general teaching method is being used. For this reason Chapter 6 is called 'Bringing learning about' rather than 'Teaching' or 'Teaching methods'.

The assessment of learning

One of the greatest problems in institutional forms of learning is that students study for the tests and exams, instead of studying to grasp the object of learning and instead of studying for life. The surface approach described briefly above (and in detail in Chapter 3) is a reflection of this. A somewhat surprising idea to deal with this problem has been put forward by the performance-based assessment movement (much of the competency movement's approach to assessment draws on these ideas): students should study for the tests!

This seems to be a contradiction – the solution to the problem is the problem itself. This appears to be so simple because the phrase 'study for the tests' has a different meaning in each case. In the latter case, the argument is that the test should be a true test of achievement of the intended learning outcome. Tests should be more or less identical with the goals of learning. If you want to earn a driver's licence, for instance, you have to learn to drive. And this is exactly what you do when you are tested: you drive. Similarly in sports: you prepare for the test. A race is a test of who is fastest and the only way of 'passing the test' is by being fast, and becoming fast is just what you want to become, what you are training for.

On the other hand, not all tests or exams are of this kind. Often they assess learning not necessarily associated with the intended performance. The point of studying at university may be to become an effective and competent nurse. But being good at exams, testing knowledge of anatomy or physiology, may reflect something which is different from – or perhaps even unrelated to – capabilities in nursing. To the extent that this is true, students can focus on 'making the grade' without necessarily developing capabilities of vital importance for their professional future. The idea of performance-based assessment is to make tests and exams 'authentic'. This implies that students should simply be tested on the very tasks of their future professions. So nurses should be tested in 'nursing situations', engineers should be tested in 'engineering situations' and so forth.

Such an approach lends itself more or less easily to different kinds of study orientations. 'Authentic assessments' come along more naturally when it is reasonable to judge students' capabilities based on a product. A budding photographer takes photos. It seems reasonable enough to judge their capabilities for taking photos on the basis of their photos. In the same way, in order to earn a PhD you have to produce some research. Your capabilities of doing research are judged in terms of the research you have done. In other cases the question of authentic assessment is quite a bit trickier. When it comes to your capabilities of handling varying situations it is hard to avoid the reality that the situation of assessment is likely to be, at least a lot of the time, a *simulation* of a real-life situation and not a real-life situation. Furthermore, there might be a problem with the sampling of situations. The one, or the ones, used for assessment purposes may not be representative at all for the wide range of situations the professionals have to handle in working life.

We argued earlier that our capability of handling sets of situations derives from the capability of discerning and focusing on the aspects of those situations which are critical for effective action, and then being able to handle them simultaneously to achieve an appropriate outcome. Authentic assessment would aim, in our view, precisely at finding out whether or not students manage to demonstrate such capabilities, at least under the circumstances given.

Again, with respect to assessment, we share a view with the competency movement that we should be assessing students' capacity to undertake tasks which they will have to perform in their future professional roles. However, we do differ in our ideas about how those tasks and capacities should be defined, and this is a fundamental difference.

If we manage to capture the central elements of scholarly or professional competence for the purpose of certification then it should not matter by what means students have developed their capabilities. Assessment for the purpose of certification should be separate from teaching or other arrangements for the development of capabilities – in this we side with the competency movement. This does not mean that judgements about progress in the development of these capabilities (formative assessment) should not be a part of teaching. As a matter of fact, they should. But the development of capabilities will then be more clearly seen as a joint project of staff and students. All the judgements made, all diagnostic or formative assessments carried out within the framework of the teaching and learning arrangements, will be carried out for the sake of the enhancement of learning and not for the sake of control. The consequences for forms of assessment are discussed in Chapter 7.

Collective consciousness and the ethics of learning

Judgements of the above kind have to be based, of course, on what teachers learn from, and about, students. More generally, in order to find out what it takes to be capable of handling certain situations, one has to study the variation in how those situations are handled and perceived. This is because – as we pointed out earlier – the most fundamental aspects of the capabilities are taken for granted by those in positions of relative power, such as the nominal experts – the teachers. These taken-for-granted aspects become obvious only through the contrasts inherent in the variation.

This means that not only do students have to learn from teachers but teachers have to learn from students as well. Learning from other people means that we become aware of their ways of seeing things, regardless of whether or not we are convinced by, or appropriate, their ways of seeing. We can talk about a *collective consciousness*, an awareness of others' ways of seeing things, as linking individual consciousnesses to each other. From this point of view it is highly relevant for students to learn from each other, as it is for teachers to learn from other teachers. We become aware of our own way of seeing something as a way of seeing only through the contrast with other ways of seeing the same thing.

Our views of a certain phenomenon can therefore be shared or they can be complementary. Combining differing views implies richer, more powerful, ways of understanding a phenomenon or a situation and is likely to offer more options for handling varying conditions.

A higher level of collective consciousness seems to enhance research as well. The optimal situation seems to be a group of people having the object of research in common and adopting somewhat varying perspectives on this object. The collective consciousness therefore established appears to be a very powerful means of bringing about learning on the collective level.

In a university as a whole there are a great number of varying objects of learning and research. We could think of collective consciousness across different objects and across disciplinary boundaries. Students learn about different objects of learning and different disciplinary fields in their studies. To a much more limited extent, researchers who are dealing with similar phenomena in different fields, or vice versa, could be seen as connecting those phenomena and fields. It depends on the level of interaction and sharing among those researchers.

Within the western cultural tradition, the power of research rests very much with specialization. On the other hand, this same focus on specialization may be an inhibiting factor, because breakthroughs often occur at the boundaries between different fields of knowledge. Researchers, too, need to be open to new ways of seeing if research is to be a truly rich source of collective and individual learning. Since collective consciousness is, to a large extent, an awareness of different and complementary ways of seeing, we need to develop a richer, more flexible understanding of the world around us with a greater potential for new ways of seeing to evolve, without blurring the precision of specialized, particular ways of seeing.

This line of reasoning presupposes respect for different and complementary views of phenomena or situations, whether these views are expressed by students or by our colleagues. This celebration of diversity and variation is closely related to the ethical stance that although certain ways of seeing certain things are more powerful than others in certain situations and in relation to certain criteria, all the different ways not only contribute to the richness of our world, they constitute that world.

A profound respect for other people's views, and in fact a profound respect for other people, is inherent in the view of learning we are advocating. Furthermore, we believe that the scientific enterprise as a whole is suggestive of the principle of tolerance: scholarship cannot exist without the realization that you can be wrong! This will be discussed further in Chapter 8.

Quality and qualities

Society has become more concerned in recent decades with what universities achieve within their growing budgets. The university as a highly autonomous institution is being replaced by an institution which has to prove its account-ability. On the whole there has been an increasing concern with the quality of the work that is being undertaken at universities: does society get value for money?

From our point of view the term 'quality' refers to the quality of learning brought about within the university, both in the sense of entirely new knowl-edge and in the sense of learning about something already known. Readers will see more of these ideas in Chapter 9.

To the extent that quality arrangements in industry focus on the quality of the processes by which products are brought about, the product is well defined in advance and one has to optimize the conditions under which it is produced. Other products and services may not be so easily defined in advance. Higher education outcomes are in the latter category. In research we cannot precisely define the product ahead of time. The product itself is, in a way, the definition of the product. And this is exactly what we are trying to come up with: the solutions to the problem, the answer that is developed. Research is successful to the extent that we are able to declare what it has produced. The quality of research has, of course, also to do with the quality of the answer we have come up with: is it convincing, interesting, fruitful?

What studying is supposed to yield is not easy to define, either. In this book we are arguing for considering the development of 'ways of seeing' as the most important form of learning. What we refer to as ways of seeing are usually taken for granted by the scholars and appropriated to a limited extent by students. The paradoxical fact is that the more fundamental a layer of knowledge is, the less visible it is. The more important the knowledge is, the less likelihood there is of even noticing it. Such taken-for-granted ways of seeing become visible if we pay close attention to students' ways of reasoning and see them in relation to each other and to alternative ways of reasoning – the teacher's for instance. The most important thing we can do in order to develop, raise or assure the quality of the learning produced in higher education is to reveal the kind of learning we should bring about, the ways of seeing we think it is important for students to develop, for instance. Expected outcomes have to be found and finding them is by far the most important step towards bringing them into being. We have more to say on this issue in Chapters 2 and 11.

The organization of learning

If we accept the idea of the university as a purpose-driven organization, if we accept the idea that the main purpose of the university is to produce learning on the individual level as well as on the collective level, if we accept the idea that the most fundamental form of learning enables us to see phenomena or situations in new ways, thereby widening the world we experience, if we accept the idea that ways of seeing can be understood in terms of what aspects are discerned and focused on simultaneously, if we accept the idea that discernment is a function of the variation experienced – then all this should have implications for the ways in which learning is organized.

The aims, as well as the achievements, of the university should be described in terms of the learning that is expected to be brought about and in terms of the learning that has been brought about. Budgetary processes should be driven by learning aims and results, not by the means used to achieve them. In such a system there should be much greater flexibility for the staff to choose means but there should also be much greater flexibility for students to choose their paths through the system.

By being clear about what we are trying to achieve and about what we have achieved, the university would become not only the University of Learning but also a Learning University. We could see the effects of the measures taken and of the options chosen. We would also be better off when it comes to forming alliances with other universities, choosing educational tools and making our work more transparent to other parties. All this simply because we would have a better idea of what we want and could then explain it better to others. And we would have better grounds for evaluating alternative means or arrangements. We will discuss this further in Chapter 10.

The University of Learning

The above line of reasoning implies that the kind of learning we want to bring about, and the kind of learning we do bring about, should be the point of departure for keeping track of how we are doing, for designing learning environments, for the kind of studying intended, for how learning is assessed and organized. Learning aims and learning outcomes should constitute the driving force of the university.

In a general sense we have a strong view on what the fundamental forms of learning are, the forms of learning which should make up the primary aims. We will even argue that we have a pretty clear idea of how this kind of learning can be brought about.

At the same time we want to argue that in a specific sense, in particular cases, we do not know, that we cannot know, what critical aspects of phenomena or situations the student should become able to discern and take into consideration simultaneously. We cannot know, but these aspects are likely to be able to be found within each field, and finding them is by far the most important step we all, within our various fields, can take towards dramatically improving the quality of learning at universities.

The critical aspects of phenomena or situations to be discovered correspond to dimensions of variation that are constituent parts of the architecture of domains of knowledge – disciplinary or professional. They can only be found by those who have a mastery of those knowledge domains. Such mastery is a necessary but not sufficient condition for discovering the critical aspects. In addition, a focus on the processes through which knowledge is formed is needed. Discernment, simultaneity and variation have to do with the formation of knowledge and they are not present in an obvious way in the knowledge produced. But we have to remember that making use of knowledge in future, novel situations take an understanding of those situations, it requires the forming of knowledge about them. Living knowledge always includes a capability of forming knowledge.

Questions about knowledge formation in a certain domain of knowledge – whether disciplinary or professional – should be regarded as a part or aspect of that domain. It should be something that people in that field deal with and about which some of them develop specific interests and capabilities. It should be a part of the studies of that domain as well – from the first introductory course to doctoral training. If this were to come true, questions about knowledge formation in different fields would become common topics of daily conversations, objects of systematic inquiry, a lever for raising the quality of learning on the individual and the collective levels.

The acts of knowledge formation – at least some of them – are generalizable across disciplinary or professional boundaries as well as across widely differing levels of sophistication, even if the actual knowledge formed varies vastly. Being aware of and focusing on the acts of knowledge formation have the potential to link people across those boundaries, thereby dramatically increasing the collective consciousness and releasing the power inherent in the differing views, perspectives, experiences and insights of all the people of the university. We end the book in Chapter 11 with a discussion of this vision.

Endnotes

1. Not to speak of other and much more ancient sites of higher learning such as Athens, Rome, Alexandria, Constantinople or China for that matter. A Han Emperor set up an institution within the court, for research students, called Taixue (able to be interpreted as 'the national university'), in 124 BC (Fairbank, 1992).

2. Still, it is in France where you find the clearest counter-example to the idea of the university, Rothblatt claims. In the most centralized of all Western European systems of higher education its institutions are virtually disembodied he says:

Different government ministries, external councils, agencies and disciplinary boards, regional as well as national, prescribe and regulate teaching, research, curricula, examinations and degrees. Budgets are handled discretely. Research and teaching are separated and placed in separate institutional structures, with a few crossovers (Rothblatt, 1997).

Part Two

Aspects of Learning

Chapter 2

What does it take to learn?

Learning in the sense of studying implies exploring paths in the landscape of knowledge that have been charted by others, with the charts being known to many. The knowledge developed is new for the individual, but probably not for others (such as the teachers). Therefore this learning is on the individual level.

Raising questions about learning

Better learning

Imagine a university that wholeheartedly aims for better learning and outcomes than it has achieved in the past, by finding improved ways of enhancing learning than it had found earlier. Let us also imagine that its approach springs from an open-minded and enlightened way of thinking about learning. We believe that such an approach would begin with the question of what 'better learning' is supposed to achieve.

So-called 'natural learning' is a by-product of the learners' participation in social practices (growing up on a farm or being a party-goer, for instance). These social practices do not have learning as their primary aim. Their aim might be the production of goods or services, or simply having fun. By trying to contribute to work or entertainment, for example, people become better at work or at entertaining each other. Such forms of learning were the main, or only, forms of learning in pre-industrial societies. Recently they have become objects of attention in the educational research community and have been referred to as instances of authentic learning (for example, Brown, Collins and Duguid, 1989).

Learning in a university is different, because the act of learning is usually separated from the social practices in which 'natural' learning is embedded. How can we work out what better learning in the university context should be? This is what this chapter is about, but we should let readers know that in laying the foundation for this book by elaborating our understanding of what this 'better learning' is about, we have had to be fairly comprehensive and detailed.

The remainder of the chapter follows a sequence by outlining the structure of our argument. In the next section we will focus on what we find to be a decisive feature of learning at universities. They are supposed to equip students with capabilities for dealing with situations in the future, about which we know little.

In the second part of the chapter we present an outline of a theory of learning which solves the paradox that we are trying to prepare students in institutionalized forms of learning for what is unknown (the future) by using what is known (our present knowledge). What is critical for handling novel situations is the way in which they are experienced, because anything that the learner finds relevant or applicable to the situation is in relation to the situation as it is experienced. The kind of learning we are interested in is learning which implies that the learners develop capabilities for seeing or experiencing situations or phenomena in certain ways. For every kind of situation and phenomenon it is possible to identify a limited number of distinctively different ways in which the situation or that phenomenon can be experienced. The differences between different ways of seeing a particular phenomenon (or a particular class of situation) can be understood in terms of the critical aspects that define the phenomenon (or situation) as experienced. For each phenomenon there is a limited number of critical aspects that can be discerned and focused on simultaneously. So differences in how the phenomenon is experienced reflect differences in what critical aspects are discerned and focused on simultaneously.

So, why is a certain aspect discerned and focused on while another is not? Discernment springs from the experience of variation; as later examples will show; what does not vary cannot be discerned. Students can therefore be prepared for the unknown variation among situations in the future through experiencing variation in their education (which will enable them to discern critical aspects of novel situations).

Learning is described here in terms of (changes in) capabilities for experiencing and being aware of the object of learning. Experience and awareness are not only characterized by aspects that are focused on, but also by what is not focused on (but is present). A further potential difference is the point of view or perspective from which something is seen.

Even if the core of our sketch for a theory is formulated in terms of the learner's experience of the object of learning, there are other, in a sense, wider aspects of learning as well. Some of these are dealt with in the third part of this chapter ('Beyond the object of learning') in which the taken-for-granted nature of our views of the world around us, the experience of the object of learning as compared to the experience of the act of learning, and learning as seen from the point of view of a wider temporal context, are dealt with.

Learning for an unknown future

We previously mentioned that, besides 'natural' learning, there are other forms of learning and we are interested in particular in institutionalized forms. These are societal arrangements for bringing learning about. Accordingly, their aim is precisely learning; enhancing the capabilities of children or students. This is what is supposed to happen in schools and universities.

All forms of institutional learning suffer from one, substantial dilemma, as old as institutional learning itself. While the aims of so-called authentic practices (within which natural learning is supposed to take place) are very much located within those practices, when it comes to 'less authentic practices', their aims are outside of themselves. The existence of schools and universities is justified by reference to the fact – or rather to the hope – that they are enabling students to handle situations other than the ones which they are using to gain that capability.

All this leads to the general question: how can you bring about capabilities in people in one situation which they are supposed to make use of in other situations? This is recognized as the classical problem of *transfer* in the psychology of learning (ie the question of what the learner carries from the situation of learning to other situations).

If we contemplate this issue briefly but intensely, we might end up with the conclusion that transfer is a pretty redundant concept. Anything you learn, you must make use of in other situations. You can never re-enter the very situation which gave birth to learning. Transfer is involved in every instance of learning; questions of transfer are simply questions of learning. And, if so, you do not need the concept of transfer of course. It is redundant.

This point was made by the Norwegian psychologist, Jan Smedslund, more than four decades ago (Smedslund, 1953). There is, however, another remark to be made on transfer. The framing of the problem is questionable on other grounds as well. Sorting situations into two categories – learning situations on the one hand and situations of application on the other – seems hard to defend. Every 'learning situation' includes the potential for application (of something learned previously) and every 'situation of application' implies the potential for learning (something new).

Even if we want to do away with the concept of transfer, we do not want to do away with the entire line of reasoning as mentioned above. Surely there are institutionalized forms of learning, which are very much about preparing students for situations ahead, and surely there are situations outside educational institutions in which former students are expected to draw on the knowledge they supposedly have acquired inside educational institutions. The most important thing is that there are differences between situations of various kinds. There are differences between situations within educational institutions (this is one form of variation), there are differences between situations outside educational institutions (another form of variation) and there are differences between the two classes of situations (a third form of variation). Interesting issues are the extent and nature of these different sorts of variation, and the possible relationships between them.

People are expected to appropriate knowledge (make knowledge their own) in the hope that in doing so they will be better able to master situations in the future which are impossible to define in advance. The faster society changes, both technologically and culturally, the greater differences we can expect to find between the situations in which institutionalized forms of learning are taking place and those in which people will be making use of what they have learned. Architecture and accountancy are two professions in which practitioners without computer skills now confront many clients who have technology-based materials. Nurses who undertook training decades ago now find themselves in a completely changed set of personal relationships with other health professionals and patients. In both cases, successful professional performance cannot rely on particular practices learned decades ago. For all professions, the pace of technological change and the shifts in the nature of the relationships between professionals and clients mean that a narrowly based professional education that focuses on skills in particular practices will not serve the individual well for very long.

We consider the second form of variation (between situations outside educational institutions). The higher the rate of change in society the less we can say about the situations students of today are going to face tomorrow. The greater the dynamics of the working place, the greater our ignorance of what it is going to be like in the years ahead. Or, to put it differently, the greater is the expected variation of the second kind, ie the greater are the potential differences between the situations we are trying to prepare students for.

We can express the same idea in yet another way. The future is, necessarily, always unknown but there are degrees of uncertainty. We would like to argue that the future we are preparing our students for is becoming less and less transparent, or more and more unknown. And what are the tools we can use? They are our knowledge, what we know and what is known. So, we are trying to prepare our students for the unknown by using what is known. A question – or rather the question – is then: 'how can this be done?' The general view seems to be that the rate of change keeps increasing and, to the extent that this is so, this dilemma of learning is becoming more and more problematic.

During a substantial part of this century thinking about and research on learning have been dominated by behaviourism, which demands that we restrict ourselves in our inquiry into what is directly observable, ie what people do – their behaviour (see, for instance, Skinner, 1953). From the mid-1950s onwards this orientation was challenged and subsequently pushed aside by the 'cognitive revolution'. Analogies between human beings and computers, and inner representations of outside reality as explanations for certain acts, were central features of research on learning, problem solving etc during three decades (see Gardner, 1987). The idea that the most interesting question about learning is what happens inside people's heads was, however, challenged in the mid-1980s by researchers who did not consider learning as only – or primarily – a phenomenon of the psychology of the individual, but more as a social, communicative, cultural, discursive, historical phenomenon. As a contrast to cognitivist conjectures about learning as a development of mental models of the world with a high degree of general applicability, the situated nature of learning and its contextual complexity was emphasized (for example, Lave, 1988).

There is an ongoing debate between situated cognition and cognitivism – emphasis on mental models in the latter compared with the contextual focus of the former. At the intersection between these two views we find the hottest question of research into learning today. Given the obviously situated nature of human acts, how can people through learning be equipped or equip themselves to face situations of very different kinds, mostly impossible to predict or foresee?

This is the psychological question of transfer referred to earlier in this chapter. As was pointed out, we can ask ourselves whether there ever can be two situations which are exactly alike. If nothing else, some time must have passed between the two events (otherwise the two would be the very same situation) and therefore the learner is not exactly the same person; if the learner is not exactly the same then the situation cannot be exactly the same either, because what we refer to as 'situations' are not 'situations as such' (ie defined by the researcher) but 'situations as they appear to those participating in them' (ie experienced by the participants). As we elaborate later in this chapter, to discern the variation it must be experienced as variation.

If we follow up this kind of reasoning then the question of transfer becomes a question of how we make use of what we learn. Furthermore it also follows that all situations are different and, if what we have learned in one situation can actually be made use of in another situation, then we must have learned something which transcends the situation in which the learning has taken place. The question of how we can make use of what we have learned is actually the question of 'what have we actually learned?' This is not as strange as it may appear.

For example, if a seven-year-old girl learns to solve mathematical problems by working through, say, 400 problems or tasks, in all likelihood it implies that she has not only learned to solve those 400 tasks. She can surely solve other problems, tasks she has never seen. If she can, she must have learned something more than how to solve those 400 tasks. The question is about what she has learned.

Contours of a theory of learning and awareness

Learning to experience

Consider the possibility that what we keep calling the new task may not seem very much like a mathematics task. The student may be trying to solve a real-life problem such as finding out if she can form two football (soccer) teams, with 11 members in each, from three volleyball teams of six members each. Will she have enough players? Will she need more? If so, how many more? If we were to think of an entirely different context, such as the capability of graduates with degrees in engineering to use in the workplace the knowledge and skills they have developed in their education, it becomes pretty obvious that the problem of connecting what you have learned earlier with the new situations is by no means trivial. This is exactly what they find difficult. They do have the knowledge, but they do not know how to make use of it (see Harvey and Green, 1993).

To return to our first-grader, the connection originates from the fact that she sees the new task in a way which is different from the way she would have seen it without the previous experience of the 400 problems. In the case of three volleyball teams and two football teams it may look something like:

$$6 + 6 + 6 = 6 + (4 + 2) + 6 = (6 + 4) + (2 + 6) = 10 + 8 = 18$$

An adult would simply have multiplied 6 by 3 to get 18 and 11 by two to get 22, then subtracted 18 from 22 to get 4. But the seven-year-old has not yet learned to multiply and she has developed the capability to add by making up to 10 first, as she learned to do in many of the 400 problems she had earlier worked out (such as how many eight-cent bubble gums can you buy if you have three ten-cent coins and one five-cent coin?). So what she did above was to begin by considering the players she had in the three volleyball teams. She divided the three teams such that she had a '10' plus a 'remainder'. Next, the football teams:

$$11 + 11 = (10 + 1) + (10 + 1) = (10 + 10) + (1 + 1) = 20 + 2 = 22$$

Here she is dividing the two football teams so that she gets two '10s' plus a 'remainder'. She has to compare the number of players she has with the number she needs and she might do it this way:

$$18 :: 22 = 18 + 2 + 2 = 18 + 4 = 22$$

Therefore, there are 4 missing.

What she has done is to make the 18 up to 20, which takes an additional two players. Then to go from 20 to 22 requires two more. The number of players missing is the sum of two plus two, that is, four.

It can be worked out differently, but in the end it will turn out to be the same: 'If you want to make two football teams out of three volleyball teams, four players will be missing'. So what is it actually that she has learned and made use of to find the answer? Well, she has been able to see the problem in terms of relations between numbers and the numbers in terms of parts and wholes, especially in terms of '10s' and 'remainders'. More specifically she was able to see '6' as '4 and 2', '10' as '6 and 4', '8' as '2 and 6' and so on, which is very much different from knowing by heart that $4 + 2 = 6, 6 + 4 = 10$ or $2 + 6 = 8$. She splits the second '6' into '4 and 2', because she can 'see' that the '4' will add up to '10', together with the first '6'.

In order to handle a certain situation in a certain way you must experience it in a certain way. An important difference between being able to do something and not being able to do it lies in the difference between being able or not being able to see or experience something in a certain way. Hounsell (1997) shows that students who succeeded better in their essays at university have ideas of what it takes to write an essay different from those who do not succeed.[1] The meaning of writing an essay varies and co-varies with the quality of essay writing as judged by the teachers. In the same way Whelan (1988) found that making a diagnosis means different things to different medical students and their ideas co-vary with what they actually do and how well they succeed (in making the right diagnosis). Sandberg (1994) shows that motor optimizers (ie engineers developing new motors in the car industry) have distinctly different ideas from each other about their own work. Again these differences co-vary with what they actually do (in actual fact their ideas are expressed through their acts) and how they succeed (as judged by their peers).

People develop ways of experiencing or ways of seeing at different levels of their domain of expertise. A chess player develops a chess player's way (perhaps one of the different ways) of seeing the board positions; a physician develops a physician's way of seeing medical situations, hearing the heart's sound using a stethoscope, seeing an X-ray or feeling the irregularities under the skin. A forestry officer, an artist, a photographer, a landscape architect, a biologist, a child from Abu Dhabi, each of these sees a particular forest in different ways, they see different things. To a great extent they have learned (or they have not learned) to see the forest in their own way. These examples point to what may seem to be a self-evident aspect of learning. This aspect is at the core of students' success or failure to learn what was intended at university.

Even skills which apparently are just motor skills spring from certain ways of experiencing the activity or the field in which it is embedded. To learn to swim properly means that the tacit meaning of breathing changes (when swimming we refrain from emptying our lungs when breathing out and inflate them more than usual when breathing in); to learn to ride a bicycle implies a discovery of the relationship between speed and the necessary correction with the handlebars and body positioning in order to maintain balance – '... for a given angle of unbalance the curvature of each winding is inversely proportional to the square of the speed at which the cyclist is proceeding' (Polanyi, 1958).

The form of learning which is in the focus of our interest is learning which implies a change in people's ways of experiencing a phenomenon in, or an aspect of, the world around them. In this context we are not arguing about whether this form of learning is all there is; it would suffice to say that this is a fundamental aspect or fundamental form of learning which, in relation our point of departure – 'How can we handle situations which we do not know?' – is of decisive importance. This remains to be demonstrated but demonstrate it we will, we believe.

Ways of experiencing

In the previous section we talked about ways of experiencing phenomena. What is a way of experiencing something? Its nature can be defined in terms of two intertwined aspects. When we talk about qualitatively different ways of experiencing something we have to deal with differences in structure and differences in meaning. To experience something implies discerning it from the context of which it is a part and to relate it to that context or to other contexts. To experience something also implies discerning the parts of what we experience and relating these to each other and to the whole (Svensson, 1984). This has to do with the structure of both the experienced and the experiencing. We consider the following example.

> This example is taken from Johansson, Marton and Svensson (1985). A group of engineering students at a technological university were interviewed at the beginning and end of a course in physics that they had participated in, with the aim of depicting changes, if any, in their understanding of certain aspects of the physical world. One of the questions used in the interviews was: 'A car is driven at a high constant speed straightforward on a motorway. What forces act on the car?'

> One subject (S2), listing motive power from the engine, air resistance, frictional force on all the bearings, gravity, and normal force as relevant, suggested that gravity and normal force are equal and that the engine is used to counterbalance the sum of the air resistance and the frictional force. As S2 saw it 'when he drives at a constant speed, all the forces counterbalance each other... when it accelerates, more power is needed forward than when it is moving at a constant speed'.

> We can now compare this with the response from one of the other subjects (S3) who spent a lot of time early in the interview drawing lines depicting such forces as gravity, air resistance and friction against the road surface (at each wheel). Subject S3 concluded that the force that moves the car forward is larger than the friction at the wheels and the air resistance combined.

> There were two major differences between these two students' ways of dealing with the problem. According to the former, the magnitude of force in the direction of the movement equals the magnitude of the forces in the reverse direction, so that the moving body is in equilibrium at a constant velocity. According to the latter student, the resultant of the forces acting upon the car must exceed zero and must have the

direction of the motion, otherwise the body would not move. Such an understanding implies that a body is in equilibrium only when it is at rest. Johansson, Marton and Svensson observed from all the interviews combined that the students who seem to realize that opposite forces are in balance have chosen 'velocity' as a point of departure and they have contrasted constant velocity with acceleration or deceleration. They have explained that the equilibrium of forces makes the velocity remain constant (rather than cause acceleration or deceleration). The other students, however, seem to have considered the problem from the point of view of 'motion' and they have compared motion with rest. They have explained that the greater force forward makes the object move (rather than remain at rest).

The two qualitatively different conceptions of a body moving at a constant velocity, corresponding to seeing a body in this kind of motion either as (a) having a constant velocity, due to the equilibrium of forces or (b) moving, due to a 'motive inequilibrium' of forces, represent two kinds of correlated differences which we may call 'structural' and 'referential (meaning)' aspects of the event. One aspect relates to what is focused on (velocity or motion). The other refers to how the explanation is given; in terms of equilibrium at constant velocity or equilibrium at rest.

To experience something is also to experience a meaning; structure and meaning mutually constitute each other. To experience, understand and make sense of a text in a certain way, for instance, must imply that the reader discerns the main theme of what the text is about, discerns sub-themes within the whole and examples by means of which themes are illustrated or illuminated. The examples and the illustrations are then subordinate to the themes, which again are subordinate to the main theme. By discerning the different parts in different levels in the text and by relating them to each other, the text gains a certain meaning. On the other hand, the parts and levels cannot be discerned and related to each other except in terms of the meanings. So neither structure nor meaning can be said to precede or succeed the other. Nor can we imagine them other than in relation to each other.

One could also envisage the same text being read by another reader discerning the same parts as the former reader but without seeing any hierarchical relations between them. The second reader is simply following the sequence of the book but nothing is superordinate or subordinate. If we were to ask this reader what the text is about, the answer would probably be 'Well first it said this, and then that, and then that'. If the question is restated, the reader will say again 'about this, and that, and that'. Here we are dealing with a structure that is sequential, not hierarchical as in the former case. In the same way, the meaning of the text is different in the two cases. In spite of both readers being able to recall the same parts, it appears as if they read two different texts. In the second case the reader is dealing with one thing at a time while in the first case each example, for instance, deals with what is described, in concrete terms, and the sub-theme, which is illustrated, and the main theme for the whole text.

The different levels are present in the first reader's awareness simultaneously. One could say that, as compared with the second way of reading the text, this way of reading it is more complex and more inclusive.

The differences described were found first in a study carried out by Wenestam (1980) who used a text taken from Hempel (1966) about the scientific method, which, according to the author, is the hypothetical-deductive method. You start by deducing a hypothesis and you test it by keeping all variables constant except for the one you assume to be the cause of what you want to explain. This was illustrated by the story of Dr Semmelweiss and his search for the cause of childbed fever. He examined a number of hypotheses, and the way he tested the various conjectures exemplified the main point in the text (the scientific method). This is the way one of the students participating in the study described above recalled the text:

> The text begins with how one sets about testing a hypothesis. One investigates two different groups, one of which will give a positive result and the other a negative result in relation to the hypothesis. If the hypothesis is faulty, then this difference won't be obtained and one will have to start again with a new hypothesis. This was illustrated by an example about Semmelweis. Semmelweis wondered why the mortality rate from childbed fever was so different (about 9 per cent and about 2 per cent in wards 1 and 2 at the hospital in Vienna (1840s). (Student S45)

Another student recalled the text in the following way:

> The text is about a professor who is going to find out the reason for childbed fever being so much higher in the first ward than in the others. It was about nine per cent while the others had only 2 to 3 per cent. He tested a lot of different reasons, one of which was that he thought that it could be a priest who caused it all when he went through the ward with ... (Student S54).

In the first case the student could see how the main point was reflected in the example. In the second case the text was read as being a story about Semmelweiss. This kind of recall was in several cases preceded by the student saying: 'First it talked about the scientific method and then he talked about a Hungarian professor, Semmelweis'. So the main point and the example are read as two separate parts on the same level without any obvious connection, or the main point may be lost altogether as in the example above. Discerning two levels in the story and seeing the (hierarchical) relation between them is one way of structuring the text. Discerning two parts of the text and seeing them in isolation from each other is another way of structuring the same text. And two radically different meanings correspond to the two ways of structuring the text (reading it as a text about the scientific method or reading it as a text about the discovery of the cause of childbed fever).

We will look at another example of experiencing something; something very concrete and ordinary like trying to hit an object with a ball. While growing up, we keep throwing things of different sizes and different weights such as toys, different kinds of balls, pebbles or pieces of wood. Often we try to hit something, a target, from different directions and different distances. Sometimes it is windy, sometimes it is raining. In this way we learn to discern the relevant aspects of situations that are critical in relation to our objective of hitting something; aspects such as distance, weight, position and possibly even wind strength. When throwing, we try to capture all those different aspects simultaneously. If we fail to capture all critical aspects we probably will not succeed. So the experience of trying to hit a target with a ball can be characterized in terms of what aspects of the situation are discerned and are simultaneously in the focus of awareness, and how they are related to each other, ie in terms of the structure we are imposing on this kind of situation.

We learn our mother tongue in a similar way. A baby hears different people speak, with different voices, some louder, others softer, they may speak with different tones and perhaps even with different dialects. Also, the very same person, even the mother, may sound different at different times; she might be closer or further away, she may raise her voice or lower it, she might be happy, angry or sad. It could be said that with all that variation, all that inconsistency, it is a wonder that a baby learns to speak at all. Marton (in press) argues that, in fact, it is the variation itself in the baby's experience which enables it to understand and use language.

What happens in normal circumstances is that the variation in a baby's experience is just what enables it to differentiate the common, essential features of language structure from the idiosyncratic aspects associated with each individual's speech. It is what enables babies to experiment with language and to infer rules. It is what enables babies to hear something with different aural characteristics but nevertheless interpret it within the inferred structure. In order to understand when the same thing is said in different ways, we must be able to discern various aspects and to take them into account at the same time (ie imposing the same structure on the different instances). Language will then gain the general sense (in addition to the specific sense of what is said): 'Though it may sound different, it might be all the same'. At the same time the idea of invariance in language is born. So, once more, structure and meaning constitute each other mutually.

Discernment and variation

To experience something is to discern parts and the whole, aspects and relations. But what does it take to discern something? This question points to another question: how do we learn to experience something in a certain way? What we discussed in the previous section was what it means to experience something in a certain way. One could think about how we learn to understand our mother tongue. We can make sense of what is said with a wide range of variation in pitch, tone, loudness, pronunciation, mode of expression, style etc. So how can that be?

We now contemplate a chilly thought experiment. If a baby's only linguistic experience was with a voice synthesizer speaking with exactly the same pitch, tone and loudness all the time, the baby would fail to notice those aspects corresponding to dimensions of potential variation. Consequently, the baby would have great difficulties in understanding speech that differed from what it has been used to (if it could understand at all) – say if confronted by speech from its mother for the first time after this long experience with the voice synthesizer.

So, our suggestion for an answer to the question 'what is learned?' is that it is the variation that is learned, although we mean that in a particular sense. As far as our mother tongue is concerned, for instance, the regularities and the invariances we learn are embedded in a great number of dimensions of variation. This can be said differently: the dimensions and the relationships constituted between them are the invariants. Or, moderating the claim slightly, they are invariants, they do not vary, and because we have learned the variation we can deal with not only what we have encountered previously but also with things we have not yet encountered. We can make sense of new situations in terms of their critical features. These critical features are dimensions of variation constituted by the new situation and the previous ones which it resembles in critical respects. The thesis is that we will be capable of dealing with varying (and novel) situations in the future because we have experienced varying (and once novel, but now known) situations in the past.

Is all this only philosophy and playing with ideas? Not at all. The relation between discernment and variation is observable empirically. Sachs' (1983) study offers an interesting example. As an anthropologist she visited a small Turkish village where she found that the water there contained a particular kind of bacteria causing what appeared, to the observer, to be quite an unpleasant stomach problem. Everyone in the village suffered with the problem and it remained throughout their lives. When interviewing the villagers about their lives, Sachs found to her great surprise that no one said anything about stomach problems. Because it was something invariant, nobody could distinguish it from living in a general sense. No one was aware of the possibility of feeling differently, no one was therefore aware that they had a disease.

Moxley (1979) tested what she called 'the variability of practice' in motor learning. Young children were invited to practise hitting an object on the floor with a badminton shuttle. Those in the experimental group had their practice distributed at four different places at the same distance from the object. Because the children's feet pointed to the same fixed point in the room each time, they experienced four different conditions of throwing. Children in the control group did the same number of trials from a single location as the children in the experimental group did from the four different locations together. Thereafter the two groups were compared when the children were trying to hit the target from a location which was new for them all (although the distance to the target was the same as in the practice trials). The performance of the experimental group was dramatically better on the criterion task (at the new location). This could be interpreted to mean that the children in the experimental group experienced variation in direction and could therefore discern it as a significant and variable aspect of the situation. Children in the control group, on the other hand, could not distinguish 'direction' from the very throwing, as the two were perfectly correlated (they threw from the same location every time during their practice). Also, other aspects of the situation, such as distance, the weight of the ball etc, can be varied, also simultaneously. Other experiments in which this was done point to the same conclusion: varied practice is superior to constant practice when the criterion task means change in the aspect that was varied during the experiment. Kerr and Booth (1977) found varied practice superior to constant practice, even when the criterion condition was identical with the constant practice condition.

What this whole line of reasoning is about is that discernment is a defining feature of learning in the sense of learning to experience something in a certain way. Variation is a necessary condition for effective discernment. So how does all of this take place?

Variation or experienced variation?

When some aspect of a phenomenon or an event varies while another aspect or other aspects remain invariant, the varying aspect will be discerned. In order for this to happen, variation must be experienced by someone as variation. A necessary condition is that the person in question experiences at the same time the different 'values' (ie instances) in this aspect or dimension that varies. If the person did not do that but experienced one instance at a time then there would not be any variation experienced.

We have talked about simultaneous experience in the sense of experiencing different things at the same time (for example, direction, distance, weight etc, when throwing a ball; main theme and example when reading a text). To experience variation we must experience instances that we have encountered, on different occasions, at the same time. This means experiencing the contemporaneousness of things that are not contemporaneous in the objective sense. We notice a person's height, for instance, when that person is especially tall or short. This we do against the background of our previous experience of variation in height. To experience that variation we have to experience contemporaneously the height of people whom we have met at different points in time.

Through the experience of contemporaneousness the different values are synthesized to make up a dimension or an aspect. Then a person in a new situation is aware of the here and now, and of the past, at the same time. The latter can, in principle, be the person's entire life, everything experienced earlier in life. It is obvious that no one can be aware of everything that has been experienced previously – not in the same way at least. Awareness has a certain structure. You are focally aware of certain things; they are in the foreground, they make a figure; these things are few. Other things you are more or less peripherally aware of on, in principle, an infinitely diminishing gradient. Such a characterization of the anatomy of awareness is in agreement with Gurwitsch's (1964) way of depicting consciousness.

In this line of reasoning there seems to be the embryo of the answer to our main question: how can we develop capabilities to handle new situations? As we are simultaneously aware of the new and the old, and as the new in this way gains its meaning through the old, and as meaning is constituted through the discernment of different aspects of the situation, and as discernment is born out of awareness of dimensions of variation, it is by experiencing variation in certain respects that we can equip ourselves for the future.

When we encounter a new situation we gain meaning from it by recognizing different aspects of the situation as values in dimensions of variation originating from our previous experiences. For instance, we can handle a new physical situation in terms of speed, time, distance, frame of reference, energy, force etc because these aspects of the situation correspond to dimensions of variation in our awareness; they correspond to our way of experiencing the world and to the way in which the world appears to us.

The application of something we have learned takes place, according to this view, through simultaneous awareness of the new and the old, whereas the meaning of the situation is constituted by both. Application amounts to creating something new each time. Furthermore, when the new situation differs in every way from our previous experiences (eg when we for the first time adopt a perspective on the universe from a point outside the earth) it can be the beginning of a new dimension of variation (a new way of seeing) developing in our awareness (for instance, infinitely variable positions from which the universe can be observed).

Yet another implication of what has been said is that the meaning of every phenomenon is a function of what it is related to, or of the dimensions of variation through which it can be seen. The same object can be experienced as fast (against a background of varying speeds), purple (against a background of varying colours), small (against a background of varying size), hairless (against a background of more or less hairy objects) and so on. It follows from this that the meaning potential of any phenomenon and of any human being of course is infinite because there can always be other potential variation surrounding it.

Focal differentiation

The relation between structure and meaning was described earlier: how awareness of the aspects and relations between aspects of a situation or phenomenon determine its meaning, and how simultaneously the meaning of the situation determines what aspects and relations between aspects the person is aware of. But the presence or absence of aspects and relations between aspects in awareness are not the only source of differences in structure and meaning. Gurwitsch's (1964) theory of awareness (or of consciousness – we use the two terms interchangeably here) was mentioned in the previous section. In addition to the aspects of a situation we are aware of, there are differences in the prominence of these aspects in our awareness.

Take as an example the reading of this text. What the reader is focusing on are the things dealt with here: learning, experiencing, awareness, structure and meaning. During the reading different aspects come to the fore (they are the figure) while others recede to the background, but they are still there all the time. The different questions are seen against the background of different thematic fields (this is Gurwitsch's term), that is, against the background of the reader's earlier experiences of what is dealt with. We stress here the relevant dimensions of variation; these make up the anatomy of the thematic field in our interpretation. In addition to being aware of the content, the reader is at least peripherally aware of the physical surroundings, that the children have to be picked up from the day-care centre in two hours, that preparation for work tomorrow still needs to be done, and so on. The reader's awareness is not directly focused upon these things, but they do co-exist in time and space. Gurwitsch calls it 'the margin'. Awareness has a structure and structure has dynamics. There is normally a figure–ground relationship (ie between what is focused on and what is in the background). The contents of figure and ground keep changing all the time. Furthermore, we make sense of every moment against the background of everything we have experienced earlier or at least against the background of very much of what we have experienced earlier. Therefore we can say that awareness extends in time and space, in principle, infinitely. When the situation changes (it is 5 pm, for instance), or something entirely new pops up in the text which one keeps reading, the structure of awareness can change dramatically. Something that is, or was, very peripheral becomes something very central.

This play in awareness (between figure and ground and between central and peripheral) we call focal differentiation. The term refers to how figural or prominent something is in awareness. This play is absolutely necessary in order to experience reality as we do. Well, in order to experience reality at all.

Consider simply the alternative. Namely that if we experienced everything, every aspect with equal intensity, equally figural all the time, all and everything would be in the foreground. If we were aware of everything in the same way all the time then we would not be able to experience any difference in meaning. We would not be able to experience any meaning at all, because if meaning springs from the aspects of reality which we are aware of and from the way in which we are aware of them, to be aware of everything in the same way would amount to not being aware of anything at all.

Centring and relevance structure

There is still another differentiation that can and ought to be done in relation to the way in which we are aware of things. We have always a point of departure from which we see or experience the world around us. When we experience the world, we always do so from a position. Differences in this respect are of two kinds. A way of experiencing something can be defined in terms of 'How a phenomenon is delimited from and related to its context, on the one hand, and how parts of the phenomenon are delimited and related to the whole', on the other hand (Svensson, 1984). Slightly distorting phenomenological terminology, the former might be called 'external horizon' and the latter 'internal horizon' (Spiegelberg, 1982). In a similar way we can talk about centring in an external and internal sense.

Centring of the former kind concerns the point (in time and space) from which the object of one's attention is seen or experienced. As far as the time aspect is concerned, our awareness is at every moment a reflection of what we have experienced earlier. But, as a rule, we also have some premonitions of what is going to happen and we are driven by some intentions, things that we are trying to achieve. In the jargon of phenomenology we have our *projects* (where 'project' has a general, existential meaning). This temporal embeddedness constitutes the personal context of our experiences and our acts. The personal context springs from our earlier experiences, but also from our aims and from the future which we expect and want to encounter. The way in which a particular experience relates the personal context and the way in which the personal context is making certain aspects of the particular situation appear more important than others, making them come to the fore, while others remain in the background, defines the *relevance structure* of the situation.

From the perspective of learning, it seems to be a profound advantage if the very same situation can be seen both from the point of view of the past and the future. A learning experience should evolve from some previous familiarity with what is learned about and it should serve purposes pointing forward. The difference between the surface and the deep approach to learning through reading, for instance, reflects differences in this respect. When adopting a surface approach, the readers are driven by demands they anticipate: to be able to recall the text and answer questions about it later on. When adopting a deep approach the readers are driven by an interest in finding out something new about something already known somehow (see Chapter 3).

Szekely (1950) carried out a simple, but striking, experiment. Two groups of students were asked to read a text about some physical concepts and principles, and to observe a physical event. The only difference in conditions was that one of the groups encountered the counter-intuitive physical event first. It ran contrary to their expectations and they were subsequently asked to read a text with the instructions 'Read this and you can find out why things went the way they did'. The other group was asked to read the same text first with the instructions 'Read this and try to understand what it says!' After having read the text they were told: 'Now you are going to see something that illustrates what you have just read about'. Then they viewed the same demonstration as the first group. The only difference between the two groups was the order of their experiences: reading the text and observing the demonstration. Nevertheless there were dramatic differences between the two groups when, one week later, they were facing a new problem that could be solved by using the principles illustrated by the demonstration and explained by the text. The first group (demonstration then text) did much better. They seemed to have appropriated the principles to a much greater extent than the second group (text then demonstration). An explanation could possibly be found in differences in the way the text was read. Reasonably, the first group read from the point of view of the demonstration. Things appeared more or less relevant to the extent that they threw light on the perplexing event just encountered. The other group had no point of departure. The extent to which something appeared more relevant than something else in the text must have been grounded in their more or less arbitrary interpretation of the situation. This way of reading a text is unfortunately typical for institutional learning: you have to read texts for reasons which you are not always particularly clear about.

So every situation is experienced from the point of view of what preceded it and from the point of view of what is still to come, but it works the other way as well. The past and the future are seen or experienced always from the point of view of the specific concrete situation which the experiencer is in. Therefore, the structure of awareness, its nature, can only be described with reference to specific situational conditions. In consequence, Hofstadter's thought experiment with Einstein's brain is an impossibility. The idea was that if you could describe the content of Einstein's brain, ie his mind, in detail, then you could build up a database and develop a program which could come up with the same answers to questions which Einstein would have given (Hofstadter, 1979). Apart from all practical difficulties, one can safely argue that the whole idea is logically impossible. It appears reasonable to say that 'the content of someone's mind' is tantamount to 'someone's awareness', in accordance with the way we defined awareness above. Awareness, however, does not have a structure in general. It is always situated and transitory. So, when it comes to Einstein's brain or, more correctly, to his awareness, we have to ask questions of the kind: at what place? where? at what point in time? His awareness, just like anyone else's awareness, was in continual flux throughout his life.

The other kind of centring refers to part of the phenomenon from which the rest is seen. It is the case that experiencing not only has a centring outside the object of experience but often also within the object itself. When this is the case there are different centrings possible. In an experiment with repeated readings of a very difficult text in which the views of two schools of philosophy on the relation between words and reference were discussed, Marton and Wenestam (1988) showed that the successful way of approaching the task meant to take the point of departure in the view of one school and look at the other and then shift the centring again and again.

A spectacular example of the internal centring of experience we find in the book about the famous geneticist and Nobel laureate, Barbara McClintock. There is an episode when, while studying chromosomes intently under a microscope, all of a sudden she finds herself among them: 'I found that the more I worked with them the bigger and bigger [they] got, and when I was really working with them I wasn't outside, I was down there with them, and everything got big. I even was able to see the internal parts of the chromosomes – actually everything was there. It surprised me because I actually felt as if I were right down there and these were my friends'. (Keller, 1983).

Beyond the object of learning

The above sketch of a theory of learning is formulated in terms of the ways in which the learner may experience or be aware of the object of learning. There are many other aspects of learning, of course. We are going to deal with some of those in this third, concluding, part of this chapter.

Making ways of seeing visible

Experiencing has, in this presentation, until now, meant the experience of the individual of phenomena in the material or cultural world, directly or by means of linguistic symbolization. But we do not only experience the material and cultural world, but also experience each other and even each other's experiencing. Not least, the latter is of central importance for the questions dealt with here. Learning is seen here primarily as a change in our way of seeing or experiencing something in the world around us. What works against such changes is what the phenomenologists call the *natural attitude*. This refers to our taken-for-granted and deeply felt assumption that what we see and experience is the world exactly as it is, and that others see and experience exactly the same world. From such a point of departure it would of course be a contradiction to change one's way of seeing something in the world.

The awareness of such a change forces you to put the natural attitude aside. On the other hand, putting the natural attitude aside facilitates changes of this kind. A simple and powerful way of countering the natural attitude is to make other peoples' ways of experiencing a certain phenomenon visible. If you do that, it becomes obvious that there are different ways of experiencing reality. This is used as an efficient educational method to facilitate learning of the kind which is the object of interest here (see, for instance, Lybeck, 1981; Pramling, 1990; Ahlberg, 1992). Making different ways of experiencing or understanding a certain phenomenon visible can serve aims other than countering the natural attitude. By people in a group or an organization becoming conscious of others' ways of thinking and experiencing different phenomena, each consciousness gets linked to others and a collective consciousness arises, richer, more inclusive and, under certain circumstances, more powerful than any singular consciousness or the sum of them (see Chapter 8).

Intentionality

Franz Brentano, the teacher of the founder of phenomenology, Edmund Husserl, asked an apparently very simple question. What is the difference between what is psychic (or psychological) and what is not? The answer he arrived at was that all psychological acts are intentional, that is, they are directed towards something else, beyond the acts themselves. There is no learning without something learned, there is no thinking without something thought, there is no experiencing without something experienced. In accordance with this, our awareness is primarily directed towards the object of the psychological acts and we become conscious of the acts themselves through a reflexive movement in our awareness. We can simply reach the psychological acts through reflection (Spiegelberg, 1982).

Sometimes the very acts become primary objects. This implies, for instance, that it is the act of learning, instead of its object, to which awareness is directed in the first place. Ekeblad (1996) shows how a change takes place in children's awareness from being primarily directed at the object of learning towards being primarily directed towards the acts of learning, during the first school year. Under favourable conditions, reverse movement can appear later, the object of learning getting into focus again. (Marton, Watkins and Tang, 1997).

In experimental studies it has been shown that if the learner's attention is focused on the act of learning instead of its object, through inserted questions or instructions, for instance, the likelihood of attaining the meaning is diminished. By extrapolating from such studies and by a theoretical analysis of learning we arrive at the conclusion that when it comes to the most open form of equipping people for an unknown future, that is, when it comes to developing people's capability of learning, it is not a good idea to encourage the learners to focus on specific acts of learning. A far better idea is to widen the ways in which learning is seen (see Marton and Booth, 1997).

Introducing and making visible variation in the ways of learning is likely to increase readiness to handle situations in the future which require new forms of learning. So learning to learn implies, according to this way of seeing, developing awareness of and a familiarity with different ways of learning and an openness in the face of future learning situations and the unknowable problems yet to be faced. Every situation has its own truth, as Wertheimer (1945) pointed out, and the will and the capability to do justice to the conditions specific for every context are likely to be the best ground for learning in and from situations that vary in many dimensions. Such a ground can only develop through confronting situations that vary in many dimensions.

That the act of learning rather than its object often becomes the focus in institutional forms of learning does not only apply to students but also to teachers. In a number of studies (see, for instance, Alexandersson, 1994; Marton, 1994 for a summary) it was found that teachers often are not primarily focusing on, and driven by, what their work is supposed to yield (the students' learning), but rather focusing on, and are driven by, what is taking place in the classroom, their own acts, handling the teaching situation and what the here and now – the work, the general sentiment in the classroom – is like and what it ought to be like. One could perhaps say that the means rather than the goals come to the fore, a means–ends reversal.

The path of learning

We now point out two fundamental metaphors for learning. One is the organic metaphor and, according to this, learning goes from the whole to the parts. Heinz Werner formulated more than half a century ago his orthogenetic law, which happens to be about development and not about learning. Development goes, according to him, from an undifferentiated whole to greater and greater differentiation and integration of the parts. In addition, of course, it is the case that a seed or an embryo contains the potential for the full-grown plant or human being with all its parts. The whole precedes the parts. One could imagine that the same is true so far as learning is concerned (Werner, 1948).

It seems to be the case that human beings instinctively focus on general features in a new situation and therefore on the frames of learning, to begin with, in a new learning situation. When children start school they try to get a grasp of the school environment before they focus on the content, on what they are supposed to learn. People participating in psychological experiments focus on what frames the experiment to begin with – the environment, the room and the people involved (Colaizzi, 1973). In order to learn to read and write one has to grasp the very idea of reading and writing and one must have an understanding of what the whole thing is about. Dahlgren and Olsson (1985) carried out interviews with children in pre-school (5–6 years old), who had not yet learned to read and write, about the point of learning those skills. They also asked the children about how reading and writing work. When these children were followed up later on at school, it was found that those who had problems with reading and writing were mainly the children who in pre-school did not have an understanding of what reading and writing were all about.

Much earlier a very observant and engaged teacher, Sylvia Ashton-Warner, was wondering why many Maori children in New Zealand did not learn to read and write. She concluded that many of these children, coming from illiterate environments, had not grasped the idea of reading and writing, what it was all about and how it could work. Ashton-Warner decided therefore to take the children's own words as the point of departure, words they were used to and words linked to strong emotions. The words were frequently about violence and sex. The teacher wrote the words on the black-board and read them, children collected their own words, they learned to recognize them and eventually they started to analyse them; they discerned constituent sounds, constituent signs and started to correlate the two with each other. In this approach the whole preceded the parts. First, the development of the idea of reading and writing preceded the teaching of reading and writing, the communicative and symbolic function of reading and writing preceded the acquisition of the technical skills of drawing letters, and of reading and combining them. Second, whole words preceded their constituent parts, the letters (Ashton-Warner, 1963).

But also in fairly well-defined situations, it seems to be necessary or at least to be an advantage to have an idea of the whole at an early stage. We return to the example dealt with earlier about the reading of a text. Already when we read the heading, or presumably even earlier through some information in advance and through the very context, we have an idea of what the text is about. As different parts or different levels are differentiated, the meaning of the whole develops. At the same time we interpret the parts in relation to our ever-changing and growing understanding of the whole. The alternative metaphor for learning is the building of a house, putting together a mechanical device. The parts are there to begin with and gradually the whole is developing, but the whole was not there to begin with. It is an extremely common idea in science teaching that as the knowledge is of a technical nature one has to start with acquiring the parts initially not very rich in meaning, neither by themselves, nor in terms of the future whole. Only when there is a critical mass of parts does the learner have a possibility of seeing the point with the whole.

Two objections – at least – can be raised against this second metaphor. It should be easy to realize that even if the whole is not there to begin with when you build a house or you put together a machine, the idea of the whole is. There is a thought, an image, a plan and a drawing. It is not very likely that you put one brick on the other without having some idea of the completed house. The other objection has to do with the nature of awareness. It was pointed out earlier that the meaning of each part springs from a simultaneous awareness of the different layers of the text. If a part, an illustration or an example, serves the aim of illuminating the subject that is a subsection of the text, and the subsection is there to illuminate and develop the theme which the text as a whole deals with, the meaning of the parts and the whole grows or develops in parallel and dialectically in a dynamic interaction between the parts and the whole. Should the meaning of the parts be fixed to begin with, it would imply that the meanings of the parts can be defined in advance, independently of the whole and also without need for subsequent change when the parts are integrated to form the whole. This seems a somewhat odd idea to us. Clearly, odd in relation to the meaning of the text and its parts, but, in fact, odd even in relation to a domain of knowledge and the parts which constitute it.

The sequence between the whole and the parts is a critical aspect, indeed so far as the dynamics of learning are concerned. Another, perhaps less obvious, but equally critical, aspect is what we referred to earlier as focal differentiation, that is, what is figure and what is ground in awareness.

An aspect of a phenomenon which is focused on can be seen as a dimension of variation. It is focused on because we have experienced and are experiencing variation in it. The expression 'we are experiencing variation in it' refers to potential variation. If we are, for instance, focusing on the 'manyness' of the set of objects it is because we are implicitly aware of the fact that they could have been more or less. If we are focusing on the speed of an object it is because we are implicitly aware of the fact that the object could have travelled faster or slower. Had we never experienced variation concerning manyness or speed we would not be able to discern, let alone focus, on these aspects.

Experiencing a phenomenon in a certain way implies, according to the line of reasoning above, that the different parts and aspects and the relations between them are discerned and simultaneously are objects of focal awareness. Our specific interest here is about how we learn to experience different phenomena. According to some preliminary observations, we have detected some orderly, systematic regularities. Some aspects are discerned earlier, others later. Think of a particular aspect not yet discerned (no aspects are discerned from the very beginning, of course). It enters the field of awareness in a non-focal position to begin with; at a point in time the learner experiences variation in that particular dimension, the aspect opens up and the learner becomes focally aware of it. Later on, it recedes to a more peripheral position in awareness again, it becomes taken for granted (but differentiated). Other aspects come to the fore at the same time.

Our experience of a phenomenon develops through this temporally extended play between figure and ground as a function of what aspects we are focally aware of at one time. Bond's (1996) longitudinal study in progress about how conceptions of learning develop can be interpreted in this way. Somewhat daringly we could argue that a similar development can be observed on the collective level when we consider how the concept of force has changed and developed historically (Stinner, 1994).

Endnotes

1. Rightly or wrongly, we are using expressions such as 'different ways of seeing', 'different ways of experiencing', 'different meanings', 'different ideas' etc, as synonyms.

Chapter 3

Approaches to learning

Approaches to learning in different situations

We are dealing with learning that widens the ways in which certain kinds of situation are seen. 'A way of seeing' can be characterized in terms of the pattern of critical aspects of the situation that are discerned and focused on simultaneously. In every particular situation we make use of things we have learned earlier and in principle we can learn something in every situation, therefore every situation is potentially both a learning situation and a situation of application. While neither learning nor application can exist independently, it is convenient to talk about learning situations in the context of studying and to talk about situations of application when it comes to making use later of what one has learned through studying.

How do the learning situations contribute to the ways in which future situations, or certain phenomena involved in those situations, will be seen? By enabling the learner to understand the dimensions of variation that define those phenomena. For example, children may like to eat fruit and various fruits have a number of characteristics, of which colour, shape and taste are a few. In our terminology we would call them 'dimensions of variation'. Children who have learned about colour are better able to discern that particular dimension of variation in fruit they might want to eat. They could now decline even to taste a green banana, simply on the basis of its colour. Having recognized the banana by its shape, they can now differentiate between green and yellow (or unripe and ripe) bananas.

The extent to which the dimensions of variation of various phenomena are seen depends on the learner's ways of experiencing the learning situations. The dimensions of variation that define a certain phenomenon are dimensions of experienced variation and experience requires something to be experienced as well as a way of experiencing it. We will now elaborate that idea.

In Chapter 2 (pages 30–32) we illustrated two examples of different ways of seeing the object of learning: a body in uniform motion in the study (see pages 30–31) by Johansson, Marton and Svensson (1985) and a text with a principle–example structure in Wenestam's (1980) investigation (see page 32). The object of learning is not experienced as an abstraction, it is experienced in a situation. Therefore, the experience of the object of learning is just one of at least two aspects of the learner's experience. There is another aspect, the learner's experience of the very situation, in particular the experience of what they are trying to achieve in that situation, and the experience of what they are actually doing. This second aspect is what we call 'approaches to learning'.

We now consider some studies which show the functional relationship between the approaches to learning adopted by the learners and the outcomes of learning arrived at by them. This was perhaps the best known discovery in the research tradition on which this book primarily builds.

Approaches to learning from texts

Consider learners who all have the necessary linguistic, factual and conceptual prerequisites to grasp a particular text fully and yet they still understand it in a number of qualitatively different ways. How could the outcome vary, unless what is happening during their reading of the text is varying? What is it that varies in their way of going about the learning task? Studies in the mid-1970s established that people learn different things when presented with the same learning opportunity, the reason being that they approach their learning in different ways.

> In one of these studies, 30 university students read a closely argued newspaper article written by a professor of education, Urban Dahllöf, concerning and criticizing proposed university reforms in Sweden. Marton and Säljö (1976) write:
>
> The newspaper article was 1400 words long and included three tables. The article was mainly a critique of the approaching curriculum reform in the Swedish universities (UKAS), which aimed at bringing studies more into line with those at the polytechnic institutes through the introduction of set combinations of subjects and stricter regulations as regards duration of studies (termination in the case of unsatisfactory examination results). The reason for the reform, as explained by the authorities, was that the examination pass rate at the universities was considerably lower than that obtained at the polytechnic institutes. The author of the article had, after examining the underlying statistics, divided university students into sub-categories and was thereby able to show that, even though the pass rate was very low for certain categories of students, for other categories it was as high as, if not higher than, that achieved by technical students. The author argued that the blanket approach of the university reform, which would affect all equally, was misguided. If the pass rate was to be raised (and this was not considered self-evident by the author) selective measures should be taken by concentrating on those groups that did have a low pass rate.

After subjects had read the article, they were asked in individual interviews not only to recall the author's main argument but also to describe how they had gone about studying it. Four distinct ways of understanding it were identified by the researchers and are summarized in Figure 3.1.

A	*Selective measures*: measures have to be taken only for those groups of students that do not fulfil the necessary requirements	
B	*Differential measures*: measures to be taken which allow for differences between the various groups	
C	*Measures*: measures need to be taken	
D	*Differences*: there are differences between groups	

Figure 3.1: *Ways of understanding the Dahllöf text*

These four different ways of understanding the Dahllöf text are logically related to each other in that they can be brought together into a 'composite understanding', of which each is one part. The question, 'What was this article about?' can be answered as follows: There are *differences between groups* (= understanding D) such that *measures need to be taken* (= understanding C) which allow for the *differences between the various groups* (= understanding B) and applied *only for those groups of students that do not fulfil the necessary requirements* (= understanding A).

Understanding A is a special case of understanding B and therefore A implies B. Understanding B implies both C and D because they are combined in B. The logical relations that exist between these differing understandings provide a basis for establishing a hierarchy among them. The levels of C and D are indeterminate in relation to each other. In Figure 3.2, we show the set of relationships among A, B, C and D.

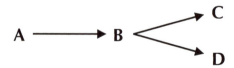

Figure 3.2: *Hierarchy of logical relationships between ways of understanding the Dahllöf text (from Marton & Booth, 1997)*

Svensson (1976) argues that the critical difference lies between A and B on one hand and C and D on the other. A and B focus on the text's structure, which is a presentation of some facts (about differences in pass rates between groups) and a conclusion based on those facts (about selective measures), while C and D do not.

Therefore, differences in learning outcomes are able to be described in terms of logically related and qualitatively different ways of making sense of the text but how can we explain the differences found? All the students participating had the intellectual capacity and the background knowledge necessary to understand the text and yet quite dramatic differences were still found.

A series of studies (Marton, 1974, 1975; Dahlgren, 1975; Säljö, 1975; Svensson, 1976; Fransson, 1977) found consistent and significant differences in the way learners experienced learning tasks and dealt with them. The outcomes of the students' engagement with a particular learning task differed spectacularly because the nature of their engagement with that task differed spectacularly. Whatever differences there might be in the learner's background, capabilities and other general attributes, they cannot affect the outcome of a particular learning experience unless they are reflected in differences in what the learners are doing in that situation.

In the specific study discussed here, two distinctively different ways of relating to the reading of the text were found. The differences are highlighted by students when they talk about how they tackled their reading task. Compare the statements, 'Well, I just concentrated on trying to remember as much as possible' and 'There were a lot of different lines of thought to follow and to try to memorize' with these: '... I tried to look for... you know, the principal ideas ...', '... and what you think about then, well it's you know, what was the point of the article, you know' and '... I thought about how he had built up the whole thing'.

In the first two statements, the students are focusing on the text itself, or on the discourse itself, or on recalling it; they are trying to memorize the text. In the second set, the students are focusing more on the author's message, what ideas he was trying to convey, what line of argument he was pursuing and the structure of the argument.

These are examples of a dichotomy that has been widely reported in many contexts – a dichotomy between a *surface approach to learning* and a *deep approach to learning*. The essential distinction between them is that a surface approach focuses on what can be called the *sign* (in this case the text itself) while a deep approach focuses on what is *signified* (in this case the meaning of the text). To be focally aware of the meaning of the text implies that the reader is not also focusing on the text as such (how it is worded), but not vice versa, therefore there is a hierarchical relationship between the two approaches to learning.

Marton and Säljö found that when they considered individual learners in this study, the most advanced outcome, of type A, was only achieved by subjects who also described a deep approach to the task, and the least meaningful outcomes, types C and D, came only from students who described surface approaches (see Table 3.1). Therefore the qualitative differences in approach to learning were associated with discernible differences in the outcome of learning: deep approaches were related to grasping the author's message and surface approaches were related to miscomprehending or missing the message altogether.

Table 3.1: *Relation between approaches and level of outcome (adapted from Marton & Säljö, 1976)*

Outcome of learning	Approach to learning			Sub-totals
	Surface	Not clear	Deep	
A			5	5
B	1	6	4	11
C	8			8
D	5	1		6
Sub-totals	14	7	9	30

We have represented the relationship between qualitative differences in approaches to learning and in outcomes of learning as an empirical finding. This finding is based on two kinds of data: the participants' description of their experience of the learning situation and their account of the text they read. This is an empirical finding but there is a logical relationship, too. Approaches to and outcomes of learning are two functionally related aspects of learning: in order to arrive at a certain outcome you must have approached the learning task in a certain way. The less than perfect relationship between the two aspects found through research probably reflects less than perfect data rather than what the relationship between the two is actually like.

The example mentioned above has been used many times and, in fact, our presentation here closely resembles Marton and Booth's (1997) presentation of the same investigation. The reason for the frequent reproduction of the study is that it was the first one of a large number of studies demonstrating that the understanding of a text read, the solving of a problem given or the gain from a lecture attended is, to a most substantial extent, a function of the learner's way of experiencing and dealing with the text, the problem or the lecture (see, for instance, Marton, Hounsell and Entwistle, 1997). 'Experiencing and dealing with...' – yes, exactly so. We argued above that our way of acting in a situation springs from our way of experiencing the situation. Act and experience are therefore intertwined and the term 'approach' denotes both.[1] An approach adopted is a way of experiencing something and dealing with it. What is experienced and dealt with is the learning situation, the task, the text, the problem and lecture.

In the above example some of the learners adopt a surface approach – they focus on the text itself. Focusing means experiencing variation. In Chapter 2 we gave examples of things that vary – or not – direction when throwing a ball, frame of reference etc and accordingly are being discerned (if variation is experienced), or not (if variation is not experienced). So what is it that might vary when the text itself is focused on? Obviously there is a sequence of words and expressions and they certainly vary. But in addition to that we would argue that there is an implicit variation in the learner's awareness. One has to capture the words, the expressions and the text. The wording could have been different and there is therefore a potential variation from which the actual text is drawn.

Learners adopting a deep approach, on the other hand, are focusing on what the text is about. Again there is an implicit variation in the learner's awareness, but in this case the perceived meaning of the text read is seen as one of several potential meanings.

This is why those adopting a deep approach arrive at a more complex understanding of the text they read, compared with those adopting a surface approach. It is simply much more likely that you would manage to discern critical aspects of what the text is about if you focus on it and quickly play around with alternative interpretations while reading, than if you do not focus on it and do not try to get hold of its different aspects.

By yielding a richer experience, the deep approach therefore helps to equip the learners better when it comes to viewing future situations through prior experiences. According to what was said in Chapter 2, the capability of dealing with varying situations in the future, through discerning their critical features and focusing on them simultaneously, originates from experienced variation in the past. The variation has to be experienced. Experienced variation can come about in two ways: either there is a varying environment that is perceived or we vary our way of dealing with the environment and perceive variation in that way. An object may move around us and therefore it appears differently or we may move around the object and therefore it appears differently. When it comes to reading, the latter is the case. The text as such does not move but our minds might. The self-generated variation mentioned above is of the implicit kind (experiencing that what we see could have been something else – therefore there is a potential variation). In the case of repeated reading, however, the variation brought about by the learner may be quite explicit.

We have used the term 'variation' in somewhat varying senses. A meaning which comes close to the common usage of the word is exploring something by more or less systematically looking at it from various perspectives. Children explore objects by turning them around, by throwing them, sometimes by tasting them and usually by feeling them. Researchers do something similar, metaphorically speaking, when they explore their objects of research. We become familiar with objects in our world in this way, and with the abstract phenomena of scholarship. It is in this way that appresentation[2] develops and that we become capable of experiencing the whole when only a part of it is given. In the study mentioned in Chapter 2 (page 40), Marton and Wenestam (1988) showed that adopting a deep approach was not a sufficient condition for grasping the conceptual structure underlying an advanced philosophical text, even when it was read as many as five times. They found that for students to understand a text of such an advanced nature, in addition to a deep approach to learning, they needed to adopt a perspective within the text. The text had to be looked at from the point of view of one of its parts and, indeed, the part from which the rest was looked at had to be varied too. This is, by the way, a clear instance of the importance of (varied) 'centring', discussed briefly in Chapter 2.

In a study by Marton, Asplund-Carlsson and Halász (1992), Franz Kafka's famous parable 'Before the law' was read by secondary school students in Hungary and Sweden. The students read the text three times, with one week between the second and third readings. The story they read concerns a man who tries many times to gain admittance to the Law. There is a door which is open but the man is refused entry time and again by a guard. He is told that he is not allowed to go through the door and should wait. No matter how many times and in how many ways he tries, he is unable to get through the door. After many years, now an old man, he tries one last time, and asks the guard why no one else has ever tried to go through the door. The guard tells him that the door was only for him, and that now that his life is reaching its end, the door is to be closed.

The group of readers can be thought of metaphorically as a prism through which the text passed, to be refracted and to exit with distinctly different meanings. Four different ways of understanding the story were found, which we will call A, B, C and D, without elaborating them. Two of the ways of understanding the story (D and C) were included in a third one (B) which in its turn was included in a fourth way of understanding (A). This fourth way was the most complex of all (similar to what was found in the Marton and Säljö (1976) study discussed earlier in this chapter, see Figure 3.2). A number of the students were found to have engaged in what was called *reflective variation*. This appeared:

... within the very same understanding by the very same individual on the very same occasion. A number of students used a form of variation to make sense of what they were reading and we find a certain *movement* in some understandings of the story; they have certain dynamic qualities. These students seem to wish to explore what is meant, what is implied in the text by trying alternative ways of understanding the whole text or its parts on the one hand and making explicit the implications of their way of understanding the whole text or its parts, on the other. This way of handling the text is strikingly different from that behind the more or less taken-for-granted understanding that most of the students put forward (Marton, Asplund-Carlsson and Halász, 1992).

Two different forms of this variation were identified. In some cases, the student varied the meaning of the whole story or some of its constituent parts and the label *variation in meaning* was applied to this form. For example, consider the following extract from one student:

The author constructed this in such a way, I believe, that everyone should understand it in accordance with his own thoughts, his own personality. Thus it means different things for everyone. The law could mean absolute knowledge, the laws of nature, our own essence itself, the goal of life or the meaning of life. If the author (or whoever reads it) is religious, you can interpret the door to the law as the gate to Heaven, to which everyone should find his own way. Of course, we can accept the law as it is, law. It would then mean that the law is not equal for all (Marton, Asplund-Carlsson and Halász, 1992).

There were other cases in which a line of reasoning was developed and the implications of certain details in the story were made explicit; this led to yet further implications. This is given the label *elaborative variation* and is illustrated by a case in which it yielded a complex understanding of the story, as judged by the authors of the paper:

This is a rather contradictory situation. The man wants to get to the law, but the guard hinders him by the door of the law. Why? This is the first question we ask ourselves. But we do not understand the answer very well. The man will probably never get through the door; law itself stands in his way. If he enters in spite of the prohibition, then he breaks the law, because the law says that he (now or whenever) cannot get in. The man can't take this contradiction since he does not want to break the law. But he must enter at any price and there is no possibility other than to get the guard to reconsider. At first he tries persuasion, but has no success. Then he tries bribery. That is not very 'legal'. This could be important, that is, if the man tries to obtain something, he won't give in at the first difficulty; if there is no straightforward way, he tries the dishonest way, illegally. Nothing is beyond human beings – neither crime nor violence – when they are trying to reach a goal. Most people are like that. But our man feels that as soon as he has entered the door, he will have to answer for his actions, since he has come to 'the law'. Therefore he waits. When he gets old, the guard mentions a kind of solution. The door was open. There are such contradictions which have no solution, it is a paradox (he can enter, but he cannot!). That is why it is such shocking reading (Marton, Asplund-Carlsson and Halász, 1992).

There was a close correlation between the use of reflective variation and the level of understanding of the story. This is shown in Table 3.2 where the occurrence of the two most complex forms of understanding is cross-tabulated against the use of reflective variation in the course of the different readings.

The two examples dealt with in this chapter have been about learning from texts. You might say they were about understanding texts. But, as we argued above, by reading people widen the experiences through which they view situations in the future. The 'learning situations' and the 'situations of application' are therefore likely to be different in this case. In other cases the two kinds of situation belong to the same class. In those cases one could say that in addition to learning about some specific content you learn the way of going about the task. By adopting a certain approach you learn to adopt that approach. The next example is about approaching programming tasks. Here, in addition to the specific programming language used and the details of the programming environment, you actually learn to adopt a certain approach – or certain approaches – to programming tasks.

Table 3.2: *Relation between best understanding and use of reflective variation. (Marton, Asplund-Carlsson & Halász, 1992)*

		Use of reflective variation on some occasion		
		no	yes	Total
Understanding A or B on some occasion	no	48	4	52
	yes	-	8	8
	Total	48	12	60

Approaches to learning to program

When students are learning to program, one of their primary activities is to write programs which address problems presented to them in prose format. The education of potential programming professionals has the aim of getting students to undertake careful consideration of a problem prior to thinking about the program that has to be written. The 14 students involved in Booth's (1992a) study were just such potential computer professionals, and the educational strategy which had been adopted involved introducing programming in the first term of a degree course in computer science and computer engineering through the very high level language called Standard Meta-Language (known as ML; see Wikström, 1987).

> The students were asked to write programs aimed at solving particular problems of current interest in the course. They were asked to read the worded problem and then say what they thought the problem was about, before trying to produce a program. Four distinctly different ways of handling such problems were found, across two different problems. These four ways fall into two groups – again the surface-deep dichotomy – as elaborated in Table 3.3.
>
> The surface approach is indicated in what have been called opportunistic approaches in the context of writing programs. On the one hand, the expedient approach is typified by the student, on reading the problem, immediately alighting on a potentially ready-made program which fits the bill. It might be one that the student wrote last week and just needs tinkering with (generally a mistaken belief), or a standard program that is indicated because of some similarity in nomenclature. In no event observed was it followed by a successful outcome; students either gave up the attempt totally or went back to the problem and thought again. On the other hand, the constructual approach is typified by the student not assuming a complete solution from the start,

but selecting constructs from the repertoire studied so far that might be relevant to constructing a program for this problem. In both approaches, the student is not interpreting the problem as such but focusing on the program that has to be written, with neither a formal nor an informal specification in mind.

Table 3.3: *Student approaches to computer programming (from Booth, 1992)*

Opportunistic (surface) approaches		
Expedient approach	On reading the problem, the student seeks a ready-made program that seems to fit; never a successful outcome.	In both approaches, students do not interpret the problem but focus on the program that needs to be written, with neither a formal nor an informal specification in mind.
Constructual approach	Student selects from repertoire studied so far of any constructs that might be relevant.	
Interpretative (deep) approaches		
Operational approach	Deep approaches in this study, here called *Interpretative approaches*, focus more on the meaning of the problem as it stands. There is the *Operational approach*, on the one hand, in which the students interpret the problem in terms of what the program will have to do or what operations it will have to accomplish in order to satisfy the problem – an informal specification for the program.	In both approaches, students focus at the outset on formulating a framework for the developing program – an operational framework for the program's way of working and a structural framework in terms of the problem's own structure.
Structural approach	On the other hand, there is a *Structural approach*, where the student's reaction to the problem is to interpret it in its own domain, referring to the problem's own features and constraints rather than what the program will be like.	

There are commonly seen to be three phases to devising a computer program: 'problem', 'specification' and 'program'. Dealing with the problem phase involves studying the problem and coming to terms with its structure in such a way that it is possible to write a program for it. This leads eventually to a specification, which is a statement of the program's requirements in terms of data structures, algorithms, internal relations such as routine interconnectivity and external relations such as programming environment and input/output devices. The actual program can be written from the specifications, provided that all of its aspects fit the kind of hardware on which it is to be run. As shown in Figure 3.3, the approaches found in Booth's (1992a) study link clearly to one or other of these three phases: the structural approach points to the 'problem' phase, the operational to the 'specification' phase, and the constructual approach (and to some extent the expedient approach) to the 'program' phase.

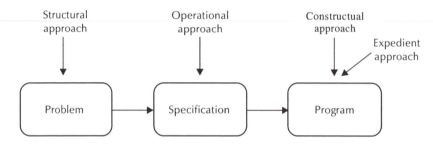

Figure 3.3: *Relation between approaches and phases of the program writing process (Marton and Booth, 1997)*

It seems unlikely that a constructual or expedient approach would lead to considered programming. That is one criticism that can be levelled at the opportunistic approaches. Booth (1992b) has shown that the opportunistic approaches are closely related to experiencing programming as being about making use of the computer in an unspecified way, hacking, and experiencing learning to program as being about learning the codes of the languages rather thoroughly. These views are just what the sort of programming exercise was intended to eradicate. While the student who deliberately considers the structure and the principles of the problem is learning that lesson, the student who tries to expedite a quick fix, or runs through the current repertoire of constructs, is merely avoiding the lesson.

This study is different from those described earlier in the chapter in two respects. First, the term 'approach' has apparently different usages. Approach to reading a text refers to the overall strategy (whether adopted consciously or not) that students say they have used when reading. In the study of learning to program, 'approach' is used with reference to the initial response to the problem, which establishes the basis for writing the program. Therefore while the approaches to reading text were found in students' reports of how they had gone about the task, approaches to writing programs have been observed and discussed in the very act of writing the program. Second, while it is less easy to be specific about learning outcomes of the programming tasks than the outcomes of reading the texts, developing a principled way of writing programs is clearly linked with certain approaches and not with others.

The origin of approaches to learning

What we learn from dealing with problems, from reading texts, from listening to lectures, from working with others or from writing computer programs is very much a function of the approaches we adopt to those situations.[3] In addition, we may adopt one approach or the other not only because we have a particular biography but also because we are in a particular situation.

Approaches to learning reflect our views of learning and, as the approach we adopt may vary from situation to situation, so does the view of learning expressed. This is so because learning might mean different things not only for different people but also for the same person in different situations.

Human beings are, as a rule, oriented towards the world around them, towards various phenomena populating it and towards the meanings with which the world is imbued. So why do learners under certain circumstances focus on the sign instead of what it signifies, on the words rather than on the meaning and on the surface rather than on what the surface is the surface of? Paradoxically enough the surface approach seems to originate from experienced demands to learn. This is a kind of means–ends reversal. A text, a problem formulation, which is supposed to be a means to learn what the text or the problem is about, becomes the primary focus of the learner, an end in itself. Learning, which is the aim of the whole exercise, is experienced as a demand, and living up to the demand of proving that one has learned (for instance, by recalling the text read) becomes dominant in the learner's awareness. This resembles means–ends reversal at the institutional level in the context of quality assurance (see Figure 9.2 in Chapter 9).

It could be argued that the most frequent and most important forms of learning are by-products of other activities without particular arrangements being made to facilitate learning (see the introduction to Chapter 2, page 23). For example, we learn our native language by interacting with others and becoming a part of the world permeated by language; we develop motor capabilities by interacting with the physical world and we develop social capabilities by interacting with the social world. Even developing professional competence can be seen more or less as a by-product of becoming a member of a professional group. Acquisition of required skills and knowledge occurs as part of the developing familiarity with ways of being, ways of thinking, ways of seeing the world characterizing the group and with the context that is gradually and increasingly inhabited.

This is illustrated in a book by Christie (1985), in which he contrasts what he calls 'white learning' with 'Aboriginal learning' in Australia, with the latter being an intrinsic part of life, while the former is separated and institutionalized. Jean Lave, an anthropologist, puts a similar view. Lave studied tailor apprentices in Liberia and became aware of the occasional nature of learning in the technical sense (becoming capable of producing cloth, for instance, Lave,

1996). Lave contributed to the emergence of the apprentice almost as the prototypic learner during the 1990s. This was a result of the convergence of the interest in learning in natural (as opposed to institutional) settings, the interest in the socio-historical school of psychology and the post-modern zeitgeist. Lave and Wenger (1991) went further with their view of learning as a by-product of socialization and as part of a transition from being 'a legitimate peripheral' to a less peripheral participant in a particular field of social practice.

The common feature in all of these studies is the emphasis on the cultural, social, linguistic and contextual embeddedness of human thought and human action (and therefore human learning as well). The basic idea of learning is that the meaningful learning of concepts, ideas or principles has to be situated in real-life practices where these concepts, ideas and principles are functional and where they constitute discursive resources for the learners. The term 'cognitive apprenticeship' is applied to this model.

It is in situations set up with the explicit purpose of learning and therefore, adverse to this view, situations which the entire educational system is there to cater for, that the very distinction between surface and deep approaches can be observed.

Can we observe the origin of the difference between approaches to learning even in the pre-school, among children 5–6 years old? Pramling (1986) argues that we can. She illustrates this in an observational study of a group of children being 'taught' (but not necessarily learning) about colours and shapes. The teacher in her study wanted the children to develop distinctions between basic and blended colours, knowledge of different colours and the idea of shades of a colour. She also wanted them to develop the idea of different shapes such as the circle, square or triangle and to appreciate the relationship between big and small and between narrow and wide (Pramling, 1986). The children interacted with objects of different colours and different shapes in both work and play situations and the teacher explained the concepts in words. Pramling found that the children focused on the situation in two distinctively different ways, the difference resembling the difference between the surface and the deep approach.

Some children focused on the activities (painting, drawing, doing) – things that they thought the teacher wanted them to do – rather than on the shapes and colours the teacher was actually interested in. In other cases the children did focus on the phenomenon they were supposed to learn about.

Ahlberg (1992) studied 10-year-olds' approaches to dealing with problems, some overtly mathematical, others covertly mathematical and still others that were non-mathematical in nature. She found two different approaches to dealing with mathematical problems, again linked to the deep and surface approaches described above. The first approach is mainly directed towards grasping the problem. The focus is on the problem-solving process, different ways of solving problems are tried. The children hypothesize and they can vary their perspectives on presented problems. They are oriented towards seeing some or all of the parts of the problem and the numbers in the problem and investigating the internal relationships between them. Children taking the second approach try to apply a well-known method of solution which they have used before, and solve the given problem according to a given pattern. They do not try alternative methods.

Both of these studies, Pramling's and Ahlberg's, indicate the adoption of deep and surface approaches to learning from an early age, and that it is not a concept exclusively useful in studies of adults learning in higher education.

As we mentioned earlier, we see the surface approach very much as a result of a means–ends reversal, brought about by institutional demands for learning. When children experience the requirements to learn, to achieve, to be clever and to show it to be the case by recalling, saying or doing something, there is a risk that the means (recalling, saying or doing something) becomes an end in itself instead of the means that were supposed to indicate the outcomes (insights, capabilities, understanding).

Even if the surface approach is very much a function of the explicit focus on learning and of the demand to demonstrate that one has learnt, is it a characteristic feature of formal schooling? Not all formal schooling has such an effect on the learners, and basically no formal schooling has such an effect on all learners. As a matter of fact we can identify the characteristics of the educational environment that are associated with different approaches.

Approaches to learning in different contexts

So far we have described research into how students approach learning in a number of specific circumstances. In this section we ask ourselves the question: can we investigate student approaches to learning at a more general level and in different contexts? In fact, we can. In the early 1980s at Lancaster University, Entwistle and Ramsden (1983) developed an inventory of students' approaches to learning with the purpose of subsequently using inventory scores to gauge the effects of learning environments on university students' approaches to study. The inventory produces scores for deep and surface approach by analysis of students' responses on a five-point scale to a series of items, including the following:

- I generally put a lot of effort into trying to understand things which initially seem difficult.
- I often find myself questioning things I hear in lectures or read in books.
- I usually set out to understand thoroughly the meaning of what I am asked to read.
- When I'm tackling a new topic, I often ask myself questions about it which the new information should answer.
- I find I have to concentrate on memorizing a good deal of what we have to learn.

- The best way for me to understand what technical terms mean is to remember the textbook definitions.
- Often I find I have read things without having a chance to really understand them.
- I usually don't have time to think about the implications of what I have to read.

High scores on the first four items and low scores on the last four items are linked to a deep approach which is also referred to as a meaning orientation (Ramsden, 1992). The reverse scoring is linked to a surface approach which is also referred to by Ramsden as a reproducing orientation.

This difference in terminology (between approaches and orientations to learning) is also related to a difference in what is being measured. Earlier in this chapter, the qualitative studies of approaches to learning were concerned with specific learning experiences. That is, conclusions could be drawn that certain students were taking a surface approach to, say, reading a particular text. The evidence came from what they said they were doing when they were carrying out the reading task. This was the original basis for the deep-surface distinction and approaches to learning were found to vary with context, more or less. The same person might adopt different approaches under different circumstances. The Lancaster inventory measures more general aspects of approaches to learning in that the responses made by students in completing the inventory normally are not related to a particular task, but rather to the general approach to learning taken by the student in the whole subject or programme. Nevertheless Ramsden (1992) reports that in numerous studies the inventory has been found to be context-sensitive. He has researched the relation between educational context and approaches to learning. He noted (Ramsden, 1984) that a particular student might well generally take a surface approach to learning in one subject and yet take a deep approach to most learning tasks in another subject studied in a different department in which the educational environment is more supportive. He also found that, within a single subject area, the tendency to take a particular approach to learning varies from one institution to another, depending on the educational environment in the particular departments.

Biggs (1987a 1987b) has also developed an inventory relevant to higher education students' approaches to learning by adapting one of his earlier inventories to produce the Study Process Questionnaire (SPQ). Biggs adopted the Marton and Säljö (1976) labels, deep and surface, to designate two of the three scales in the SPQ. However, the SPQ appears to be used at an even more general level than the Lancaster inventory as if it were a learning styles instrument, measuring some characteristic of the person rather than their relation with the object of learning. The Lancaster inventory appears much closer to the original Swedish research and it is helpful that it has introduced new terminology (meaning and reproducing orientation) which distinguishes it from the original qualitative research into deep and surface approaches to learning.

How does the learning environment affect students' approaches to learning?

It is clear that teachers and others involved with higher education would like students to achieve more than minimal learning outcomes. Yet many teachers lament the fact that their students do not approach learning with higher level aims in mind. Students are criticized for their tendency to memorize information, often by swotting just prior to examinations, and to forget it promptly afterwards. Subsequent testing often demonstrates that, despite students' having successfully negotiated the assessment system, little understanding of fundamental concepts has been gained (Bowden *et al.*, 1992). Learning has often been of lower quality than teachers expect, which leads to an important question that should be addressed. How can teachers encourage students to focus on the higher level objectives?

What teachers do in their classes and what students achieve are affected by many factors. Some of the more tangible factors among these are the previous learning experience of students, the type of performance in assessment that has brought rewards to students in the past, the expectations of various bodies such as employers, professional associations and the educational institution itself, the types of activity that bring reward to teachers in their institution, the educational ethos of the institution, teachers' understanding of learning theory and their capacity to apply such theory to practice (Ramsden, 1984; Bowden, 1988). Teachers are not always aware of the influence of these factors on their teaching and, while they need to approach their work with flexibility, they also need a framework that guides their action. What is likely to succeed in practice is not teaching recipes but decision making based on clear principles related to student learning.

Approaches to learning describe the relation between the learner and the object of learning within a particular context. Therefore a person may be described as having taken a surface approach to a task but should not be described as a surface learner. In a more supportive learning environment, that same student may take a deep approach to learning, a proposition supported by research evidence (Ramsden, 1984). A surface approach is related to a reliance on rote learning. Students taking a surface approach tend to be assessment-conscious, fact- and syllabus-bound and not searching for relations between ideas. There usually is a concentration on procedures, time limits and learning of details, with different parts of the learning being dealt with in isolation from each other (Marton, 1983). Ramsden (1984) reported that the factors that most influence students to take a surface approach to a task are inadequate previous knowledge, time constraints, an over-demanding syllabus, frequent assessment for credit, lack of feedback, assessment methods that emphasize recall and previous rewards for learning of this sort. Factors that encourage a deep approach to learning include teaching and assessment methods that foster active and long-term engagement with the learning tasks, clearly stated expectations, teachers' commitment to the material and emphasis on meaning and relevance to students, opportunities for students to exercise responsible choice in how and what to learn, interest and background knowledge of the material and previous rewards for learning of this sort.

Many students enter university through competitive examination systems which have led to learning environments of the kind that foster surface approaches to learning. The only way that students will learn to approach their learning differently is by experiencing a different kind of learning environment. Yet many university teachers acknowledge that it is common for courses in their own university, or even courses that they have taught, to have the following characteristics: many short units, immediate assessment, assessment for recall, grades being the only feedback, students never assessed again on topics and few links to other units (Bowden, 1990). Such characteristics are exactly those which will encourage students to take a surface approach to their learning. Clearly there are links between the way universities and teachers structure and manage educational programmes and how students approach their learning, often negative links. Academic teachers may stress to students how important the search for meaning in learning is but students will judge the university by its actions and not its words. Only by changing the learning environment will a university have reason to hope that the majority of its students will approach their learning in the manner desired.

The Course Experience Questionnaire

It is possible to find out how students perceive the learning environment. Many academic teachers will have discovered something about their own students' perceptions of the environment they have provided through standard 'evaluation of teaching' surveys undertaken in many universities, but also through informal comments by students or through organized group feedback sessions. Another way in which such feedback is commonly obtained, especially at the educational programme level, is through the Course Experience Questionnaire (CEQ) developed in Australia by Ramsden (1991). The advantage of the CEQ is that it is based on the very research that informed us about the factors in the learning environment which encourage or discourage deep and surface approaches to learning.

The CEQ provides a series of 30 statements with which students are invited to agree or disagree on a five-point scale. The statements fall into five groups which have been labelled as shown in Table 3.4.

The characteristics of programmes that rate highly on the Good Teaching scale (Ramsden, 1992) are not surprising: teachers try to understand the problems students are having and give helpful feedback; they try to make the subject interesting and explain things well; they care that students do well and try to motivate them to do their best.

Table 3.4: *CEQ scales and sample items*

Scale	Sample item
Good Teaching	Teaching staff here normally give helpful feedback on how you are going
Clear goals	You usually have a clear idea of where you're going and what's expected of you in this course
Appropriate Workload	The sheer volume of work to be got through in this course means you can't comprehend it all thoroughly (negatively scored)
Appropriate Assessment	Staff here seem more interested in testing what we have memorized that what we have understood (negatively scored)
Emphasis on Independence	Students here are given a lot of choice in the work they have to do.

The CEQ was trialed in 1989 with students in Australian universities across the full range of disciplines, including both general and professional programmes, and it was found that there were significant differences between fields of study, with the health sciences (including medicine) and engineering scoring lower on all scales than the humanities and the visual and performing arts at the other extreme. There were also variations within fields of study, with electrical engineering scoring lower than other engineering fields and psychology lower than other social sciences. A validation study in the same institutions by Bowden and Martin (1990), in which academic staff rated the teaching in their own departments, revealed the same within-field and between-field variations. In addition, the CEQ outcomes revealed differences in students' views of the teaching of particular subjects across institutions. For example, there is more than a standard deviation between the worst- and best-rated accountancy departments across 13 Australian universities.

Because of its capacity to measure such variations, a modified version of the CEQ is used on a biennial basis in every Australian university in every educational programme. The survey is administered by the Graduate Careers Council of Australasia under the auspices of the Australian Federal Government's Department of Employment, Education, Training and Youth Affairs. The data are fed back to the universities and are used in various ways. The first way, which is supported by the originators, is as a set of longitudinal data through which student perception of quality improvement interventions can be measured. Is the change made in assessment procedures last year, at all levels of the programme, reflected in a change in the 'Appropriate Assessment' scale of the CEQ, as rated by this year's graduates compared with the previous cohort? Are the recent complaints by students about work overload in this programme reflected in the graduate scores on the 'Appropriate Workload' scale of the CEQ data that just arrived? Should we contact some comparable departments at other universities to see how our scores on these scales compare? Should we collaborate with them on ways of mutually improving relevant aspects of the teaching and learning environment in our courses? These are the kinds of question for which the CEQ data is a useful source of information. However, it needs to be emphasized that the CEQ data provides a first layer of evidence only. The CEQ was developed as, and is only, a source of performance indicators. The performance indicator, by definition, does not provide the solution. Other necessary processes, including direct discussion with students, graduates, professionals, other academics and educational experts, are necessary if the problem is to be defined and solutions designed and implemented. The object of study is also important and more will be said of this later in this chapter.

Another application of CEQ data which is not advocated (by us or by the originators of the CEQ) is to use the scale scores in 'league table' ratings. The CEQ data are at their best when comparing identical situations with single or limited factor variations as mentioned above. Longitudinal studies in the same educational programme, or comparison between similar educational programmes in different universities at the same time, can benefit greatly from use of one or more scale scores from CEQ data. However, averaging the scale scores across the whole CEQ or averaging scale scores across a university produces numbers with doubtful validity. Certainly, comparison between whole universities on such averaged scores is inappropriate. The dependence of the scores on field of study means that a university with more students enrolled in visual arts or humanities will normally do better than a university with the majority of its students in engineering or the health sciences, irrespective of efforts made to improve the quality of teaching and learning in either institution. There is no independent data to prove one way or the other that those differences reflect anything other than some cultural or other effect on the perceptions of students. This is likely to be only a partial explanation but it tends to invalidate most 'league table' uses of CEQ data. We would counsel universities to use the CEQ data for its richest purpose, to contribute to the improvement of the quality of student learning.

Approaches to learning and changes in ways of understanding

In Marton's and Säljö's (1976) study described above, it was found that differences in the outcomes of learning in a particular situation were closely related to the ways in which the learner approached that situation. When we are dealing at a more general level with 'orientation' rather than 'approach', we might ask whether changes in how learners see and experience the object of learning over longer time intervals are related to the learner's orientation to learning. We would therefore expect learners who tend to adopt a deep approach, who have such an orientation, to be more likely to change their way of experiencing the phenomena dealt with in their studies.

Prosser and Millar (1989) found this to be so. They investigated the relation between approaches to learning and coming to see, ie to understand, the object of learning in a particular way. The study focused on a six-week course including a topic known to be conceptually difficult for physics students – force and motion. Newton's first law states that a body remains in its state of rest or uniform motion unless a force is applied to change it. This makes a critical distinction between the idea of rest or uniform motion, implying the net absence of force, and the idea of change in uniform motion (acceleration or deceleration), implying the net presence of a force. Johansson, Marton and Svensson (1985), had earlier shown that while students can learn to apply and manipulate the formulae derived from Newton's laws, they tend to retain the qualitative understanding of Aristotle (see Chapter 2, pages 30–33). In the course studied by Prosser and Millar, the focus was on qualitative understanding rather than formula manipulation skill, through discussion sessions aimed at revealing the variation in understanding, and laboratory work focused on problem solving. Students were interviewed both before and after the course, first, to test their understanding of the key concepts and, on the second occasion, to reveal their approaches to learning.

One example concerns a question already used in illustration in Chapter 2: 'A car is driven at a high constant speed along a straight line on a highway – what forces act on the car?' The Newtonian description is of forces in balance – motive force balancing resistance – while the Aristotelian description is of a net force in the direction of motion – motive force exceeding resistance. When students were interviewed prior to the course, none showed the Newtonian understanding in tackling the problem, whereas 4 of the 14 participants indicated it afterwards. Other questions used were 'A golfer hits a ball and it lands on a completely level green – what kind of path will it follow and why?' and 'A puck leaves an ice hockey stick and glides straight ahead on smooth ice – what happens to the puck and why?'

Following the second set of interviews, students were classified as having had a deep or a surface approach to their learning in the course as a whole, rather than on a single occasion. In this particular case, the students who indicated that they tend to take a surface approach were seen as trying to: 'categorize and memorize disconnected pieces of material so that they could increase the amount of knowledge they had and meet course requirements'. Those tending to take a deep approach were seen to 'abstract meaning from, change their understanding of and develop a personal commitment to the material being studied so that they could explain and better understand reality'. Three students showed no clear orientation to any one approach.

The four students who showed a more developed conception of the problem in the post-test were the only four who had clearly indicated a deep approach to learning.

A summary of the results combined over four tasks is shown in Table 3.5. It excludes those students who had the most advanced conceptions from the beginning.

Table 3.5: *Summary of development of understanding by approach to learning (adapted from Prosser & Millar, 1989)*

	Approach		
	Clearly deep	Unclear	Clearly surface
Did develop	8	6	2
Did not develop	1	3	21

These findings indicate that learning in the sense of students' changing their way of experiencing a phenomenon is contingent on their approaches to learning. Prosser has since replicated these findings (Prosser, 1994) about the relation between approaches and ways of experiencing, which he calls conceptual change, in another field of physics: electricity.

Students' approaches to learning and teachers' approaches to teaching

We have shown that the learning environment has a significant effect on students' approaches to learning. It would be reasonable to conclude that the way in which university academics undertake their teaching would be one of the important factors.

Trigwell, Prosser and Lyons (in press) have investigated that proposition and their paper reports an empirical study which shows that different approaches to teaching are associated with different approaches to learning.

The study made use of a teaching approach inventory derived from interviews with academic staff, and a modified 'approaches to learning' questionnaire. Over 2,000 science students, who adopt significantly deeper approaches to learning than a similar number of their colleagues, are found to be taught by staff who adopt approaches to teaching that are significantly more oriented towards students and to changing their conceptions. Conversely, in classes where teachers describe their approach to teaching as having a focus on what they do and on transmitting knowledge, students are more likely to report that they adopt a surface approach to the learning of that subject.

The Approaches to Teaching Inventory (Trigwell and Prosser, 1996) contains two scales, each of which has both an intention item and a strategy item.[4] For the Information Transmission/Teacher-focused approach, measured by one of the scales, one pair of items (Trigwell, Prosser and Lyons, in press) was:

Intention item: I feel it is more important to present a lot of facts in the classes so that students know what they have to learn for this subject.

Strategy item: I design my teaching in this subject with the assumption that most of the students have very little useful knowledge of the topics to be covered.

The Inventory also has items corresponding to a conceptual change/student-focused approach to teaching measured by the other scale. One pair of items aimed at measuring this approach was:

Intention item: I feel a lot of teaching time in this subject should be used to question students' ideas.

Strategy item: We take a lot of time out in classes so that students can discuss among themselves the difficulties that they encounter studying this subject.

The students' approaches to learning were investigated by using a modified version of Biggs' Study Process Questionnaire (Biggs, 1987a 1987b) referred to earlier in this chapter. The version used had two scales – a Deep Approach to Learning scale and a Surface Approach to Learning scale. The conclusions, derived from correlation, factor and cluster analyses at both the class ($n = 48$) and individual student ($n = 3956$) levels in Australian universities, show the connectedness of teachers' approaches to teaching and students' approaches to learning and led Trigwell, Prosser and Lyons (in press) to comment as follows: 'Given the numerous studies that show correlations between students' deeper approaches to learning and higher quality learning outcomes, these results demonstrate the importance of attempts to improve the quality of student learning by encouraging higher quality, Conceptual Change/Student-focused approaches to teaching.'

They make the point that theirs is the first study to investigate teachers' own reports of their approach to teaching rather than the students' perceptions of their teachers' teaching and to show relations between teachers' approaches to teaching and students' approaches to learning. The teachers who describe their teaching as corresponding to a student-focused approach are more likely to be teaching students who report adopting a deep approach to learning in that subject. On the other hand, teachers who say they take a teacher-focused approach to teaching are more likely to have students who say they take a surface approach to learning in the subject. Given the correlation between students taking a deep approach to learning and higher level learning outcomes, this finding about teachers' approaches to teaching is highly significant. They support the CEQ findings reported earlier in this chapter on the relation between students' approaches to learning and their perceptions of the teaching they experience, both in terms of the relationship and in terms of what constitutes good teaching.

Conceptions of learning

The point of departure of this chapter was a series of studies published in the mid-1970s and onwards. These were in-depth investigations of what students learn from reading texts, solving problems, and listening to lectures, and how they learn. The first question was answered in these studies in terms of the different ways in which the learners made sense of the texts, problems, lectures and so on. Such differences were characterized in Chapter 2 – and less comprehensively in the present one – in terms of the aspects of the situation that are discerned and focused on simultaneously. Furthermore, what is discerned and focused on was seen as a function of the previous experiences (dimensions of variation) through which the present situation is seen. What the present chapter adds to Chapter 2 is that those past experiences used are a function of how the present situation is experienced and dealt with, or in other words, how it is approached. Not only is the present seen from the point of view of the past, but the past is seen from the point of view of the present.

Differences in the approaches adopted to the situation answer the second question, about how individuals learn what they learn. Furthermore, to the extent that the situation is seen as a learning situation, the approach the learner adopts originates from the way in which learning as a phenomenon appears from the point of view of that situation. The learner's approaches to learning are therefore closely related to their views, or conceptions, of learning. This is a finding that has been confirmed repeatedly (see, for instance, van Rossum and Schenk, 1984; Gibbs, Morgan and Taylor, 1984). What are conceptions of learning like? We will address this question by summarizing a fairly recent study.

Twenty-nine of the students who enrolled on the Social Science Foundation Course of the Open University in 1980 were selected for study over a wide range of aspects of their experiences as students (Gibbs, Morgan and Taylor, 1984; Taylor and Morgan, 1986; Beaty, 1987). They were interviewed up to seven times throughout their enrolment and over six years for some (including twice in the first year – at the beginning and end of the academic year). In each interview, the students reflected on their own learning and their progress as learners. That aspect of each interview formed the basis for a thorough analysis (Marton, Beaty and Dall'Alba, 1993) of how these students conceptualized learning overall.

Säljö (1979, 1982) had earlier addressed the same question and he identified five qualitatively distinct conceptions of learning, and Giorgi, who tackled similar material from the research perspective of phenomenological psychology, verified them (Giorgi, 1986).

Marton, Beaty and Dall'Alba (1993) identified virtually the same five conceptions of learning as Säljö (1979) and Giorgi (1986) but also found a sixth. Again the six conceptions were in two groups (see Säljö, 1982). One group focuses on learning itself in the context of tasks of learning – on the act of learning and the consequences of that act. The other group focuses on the object of learning – finding meaning through the learning tasks. The term 'conceptions' in this context refers to qualitatively distinct ways in which the subjects were found to voice what they thought about learning, whether in respect to themselves, their reflections over their progress, or any other expression. Conceptions are not assigned to an individual as some sort of mental entity; rather they are seen as telling features of the whole picture drawn by the group.

In the first group of conceptions, the focus is on the act of learning itself. For instance, in the first conception: *learning as increasing one's knowledge* (A), students refer to 'accumulation of knowledge' (Vincent 1b) or 'filling my head with facts' (Field 2). (The number following the name of the participant – actually a pseudonym – refers to the interview occasion, for example, 1b refers to the second interview in first year .) Learning is seen to be about knowledge in the form of facts and information that are acquired. Consumption is the principal metaphor: filling up, being absorbed and picked up. Learning is seen as an increase of knowledge.

In the following quotes, a different idea of learning emerges: 'learning it up for exams and reproducing it' (Field 1a); 'drumming it... into the brain and reeling it off' (Nelson 1a); 'When you have achieved whatever it was learned for, then that's it, it can go away, it's disposable, you can get rid of it' (Downs 4). The focus here is not only on acquiring knowledge, but equally on what is to be done with it, but again purely in a study context. Students taking this approach see *learning as memorizing and reproducing* (B). There is still a consumption metaphor but it is extended to include the way in which it is consumed – drumming in, learning by rote, cramming – and its eventual use – repeating it, reproduction in exams, disposal when used.

Another difference is illustrated by the following student comments: 'take in information, see how it can be used' (Childs 2); 'turn it around and make use of it in other ways' (Parker 1b). These two quotes exemplify *learning as applying* (C), in which the focus is on application in addition to getting the knowledge and storing it. In this view, learning is no longer confined to study situations, as the learner becomes prepared to consider the new acquisitions in other, as yet unspecified, contexts.

These three conceptions make up the first group of conceptions of learning, in which the learners thematize the task of learning *per se*.

Consider the next group of quotes of which Marton, Beaty and Dall'Alba (1993) wrote 'the watershed is meaning': 'finding out lots of ways of thinking about things, and what view you have yourself' (Charles 1a); ' looking again at things that you know about but with a slightly different perspective – or seeing other people's views on things' (Parker 1b); 'to have a process of thought that sort of "sets in motion" when you look at something... tackle looking at something in a far more logical way' (Field 2).

These three students are talking about having a view or taking a perspective or looking in a particular way at the things they are learning. Their horizons have broadened with respect to learning; they stand back from the knowledge they are acquiring, or memorizing, or applying and reflect over it. They see *learning as understanding* (D). This involves putting their newly gained knowledge not only into the context of the demands being made by the educational system they are part of, but also integrating it into their own worlds through comparing and contrasting. The consumption metaphor so dominant in the first two conceptions is replaced by more of a visualization metaphor, in which learning has the character of looking at things, seeing things in a new light, taking a view and having insight. Learning is now centred on the learner; it goes from the learner – who examines things critically or considers arguments – into the stuff to be learned, which is tossed around or viewed from different angles.

The fifth conception, illustrated here, takes understanding a stage further: not only does the new knowledge act as a catalyst for taking a perspective or view, but it actually makes the world appear in a different way: 'all the time it [what was learnt] keeps cropping up; you might just have seen it [what happens around you] in one way before, you sort of see it in different ways' (South 1b); 'opening your mind a little bit more so you see things [in the world] in different ways' (Field 2); 'being able to look at things, from all sides, and see that what is right for one person is not right for another person' (South 2).

Therefore *learning is seeing something in a different way* (E) not only takes a perspective or view on things, but takes a wider perspective or multi-faceted view, thereby bringing about a more fluid or dynamic perspective on the world. Compared with the previous conception, 'learning as understanding', the context of learning has expanded away from the area immediately demanded by the subject of study and towards the world as a whole.[5]

The five conceptions described so far are virtually the same as those identified by Säljö and by Giorgi. Marton, Beaty and Dall'Alba found a sixth: 'I suppose it's what lights you... it's something personal and it's something that's continuous. Once it starts it carries on and it might lead to other things. It might be like a root that has other branches coming off it... you should be doing it [that is, learning] not for the exam but for the person before and for the person afterwards' (Downs 4); 'expanding yourself... you tend to think that life just took hold of you and did what it wanted with you... you should take hold of life and make it go your way' (Field 6).

This is *learning as changing as a person* (F), the most extensive way of understanding learning in that it embraces the learner not only as the agent of knowledge acquisition, retention and application, and not merely as the beneficiary of learning, but also as the ultimate recipient of the effects of learning.

The six conceptions described and illustrated fall into two groups as shown in Figure 3.4. While there is a focus on the meaning of what is learned present in the last three conceptions, meaning is not stressed at all in the first three. At the same time we can see why approaches to learning adopted are again and again found to be closely related to conceptions of learning expressed. Although 'approaches to learning' refer to the ways in which learners experience learning situations (in particular, what they are trying to achieve and what they are doing), while conceptions of learning refer to the ways in which learners make sense of learning in general (ie when they are reflecting on what learning on the whole means to them) there is a *synonymi* (term used by Linder, 1997) between them: they depict variation in the same dimension. The first group of three conceptions of learning corresponds to the surface approach to learning; the second group corresponds to the deep approach to learning. There are distinct parallels between this second group of approaches to learning and Boyer's scholarship of integration – stepping back, looking for connections and fitting one's own ideas into larger intellectual patterns.

Learning as...

A   ... increasing one's knowledge

B   ... memorizing and reproducing   Learning as primarily
                                                         reproducing
C   ... applying

D   ... understanding

E   ... seeing something in a different way   Learning as primarily
                                                         seeking meaning
F   ... changing as a person

Figure 3.4: *Summary of six conceptions of learning (from Marton, Beaty & Dall'Alba, 1993)*

There is a further detail in the study by Marton *et al.* (1993) that we should notice. The fifth conception, 'learning as seeing something in a different way', and to some extent also the sixth conception (in which the fifth is included), 'learning as changing as a person', resemble the view of learning advocated by us. This is in accordance with the discussion of the continuity of human thought in Chapter 8 – and implicitly also in the next chapter – according to which the ideas developed and used in research originate in our general human understanding of the world around us.

A pattern of relationships

Our sketch of a theory of learning put forward in the previous chapter is formulated in terms of the learner's experience of the object of learning. According to the principle of intentionality (see page 42), when learning we are habitually oriented towards what we learn about. But occasionally we may reflect on our way of going about learning or on what learning in general means to us. In the studies referred to in this chapter such reflection was always triggered by the investigator's question. This chapter is therefore wider in scope than the previous one. In addition to discussing the learners' ways of experiencing, understanding and making sense of what they learn about we have also been dealing with the learners' ways of experiencing the acts of learning, the context of learning and learning as a general phenomenon. We have also discussed studies of relationships between approaches to learning and outcomes of learning, approaches to learning and the learner's experience of the context of learning, approaches to learning and changes in understanding of the object of learning, students' approaches to learning and teachers' approaches to teaching, learners' approaches to learning and their conceptions of learning in general.

Furthermore, we have referred to qualitative studies based on in-depth individual interviews as well as to large-scale questionnaire studies. On the whole the highly heterogeneous collection of studies points to a remarkably convergent pattern: all the variables are interrelated. After all, they represent different aspects of the very same learning experience. Outcomes of learning in our description refer to how the object of learning is seen or experienced by the learners. Now the experience of the object of learning and the experience of the act of learning are not two separate things, but two different aspects of the learner's engagement with a learning project ('project' is used in a wide sense – as something one is trying to achieve). In addition, the learning project is always situated in a context, the experience of which is yet another aspect of the learning experience. This context is to a considerable extent constituted by the teaching arrangements and the examinations. Teachers' approaches to teaching very much represent these parts of the context of learning – as seen by the teachers. So the pattern of relationships depicted in this chapter is between different aspects of the same experience as seen by the same individuals and between the same aspects of the same situation or phenomenon as seen by different individuals. Not only are the relationships found expected but occasionally they are of a logical nature (as far as relationships between different aspects of the same experience are concerned). Does this imply that pointing out the relationships adds little – or nothing – to the questions discussed here?

We aim at capturing the idea that different fields of knowledge should include epistemological aspects of knowledge. 'Epistemological' is used here in a very wide sense, referring to questions about how knowledge is constituted, formed and how it is brought into being. In accordance with the terminology introduced in Chapter 1, this chapter and the previous one are about learning or knowledge formation on the individual level. In Chapter 2 we wanted to show how knowledge about the object of learning is constituted through the dynamic properties of human experience, human awareness: discernment, simultaneity and variation. While Chapter 2 was about the experiential origin of the object aspect of learning, this chapter is about the experiential origin of the act aspect of learning, which in its turn is embedded in the experience of the context of learning. We can never affect learning except through the learner's experience of the object, act and context of learning. So the relationships described in this chapter and the previous one point us to the aspects necessary to attend in order to enhance learning: how the object of learning is presented (in terms of the pattern of variation and simultaneity), how learning tasks and learning context appear to the students (above all in terms of demand characteristics and possible ways for acting) and what learning, studying and solving problems mean to the learners.

Endnotes

1. Earlier we said that an approach to learning comprises the learners' experience of what they are trying to do and what they are doing. In one case it is the intertwined nature of experience and act and in the other case the intertwined nature of the experienced intention and the experienced act that are emphasized. In fact, intention, experience and act – all three are intertwined aspects of approaches to learning.

2. 'Appresentation' is a phenomenological term referring to the fact that in our experience of a part of something the experience of the whole is given. When standing in front of the house where we live we do not only experience a facade but also what is behind it – rooms, furniture and, even more so, people.

3. In Chapter 5 competence in making clinical diagnosis is described in terms of the approaches adopted by medical students (pages 109–10). Similarly differences in engineering competence in developing car motors are described in terms of varying approaches adopted for the task (pages 112–113).

4. Based on the idea that an approach to learning comprises an intentional and a strategic aspect. This relates to our claim above (see note 1) that what you are trying to achieve in a learning situation and how you handle it are two aspects of the approach adopted to that situation. The somewhat differing definitions of 'approaches to learning' do not contradict each other, but highlight different combinations of aspects to the concept.

5. Note that an individual is not necessarily restricted to one conception at a time; in this study, Field is categorized as having voiced two distinctly different conceptions of learning in the second interview.

Chapter 4

Learning and research

The previous two chapters discussed how knowledge is constituted through studying, which we refer to as 'learning on the individual level' (in the title of this chapter, simply as 'learning'). In this chapter we will deal with how learning is constituted through research, which – again in the terminology introduced in Chapter 1 – yields 'learning on the collective level'.[1] We will argue that these two kinds of knowledge formation can be seen from the very same perspective and doing so gives us a better understanding of the relationship between the different aims of the university than recurring opinions about the allegedly inevitable or mythical relationship between teaching and research. We will continue to use the term 'research' because we anticipate negative reader reactions if we continually refer to 'learning on the collective level'.

Learning on the collective level

We take our point of departure from the philosopher, Norwood Hanson, whose book, *Patterns of Discovery*, which was published 40 years ago, describes research in terms congenial to our way of describing learning. To begin with, the metaphor he uses for breakthroughs in frontier research (in physics) is 'seeing'. You see, discover, arrive at a pattern, a conceptual gestalt, which makes the observations you have made earlier appear intelligible. They are endowed with meaning by the pattern. It refers to the way in which the field is organized. The pattern is therefore genuinely 'more than the sum of its parts' (Hanson, 1958).

One of Hanson's many examples is a thought experiment comparing Tycho Brahe and Johannes Kepler watching the dawn. Brahe regarded the Earth as fixed, with all other celestial bodies moving around it. Kepler thought the other way around: the Sun was fixed with the Earth moving around it. Well, would Brahe and Kepler see the same thing in the east at dawn?

The retinal image would most likely be the same but, as Hanson points out, 'Seeing is an experience' and 'People, not their eyes, see' (Hanson, 1958). So even if the elements of their experiences are identical, their conceptual frame-works are different. While Brahe sees the Sun beginning its journey from horizon to horizon, Kepler sees the horizon dipping, or turning away from the Sun (Hanson's treatment of this example (Hanson, 1958) ignores the contri-bution of the rotation of the earth). The latter way of viewing the scenario implies an awareness of alternative frames of reference. In addition to the Earth, or the ground, as a taken-for-granted frame of reference, inherent in Brahe's way of seeing the dawn, there is a frame of reference adopted implicitly by Kepler, from a point outside the Earth. From this perspective the Sun appears fixed. In this case the frame of reference is not taken for granted, but constitutes a dimension of (possible) variation.

Seeing as and seeing that

Hanson makes a logical distinction between 'seeing as' and 'seeing that', arguing that these are two intertwined aspects of seeing. The former refers to the way something appears to someone: the pictorial component of seeing. The latter refers to what someone holds to be true about something: the knowledge component of seeing. What this distinction suggests is that, from our perspec-tive as observers of Brahe and Kepler watching the dawn in the thought experiment, Brahe perceives the Sun to be moving upwards from the horizon, while Kepler perceives the horizon to be dipping, moving away from the Sun. We may of course be wrong in our assumptions about what Brahe and Kepler would see, but the perceptions themselves are neither true or false, they are ways in which something appears to someone. But Brahe himself sees *that* the Sun is going up and from all that we know we have to declare him wrong to the extent that a statement about the relative motions of the Sun and the Earth is implied. The case of Kepler is less straightforward. He, like all other humans, must have habitually used the Earth, the ground, as the frame of reference in his daily life. So to see the horizon moving away from the fixed Sun must have taken quite a bit of effort and had to be heavily supported by the organization of his conceptual framework. But, to the extent he managed to see it in this way, we must conclude on the grounds of our current knowledge that he was right in his perception that the horizon turns away from the Sun.

Developing new ways of seeing

According to Hanson the science of physics is not just '... a systematic exposure of the senses to the world; it is also a way of thinking about the world, a way of forming conceptions' (Hanson, 1958). It is not just seeing and reporting what all normal observers see and report, but seeing in familiar objects what no one else has seen before.

According to this line of reasoning, ways of seeing phenomena of interest are fundamental to learning on the collective level, which research is supposed to contribute to, just as they are fundamental to learning on the individual level, which teaching is supposed to contribute to.

Developing new ways of seeing is difficult. As was pointed out in Chapter 2, we see the world through our previous experiences. Our past is our main resource when dealing with the present but it constitutes our constraints at the same time. The space of what we can possibly see is to be found in the very intersection of the past and the present. This is true for every human being. The difference between high-school students' attempts to expand their ways of grasping the physical reality, and the attempts of researchers at the frontier of human knowledge to expand their (and thereby humanity's) ways of grasping the physical reality, is a difference of time scale, persistence, resources, level of difficulty and impact.

One of the major achievements in the history of physics was that of Galileo Galilei. Dewey writes: 'The work of Galileo was not a development, but a revolution. It marked a change from the qualitative to the quantitative or metric; from the heterogeneous to the homogenous; from intrinsic forms to relations; from aesthetic harmonies to mathematical formulae; from contemplative enjoyment to active manipulation and control; from rest to change; from eternal objects to temporal sequence'. (Dewey, 1929).

In 1604 Galileo formulated a law of falling bodies, according to which velocity was proportional to the distance the body has fallen. Galileo was, however, wrong (as we see it today): the velocity of a falling body is proportional to time, not to distance. As a matter of fact it took Galileo another 34 years to arrive at that more accurate principle.

If we consider the problem as a real-world phenomenon we can conclude that a pile driver, for instance, would drive a given weight further into the ground as its height is increased. As Hanson points out, at distances less than 50 feet differences between distances or between velocities are more likely to capture one's attention than differences in time. Expressed in terms of the conceptual framework developed above, there is much less variation experienced in time than in distance or velocity, within the range mentioned.

On the whole, scientific thinking in Galileo's time was very much about spatial relations and 'the time coordinate' did not have very much significance. Galileo's project was in fact to geometrize motion, thereby liberating it from impetus theory (according to which a projectile maintains its motion due to an inert driving force, the impetus). In order to solve the above problem he had to transcend the conceptual framework and idiom of his time.

By 1609 he realized his mistake and argued that velocity was proportional to time elapsed rather than to distance travelled in free fall. In 1638 he formulated the idea of constant acceleration (according to which an invariable force produces variable velocity). This idea, put forward as a hypothesis, patterned diverse observations obtained during 30 years.

Abduction

'Physical theories provide patterns within which data appear intelligible'. They constitute 'conceptual Gestalts', Hanson says (Hanson, 1958). In addition, Galileo's constant acceleration hypothesis is an excellent example of such a conceptual Gestalt. So how do you arrive at something like that?

Galileo clearly did not work deductively with the point of departure in *explicanda* (those which are to be explained); he was looking for *explicans* (those which are used to explain). Neither did he work inductively, not in the sense of the empiricists (ie assuming that by means of observing an increasing number of individual cases we can increase the likelihood of gaining valid knowledge about what is generalizable across the cases). Aristotle listed three types of inferences: deductive, inductive and what Pierce (1931) called abduction (or retroduction) and through which all the ideas of science come about. It consists of observing the facts and trying to find a theory (Pierce) or a pattern (Hanson) that makes the facts appear intelligible.

And, indeed, deductive inference already presupposes a theory, a framework or a pattern from which the hypothesis can be deduced and the inductive inference is not very likely to yield a theory, a framework or a pattern, as Einstein (1933) so forcefully argued: 'There is no inductive method which could lead to the fundamental concepts of physics... in error are those theorists who believe that theory comes inductively from experience'.

Galileo's arrival at the constant acceleration hypothesis is an excellent example of abduction. He discovered a principle from which all of his earlier observations could be derived (and not the other way around). If the principle were valid the observations must look exactly as they did. In this way they were explained by the principle. The principle is thus not a summary of the observations; it belongs to a level below or underlying the observations and cannot rest upon features that require explanation. Neither is the principle a discovery of some underlying regularities. It is simply a concise formulation from which diverse observations followed.

But it took 34 years to find it. We have already mentioned some of the conceptual constraints under which Galileo had to advance his thinking. Lack of closure, probably observations that were not reconcilable with the earlier formulation were, we believe, driving forces and perhaps a vague, intuitive apprehension of the idea which he was on his way to. He had to be persistent and open-minded. He had to open up the space of variation he was studying: first, in order to include time as a critical aspect of bodies in free fall and second – on a higher level – for a different form of relation between dimensions of variation: for something invariable (acceleration) producing something variable (velocity, distance).

Another example of abduction is Kepler's discovery of the elliptic orbits of planets, in particular of Mars. He, too, when studying variation (in aspects of planetary movements), had to open up for variation on a higher level – in the nature of the orbit. This opening up for variation is what Hanson calls 'pulling the pattern away from all the astronomical thinking there had ever been'. He adds: 'Before Kepler, circular motion was to the concept of planet as "tangibility" is to our concept of "physical object"'. Taking Brahe's observations as the point of departure when considering Mars' orbit around the Sun, Kepler came to the conclusion that the observations could not be reconciled with a circular orbit. So the situation he was facing was: how can the orbit of Mars be described in such a way that all the observations would follow logically from it? Kepler came up with the idea that Mars followed an oviform (ovoid) around the Sun. This is a curve, similar to an ellipse but with one focus only. Historians of science have always believed that Kepler went from a circle to an ellipse (in fact he called the oviform ellipse). According to Hanson, Kepler used an ellipse (ie a real ellipse) as a mathematical model to which the oviform was seen as an approximation: 'The move of treating observed physical phenomena as approximations to mathematically "clean" conceptions developed after Kepler into a defining property of physical inquiry' (Hanson, 1958). In this way he took one major step and opened one dimension of variation – for other than circular orbits, but he refrained from taking another step and opening another dimension of variation. In accordance with his predecessors as far as Martian theories go – whether using a geocentric or a heliocentric model – he used one focus for the orbit.

But the data did not square with the idea. The oviform orbit was not possible to reconcile with the observations. Kepler understood that what he needed was something between a circle and an ovoid. Eventually the insight dawned on him: the orbit is an ellipse! Now he opened up a new dimension of variation (from one focus to two foci) and made a move in a dimension of variation established earlier (between a mathematical and a physical hypothesis). This was a profound figure–ground reversal: what was there to begin with as a mathematical instrument was now seen depicting the physical reality. In this way Kepler could account for all of Brahe's observations as to the various positions of Mars at different points in time as well as for the reason that Mars appeared to accelerate at 90° and 270° (Hanson, 1958).

Scientific intuition

Each year in Sweden, when Nobel prizes are awarded in Stockholm, Swedish Television broadcasts a round table discussion with the prize-winners. Always, the issue of how they see scientific intuition is discussed. In a study of transcripts of these discussions from 1970–86, Marton, Fensham and Chaiklin (1994) found that two kinds of experience dominated the Nobel laureates' accounts of instances of scientific intuition. The first one was a strong sense of direction, of a path, of being on the way towards something as yet unknown. There is a feeling of certainty about the choice of path, despite the absence of conscious reasons for that choice. The second kind of experience laureates refer to is the sudden insight that occurs without any obvious reasons for it, the experience of pieces of a jigsaw suddenly falling into place or the sudden revelation of the solution. There is a feeling of certainty present here too, in this case that the answer has been found despite the fact that it has yet to be verified.

Can we explain these two kinds of experience? Well, we think we can. Typically in research, a crucial observation is made which is recognized as significant and which causes the researcher to make certain choices about the next step – choices which direct the research in both the short and long term. What is it that makes the researcher select one of an unlimited range of options and pursue it for years, sometimes for a lifetime? This can be understood if we think of the particular observation as a part of a greater whole, the answer to the research question. This answer does not actually exist when the observation is made, yet it is provided in some way and in some form, in the experience of the part.

In phenomenology there is the idea of *appresentation* which we can use as an instrument to make sense of what happens. We introduced the idea briefly in Chapter 3 (see footnote 2 in that chapter). Appresentation refers exactly to how the experience of the whole is given in the experience of the part. If we look at a tabletop from above, for instance, we do not experience it as a two-dimensional surface floating in the air, in spite of the fact that what we see is, strictly speaking, a two-dimensional surface separated in some mysterious way from the ground. But in looking down on a tabletop we experience the legs that support it as well, because the experience is not of a two-dimensional surface, it is of a table. Thanks to our previous experiences of tables, and of the particular table we are looking at, we have learned to know tables in general and hence this particular table as well. We are familiar with them so that when we see a part of a table we are aware of the presence of the table as a whole. The aspects that are not actually seen, which are not even visible, are *appresented*. When we look at a house from the street, in particular our own home, we do not experience the façade as merely a façade, but we experience it as a house, while its elements such as rooms, doors or floors are inherent in our experience – they are *appresented*.

We would argue that appresentation is not restricted only to such sensuous experiences but also applies to the experiences of abstract entities as well. When scientists think of the gravitational constant g, for instance, then the highly abstract formulation made by Newton of how bodies affect one another at a distance is appresented – provided the scientists have sufficient understanding of classical physics.

We suggest that what is called scientific intuition refers to the fact that the researcher's observation of something, which subsequently turns out to be a part of a greater conceptual whole, may trigger off a vague awareness of the whole which the researcher has not yet seen but which is somehow implied by the part experienced. This vague, tacit experience of the whole guides one's steps: 'And so... as we did our work, I think, we almost felt at times that there was almost a hand guiding us. Because we would go from one step to the next, and somehow we would know which was the right way to go.' (Michael S Brown, Nobel Prize for Medicine, 1985).

When you eventually arrive at the answer, you suddenly see the whole and you know that it is right, you feel the shock of recognition: '... you've been thinking about something without willing to for a long time. Then all of a sudden, the problem is opened to you in a flash, and you suddenly see the answer'. (Rita Levi-Montalcini, Nobel Prize for Medicine, 1986).

There is one contrast to be made between our earlier examples of appresentation and the scientific intuition discussed by the Nobel laureates. Compared with the appresentation of your home from the street, in which the well-known whole is appresented in the part, in the experience of scientific intuition it is the previously unknown whole that is suddenly appresented from a well-known part.

Learning on the individual and on the collective level

As mentioned above, we called research 'learning on the collective level' because through it humanity learns and the frontiers of our knowledge are widened. As a contrast we are referring to learning in the context of studying as 'learning on the individual level'. Of course, we need to acknowledge that, for the individual researcher, the research endeavour also involves learning on the individual level, but in a context of intended collective advancement.

We argued that we should consider the relationship between these two forms of learning, instead of – as is more common – considering the relationship between teaching and research. A frequent, but in our view not very enlightening, way of looking at the latter is represented by the question 'Are better researchers better at teaching than those who are not so strong in research?' When such a question is examined it tends to show that there is little correlation between teaching and research. Hattie and Marsh (1996) carried out a so-called meta-analysis of 58 studies of the relationship between research and teaching. In most of the studies, productivity and citations were used as a measure of excellence in research while course evaluations by students were used as a measure of excellence in teaching. The weighted average of 498 correlations in the 58 studies was 0.06. As Hattie and Marsh point out, quality of research and quality of teaching (as measured in the studies included) have less than 0.1 per cent of the total variability in common. In a meta-analysis we are not very likely to detect subtle relationships, but we can at least conclude that there is no empirical support in Hattie and Marsh's study for any relationship between research and teaching, when these are seen in terms of individual capabilities.

But we want to emphasize once more that their question is not our question. We would like to explore the relationship between learning and research as human activities instead. How does the nature of learning on the individual level relate to the nature of learning on the collective level?

The central point of this book is that the most important form of learning is that which enables us to see something in the world in a different way. According to Hanson (1958) and Kuhn (1970), it is characteristic of frontier research that it opens up new ways of seeing the world. In addition, being able to see something in a certain way amounts to being able to discern critical aspects of the phenomenon and keep them in focal awareness simultaneously. This is true whether we talk about learning or research. The point is, however, that in the study situation the act of discernment is frequently excluded. By presenting the relevant aspects of the phenomenon only and the relations between them, the finding of the relevant aspects and the pattern of which they are constituent parts (which are the heart of the matter in research) disappear in the study situation. Instead of the figure–ground structure of aspects that are relevant and those which are not, you get a kind of lifeless two-dimensional picture with the relevant aspects only. The principle that Galileo arrived at is probably presented quite often to students simply as a relation between time and velocity. By doing so the tension between selecting distance and velocity as relevant aspects to begin with and, subsequently, time and velocity, is gone. The problem that students are facing (with due support from their teachers) should be about a body in free fall and the discussion should involve the discernment of various aspects of the situation.

Hanson argues that scientists arrive at new ways of seeing the phenomenon of interest through abduction, ie by finding a pattern which makes their observations appear intelligible. He does not say very much about how the pattern is found. The findings reported in the previous section possibly shed some light on how such patterns might come about. The scientist in the study talked about a strong sense of direction, a quasi-sensuous experience of the object of research, extended and varied experience and, finally, sudden illumination. In Chapter 2, we pointed out that there can be no discernment without variation or, to put it the other way around, discernment originates from variation. Focusing on a particular aspect of a phenomenon implies an awareness of the corresponding dimension of variation: it is open instead of being taken for granted. As we implied at the end of Chapter 2, during learning there seems to be a change in certain aspects, from a peripheral to a focal position in awareness. This could possibly explain the strong sense of direction and also the quasi-sensuous nature of the experience of the object of research before the pattern becomes visible and appears fully illuminated.

The experience of variation has to be constituted somehow and this experience is reasonably less obvious before it gets more obvious. As a matter of fact,

Entwistle and Marton (1994) found that students who were engaged in intense study activities had quasi-sensuous experiences of something object-like. This was simply the knowledge they kept developing and Entwistle and Marton used the label 'knowledge object'. The experience of the knowledge objects thus had interesting similarities with the experience of the object of research the Nobel laureates were discussing in Marton, Fensham and Chaiklin's (1994) study.

On the origin of The Origin of Species

Acts of studying and acts of revolutionary research are different, of course. But this is necessarily so in terms of complexity, time scale and driving force. To the extent that new ways of seeing something are developed, much of what is taking place can be understood in terms of variation, discernment and simultaneity. We would like to suggest that developing new ways of seeing should have a higher priority in university education. The point we are trying to make is that scientific discoveries can be characterized in terms of the aspects of the phenomenon that are focused on simultaneously, and that to learn about a discovery should imply being able to discern the relevant aspects and have them in focal awareness at the same time.

We turn at this point to discuss briefly the theory of evolution as an example. Brumby (1979) showed most convincingly that university students of biology might well come up with reasonable wordings of the theory of evolution but very few of them appropriate it and are able to use it as an instrument to look through when they encounter problems such as the following example.

A patchwork picture of human skincolour variation was placed in front of each student participating in the investigation and the question was asked: 'If we suppose that man originally arose in one place, say in Africa, where some of the oldest human skulls have been found, then how do you account for the different skin colours that exist in the different races round the world today?'

After the students had given their explanation two further questions were asked: 'What would you predict to happen to this couple's skin (dark-skinned), if they went and lived permanently in Norway?' and 'If they had children born in Norway, what would their children's skin look like?' Further: 'What would you predict to happen to the skin of this little girl (very light-skinned) if she went and lived in Africa for the rest of her life? If she married someone of her own race, they lived in Africa, and had children there, what would their children look like, at birth?' (Brumby, 1979).

Only 15 per cent of the students gave accounts in accordance with evolutionary theory. The rest of the group interpreted the question in Lamarckian terms, ie in terms of change on the basis of need. They thus failed to appreciate the difference between changes acquired during the lifetime of an individual, and changes in the proportions of individuals with certain characteristics in a population, occurring over many generations. They did not realize that changes occur in a population with more and more individuals having a certain characteristic. They thought instead that it is by single individuals having more and more of that characteristic (and they genetically pass it on to their offspring). A substantial number of the students believed, for instance, that the baby of a white couple moving to Africa would be born with a darker skin (darker than the parents themselves had at their birth). Far fewer thought that a black couple moving to Norway would have a baby born with lighter skin. These responses can be understood in terms of the difference between the natural gain of pigment within a lifetime (suntanning) being familiar, and loss of pigment not being familiar within a single lifetime.

Having appropriated the theory of evolution and having made it a tool for making sense of the world – something that most of the students failed to prove having done – amounts to being able to identify a number of critical aspects. Being able to discern them and focus on them simultaneously would amount to seeing what Darwin saw.[2]

There is no way we could do justice to the subtle and complex process through which Darwin arrived at his formulation. Gruber (1974) and Mayr (1982) are excellent sources and we use them to point out just three critical aspects of the theory of evolution as an example.

The first volume of Lyell's *Principles of Geology*, which instantly became Darwin's bible, appeared in 1830. Lyell started with two fundamental obser-vations: first, that species are extremely well adapted to their environment; second, that they live in a constantly (but slowly) changing world. As Lyell believed that species are constant and cannot change, his conclusion – in agreement with almost all geologists by the 1820s – was that species must become extinct and have to be replaced by new species, but how the latter can happen he could not tell.

By the end of 1831 Darwin sailed from England with HMS *Beagle*. Half a year after his return home, in March 1837, the well-known ornithologist, John Gould, when working with Darwin's bird collection, alerted him to the specific distinctness of the mockingbirds (Mimus) collected on three different islands in the Galapagos.

The remark had a profound effect on Darwin's thinking. To begin with, geographically distributed variation within a species contradicted Lyell's idea of invariant species. It also directed Darwin to consider geographic speciation, ie instead of comparing populations and species in time, as most of Darwin's forerunners did, he opted for comparing species and populations geographi-cally.

A few months later Darwin was convinced that species are modifiable and that they multiply by natural processes. He was still unclear about what factors could account for the transformation of species. Another year later, he was reading Malthus' (1798) famous book:

In October (actually September 28) 1838, that is, fifteen months after I had begun my systematic inquiry, I happened to read for amusement, Malthus on Popula-tion, and being well prepared to appreciate the struggle for existence which everywhere goes on from long-continued observation of the habits of animals and plants, it at once struck me that under these circumstances favourable variations would tend to be preserved, and unfavourable ones to be destroyed. The result of this would be the formation of new species. Here, then, I had at last got a theory by which to work (from Darwin's autobiography, quoted by Mayr, p. 478).

From Darwin's notebook we learn about the particular passage that made such an impression on him: 'It may safely be pronounced that population, when unchecked, goes on doubling itself every 25 years, or increases in a geometrical ratio'. In the contest for scarce resources 'the survival of the fittest' hampers, however, the uninhibited growth of the population. There is thus the mechanism for the adjustment (and differentiation) of the species to varying environmental conditions.

The point we would like to make is that seeing what Darwin saw takes the discernment and simultaneous awareness of the same aspects of the phenomenon that he discerned and focused on.

As it happens this is exactly what Alfred Russell Wallace (1823–1913) did completely independently from Darwin, who had not published his findings for some 20 years. Wallace set out, in the beginning, to search for an answer to the question Lyell was unable to answer, about 'the introduction of new species'. He left England in April 1848 for the Amazon Valley, and was struck by the variation within the very same species that he found there. Thus by focusing on geographical distribution of species instead of variation in time, he came to reject Lyell's idea of invariant species, as had Darwin more than 10 years earlier. At last Wallace too read Malthus' *Essay on Population*... As was the case with Darwin, the reading sparked off a sudden illumination and he could formulate his version of a theory of the origin of species which closely resembled Darwin's.

One interesting detail here is that the switch in focus to the geographical dimension from the time dimension resembles somewhat the switch in focus from distance to time in Galileo's case. Another matter is the stepwise manner in which the theory developed, opening up for one dimension of variation at a time, as it were, in accordance with our remark about the stepwise path of learning earlier.

The picture we have painted is very much oversimplified. A close analysis shows that the seemingly sudden shifts were very much prepared and intensely foreshadowed. Further, our intention was only to give some examples of critical features in the Darwin–Wallace discovery. Both Darwin and Wallace discerned three critical aspects or dimensions of variation (at least): the adjustment of species to changing environmental conditions, the heterogeneity and geographical distribution of the very same species and the uninhibited growth of populations exponentially exceeding food supplies. Both Darwin and Wallace saw the same pattern and arrived at the seed of the theory of evolution independently from each other. The point we want to make is that it is very difficult, if not impossible, to understand a scientific theory simply by looking at it in its final form, without being aware of the original question that set its development in motion, of other attempts to answer the same question, of the critical discernment of aspects – among other aspects and so forth. In order '... to open the scholarly discourse to the student, inducing her to see as her own arguments, the arguments for and against standpoints constituting the scientific exchange of opinion' (Björklund, 1990). The acts of research and not only its products must be made visible, even if the original actors are not among us any more.

Making the acts of research visible

A fascinating example of what 'making visible the acts of research' may look like is offered by one of the most heroic undertakings in the history of academic teaching: Feynman's reconstruction of the original derivation of Newton's theory of planetary motion.

Richard Feynman, a Nobel laureate, inventor of quantum electrodynamics, gave a course of lectures to undergraduates at the California Institute of Technology (Caltech) in the early 1960s, subsequently turned into the Feynman Lectures series of textbooks. Fellow Caltech physicist, David Goodstein, recalls:

> In all those years, only twice did he teach courses purely for undergraduates. These were the celebrated occasions in the academic years 1961–62 and 1962–63 when he lectured... on the materials that were to become *The Feynman Lectures on Physics*... As the course went on, attendance by the kids at the lectures started dropping alarmingly, but at the same time, more and more faculty and graduate students started attending, so the room stayed full, and Feynman may never have known that he was losing his intended audience... The lessons in physics he prepared, the explanations of physics at the freshmen level, weren't really for freshmen, but were for us, his colleagues... It was more often us, scientists, physicists, professors, who would be the main beneficiaries of his magnificent achievement, which was nothing less than to see all of physics with fresh new eyes (Bartlett, 1992).

The same David Goodstein together with his wife, Caltech archivist Judith Goodstein, has recently published a book, which is an attempt to reconstruct a lecture given by Feynman in 1964, not included in the original series: *Feynman's Lost Lecture: The Motions of the Planets Around the Sun* (Goodstein and Goodstein, 1996). It is about Feynman's attempt to reconstruct Newton's geometrical proof for the claim that '... the planets travel in ellipses because they are compelled to do so by an inverse square force coming from the direction of the sun' (Wertheim, 1996). The book is thus an attempt to reconstruct – having

Feynman's lecture notes but not, for a geometrical proof, the crucial diagrams – Feynman's attempt to reconstruct Newton's original derivation.

As mentioned above, we referred to Kepler's discovery of the elliptic orbits of the planets. Newton offered an explanation as to why the planets must necessarily travel like that. The shape of their paths follows from the formula for the gravitational forces acting on them – being a function of the mass of, and the distance between, the two bodies (eg the Sun and a particular planet) affecting each other. The gravitational force was used by Newton not only to explain the elliptic orbits of the planets but also how the moon orbits the Earth and why apples fall from trees. It connected thus the Earth and the sky, previously dealt with as two metaphysically distinct regions, where the planets' orbits were attributed directly to God. By presenting a forceful argument for seeing the Earth and the surrounding universe being governed by the same laws, Newton definitely introduced a new way of seeing the world.

Linking the elliptic orbits of the planets to gravitational force is easily done by using calculus – invented by Newton himself – as a mathematical tool. The proof runs for one or two pages, but Newton made use of geometry instead. In this case the proof runs for more like 80 pages. So why would Newton choose the difficult path? According to Margaret Wertheim in her review of Goodstein and Goodstein's book he wanted to ground his new mechanics on a rock-solid foundation and, although calculus originated from algebra, at that time not even regarded as a part of mathematics proper but more as an extension of logic, geometry stood as the model of eternal truth. In Kepler's words: '... geometry provided God with a model for the Creation' (Wertheim, 1996). In the beginning of his lecture Feynman discussed the apparent madness of using geometry when the tools of calculus are available. But he wanted his students to be enthralled by the sheer beauty of the geometric proof and he wanted them to see what Newton actually did and he wanted them to see what Newton actually saw.

Proving the link between gravity and Kepler's ellipses by using simple geometry is very hard and not even Feynman himself managed to follow Newton's derivation in the *Principia Mathematica* beyond a certain point. He had thus to develop his own proof by using a path slightly different from the one Newton had used. Feynman could thus declare to his students that he would prove the link between gravity and Kepler's ellipses using only simple high-school geometry, which he did. But not even those brilliant Caltech students could follow him with anything other than great difficulty, as is probably the case with the readers of Goodstein and Goodstein's reconstruction.

Feynman's teaching on the undergraduate level may not have turned out to be an instantaneous success story if measured by the reactions of the majority of students. Nevertheless he certainly made a lasting contribution to the teaching of physics by linking the level of collective and individual learning. Above all, in his 'lost lecture' he managed to demonstrate that you can actually see what critical steps in the history of human thinking about the physical world meant when those steps were taken. In the series of lectures preceding it he managed to demonstrate that you can develop new, fresh ways of seeing physics, which lend a more powerful understanding of it. Such contributions are, of course, better appreciated at a university where the aim is to develop as deep and as powerful an understanding of what is being learned as possible.

A similar idea was succinctly expressed by a university lecturer in physics participating in Marton, Runesson, Prosser and Trigwell's (1997) study of university teachers' conceptions of the students' problem solving in science:

> The process of learning is a process of invention and that implies quite a number of things about one's behaviour. It means that if you're really going to learn something, then you have to invent it for yourself. It doesn't matter that someone three or four hundred years ago was the first person to invent this. You are now engaged in the inquiry that they were and probably over a much shorter time span, because for some people it was their life's work, but the fact that you're engaged in the same sort of inquiry as they were doesn't take away from your capacity to invent more, or the act of invention on your part. If you look at the explanations that people provide for various things when you question them in tutorials, people have got idiosyncratic... very individual ways of explaining things, and ways of understanding things and really it's a matter of defining, sorry it's a matter of redefining or keep reinventing them. They have some interpretation already...

So this is the way we prefer to see the relation between learning and research, through coalescing ways of seeing. 'A way of seeing' is always a way of seeing something somehow. Shared understanding takes a shared object of knowledge and it takes shared acts of knowing as well.

Endnotes

1. Again, we have to point out that finding out new things about the world through research is a learning experience for the individual – or the individuals – involved. However, to the extent that what has been found is new in relation to the collective knowledge of humankind (ie in relation to all that is known by humans), we can speak of learning on the collective level as well.

2. This is not completely true, of course. A theory, or a way of seeing something, has always a more or less unique personal, cultural and social context as well and the exact meaning of the theory derives from these, too.

Part Three

The University
of the Students

Chapter 5

What should be learned: competence and competencies?

What should be learned?

This chapter addresses the purposes of university education. What should be learned? What is the nature of the competence that graduates should develop? What sort of capabilities are necessary for them to take their place in the world as professionals? For us, this is a question of the university curriculum and is the most important question that can be asked about learning at universities.

In Chapter 1 we challenged the common view that universities are about teaching, research and community service. In particular we questioned the idea that teaching is one of the defining purposes. Teaching is obviously not an aim but a means. The aim is to bring learning about and teaching is one of the means by which this might happen. We see our book as a contribution to a general, international shift in focus from teaching to learning (this theme is discussed in Chapter 10). One implication of such a shift is to describe the aims of academic courses or programmes in terms of learning goals, independently of how they are brought about.

We will first deal with the general problem of how to formulate learning goals. Second, we will deal with a well-known, explicit and fairly consistent attempt to define learning goals in terms of what graduates should be able to do, ie in terms that are independent of the means by which they are achieved and which refer to the context of working life. These are so-called competency-based descriptions, and we agree with one of the main driving principles of the movement behind them, namely with the idea that we should try to make explicit the kinds of capabilities we hope students will develop.In addition, the question of how these capabilities are developed should be dealt with as a separate issue (assuming that they can be developed in more than one way). On the other hand our views about the nature of the capabilities the university should aim for and the way they should be described differ radically from the view of the competency-based movement. In the third part of this chapter we will contrast with the competency-based approach our own position, which is derived from our theory of learning, and our way of characterizing competence which follows from that position. We will conclude the chapter with a section on the curriculum perspective on the question of what should be learned: we will illustrate a description of the nature of experiences the learners need to have in order to develop a certain competence.

In Chapter 2 we tried to make it clear that our point of departure, when it comes to illuminating the nature of learning, is the question of what is actually learned when something is learned. Breaking with taken-for-granted assumptions and exploring the question in an open and unprejudiced way is the heart of the matter of our theoretical account.

In this chapter we argue that the question about the kind of learning universities should aim at bringing about is the most fundamental question when it comes to the development that students are supposed to go through during their years in higher education. We should not take the answers for granted in this context either, but examine them thoroughly and in an open-minded way again and again.

As mentioned above, we said that what capabilities the students should develop are a question of university curriculum. It is just as much a question of learning theory as well. This is actually a point where the practical and the theoretical coalesce and have the same need for an answer, and for the same answer, we would claim. Curriculum and learning questions have to be addressed together.

Academics' views of the desired learning outcomes

At a number of universities in Australia, Hong Kong, Sweden and the UK over several years, academics were asked questions in a workshop setting (Bowden, 1989) about what they would like their students to have achieved at the end of a subject they teach and also upon graduation.

Academics were asked to list the key understandings they wanted students to develop during their learning in such a subject. Some of the responses were simply statements of topics, even if on occasion the word understanding was added, without adding much to the meaning. The following is an example:

> Electricity
> What is a field?
> Understanding concept of current, voltage.
> Kirchoff's laws.
> How fast does an electron move in a wire?

The difficulty that many teachers had with this task was common to all participant groups, no matter where the workshop was held – in general or technological universities in Asia, Australia or Europe. There were some, however, who were able to express the core understandings more clearly, such as the following:

Second Year Optics
Development of 'mental model' of light waves and how they behave: conceptual–geometric picture.
Develop strong correspondence between geometrical picture and the equivalent mathematical expression: use insight in one to assist the other.
Become familiar with 'type examples' of light behaviour in different circumstances: understand what model is appropriate in which case. Be able to extend to more complex situations.

In this expression of intended learning outcomes, the academic has gone beyond organizing the content into topics and has both drawn out relationships between different aspects of the content and also focused on the relationship between the learner and the content. This academic talks about the learner using insight to link the parts and being able to extend the learning to other, more complex, situations.

Another example (Marton, Runesson, Prosser and Trigwell, 1997) of the intended learning outcomes for students of some scientific subjects, as expressed by the academics who teach them, is also of this more highly developed form:

Electrical engineering
understanding the idea of measurement, how to actually do measurements and that measurement influences what you actually get out of an experiment.
Thermal physics
a much deeper understanding regarding the nature of heat and thermal processes
also facility in being able to manipulate quantities
as a consequence of the understanding to be able to solve problems, predict behaviour

Here again, the academics are going beyond the content and thinking in terms of the student's capabilities that are being developed.

Ways of seeing

The focus on understanding referred to above has been extended over the last decade or so to the consideration of variation in 'ways of seeing', some of these being more powerful than others in explaining aspects of the world. Teaching and learning therefore came to be focused on discovering students' ways of seeing a phenomenon and helping them to develop more powerful ways of seeing. The contrast of rote learning with learning for understanding shifted to a focus on the idea of a range of understandings (the plural being important in appreciating this shift), with learning taking place as understandings change.

While most participants in the workshops described earlier (Bowden, 1989) had some difficulty with the way they expressed desired student learning outcomes in their subjects, they usually carried out a subsequent task more readily. This second task involved participants in writing down a statement of one aspect of the subject where students needed to develop their understanding, along with several alternative conceptions of that particular phenomenon that were commonly held by students. In the workshops, this listing of alternative student ways of seeing always followed a discussion of the outcome of the previous activity and further examples provided by the workshop leader. Furthermore, the influence of assessment on student learning was normally included in the discussion. The following example from one participant illustrates the greater richness of responses to this question:

> Electricity
> You are an electron in the middle of a copper wire. At a certain time, I will connect a battery across your wire. How will you react before and after connection?
> My neighbour bumps me immediately and I then bump the neighbour on the other side.
> I sit still before connection but gradually move together with the others after connection.
> I gradually accelerate.
> I take off with the speed of light.
> Before connection, I am dancing around randomly. I do not feel the field from the battery immediately, but when it gets here (at the speed of light) my dance is biased a bit in the direction of the field.

These are expressed, in this case in an aesthetically pleasing way, in terms of different ways of seeing the phenomenon. Some are more powerful ways than others but the value of this exercise is that the academics concerned have come to grips with the essence of teaching. They see it as a process in which they need to understand how their students conceive particular phenomena in relation to important concepts being taught. They need to know this in order to be able to organize experiences for students that will enable them to move from those conceptions towards others that are more powerful. This is in fact the way that science in general moves forward.

Generic skills

In Chapter 1, we suggested that the curriculum for any university programme needs to be developed around the idea that students are being prepared for a future which is largely unknown. Now this is not an idea that is unrelated to other developments in education over the past decade. In recent years, many reviews of education (eg Mayer, 1992; Bowden and Masters, 1993) have discussed the idea of generic skills as desirable outcomes of education. If you do not know what the future situation will be, then teach students some fundamental skills which they can apply to any situation.

This idea has been taken up almost universally by governments and by employer associations who commonly talk about the need for generic skills such as problem-solving skills, communication skills, team skills and the like (see, for example, Harvey, Burrows and Green, 1992; Burrows, Harvey and Green, 1993; Harvey, 1993). A policy discussion paper on higher education, published by the Australian Government Department of Employment Education and Training (1987), argued that 'the major function of education is... to increase individuals' capacity to learn, to provide them with a framework with which to analyse problems and to increase their capacity to deal with new information'. Bowden and Masters (1993) report that some commentators even go on to say that it does not matter what the subject content is, so long as the generic skills are developed.

Harvey (1993) reported on a survey of both university academics and relevant employers in the UK, all of whom were asked to rank the importance of 15 possible criteria by which employers assess graduates. Both employers and academics rated effective communication, problem-solving ability and analytical skills among their top five. Employers also included team work, flexibility and adaptability while the other two in the academics' top five were independent judgement and enquiry and research skills. Specialist subject knowledge was among the last two for both employers and academics.

Harvey points to the low rating of specialist subject knowledge and asks whether perhaps employers take a minimum level of specialist subject knowledge for granted, whether they were focusing in their responses on 'specialist' rather than 'subject' or whether, rather, employers seek understanding of basic principles. A new survey of employers was undertaken, disaggregating not only specialist knowledge but also other categories to produce 62 criteria, and was augmented by discussions and interviews.

Some detailed rankings from this second survey are given in Table 5.1. There was a high correlation with the previous survey, with specialist factual knowledge remaining low both on importance and satisfaction.

Table 5.1: *Employers rankings of two of 62 criteria for recruitment of graduates*

	Specialist factual knowledge (ranking out of 62)	Understanding of core principles (ranking out of 62)
Employers who see subject area of degree as relevant to recruitment	46	8
Employers who do not see subject area as important	57	44

This was true for both the group of employers who regarded the subject area of the degree as relevant to their recruitment decisions (they ranked specialist factual knowledge forty-sixth in importance) and the group of employers who regarded the subject area of the degree as irrelevant to their recruitment decisions (they ranked specialist factual knowledge fifty-seventh in importance). In contrast the two groups ranked 'understanding of core principles' as eighth and forty-fourth respectively. Harvey suggests that the interview data show that the low ratings of specialist factual knowledge relates to the perception by employers of the short shelf-life of factual knowledge. The low satisfaction with specialist factual knowledge, which was also found in the second survey, appears to be more related to the perceived inability of graduates to apply their knowledge in practical situations. This is linked to employers' dissatisfaction with problem-solving ability: 'Technically our graduates have a good theory of the subject and are good at solving problems in theory. But in practice they are not sure how to proceed' (Discussant RS1 in Harvey, 1993); 'Graduates learn skills but are often unable to apply them' (Discussant SV5 in Harvey, 1993).

Employers rated communication skills as very important but not very satisfactory so far as graduate performance was concerned. They suggested that students should get experience of writing different kinds of documents for different kinds of audiences while at university and also have experience in giving oral presentations. In addition, they suggested that universities integrate communication skills development into normal subject units and provide staff development for academics so they can tutor students on these matters.

The academics referred to earlier (Bowden, 1989) were also asked about learning goals for degree programmes. On every occasion, whether in Australia, Hong Kong, Sweden or the UK, academics from every discipline made a distinction between the mere memorizing of information or skill development and more desirable, higher level goals which include, but are not dominated by, a knowledge of facts, procedures and skills. Their lists, which are very similar despite the cultural and system variations, commonly included:

- knowledge of core facts, procedures and skills
- understanding the core concepts
- understanding the relation between core concepts
- understanding of structure of knowledge in related disciplines
- understanding of the theory-practice relation
- appreciation of real-world variations
- general knowledge
- ability to define a problem
- problem-solving ability
- communication skill
- literacy and numeracy skills

- lateral thinking
- insight
- perspective
- self-motivation
- capacity for self-learning integrity.

These correspond in general terms with the UK findings (Harvey, 1993). Indeed, the distinction between 'understanding of core concepts' and 'knowledge of facts, procedures and skills' mirrors Harvey's report on employer views. Academics in Bowden's report also made a distinction between problem-solving skills and the ability to define a problem, which was of concern to the employers quoted above.

These kinds of comment by academics and employers seem to support the concept of generic skills as desirable goals of university education. However, Bowden and Masters (1993) have argued that the concept necessarily needs to be rooted in content, that is, educational goals such as communication or problem-solving ability necessarily must be related to communicating something or to solving some particular kinds of problem. A professor who is good at solving research problems is sometimes not at all capable of solving social problems in the community or financial problems at home. The idea of problem-solving ability that has not been developed within a content area, or is independent of content, does not fit with our experience. The UK employers' suggestion in Harvey's (1993) study that, for instance, communication skill development should be undertaken within normal subjects, is consistent with that view.

Bowden and Masters use the term 'generic capacity' to refer to those more general abilities that are developed through an integration of discipline knowledge, learning and practical (workplace) experience, and which enable individuals to deal with novel situations. They argue that the idea that generic capacities can be developed independently and applied to the professional situations (as is often claimed for generic skills) is unfounded and that, rather, they develop exclusively through experience of the professional field to which they are meant to relate. Bowden and Masters use the term 'generic capacity' to emphasize the difference of their ideas from those associated with the idea of largely content-free and context-free generic skills, an idea which they dismiss.

Stephenson (1992) expresses similar ideas to those of Bowden and Masters when he suggests that the fundamental objection to a separate generic skill, which he refers to as 'bolt-on capability', is that it denies 'the holistic nature of capability, the essential integration of personal qualities, skills and specialist knowledge which enables students to be effective'. Stephenson (1992) uses the term 'capability' to refer to the ability of professionals to take 'effective and appropriate action within unfamiliar and changing circumstances'. The book edited by Stephenson and Weil (1992a) reports the outcomes of the Higher

Education for Capability Project undertaken in the UK. Four themes are identified (Stephenson and Weil, 1992b) for student activities that lead to responsibility and accountability for their learning. They are:

- building on previous experience, knowledge and skills
- planning and negotiating approvals
- active and interactive learning assessment of outcomes in terms of agreed criteria.

Stephenson (1992) emphasizes the need to prepare students for 'coping with uncertainty and change in the workplace'. However, Stephenson and Weil (1992b) do not address the fundamental role of curriculum design, which is the point of departure for this chapter.

So how are we to define the capabilities which we are trying to help students develop? There has been a movement which has been very explicit about that. The competency movement has, over recent decades, developed a formal process for specifying the kinds of capabilities students should develop, but the problem is that, in practice, many of their formulations have been very narrow, both in terms of the kinds of capabilities and the contexts to which they apply. We share their view about making the development of capabilities central to the teaching and learning activities of universities but we differ when we consider the kinds of capabilities and their contexts. In this chapter we will describe the competency approach to curriculum development, largely based on an account by Bowden (1997), and then introduce our alternative.

Competency-based approaches

Historical perspectives

A competency-based approach to curriculum design focuses on defining the workplace skills needed by graduates and planning the curriculum to meet those needs. The concept of a competency-based education system is both an old and an evolving idea. Competency-based education programmes were first introduced in the USA, beginning in teacher education in the late 1960s, and evolved through applications to other professional education programmes in the USA in the 1970s, vocational training programmes in the UK and Germany among others in the 1980s, and vocational training and professional skills recognition in Australia in the 1990s.

The origins of this approach are found in the thinking of educators such as Benjamin Bloom. The behavioural objectives movement sought to focus attention on the intended outcomes of learning programmes and, in particular, to encourage teachers to express their instructional objectives as changes in observable student behaviours. Proponents of the movement advocated the specification of objectives as 'directly observable behaviours which can be reliably recorded as either present or absent' (Bloom *et al.*, 1971). An important feature of the movement was the desire for reliability of observation and judgement. Writers of behavioural objectives were encouraged to state outcomes 'in terms which are operational, involving reliable observation, and allowing no leeway in interpretation'. In an attempt to achieve this degree of reliability, statements of educational objectives begin with verbs describing student behaviour such as 'states', 'lists', 'names', 'selects', 'recognizes', 'matches', and 'calculates' (Bloom *et al.*, 1971). It is this narrowness that has led to much of the criticism of such approaches, then and now. The behavioural objectives movement of the late 1950s and 1960s gave rise in the 1970s to four related developments: mastery learning (Bloom, 1974); criterion-referenced testing (Popham, 1978); minimum competency testing (Jaeger and Tittle, 1980); and competency-based education (Burke *et al.*, 1975).

Although the imperatives for the introduction of competency-based education have been different in different countries at different times, and the ways in which this concept has been operationalized have changed over time, the basic principles and intentions of competency-based education have remained essentially unchanged since the 1960s. They are a focus on outcomes, greater workplace relevance, outcomes as observable competencies, assessments as judgements of competence, improved skills recognition, as well as improved articulation and credit transfer.

There are two themes through these. The first, which is concerned with access to education and recognition of experience outside educational institutions as equivalent to formal education, derives from economic and social theories and is the basis for the political debate which has threatened to overwhelm the pedagogical questions. So it focuses on processes to enable enrolling students to obtain credit in the programme for experience in the workplace and for subjects studied elsewhere, the links between performance assessment and job design, as well as efforts to make it easier for students to move from one programme of study into another at a higher level.

The second theme concerns the relation between the world of learning and the world of work and the mechanisms by which experience of one is a preparation for participation in the other. Here we focus on the second rather than the first of these two themes. A more complete analysis of the history of the competency movement and the principles of competency-based approaches may be found in Bowden and Masters (1993), from which this account draws, and which describes developments in Australia in the 1990s. Houston (1985) describes the early movement in the USA in the 1970s while Jessup (1991) and Tuxworth (1989) deal with UK developments in the 1980s.

A focus on outcomes

A first characteristic of competency-based education is its emphasis on the specification and assessment of outcomes (referred to as competencies). This focus on outcomes is often contrasted with more traditional concerns of educational programmes with inputs such as methods of student/trainee selection, lengths of courses and training programmes, class sizes, teacher–pupil ratios, and so on (Spady, 1977; Johnston, 1992). This corresponds to general reforms in public finance which have shifted from inputs to outputs.

Of course, competency-based education is not unique in its intention to focus more sharply on educational outcomes. This intention is central to many initiatives in education in many countries, including the development of educational performance indicators, the setting of national educational goals, the introduction of statements and profiles for key areas of the curriculum and the development of programmes to assess and report levels of student achievement and to monitor educational standards over time. These initiatives share an intention to clarify and communicate educational outcomes and to establish frameworks for setting goals and monitoring progress towards the achievement of those goals. This kind of framework applies both to the system and the individual level. Our own position and that advocated by Stephenson and Weil (1992b) could also be classified as being focused on learning outcomes.

What distinguishes competency-based education from this broader orientation towards the clearer specification and monitoring of outcomes is its concern with outcomes specifically relevant to employment. While one of our interests, but not the only one, is also related to the relevance of learning to employment, it is not so narrowly focused as the competency movement has been.

Greater workplace relevance

Running through the literature on competency-based education is an ongoing concern over the workplace relevance of much of the content of formal educational programmes. There is a commonly expressed belief that institution-based courses too often emphasize theoretical or 'book' knowledge at the expense of the ability to apply knowledge to perform practical tasks and to fulfil workplace roles (Jessup, 1989; Tuxworth, 1989). Recent initiatives in Australia to promote competency-based education have similarly been based on concerns over the workplace relevance of many formal educational qualifications: 'Dissatisfaction with the workplace relevance of many credentials derived in the traditional model of curriculum development based on the inputs of "knowledge", "understanding" and "skill attainment" has led to an emphasis on working from the outcome – increasingly referred to as a competence. A competence is the ability of the learner to put skills and knowledge into action' (Humphrey, 1992).

Under competency-based approaches, the redesign of curricula to make them more relevant to workplace requirements normally begins with an analysis and identification of workplace 'competencies', which are then organized into a set of 'competency standards' for an occupation. For instance, in the UK, a unit of competence (note here the different terminology – 'competencies' in Australia, 'competences' usually in the UK) is intended to describe an employment function and is made up of a coherent group of elements which together are required to perform that function. Competency standards being developed for the National Vocational Qualifications in the UK tend to contain between 5 and 20 units of competence.

Units of competence usually consist of two, three or four 'elements'. Each element of competence identifies an area of desired achievement, but does not, by itself, specify a standard of satisfactory performance in that area. To differentiate between satisfactory and unsatisfactory performance in an area of achievement, performance criteria are required (Debling, 1989). According to Debling, it would not be unusual in work under way in the UK for a statement of competence to consist of five units of competence and about 200 performance criteria.

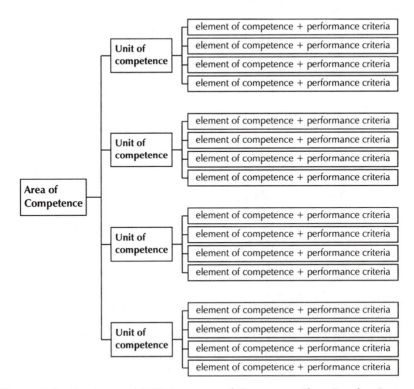

Figure 5.1: *Components of UK Statement of Competence (from Bowden &*
Masters, 1993)

In an attempt to reduce ambiguity of meaning, UK competency statements now also include 'range statements' designed to indicate the range of situations to which elements of competence and their associated performance criteria are intended to apply. An example of part of a statement of competence for a health-care profession is shown in Figure 5.2.

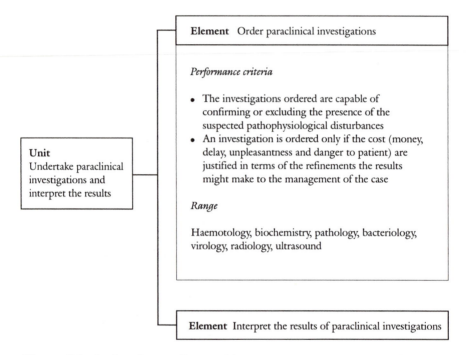

Figure 5.2: *Section of Australian Health Care Competency Statement (from Bowden & Masters, 1993)*

This example is provided by Jessup (1991) to illustrate how 'units' are to be made up of assessable 'elements'; acceptable standards of achievement in relation to each element are to be specified through 'performance indicators', and 'range statements' are to be used to provide a guide to the range of contexts in which a 'competent' person should be able to demonstrate the performance criteria. Other examples from work in Australia are provided later in this chapter. Units, elements, performance criteria and range indicators together constitute the 'statement of competence' for an occupational area. The statement spells out what candidates are required to be able to do for the award of a National Vocational Qualification. Figure 5.3 is based on work in the mid-1990s by the Australian Institute of Agricultural Science to develop competency standards in Agricultural Science (Bowden and Masters, 1993).

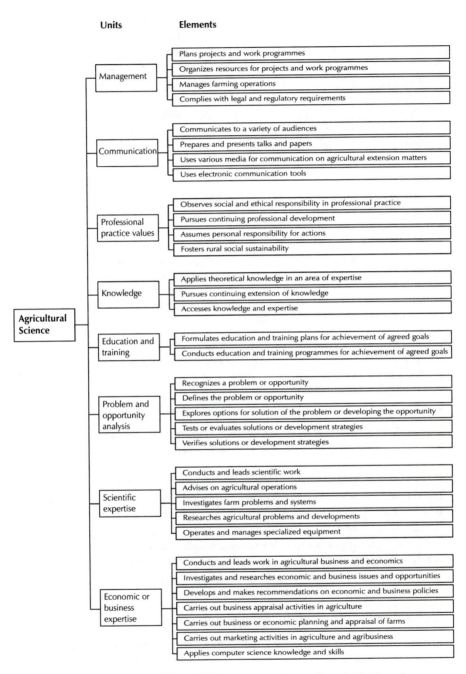

Figure 5.3: *Units and Elements of Competency: Australian Agricultural Science (Bowden and Masters, 1993)*

In Agricultural Science at that time, eight units of competency were defined and, for each unit, between two and seven elements of competency were identified. The first six units define 'core' competencies in Agricultural Science. The last two define 'specific' competencies in science and business/economics.

These eight units and 34 elements are accompanied by performance criteria which spell out the level of performance expected of agricultural scientists at the beginning of induction into the workforce and professional practice. The performance criteria for element 2 of the unit 'Scientific Expertise' (providing agricultural advice) are shown in Figure 5.4.

Element: Provides an agricultural advisory or extension service

---

Performance criteria

- Assists in providing integrated whole farm advice to the farming community to improve agricultural productivity, efficiency and conservation.
- Advises farmers and other relevant bodies on aspects of agriculture including crop, livestock and pasture production, soil and water conservation, irrigation and drainage and farm management.
- Provides advice on the basis of a good understanding of the techniques of information and technology transfer.
- Advises farmers by one-to-one farm visits, telephone or at the office.
- Assists in organizing and conducting field days, group discussions, seminars, lectures and demonstrations.

Figure 5.4: *An element of competency and its associated performance criteria – Australian Agricultural Science (from Bowden & Masters, 1993)*

To ensure that standards are firmly based on the needs of employment, and not merely on doubtful assumptions about workplace needs, competency-based educational reforms look to industry to take the lead in developing appropriate standards, and involve persons in the workplace as widely as possible in determining and endorsing competency standards. This, too, is something that we share with the competency movement and our approach to involving people in the workplace is discussed in Chapter 10.

Outcomes as observable 'competencies'

A third intention of competency-based approaches is to express outcomes as explicit, observable workplace performances. The intention is to express outcomes in the form of clear and precise 'competencies', so that (a) the needs of employment can be better communicated, (b) the goals of educational programmes can be redefined and communicated with greater precision, and (c) straightforward judgements can be made about the extent to which any particular competency has been attained:

> Rather than designing curricula to meet assumed needs, representative occupational bodies identify 'occupational standards' which are clear and precise statements which describe what effective performance means in distinct occupational areas. The standards are then used to develop 'new' vocational qualifications and the assessment which underpins them; plus learning programmes which deliver the achievements identified in the standards (Mansfield, 1989).

Explicitness and precision are recurring themes in discussions of competency-based outcomes. If outcomes can be expressed in precise, observable terms, it is argued, these can then be used to set clear goals for educational programmes. For Gilbert Jessup, a leading advocate of competency-based education in the UK, precision in the specification of competencies is the key to accurate communication of workplace needs: 'For accurate communication of the outcomes of competence and attainment, a precision in the use of language in such statements will need to be established, approaching that of a science' (Jessup, 1991).

It is here that we differ considerably from the competency movement. We believe that it is not possible to define precisely the specific workplace competencies that graduates will need to have developed to enable them to perform competently in the workplace. We believe it is impossible to do so and our approach, which we discuss later in this chapter, takes this as its point of departure.

Approaches to competence development

Table 5.2 shows different perspectives on what represents competence, from simple performance in the workplace, through performance plus knowledge, an additive model (each of these first two linked to competency-based approaches), to an integration of performance and knowledge and then finally a more holistic competence, which we favour and discuss below. There is a need to differentiate between the Level 2 additive approach and the Level 3 approach, which attempts to consider knowledge in context, in relation to performance rather than separate from it. The Level 4 approach represents the attempt to integrate as well the person's way of seeing themselves as a professional. It is more holistic than and subsumes the previous levels. In our view, competency-based approaches have not gone much beyond Level 2 in practice and we believe any educational approach should be directed at least to Level 3 and preferably to Level 4.

Table 5.2: *Description of levels of competence (adapted from Bowden, 1997)*

1 Behaviourist	Basic performance in the workplace
2 Additive	Performance plus knowledge (usually with knowledge assessment undertaken separately from performance assessment, an additive not an integrated approach)
3 Integrative	Performance and knowledge integrated
4 Holistic	Holistic competence (discussed further below)

Gonczi, Hager and Oliver (1990) point out that the analysis of professional work into roles, tasks and sub-tasks results in impractically long lists of specific tasks (Level 1 in Table 5.2). Attribute analysis, on the other hand, which the competency-based approach was intended to replace, runs the risk of attempting to spell out the knowledge, skills and attitudes that underlie professional competence without considering what it is that professionals actually do in the workplace. According to Gonczi *et al.* the Level 2 approach begins by attempting to identify those areas of professional practice in which it is essential to demonstrate at least minimum competence and to identify the knowledge, skills and attitudes required to perform complex professional activities.

There is a series of trends as you move from Level 1 through to Level 4. They are:

- increasing complexity of outcome
- broader curriculum requirements
- more complex assessment requirements
- increasing ambiguity in the relation between objectives and assessment of outcome
- increasing need for interpretation and professional judgement in assessment.

Level 4, for instance, represents a three-way integration among the person's way of seeing their professional role, their capacity to undertake that role and the knowledge base with which that professional identity and performance are intermeshed. The assessment of such an outcome is not simple and it is difficult to assess it directly. Competency-based approaches do not in practice address these matters.

It is not surprising that, initially, the competency movement focused on minimal ambiguity and greater certainty, viz Level 1. They were concerned with generating greater recognition of the role of education in preparing students for the workplace, within an educational world that they saw as focused on book-learning and theory. As a consequence their terminology and their practices focused almost entirely on the workplace connection. This may or may not have been strategically wise but, whether it was strategic at the time or not, such lower-level approaches must be judged in the 1990s on their merits, not on rational motives of decades before. Therefore the kinds of shifts in focus adopted by Gonczi and Hager and others are developments that would be expected to take place and some would argue, including ourselves, that there is a lot further to go. That is what the next section of this chapter is about.

Competence versus competencies

We consider that the questions 'What is learned?' and 'What should be learned?' are the most fundamental questions of learning. The competency-based approach is surely an attempt to address the second of these two questions explicitly. However, we have not found those attempts very powerful, mainly because they have not advanced very far in terms of the progression outlined in Table 5.2.

We are trying here to provide answers to the question of what we learn when we learn something. Answers to this question should reasonably provide us with a point of departure for addressing the question 'What should be learned?' Our answers to that question could be considered as a description of the competence – and not competencies – aimed for.

What is competence then and how is it related to competencies? The term 'competency' itself has two elements to it. The first is that it appears to be linked to competence in some way and the second is that it is a diminutive, ie it refers to some part of competence. The term is not used consistently although its origins mean that it refers in some way to competence in the workplace. Is a competency the capacity to adequately do some task which, along with other tasks, represents competence in the workplace? Is a competency one of a range of underlying attributes, the possession of which will ensure competence in carrying out workplace activities? Or is the concept of competence more complex than either of these indicates?

Velde and Svensson (1996) suggest that the conception of competence needed to meet the demands of the general situation seems to be a relational, interpretative, holistic and contextual conception. They focus the term 'relational' on the relation between an individual (group) and a situation, seeing competence as a holistic quality in this relation. Contextual because parts of the relation are understood in relation to the whole and the whole qualities of the relation are understood in relation to the nature of the individual and of the situation: '... what is needed is not only a description of performances which are according to standards but an understanding of the variation in whole characteristics of performances on specific tasks, both successful and unsuccessful performances, as a basis for understanding the relation between more general and more specific parts of competence'.

Sandberg (1994) extends these views of competence by arguing for the inclusion of an intentional dimension, ie the person's conception of the work and their relation to it. This corresponds to Level 4 of the earlier categorization in Table 5.2. Sandberg's notion of intentionality is content-related. This means that the general characteristics of competence that have been described acquire their meaning only through consideration of each specific case. What it means to be a competent engineer, doctor, electrician or teacher will be different from each other despite them all being characterized by the individual's way of seeing the professional situations. Those meanings have to be learned.

The nature of competence

Sandberg's (1994) point of departure is close to the argument in Chapter 2 that the most fundamental form of learning implies a change in our way of seeing something. In addition, having learnt to see something in a certain way implies becoming able to discern certain aspects of a certain kind of situation and being able to focus them simultaneously. Such a capability originates from having experienced variation in dimensions corresponding to those critical aspects.

In many examples previously discussed, we have described qualitatively different ways of seeing the same phenomenon, the same situation. In Chapter 2 we described the learner's focusing on the velocity of bodies in uniform linear motion and understanding the equilibrium being related to constant velocity as compared with focusing on movement and of forces acting on that body and understanding equilibrium being related to rest (pages 30–31). In another example we distinguished between understanding text comprising a principle–example structure in hierarchical terms, whereas (a) the example is seen as illustrating the principle which is present in the example, on the one hand, and (b) on the other hand, understanding what is stated in the principle and what is stated in the example isolated from each other, one following the other and therefore not seeing them as principle and example (page 32). These are descriptions of what people actually learn but this chapter is about what they should learn.

One of the ways of seeing the object of learning in both examples could be used as a characterization of what should be learned or what competence should be developed. The first way of seeing bodies in uniform linear motion in the first example above, and the first way of making sense of the text with a principle–example structure in the second example certainly reflect capabilities we would wish our students to have. Often, however, we have to make curriculum decisions or specify learning goals on a more general level.

Therefore let us focus on some of the examples of broader kinds of capabilities (see Chapter 3). What we referred to as approaches, comprising both ways of experiencing and handling certain kinds of situations, qualify very well. Approaches to learning, for instance, constitute some most important capabilities. In the case of approaches to learning through reading, described earlier, one of those approaches is clearly preferable (see pages 49–50). In other cases, such as approaches to programming, versatility is the aim. As pointed out, the expert programmer moves freely between the different approaches, using the one which is most appropriate. Therefore the competence aimed for has to be the capability of adopting any one of them when it is appropriate and effective (see page 56).

Competence in clinical diagnoses

Approaches to learning considered as competences provide us with descriptions sufficiently general to be applicable both to the context of studies and the context of working life. Whelan's (1988) investigation of learning clinical diagnosis in medical schools offers an excellent example.

> In most medical courses, students have to learn how to make a clinical diagnosis when confronted with a patient with a particular set of symptoms, so that some treatment can be devised. A lot of doctors think that such a skill is developed naturally (Whelan, 1988); some medical schools build it into the curriculum either in its own right or as part of other studies, but, while it usually is part of other studies, it is not the subject of particular emphasis.

> Concerned by students' apparent trial-and-error approaches when faced with the need to diagnose an illness, Whelan (1988) studied the problem systematically. He designed two case descriptions able, in principle, to be diagnosed using basic, scientific concepts. He asked several first-year clinical students (fourth-year medical students) to discuss them.

> Whelan identified some distinctly different approaches to the task. The approaches of 'ordering' and 'structuring' found by him refer to the directedness of students' awareness to the problem, and correspond very closely to the surface and deep approaches already discussed. Whelan (1988) comments on the 'ordering' approach:

> If symptoms were discussed individually without relating to one another, if symptoms were ignored, if parts of the problem were ordered and grouped but if the groupings were not put together into a whole, if the process used distorted the structure of the problem and dislocated the content from its meaning, if the student was unable to describe what she/he was doing, the extracts were considered to characterize an ordering (or atomistic) approach to clinical problem-solving. Students using this approach usually did not discover a solution that satisfactorily accounted for all the information given.

> Whelan (1988) also commented on the 'structuring' approach: 'If the student maintained the underlying structure of the problem, if extracts illustrated that the student used evidence to support his or her ideas and related ideas to previously learned basic science, then these extracts were considered to characterize a structuring (or holistic) approach to clinical problem-solving'.

> Students adopting the 'ordering' approach focus on the list of symptoms in themselves, while those taking the 'structuring' approach search for the meaning of the symptoms in terms of an underlying cause.

This study has led to a more complex analysis of approaches, interpreted in terms of the ways the students actually went about the task, a different dimension. Subordinate to the ordering approach, students were found to tackle the case either by using 'pattern matching', in which a diagnosis was attempted based on one or more clinical features found in the case, or 'exclusion', in which diagnoses were eliminated according to the absence of clinical features present in the potential diagnosis but not in the case described. The structuring approach, on the other hand, found students who used 'diagnostic integration' to reach a diagnosis. Such students interpreted symptoms in terms of conceivable underlying causes rather than jumping directly to diagnoses, thereby developing a hypothesis using a logical sequence of pathophysiological mechanisms.

Figure 5.5 shows the two case descriptions used in the study. Pattern matching is evident in quotes from two students who describe their approaches to diagnosis of case 1 thus: 'As soon as I read he was tired and weak I thought of anaemia... I thought, was that in a list (of causes) they gave us concerning such and such a disease? I thought that the problem was tiredness and weakness and from that I went onto think that the diarrhoea was something unrelated or superimposed'.

---

1. A male electrician, aged 23 years, presents complaining of progressively worsening tiredness and weakness of three week's duration. He has difficulty climbing the stairs. He believes that this is due mainly to weakness but he has noticed that he has trouble breathing whenever he attempts to walk up more than one flight. Three months ago he first noticed the onset of diarrhoea. This occurs on most days varying from four to six bowel actions daily. He has lost approximately 10 kilograms in weight over this time. Physical examination reveals a thin male consistent with his stated weight loss. There are no other physical signs of disease – specifically, none of his abdominal organs are enlarged. There is no guarding or tenderness.

2. A 55-year-old female, widowed for two years, presents complaining of shortness of breath on exertion for six months. She has also experienced three episodes of shortness of breath at night. These have been associated with a dry cough and wheeze. Attacks last from 20 minutes up to several hours. Her distress was eased by sitting up. She reported smoking 25 cigarettes a day for 20 years but ceased 13 years ago. Another doctor, several years ago, prescribed Lasix for swollen ankles. There are no abnormal physical symptoms on examination.

Figure 5.5: *Two cases used in the study by Whelan*

These students are focusing on one symptom and ignoring others. Compare this quote, dealing with case 2: 'She probably had some sort of problem with her heart which is unable to cope with maintaining a good circulation. It could be due to hypertension... because she is a smoker, hypertension and atherosclerosis could be inter-related... The heart has got to the stage where it can't cope with increased demand such as with exercise'. Here, the meaning of the symptoms described is in focus while in the previous quote the symptoms merely provide a launching pad for diagnosis.

In terms of learning, this diagnostic session led to distinctly different learning outcomes. The students were asked to describe the diagnosis they reached and this was analysed in terms of the extent to which it demonstrated understanding in terms of their basic knowledge of medical science. Understanding was ascribed to the diagnosis if 'the clinical features were explained in terms of pathophysiological links, if causal chains with explanatory intermediate steps between clinical features and diagnosis could be recognized, and if both positive and negative links were included (i.e. items for and against the chosen diagnoses were discussed)' (Whelan, 1988). If, in contrast, mere description was the main feature of the diagnosis, in which 'the discussion was characterized by short causal (associative) links between symptoms and diagnoses, if the outcome was given only in descriptive terms or if the student was unable to make a diagnosis' (Whelan, 1988), then the student was judged not to have based a diagnosis on medical science.

Consider these learning outcomes in the context of the students' whole education, especially the early years in conventional programmes that are spent studying basic science, and the clinical experience to come. The outcome of such a diagnosis exercise lies in the form of the understanding arrived at – in Whelan's terms, understanding or description. Out of the 48 students who took part in this study and the two cases they were asked to diagnose, in the overwhelming majority of instances (83) an ordering approach was adopted, and in only six of those was an outcome reached that could be classified as understanding. Of the seven instances when the structuring approach was adopted, on the other hand, understanding was reached on all occasions. Again, the approach and the outcome are seen to be clearly related.

It is possible to consider the symptoms in these cases to be a text about the patient who exhibits them. If we do that, the similarity between the ordering approach to diagnosis and the surface approach to reading a text becomes apparent – the focus is on the sign rather than the signified, focus passes from one bit to another, without relating each bit to the whole and so on. Marton and Booth (1997) continue with this metaphor in describing this example and suggest that students adopting a structuring approach are reading the symptoms as a window into the underlying disease they wish to diagnose, whereas those with an ordering approach read the symptoms for their own worth. The structure of awareness in the case of the ordering approach is one symptom after the other with no sense of the simultaneity of the symptoms. The structuring approach, in contrast, implies an awareness of the symptoms simultaneously and the diagnosis is also there all the time. The ordering approach does not move away from the level of the symbols included in the written case description, whereas the structuring approach sees the case as a real-life entity. In the structuring approach, each symptom is seen by itself, and in relation to the other symptoms, and in relation to the diagnosis.

The capability of experiencing and handling clinical problem solving in accordance with what Whelan referred to as a structuring approach, diagnostic integration and understanding strikes us as a reasonable way of describing competence in clinical problem solving – to be aimed at in medical education. However, Whelan talked about approaches to clinical problem solving, strategies used and understandings arrived at. He certainly did not talk about 'competence' and neither have some other authors to whom we have referred in this chapter. We have labelled outcomes of learning approaches 'competences'. We would justify this seemingly daring step by using Jörgen Sandberg's above-mentioned work as support. His point of departure is a thorough analysis of the concept of competence and he suggests an alternative and novel sense. He describes competence in terms of the qualitatively different ways in which professionals experience (and carry out) their own work. Sandberg is partly drawing on the same research tradition as we do and his description is in our view reconcilable with the description of qualitative differences in people's ways of experiencing and handling classes of situations, differences that in this chapter is referred to as differences in competence.

Competence in motor optimizing

Sandberg (1994) studied a group of engineers at the Volvo factory in Göteborg. They are called engine optimizers and their work is to develop the engines for new models of Volvo automobiles. The engines have a number of qualities, such as fuel consumption, durability, exhaust emission, power and it is the task of the engine optimizer to produce an engine with the best possible combination of properties, subject to a number of legal constraints, by making adjustments to the fuel and ignition systems.

There is a variation in these engineers' competence, as is true of any other body of professionals. There is general agreement on this and, moreover, the optimizers themselves agree on who is more competent at the job and who is less so. It could have been that educational background or years of experience as engine optimizers would account for such differences in competence, but that was not found to be so. Sandberg studied 20 of the optimizers, selected to cover a range of educational backgrounds and engineering experience, by analysing interviews he had conducted focusing on the nature of engine optimization and the competent engine optimizer, and by trying to get them to link their general comments to concrete examples of their work. He aimed to make explicit how this category of workers experienced their work, in terms of what it is and how it is done.

Sandberg found three qualitatively different ways of experiencing the work. The least complete of these (I), implying least competence, was one in which competence was seen as accurately optimizing separate qualities of the engine according to requirements, so that the work is organized into a number of separate optimizing steps. At each step one quality is monitored according to a monitoring parameter and, when a satisfactory value has been achieved, the next step is undertaken. This has to be repeated in cycles to take account of interaction between optimizations of the different parameters until all the adjusted qualities combine to make an engine that can be approved. The second way of experiencing the work (II) sees competence as accurately optimizing interacting qualities of the engine in the right order, which is to say that focus has now shifted away from single steps, towards working in steps that have a relation to one another and to the whole engine. Whereas (I) was an additive view of optimization, (II) is a more integrated and interactive view, in that the aim of the optimizer is now to optimize a single quality such that it interacts with the other qualities to lead to an approved engine. The third way of experiencing the work (III), as well as focusing on the single adjustments to qualities of the engine in such a way that they lead in interaction to an efficient engine, also focuses on the relation between the approved engine and the putative user. When an optimization is being carried out, the optimizer considers how the driver would experience the finished product.

The hierarchical set of ways of seeing the work of the optimizer introduces at each stage a new factor into the optimization consideration – to the individual qualities of the engine (I) are added the integration and interaction of qualities (II), and then the engine is turned round and seen from the driver's perspective (III). These are the different ways in which the engine optimizers experience their work and competence at their work, but what does it say about competence in any other way? The most interesting thing is that those engineers who were found to voice the most advanced ideas of competence (III) were actually those who were judged to be most competent by their fellow engine optimizers. Furthermore, competence is seen to depend less on education and years at work, than on the way in which the work is viewed.

We have therefore another example of how a certain phenomenon or a certain set of situations (developing a new engine) is seen in a number of qualitatively different ways. In terms of certain criteria of efficiency they can be ordered meaningfully. It is reasonable to argue that they represent differences in competence. At the same time they represent capabilities of discerning critical features and focusing on them simultaneously. Ways of experiencing and handling the work task judged to be more efficient are more complex. In addition, as the aspects discerned correspond to dimensions of variation, richer, more complex patterns of aspects correspond to wider spaces of variation. It is in this sense we can claim that we learn through variation, and in a way it is variation we learn.

Beyond competence

The subtitle of this book is *Beyond Quality and Competence*. Yet, in the previous section we gave examples of how competence could be described. This might not seem as 'going beyond competence', but in a sense it actually is. 'Competence' in the subtitle denotes what we have referred to as 'the competency movement', ie something we want to go 'beyond'; 'competence' in the title of the previous section refers to competence in a more meaningful sense, ie something we want to elaborate. All this may sound rather bewildering and to add to the confusion we would point out that the linguistic distinction between competencies and competence that we used for making a conceptual distinction does not hold across cultural boundaries: as we said earlier, in publications in the UK for instance, the term 'competences' is used in the same sense as competencies in Australian documents. So, the distinction is primarily between two senses of 'competence', one which we want to go beyond and one which we want to elaborate. Competence in the first sense refers to sets of independent, observable units of behaviour in the workplace. Competence in the second sense refers to capabilities of seeing and handling novel situations in powerful ways, capabilities that frequently integrate disciplinary and professional knowledge.

There is still one more sense in which we argue for 'going beyond competence'. Descriptions of competence are attempted answers to the question 'What should be learned?' However, this question in the educational context is basically a question of curriculum and as such it can be preferably dealt with in terms of analysis that integrates empirical, theoretical and normative aspects. In addition, it not only defines the aims of learning to be achieved, but in fact points to the kinds of experience the learner may need to engage in for those aims to be achieved. It is in the questions 'What is learned?' and 'What should be learned?' that the core issues of curriculum and issues of teaching coincide. This is why we are going to argue in the next chapter that it is the capabilities that the students are supposed to develop that have to be the point of departure when it comes to teaching, and not the particular teaching methods. Curriculum and teaching will then be described primarily in terms of the capabilities to be developed and the patterns of experiences it takes to develop them.

A central idea in the theory of learning outlined in Chapter 2 is that changes in the way in which we see a certain phenomenon or a certain class of situation is the most fundamental form of learning and that 'a way of seeing something' can be understood in terms of the critical aspects of the phenomenon discerned, and focused on simultaneously. Another central idea is that discernment and simultaneity originate from experienced patterns of variation. The present section builds mainly on the first idea, the next section on both.

Curriculum and variation

This brings us to our perspective on curriculum design, the variation model[1] which derives from our own analysis of what it takes to learn for an unknown future. It is one thing to argue for the kinds of learning outcomes implied by the particular definitions of competence given earlier in this chapter and which many deem as more appropriate for describing performance in the workplace. It is quite another to suggest mechanisms by which such high-level outcomes might be achieved. A theory of learning is needed which accounts for the ways in which learning experiences may be designed so that these particular learning outcomes are more likely to be achieved. We have elaborated our theory of learning in Chapter 2 but will recall one aspect of our argument by means of a quote addressing this issue in a way that reflects Sandberg's view of competence: 'Studies in higher education are supposed to enable students to deal with situations in the future which cannot be defined in advance. By means of appropriating what is known, students are expected to be equipped for dealing with the unknown. This can be achieved by forming the eyes through which students are going to see situations in their professional lives in the future' (Marton, 1996).

What tertiary educators must face is that students need to experience a curriculum related to a particular area of study which will enable them to develop the capacity to perform after graduation in circumstances that cannot be prescribed in advance. On the one hand, it is too difficult to define the specific contexts that a particular graduate will later confront. Students need to learn in ways that help them deal with a range of contexts, many, if not all, unique. Secondly, the world advances every day and no preparation for experiences some years ahead can rely on the accuracy of any forecasting of such advances. So university education has to be, as suggested in the quote above, about learning for an unknown future.

Curriculum design

In addition to a shift towards focusing on learning and on the learners, we believe that the nature of the curriculum *per se* needs attention. Typically, traditional curriculum design has focused around the needs of the discipline. The syllabus, that simple statement of what the educational programme is about, is normally constructed around the structure of the discipline. In physics, for example, the area of mechanics is often divided up among scalars and vectors, force and acceleration etc. In competency-based approaches, the curriculum is derived with workplace practice as the focus. What does a competent person need to be able to do in the workplace and what skills are needed for the worker to be able to do those things? Then questions can be asked, although they are not always asked, about what knowledge is relevant.

We believe neither of these approaches is adequate. Both approaches depend on two things being true. The first is that the world of work and discipline knowledge are stable, both within themselves and in relation to each other. The assumptions, either that one can specify exactly what skills and knowledge are needed to be a competent worker or that learning the discipline as it now exists prepares a graduate for the workplace, both depend on this first proposition being true and it is obvious that it is not true. Both the world of work and the disciplines are dynamic and increasingly so.

The second thing that must be true for either of these approaches to work is that either learning about a concept or developing a skill enables a graduate to apply that knowledge or skill to novel problem situations, the latter being a requirement for virtually every graduate. There is no evidence that learning about a concept or learning a skill alone can lead to such an outcome. In fact there is evidence to the contrary (Bowden *et al.*, 1992; Dall'Alba *et al.*, 1993). The most able students in their cohorts, who gain the highest scores in competitive examinations, often have difficulty with problems that are presented in a form different from any they have seen before, even when the problem is dealing with the same issues they have successfully managed in practice and in examinations. A detailed example is shown in the next section.

Force and acceleration

Differing understandings

This example is focused on a technological learning topic, viz. understanding of concepts such as force and acceleration. Typically, in a physics course at senior secondary school or first-year university, concepts of force and acceleration are exemplified through problem sets featuring, for instance, motor vehicles travelling along roads or trains on railway tracks. Students are asked to solve many problems of the kind that require calculation, say, of the acceleration of a vehicle which increases its velocity from 0 to 50 km/h in 10 seconds. Some relevant equations, which many students might have learned off by heart are:

$$v = u + at$$
$$s = ut + 0.5at^2$$
$$v^2 = u^2 + 2as$$

with u being the initial velocity, v the final velocity, a the acceleration, t the time elapsed and s the displacement.

What many learners do is to ask themselves which of u, v, a, t and s have numerical values provided in the problem description, which variable is needed in the answer and then choose the equation with that complete set of variables in it. In a sense, what acceleration means to such a learner is 'the answer to the solution of the relevant equation'. Slightly more scientific than that, it also commonly has a meaning associated with changing (usually increasing) speed. These understandings are reinforced by the large number of problems of just this kind that students are expected to solve and by the fact that those problems inevitably turn up in the examination papers.

The assumptions that are required to solve problems such as those described above are that any acceleration being calculated is uniform or constant, that the vehicle is travelling on a straight, flat surface and that other forces such as wind resistance should be ignored. One of the difficulties in helping students learn about force and acceleration using this kind of curriculum is that such assumptions are unlikely to be encountered in real-life situations.

In case you think that this minimalist approach to teaching and learning is likely to be a characteristic only of inferior educational institutions or less able students, we now discuss an Australian Research Council funded research project that we undertook because later-year students in a university physics course were having difficulty with advanced study, despite performing very well in physics examinations in their final year of school and first year at university (see Bowden *et al.*, 1992; Dall'Alba *et al.*, 1993; Walsh *et al.*, 1993). The university was a prestigious one, always ranked in the top group on any national ratings scale, and the students entered the university with secondary-school grades higher than any other cohort entering physics courses elsewhere in the region.

In this research, students were asked to solve physics problems, some of which were quantitative and others qualitative problems, without any numerical answers possible. Students were always asked to explain how and why. The researchers found the anticipated result that, while there certainly was a range in capacity to solve the quantitative problems, many students had little or no difficulty at all with them. In contrast, few students were able to deal adequately with the qualitative problems. Further, even when students were able to solve the quantitative problems, their qualitative explanations often lacked scientific rigour.

For instance, in one of the qualitative problems, the researchers described to students a situation in which a parachutist jumps from an aircraft and opens the parachute after a few seconds. They asked each student to tell them what would happen from the moment the parachutist left the aircraft and to explain why.

The scientific explanation for the motion prior to the opening of the parachute is that, without any other influences, the force due to gravity would cause the parachutist to move towards the earth at an increasing velocity. However, the parachutist does not accelerate (increase velocity) indefinitely. In fact, a parachutist would be moving towards the ground after falling, say, 2,000 metres, at the same velocity as after just 1,000 metres. Why is this so?

The reason is that there are in fact two forces acting on the parachutist. One is the force of gravity which is constant. The second is the resistance to the motion caused by the air through which the parachutist is moving and this force of air resistance is in a direction opposite to the downwards motion. That second force is not constant: as the parachutist falls faster and faster, the air resistance gets greater. Therefore the overall force on the parachutist in the downwards direction gets less and less as the velocity increases (the constant gravitational force minus the increasing air resistance). So, as the parachutist gets faster, the overall acceleration diminishes, ie the rate at which the velocity is increasing is slowing. Eventually the acceleration becomes zero when the force of gravity and the air resistance are equal (and opposite). With acceleration zero, the velocity remains constant, therefore the parachutist continues to fall at that constant velocity, which has been given the name 'terminal velocity'.

Few students in the study were able to explain the parachutist's motion in this way despite being able to calculate answers to quantitative problems depicting similar situations. Many were aware of the influence of gravity on the parachutist's velocity and they were also aware of the effect of air resistance on velocity but they often responded as if these two aspects were not related. They tended to deal with them independently but not together.

Underlying all of these results was the finding that descriptions of students' understanding of fundamental concepts such as force and acceleration cover a range of categories and that many of these understandings have much less explanatory power than the accepted scientific explanation. An important aspect of that is that many students who were unable to explain adequately the underlying scientific principles could still perform the quantitative tasks perfectly, provided they could be addressed simply by using memorized equations. So here we have an example of students being able to do something, to carry out a required task, but who are unable to cope with problems outside a narrow spectrum and unable to explain adequately why the solutions work.

Objectives and curriculum structure

The conclusion to be drawn from this and other similar studies (many of them listed by Pfundt and Duit, 1994) is that traditional courses in physics have focused on developing students' skills in solving set problems but have not done much to help students to develop the capabilities to deal with new situations, of a kind not seen before. We argued above that, for students to be able to cope with the unknown future on graduation, the curriculum would need to be designed so that students experienced variation and developed the capabilities to look at a situation, discern the relevant aspects and address them simultaneously in the design and solution of the problem.

We spoke particularly about the problem sets dealing with force and acceleration which all of us who studied physics learned to solve. Generally there is no variation to experience; students are given a particular situation with the relevant aspects identified. Often the aspects included are limited in number and different from real cases graduates will encounter in their work. These narrowly focused, almost simplistic problems can be solved by one of a number of memorized equations and the criterion of success is getting the same numerical answer, which is at the back of a textbook or in the teacher's answer sheet. These kinds of problem are unlikely to assist students to develop their understanding of concepts like force and acceleration, which are behind these situations. Variation theory would suggest that students' understanding of scientific principles and capacity to explain a variety of real-life contexts would be enhanced by including well-designed contextual variation in the learning experience. Far better to expose students to a variety of situations (see Figure 5.6) which are designed to develop the capacity to discern the relevant aspects of the situation.

Figure 5.6(a) depicts the idealized context for consideration of force and acceleration that is the subject of so many textbook treatments – a vehicle moving on a flat, straight surface. Students are usually told to ignore air resistance. This is almost an invariant context. The normal variations we experience in real life are artificially removed. Students are able to relate the concept of acceleration to changes in speed but the difficulty for students is that if the artificiality of this context is not made visible by consideration of the same concepts in more real-life contexts, then the capacity to deal with novel contexts will not be developed. This is what was found in the research study.

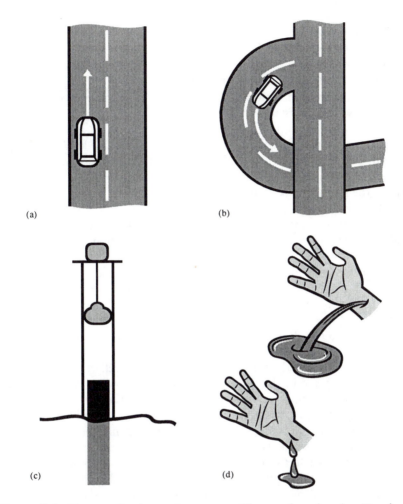

Figure 5.6: *Contexts showing various aspects of force and acceleration (Bowden, 1997)*

There are contexts which are more commonly encountered and which can be used to develop students' understandings of force and acceleration. These are shown in Figure 5.6(b)–(d). The diagrams and contexts they depict are schematic and it is not suggested that they represent an appropriate curriculum. However, they do demonstrate the idea of variation and its contribution to the development of discernment of the relevant aspects of a phenomenon and are used here only for that purpose.

Figure 5.6(b) depicts a car driving on a ramp leading to a motorway. This context raises a number of questions:

- Why do some drivers cause their cars to become slower and slower as they move down and around the ramp?
- Is the car easier or harder to control if the accelerator pedal is depressed a little more as the car moves around the ramp?
- What is the relation between acceleration and the changing of direction, with or without constant speed?

In fact, the concepts of force and acceleration are not related only to changes in speed. The term 'velocity' is used in physics rather than the term 'speed', to denote the inclusion of the directional aspect. Not only does it take force to increase the speed of a body but it also requires force to change its direction, with the speed held constant. Therefore if the accelerator pedal of the car moving around the ramp in Figure 5.6(b) is pressed down a little further, there can be sufficient force to bring about a change in direction without affecting the speed. However, if the pedal is not pressed down further, the speed will decrease as the direction of the motion changes around the curving ramp; the car slows down. (Even this is a simplification because transverse motion and road-tyre friction can also come into play. Nevertheless, the essential argument above stands.)

What this context does is to encourage a more sophisticated understanding of acceleration and force to develop – one whose relevance structure is more complex so that it includes the direction of motion as well as the speed.

Figure 5.6(c) shows the use of a pile-driver. This diagram is merely a schematic one, a real pile-driver is more complex. Nevertheless, this provides sufficient aspects to illustrate the points being made. Basically, a pile-driver consists of a frame supporting a weight held some distance above a pile, which is wedged in the ground. The weight is released and it falls towards the pile. When it hits the pile the two move down together and the pile is wedged further into the ground until the pile and weight come to rest. This process is repeated many times until the pile has been driven into the ground to the required depth.

This context raises questions which test the useful limits of the concept of acceleration:

- Is the motion of the descending weight the same as or different from that of the parachutist in free fall described earlier?
- What forces are affecting the motion of the descending weight in free flight and what is its acceleration?
- When the weight hits the pile, the weight and pile appear to instantaneously move together at a velocity much less than that of the weight before impact. Can this be a case of infinite acceleration of the pile or have we reached the limits of applicability of the concept?
- Is there some other explanation involving new concepts such as impulse and conservation of momentum that is more appropriate?

Most of the relevant issues are found in the questions above. Indeed, the answer to the first two questions is that the motion of the falling weight and the parachutist in free flight can be explained by the same scientific principles and, yes, there is a need to use new concepts to describe the motion of the combined weight and pile.

What needs to be explained is how it is that the pile is sitting at rest and, then, instantaneously when the weight hits it, it is moving (similar to when billiard or snooker balls collide). A relevant aspect of acceleration not yet dealt with is that it is concerned with the rate of change of velocity, ie not just with the amount of change in velocity but also how quickly the velocity changes. The average acceleration is the change in velocity divided by the time taken for the change to occur. With the pile-driver, it appears that the pile instantaneously goes from rest to some finite velocity. This implies infinite acceleration (change in velocity divided by zero), therefore some other way of dealing with this context is necessary. The concept of impulse and conservation of momentum principles are introduced by physicists to provide a full explanation of this phenomenon. These new principles are applied to the pile and the descending weight together, both before and after impact. The two are seen as a 'system'. So this context introduces several new aspects (acceleration as rate of change in velocity and the notion of a system) and also demonstrates some limits to the usefulness of the concepts of force and acceleration as explanations of such motion. In that way, the understanding of these concepts is enhanced and their relation to the new concepts developed. The expectation would be that the learner would develop a greater capacity to discern the relevant aspects of this and other situations.

Figure 5.6(d) merely depicts the different way that blood flows from a punctured vein and a punctured artery in the human body. When the blood from the artery spurts out (not continuously of course) it is moving faster than the blood which oozes more slowly from a vein. The motion of drops of blood falling to the ground from the puncture in each of the two cases can be explained in the terms already described for the parachutist, ie once the blood has left the body. However, what about the motion of blood circulating around the body in unpunctured arteries and veins? Does the behaviour of the blood coming from the punctured blood vessels reveal different motion within the closed systems? In particular:

- does the blood flow more slowly in a vein than in an artery?
- does the blood flow more rapidly down the body than up the body due to the influence of gravity?
- are the concepts of acceleration as applied to falling bodies like parachutists and pile-drivers relevant when the object is a fluid?

This is an even more complex situation than any of the others so far and the fact that the blood flow is not constant (related to the pumping of the heart), that there are valves in the system and that it is a closed fluid system (think of the effect of the opening of a household tap on the level of water in a reservoir some distance away) make simple analysis using the concepts of force and acceleration impossible. This, too, is a complex system and there is a need to deal with new concepts such as pressure; experience of this system adds to the understanding of force and acceleration through their relationship to the new concepts.

Most of the questions that have been posed invite qualitative answers. Our research showed that the ability to provide the right answer to quantitative questions often masks the understanding of the underlying concepts and students are not challenged or encouraged by such questions to reflect on and modify their understandings. Qualitative questions and discussion are essential for conceptual development.

Integration within the curriculum

The context depicted in Figure 5.6(b) involves the idea of circular motion and the context depicted in Figure 5.6(d) involves fluid motion. Some physicists who are reading this account will say, quite correctly, that in physics subjects, circular motion or rotational mechanics is often taught; so, too, is fluid mechanics. The trouble is that those topics are usually taught as separate idealized systems, separate from each other and from basic mechanics. Students who can solve the basic mechanics problems described earlier often also become adept at solving the quantitative problems involving rotational mechanics, using yet another set of memorized equations. However, they commonly fail to integrate the experiences in a way which enriches their understanding of force and acceleration or develops their capacity to discern the relevant aspects of novel situations involving those concepts.

Figure 5.7 illustrates this point. In Figure 5.7(a), the real-life phenomenon P, as depicted, is less likely to be understood if each of the contextual variations is treated in the curriculum as a special case with lots of contemporary experiences being required which focus on that one aspect. So clumps of specialized knowledge or skill are acquired and the way of solving a problem is to see if it fits one of the clumps. When it does not, there is difficulty in solving the problem.

However if the changing context, the variation in experience described earlier, is treated as part of the problem solution, as in Figure 5.7(b), then the contextual differences associated with phenomenon P become merely one aspect of the problem, which students have become used to including and dealing with. It is part of their way of seeing themselves as scientists.

It should be emphasized that what is being argued here is not simply that there should be a wide range of relevant examples provided, which in some way captures the range of student interest. It is not being argued that basic physics subjects should be made relevant for students of nursing, say, by replacing some

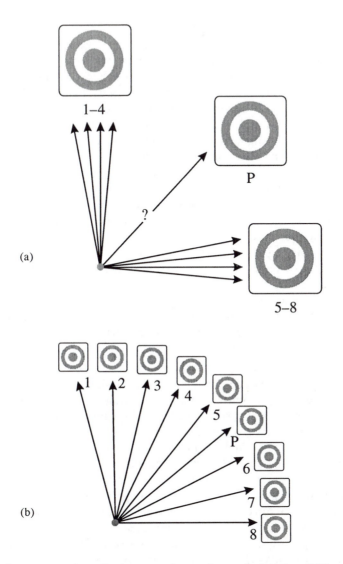

Figure 5.7: *More or less affective ways of preparing to deal with real-life phenomena (Bowden, 1997)*

of the standard 'motor cars on a straight, flat road' type problems with problems concerned with 'wheelchairs moving down a hospital corridor' or the like. Rather, the different contexts should be chosen so that different aspects of, say in this case force and acceleration, come into focus from one context to the other. The contexts in Figure 5.6 provide that kind of variation and in doing so assist the student to develop a more comprehensive and differentiated understanding of the concept and the contexts in which different aspects are more or less relevant. Perhaps more importantly, they can lead students to the conclusion that there are contexts in which other concepts become more relevant and can facilitate an even broader understanding of the whole subject in a relational way. As Dall'Alba and Sandberg (1992) express it: '... students learn skills and knowledge in accordance with their developing conception of the content related to the profession. Therefore, in order that students master the necessary knowledge and skills, they must learn to conceptualize the content in ways that are appropriate to the aims of education and to the profession'.

So it matters what kinds of learning experience students have and the responsibility of teaching goes beyond simple specification of topics to be covered. Attention needs to be given to the ways that students see the content, ie Marton's 'forming the eyes' through which students will be dealing with the future, and the example given above of contexts demonstrating aspects of force and acceleration is just that, one example. Course teams need to devise appropriate variations in learning experiences in their programmes so that students develop in ways that enable them to become competent professionals who can discern the relevant aspects of novel situations.

Learning experiences

We must repeat the argument that in order for students to discern the relevant aspects, there must not only be variation but students need to experience that variation. In traditional curricula in this field, simple mechanics, rotational mechanics and conservation of momentum (which are in turn relevant to the first three situations in Figure 5.1) are dealt with separately, with their own problem exercises and their own sets of equations. Many students do quite well in each of the three separate activities. However, to prepare for the unknown, students need to experience the variation among the three situations, to see that different aspects of force and acceleration are relevant in each of the situations and that, in some cases, other concepts need to be used to provide a full understanding of what happens. Students need to develop the skill of discerning the relevant aspects of the situation. To do so, they need to experience each situation in a way that emphasizes their relatedness and their differences. They need opportunities to compare them, to try out problem definition and solution in one situation, which they found worked in another and look for explanations as to why it might not have worked in the new situation. They need to experience the failure of the solution to work in a different situation as part of their learning.

It is important therefore for students to have ways of investigating these kinds of situation demonstrated to them. Whether this is undertaken through lectures, through multimedia packages or through tutorial discussion is a question to which we have no definitive answer except perhaps that, whichever method is used, it should be applied with the learning objectives in mind at every stage.

Students then need to experiment with such situations, to draw conclusions, trial their solutions and reflect on their experience. This may be done alone but we would counsel against it. We would argue that the observation of both the kinds of difficulty other students have and the kinds of strategy they use to deal with them are of immense importance, as well as the realization that other students are having such difficulties. Whether that interaction with other students best occurs in face-to-face tutorial classes, through Internet chat sessions or email is a matter of conjecture. However, it is doubtful that it can be undertaken effectively without some involvement of an academic teacher to help guide students through some of the issues, to provide feedback and to ensure that all students get an effective opportunity to develop their understandings in the desired direction.

Finally, it would be helpful for many students, if not all, to see some of the consequences of the failure to discern the relevant aspects through, for instance, laboratory experiments, computer simulations and the like. It would be imperative that these opportunities are organized with the whole range of objectives outlined above in mind, that students get the opportunity to try out their own solutions and see them succeed or fail and that failure in this sense be celebrated as a positive aspect of learning by the academic teachers and through the structure of the experience and the assessment.

Finally, however students are assessed, it is absolutely essential that the full range of objectives across a range of situations is included. We will discuss this further in Chapter 7.

No short-cuts

Many pages have dealt with one single example about force and acceleration. This may appear senseless, especially as most of the readers of the book are not physicists. So what is the point? We hope to have made some major points because the example was after all a means to illustrate and bring through some fairly general ideas. But there is more to it, we would say. We believe the very length of the example to be a point in itself.

We have to take our point of departure in what should be learned, we keep arguing. Many people around the world embracing such a view form groups, committees sitting in meeting rooms or go on retreats and keep producing lists of objectives like the ones in Figure 5.2.

What good does all that listing of objectives that goes on around the world do? Some think one thing, others think another – this is something you surely find out when you are sitting and listing in a group. At best the lists reflect opinions, grounded on little and they do not reveal what should be learned, they are putting up labels.

To reveal what should be learned takes a thorough analysis, an integration of empirical findings, theory and a normative stance. The questions are no easier, no less challenging and no less serious than questions within the very field of knowledge the students are supposed to learn about. The questions about what is learned, how it is learned and what should be learned are questions completely on par with questions within the domain that is the object of study. So how can we imagine that such questions can be settled by arranging meetings, preparing long lists of so-called objectives, on the ground of opinions, views, prejudices?

Our analysis of what should be learned about force and acceleration may be wrong, but the effort invested and the seriousness of the undertaking is right. This is what it takes to analyse the aims of learning and there are no short-cuts.

Still, one may object. Isn't an important function of learning aims, of objectives, to communicate what a subject, a course, is all about, to other people, especially to the students who are going to study it? And you can surely not offer them a 15-page description of just one single topic.

Yes, this is perfectly right. And in the actual case you may offer much more concise formulation, such as, in the case of the force and acceleration example:

> Students successfully completing this subject will understand how the concepts of force and acceleration enable explanation of the motion of physical entities in a variety of contexts, will be able to discern which aspects of those concepts are relevant to a particular context and will be able to use these understandings to explain and solve problems within that context. The contexts that will be dealt with in this subject are the idealized case of vehicles moving on straight, flat pathways without air resistance, more realistic contexts involving motion along the earth's surface and motion under gravity, and a small number of specific contexts in which the concepts of force and acceleration are only part of the explanation of the motion under study, along with other scientific concepts and theories. However, students will be expected to develop the capability to deal with previously unseen contexts to which the concepts and processes dealt with in this subject also apply.

In order to improve learning within a field, those within the field have to find out what their students actually learn, how they learn and what they should learn. What the teacher should do will follow from such an analysis and what the students should do as well.

What is to be done?

We are arguing for rigorous, careful analysis of specific aims or objects of learning and there are some general principles? They do not exist separate from the very content of learning and therefore we try to elaborate them mainly through examples. We will summarize some of the general conclusions, embodied mainly in specific illustrations.

Graduates are knowledgeable; they have many skills but they do not seem to know what to do in a novel situation. That seems to be what employers say and it fits with the research studies on students' learning. How do you learn what is known in a way that enables you to deal with unknown situations? Firstly, Marton (1996) argues that we learn to discern aspects that vary or, to put it slightly differently, it is variation we learn (see also Chapter 2) and it is variation that students should learn. The question is: what kind of variation should they learn? Secondly, we suggest that the curriculum be constructed by integrating two ways of organizing knowledge, from a disciplinary and professional perspective.

What does 'learn variation' mean? One of the problems with existing curricula and existing approaches to teaching and learning is that students focus on some particular issue or problem type and then practise solving such problems about that issue hundreds of times, until they are experts. They then move on to learn in the same way to solve problems about another issue, again and again. Then when they are faced with a problem they have never seen before they ask themselves: which set does this belong to? If they find it belongs to none of the sets they know and, as employers have noticed, they then do not know what to do. If only someone would give them a problem that belongs to one of those sets they have practised with – they could certainly solve it. But the real world is not like that.

What we need to do is to create a curriculum in which a lot of the problems are about novel situations, that is, situations in which at first it is not obvious what the problem is. Students should frequently be placed in contexts in which their first task is to figure out which aspects of their knowledge are relevant to the particular situation. Having done that, they need to work out just what the problem really is. Then they need to try to solve the problem by putting together the things they know that are relevant. In this way they will learn variation. Then when they graduate, they would follow the same process. It would be just like it was when they were students. The situation would be novel, they would discern the relevant aspects and then they would solve the problem by dealing with those relevant aspects simultaneously.

One difficulty with Newtonian mechanics is that the ground, that which is at rest, is in everyday life a common-sense, taken-for-granted frame of reference, therefore people easily focus on motion as needing to be explained. In Newtonian mechanics, however, the dividing line is not between rest and movement but between rest and uniform motion on the one hand and between accelerated or decelerated motion on the other. It is the change in velocity and not movement that has to be explained. In Chapter 6 we refer to Ueno, Arimoto and Fujita's (1990) study in which they considerably improved students' understanding of questions, like the one in our example, by introducing variation in the frame of reference through computer simulation of different perspectives (frames of reference) from which bodies in motion were seen. In order to develop an understanding of pricing in terms of supply and demand, one has to experience variation in both. Pong's (1998) study of Canadian high-school students' views of pricing (explored through widely varied questioning technique) offers some preliminary evidence for this conjecture.

In our lengthy example about how the concepts of force and acceleration might appear in a university programme, we drew on a number of specific contexts to which these concepts are relevant in various ways. The contexts were a vehicle moving on a straight, flat surface, a car moving around a roundabout on to a motorway, a pile-driver and blood flowing through blood vessels in the body. We considered how students can reflect on the variations as they consider what aspects are relevant in each context, why there is such variation and how it can be dealt with.

We have also given an example earlier of how the aims of learning about force and acceleration can be communicated to the students. Some readers may be thinking that what we have proposed goes 'over the top', that it is not feasible to have curricula described in this level of detail. After all, the excerpt provided earlier refers to only one aspect of an educational programme and the document describing the whole programme in this way is likely to be many pages long, perhaps 10, 20 or 30 pages, perhaps much longer still. They may be saying it cannot be done. However, it is being done in some universities. The Interior Design programme at the Royal Melbourne Institute of Technology, whose curriculum is described in Chapter 6, and whose development through a programme team-based, quality assurance process is referred to in Chapter 9, provides all students with just this level of detail (Lines, 1997). Certainly one might not expect university handbooks to contain such detail, mainly because of the amount of paper involved, but every academic team could produce such descriptions, place them on the Internet and ensure that handbooks are written in ways that are consistent with them and indicate how they can be accessed.

There is significant gain to be made by this process. The educational gain for students has been highlighted so far but the existence of such explicit statements creates confidence and increases the chance of satisfactory relationships between staff and students. Such statements represent a commitment, an unambiguous commitment, about what the university stands for and has pledged to deliver. It provides a framework for quality improvement and a fundamental base for quality assurance.

We now return to another aspect we mentioned earlier, the need to integrate the disciplinary and professional knowledge frameworks in developing university curricula. One of the characteristics of the workplace that is quite different from the university is that the way of organizing knowledge is different. In universities, our structures are usually built around disciplines and the functions tend to follow. The result has been that each discipline develops its own curricula very much in isolation from the other disciplines in the university.

Even within disciplines academics, who are appointed largely because of their expertise in one particular aspect of the discipline, also tend to develop curricula and teach in isolation from others, even others within their own discipline. It is no wonder that the fragmented learning in the examples described earlier is taking place. When physics graduates enter the workplace, the situations they face are not labelled 'Newton's first law'. They may not be 'labelled' in any way that resembles physics. When medical graduates enter the workplace, they are not faced with situations labelled 'anatomy', 'microbiology' or the like. They are faced with patients with illnesses and there are professional ways of managing those situations. For experienced professionals, those professional ways of organizing knowledge can be readily explained in terms of the disciplinary knowledge. Both are legitimate, important and linked. It would be a good thing if graduates had learned how to make those links then maybe they would no longer be described by employers as 'not knowing what to do'. In Chapter 10 we will exemplify how this can be achieved.

The variation model and the competency-based approach in contrast

These two aspects of our theory of learning, learning goals formulated in terms of capabilities for seeing certain situations in certain ways brought about through experienced variation in critical dimensions, on the one hand, and the integration of the disciplinary and professional knowledge frameworks, on the other, are what distinguishes our approach from the competency-based approach. The competency-based approach assumes that you can be prescriptive about the 'competencies' required in the workplace, while we argue that students need to experience variation precisely because you cannot predict in advance what they will have to deal with as professionals. Secondly, the competency-based approach focuses exclusively on the workplace framework whereas our theory is based on the argument that the only way to be able to use the disciplinary framework to explain and develop the professional framework, and vice versa, is to integrate the two frameworks in the curriculum. So we share a concern with the competency movement to focus on student learning outcomes but, as we said earlier, what we mean by learning outcomes is totally different.

---

1   See Marton (1998); Marton and Booth (1997); Fazey and Marton (2002) and Chapter 2 of this book.

Chapter 6

Bringing learning about

Views of teaching

The shift from a focus on teaching to a focus on learning is a theme running through this book. In the past, probably still in many universities, discussions about ways to improve the learning environment for students have been couched in terms of changing teaching methods and delivery systems. Arguments are put for and against maintaining a traditional approach to teaching using lectures, seminars and tutorials as compared with a shift towards, say, problem-based learning or workplace learning. These arguments often lead to the adoption of one, preferred approach to teaching and have the implicit assumption that that particular teaching method will lead to better learning. As we said in Chapter 1, the teaching method is only one means by which learning is brought about and, especially in these days of increasingly flexible, more electronically distributed, more open, more learner-controlled forms of learning, the 'teaching method' will decrease in relative importance.

That is not to say that it is unimportant how academics interact with students on the matter of learning. Our argument is that the 'best' approach to teaching will vary both with the nature of the learning being undertaken and the context in which it takes place, and above all with the object of learning. If the aim is to have students develop the capability to discern the relevant aspects of any situation and to address them simultaneously, the best learning method is the one which is optimal in relation to that aim. Depending on the nature of the learning goals and of the context, the most effective form of staff–student interaction should be chosen. It is unlikely that one particular form of such interaction, one teaching method, will be effective for all learning goals in all contexts hence our argument that universities need to be flexible in terms of teaching methods. They need to have a variety of possibilities, with the most appropriate one being chosen to fit the circumstances. The essential question is how to maximize learning in the circumstance; adoption of some preferred general teaching method by the university seems unlikely to help students achieve their goals.

In this chapter we will discuss teaching and learning in general, comment briefly on some general approaches to teaching such as the conventional lecture–tutorial approach, workplace learning, teaching and learning using technology and problem-based learning, and argue that exclusive adoption of any one is unlikely to assist students in achieving their learning goals. How successful teaching is should be judged in terms of the way the students come to understand the content dealt with in teaching and the decisive factor from this perspective is the way in which the content is dealt with in teaching. We will show that different teachers may handle the very same content in different ways and thereby affect differentially the students' understanding. General approaches to teaching are in our view just potential means for developing conditions conducive to effective learning. The critical aspects of the conditions for learning are the ways in which the object of learning is dealt with. Towards the end of this chapter we give some examples of how ways of dealing with the object of learning (ie the content of teaching) can be moulded on the grounds of theoretical conceptualization of learning. Finally we will argue that so-called principles of teaching or theories of instruction should be replaced by principles of learning and we will show how these principles of learning can be used to devise appropriate curricula and facilitate effective learning.

We have discussed above the evolution of ideas about teaching and learning, from a knowledge-based to a student-centred view, over recent decades. Formerly, in science education in particular, the educational process was more one of having teachers define the curriculum and students acquire the knowledge. Since that time, our ways of conceptualizing the outcomes of learning have become more differentiated and what students learn, what scientists 'know', we would like to conceptualize as 'ways of seeing'. This is not to say that everything is relative in the sense that there can never be any consensus, that any idea is as useful as any other, or that it is not possible to compare one way of seeing with another. Rather, this way of thinking provides a more powerful explanation for what we already know about learning. Every way of seeing contributes to our collective understanding of any phenomenon.

In science, there are significant parallels, indeed considerable overlaps, between the ways different scientists see the same phenomenon. These overlaps, these things held in common, have been the focus in the past. That there are also differences, however, needs to be acknowledged (see endnote 3 in Chapter 4) because in practice, the currently accepted theory is just what those words imply. While a primary criterion is that the theory is able to explain observations and measurements available at the time, science is a social construct and any contemporary theory is accepted when it represents the commonality of the ways of seeing by relevant scientists. The fact that acceptance of the new theory usually only occurs when there is agreement by the most powerful figures in the field emphasizes the social construct aspect of science. The scientific view of any phenomenon comprises the combination of views of all scientists, with the socially agreed and usually commonly held aspects being codified, albeit temporarily, as the current scientific theory. However, for the advance of science, the differences in ways of seeing are also significant. Indeed, whether we subscribe to a Popperian or a Kuhnian view, we have to acknowledge that science will only progress while individual scientists continue to see phenomena in their particular way, even while carrying out professional activities in accordance with the accepted way of seeing.

Just as scientists' ways of seeing vary, so too do those of students. Indeed, as we will show later in this chapter, teachers' ways of seeing what appear to be standard, accepted phenomena vary considerably. The lesson we learn from this is that teaching is not about transferring the teacher's understanding of a phenomenon to the student but rather it is about assisting the student to develop their way of seeing the phenomenon in a way that is more powerful for them. Students' ways of seeing may become just as – if not more – effective than those of their teachers without being identical to those of their teachers. Students' ways of seeing, as well as teachers' and scientists' ways of seeing, add to the collective consciousness and, as we argue in Chapter 8, are worthy of respect. Indeed, the ultimate goal of teaching should be for the student to go 'beyond' the teacher.

Teachers have to ask what they can do to assist students to develop ways of seeing that are as powerful as possible in helping them understand the world around them. One particular aspect, which we elaborated in Chapter 5, is the framing of curricula, the structuring of the object of learning so it is clear what the learning goals are, both generally and specifically. We suggested that the curriculum needed to be seen as problematic (in the sense of being an object of reflection over diverse potentially viable options) which in the past it had not. We outlined an example in which the development of the capacity to discern the relevant aspects of any particular phenomenon associated with the specific area of knowledge in question was seen as the key aspect of the curriculum. It was shown how experience of variation could be seen as a key aspect of their learning experience in order to achieve those outcomes.

A significant aspect of teaching within this framework is a respect for students' ways of seeing. Again, we should repeat that this is not an extreme, relativist position that we take. Rather, as students progress with their education they should come to understand their goal as being to learn to explain observations and make predictions which have a fair degree of success. They must learn to value their own ways of seeing but continue to question their efficacy. A teacher who scorns student responses as 'wrong' inhibits those students from pondering on what it was about the phenomenon that led them to see it that way and what other aspects might be relevant to a more powerful way of seeing. It is the capacity to judge the relevant aspects and to develop the most appropriate understanding of the phenomenon that is far more important a goal in education than learning to get any number of specific things 'right'.

If we are successful with the former, the latter will follow naturally; the reverse process is unlikely to be true. In this chapter, we will focus on the learning opportunities provided to students with this purpose in mind, that is, what it means to teach with such an orientation.

The task facing curriculum designers is to devise a set of key concepts or features or phenomena which characterize the educational programme area under consideration. Their relationship with each other should also be made explicit. Then key aspects of each need to be identified. For each, critical contexts need to be devised so that these key aspects are differentiated with one or more being in the foreground in one context while in the background in another context.

How these contexts can be used to enhance learning is to be discussed in this chapter, and it is fundamental that whatever teaching and learning methods are used, students need to deal with each of the contexts and, as well, make comparisons between them. Only then will they have the opportunity to discover that different aspects of a phenomenon or concept play a greater or lesser role in explaining a situation, depending on the context. They need experiences which lead them to conclude that it is important to identify early on what the relevant aspects of the concept or phenomenon are in a particular problematic context, before progressing to formulating and then solving the problem.

Underlying assumptions about teaching

There are certain assumptions on which the above analysis is based (Bowden, 1986) and on which our new ideas about teaching for the unknown build:

1. In relation to certain criteria (which we will describe in Chapter 9) certain types of learning are more effective than others; for instance, learning for understanding that involves more powerful ways of seeing a phenomenon is more effective than rote learning of information or skills; we would add that such learning for understanding needs to include the development of a capacity to discern the relevant aspects of the phenomenon prior, say, to problem formulation and solution.
2. As a consequence of the previous point, in relation to certain criteria, certain conceptions of teaching are considered more effective than others. Teaching for more powerful understanding in learners is more effective than teaching for information transfer alone and teaching to develop students' capacity to discern the relevant aspects of phenomena is more effective again.
3. If our aim is to develop students' capabilities to see certain things in certain ways, and if this means being able to discern certain critical aspects and

focus on them simultaneously, and if the capability of discerning certain aspects and focusing on them simultaneously is a function of the experienced pattern of variation, then irrespective of the teaching method there must be such variation.

4. The characteristics and behaviour of teachers, departments, institutions and educational systems, in both the current and past experience of students, have significant effects on how students of any age learn.

5. Teaching is a process that requires professional decision making at every stage, with teachers constantly being confronted by unique circumstances. Teachers need to develop the capacity to identify relevant factors and act in ways that maximize student learning. This is just the sort of capacity which the variation theory argues is needed by all professionals.

6. Attempts to improve teaching and learning processes require teachers to have both a theoretical and practical understanding of how students learn and how they can be encouraged to learn in more effective ways.

7. Attempts to change the way teachers see their role require this theoretical and practical basis as well, since these developmental activities can be seen as teaching and learning activities of a particular kind.

In Chapter 2 we argued that understanding is not seen as something which a person has or does not have. Rather, there are a variety of understandings about a particular phenomenon and when a person moves from one level of under- standing to another more complete or more powerful one, learning is occurring. Furthermore, the origin of any person's current understanding is likely to include both formal instruction and everyday experience. It is inappropriate to try to separate the aspects of students' understanding that derive from the two forms of experience. As soon as a teacher utters one sentence in a lesson or a parent or peer offers a student a logical explanation of an observed phenome- non, the student's way of seeing the subject under discussion is likely to draw on both formal and informal experience. The task for teachers is to discover students' conceptions of the phenomenon under study and to devise ways of helping their students develop more powerful understandings. It is unhelpful to consider the teacher's task as one of encouraging students, say, to dismiss their 'common-sense beliefs' and embrace scientific beliefs. This becomes even more important as we focus our attention on learning to deal with unknown situations. The integration of scientific understandings and experience of the world is paramount.

Teaching methods

The fundamental question concerning teaching for an unknown future is about the kinds of learning experiences that will best enable students to develop an

if not most, have informally developed their capacity to teach, perhaps learning to do so 'on the job'. Lecturing has been a core part of the teaching programme for long enough for that function to be the central aspect of any academic's sense of competence as a teacher. Many put a lot of effort into the process and take great pride, quite deservedly, in being a 'good' lecturer. To suggest that there should be a greater mix, with the implications that other forms of learning experience should replace some of the lecture attendance for students, is both to ask academics to stop doing (or to reduce) something which they have been doing for a long time and to replace it with other activities which, if not entirely new, are at least less familiar. In addition, lecturing is a fairly orderly process with clear lines of responsibility. Alternative forms of learning experience require more *ad hoc* decision making by academic teachers and a more blurred line between the roles of teacher and student. There is a real sense of lost competence which can encourage a resistance by academic staff to such changes, therefore any attempt to bring this change about requires support for academic staff and this is discussed in Chapter 10.

Workplace experience for students

What has been described above is just one aspect of change in recent decades. At the same time, there has been a recognition that the workplace can play an important role in the student learning experience. Six- or twelve-month work placements in the middle of what have been called 'sandwich courses' have already been discussed in Chapter 5 and it has been suggested that not all of them live up to their potential. There is a need for learning to be taking place during the time in the workplace and that, like any other learning, should not be left to chance. Project work, mini research and development tasks for real clients, course advisory groups comprising professionals from relevant work-place areas, and the involvement of similar external professionals in the teaching programme and in assessment of student work are examples of ways the workplace and campus learning have been linked (eg engineering, architectural design). The way this can be organized within a university is discussed in Chapter 10.

Teaching and learning using technology

One of the alternatives to the economy-driven drift to lecturing as the primary medium of staff–student contact that is often presented is the use of technology in teaching and learning. Various terms such as open learning, flexible delivery or flexible learning environments are used to emphasize different aspects of approaches involving the use of computers in the learning process. Some of the ways in which they are used include, among others, simple communication applications, Web access to learning materials through a programme guide, provision of full sets of learning materials on the Web, a requirement that students use information technology to access relevant information themselves, simulation packages and full multimedia learning packages.

The communication applications include email, both between students and the academic teachers as well as among students within the group, Internet chat sessions, again with or without teacher involvement in the sessions, and video-conferencing. Simulation packages enable students to practise a wider range of skills in a shorter space of time, often by providing a larger set of data to be comprehensively analysed or by allowing the collection of data not otherwise available to students, often following student collection of core data in a laboratory session.

All of the applications described in the previous paragraphs are desirable additions to the student learning experience in the relevant context. Together, they allow students to experiment with their own ideas without penalty – such as trialing processes which, if undertaken physically rather than electronically, could result in disastrous outcomes such as explosions or structural collapse. They are the sorts of alternative experience we would argue for if students are to achieve the kinds of outcome that we have suggested should be among the central purposes of university education. They involve a number of key aspects of learning. The first is that they encourage students to commit themselves to a perspective and to test that perspective or have it tested. Indeed they encourage students in the first place to realize that there are multiple perspectives, or ways of seeing, that some of these ways of seeing are more useful than others in particular contexts and that this is a testable proposition. One potential of computer simulations, for instance, which is vital from the point of our conceptualization of learning, is the possibility of varying aspects of situations which are difficult to vary otherwise. As mentioned in Chapter 5, Ueno, Arimoto and Fujita (1990) made use of computer simulation for varying the frame of reference from which objects in motion are seen, and students' understanding of aspects of Newtonian mechanics was profoundly enhanced. Laurillard (1993) gives an excellent account of how information technology can be utilized with the point of departure in a theoretically grounded view of learning very close to the one advocated in this book.

Secondly, the interactions between staff and students, and among students, has the potential to reinforce this multiple perspective notion and also has the potential to encourage students to develop arguments for their ideas, to examine them in the light of contrary argument and to draw conclusions about more and less powerful perspectives. It is only through committed argument of this kind that students can practise the important skills of discerning the relevant aspects in any particular context and defining what the situation is or what problem it represents. The skill of problem solving, to be effective in the unknown future, must always accompany and in fact usually follow those other processes. All of them involve skills and understandings that need to be developed by all students.

One of the difficulties that the advent of information technology has produced is the tendency to want to use information technology for all aspects of the education process, the idea of the virtual campus. As a pilot for development, this is a useful focus. However, it is unlikely that the broad range of objectives of university education can be achieved by information technology alone. For many students in most areas of education, there is a need for 'hands-on' activity, personal interaction with academic teachers and face-to-face discussion with other students. The kinds of application of information technology described earlier often deal with objectives for which information technology is the most effective mode. When this is true, if all else is equal (such as resource issues), then the information technology approach is likely to be the most appropriate one to use. However, we should be wary of being seduced by the glamour of technology and the status of being fashionably up to date or providing slickly prepared materials. If the materials are not educationally effective, then their glossy appearance is to no avail. Being up to date means using the most appropriate means at our disposal to help students achieve the learning necessary for them to be able to deal with the unknown future. If that is best done in the particular context by information technology, then we should use the technology and if we are using the technology, we need to ask ourselves about how glossy it needs to be to be educationally effective. These days it is argued that students are so used to technology used commercially, which is up to the minute in quality, that educational uses of technology have to match that standard. That is a testable proposition that may be true.

Another aspect is the cost of high-standard materials of this kind. Choices need to be made and unfortunately the choice is often made to limit the educational purpose in order to maximize the technological use. Educational programmes, which have stated purposes at the high end of the kind we have espoused, sometimes have substantial amounts of technological content that are limited to page-turning, drill and tick-the-box assessment. These are unlikely to lead to the intended outcomes but the expense of their production often exhausts the financial and energy resources of the teaching team. So fitness for purpose, cost and implications for other learning activities are important elements in choice of technological solutions in an educational programme. In addition, irrespective of the level of technology in the programme, educational development is an essential feature if it is to be done well. Subject experts are not always skilled technologically and a balance of staff development and provision of support services are important elements we will discuss in Chapter 10.

Problem-based learning

If there is one approach to teaching and learning that appears to be consistent with our way of seeing learning it is the approach labelled 'problem-based learning', yet we have concerns about it which we wish to share. Problem-based learning is well known in a number of countries and the most usual examples cited are in the medical field. The medical curricula at McMaster University in Canada (Woods, 1994), Maastricht University in the Netherlands (van den Vleuten, 1998), the University of Newcastle in Australia (Newble and Clarke, 1986) and the University of Linköping in Sweden (Kjellgren *et al.*, 1993) are all well known in their own countries, as well as internationally, for their problem-based approach. Of course there are problem-based programmes in many other fields, universities and countries.

There is much to be said for many aspects of the problem-based approach. By enabling students to see what is to be learned from the point of view of an experienced problem, there is a potentially inherent relevance structure of the situation conducive to learning (see Chapter 2, pages 39–40). Firstly, the centre of attention is the student acting in a professional role. In problem-based medical courses, for instance, students in their first year begin immediately to work on real cases with real patients in the hospital setting. This contrasts with what is effectively only a token contact with patients until the fourth year in many traditional medical programmes, with the first three years being spent learning the underlying chemistry, physics, anatomy, biochemistry, physiology and so on, deemed to be a prerequisite for real medical activity. In such problem-based settings, students tend to work in teams and they gather the discipline-based knowledge as they need it in dealing with the medical cases at hand. The relationship between staff and students is different, with academic teachers no longer the font of knowledge but acting as coaches and guides on an interdisciplinary journey.

Now readers may well be puzzled why this approach concerns us. It fits with the idea that all learning is in context and the context chosen here is the professional circumstance in which the early graduates will be working. The kinds of issue being addressed are the actual medical cases that the graduate will be expected to be competent to handle. Secondly, with this approach, students take on the role of active seekers of knowledge and of problem-solvers so that this approach should encourage students to develop their skill in these areas. Thirdly, the early 'hands-on' experience that students have should deal with the demotivating boredom of learning for three years in a traditional course without being in a hospital and experiencing the professional role for any extended time period.

The problem-based approach can do all those things and not without a considerable effort on the part of academic teaching staff. The selection of cases, the establishment of both resources and processes through which student groups can gather such information as they need is a complex intellectual, pedagogical, organizational, and onerous task of management and resource administration. But why are we concerned about it?

Our concern stems from the same source as our concern about the virtual campus and the lecture-focused learning environment. We are concerned whenever a teaching method or a learning environment is constructed in ways that do not both stem from judgements about what is needed to support appropriate learning and also allow for dynamic change through professional judgement by teachers interacting with their students. The traditional lecture-focused approach fails on both requirements as do many of the virtual campus approaches. Even those virtual campus approaches, which are dynamic and open to change, still usually fail the first requirement because they assume that a technological solution addresses all educational needs. The problem-based learning approach does better on the first requirement in that in general it is geared towards student learning needs, but it too assumes that the context of a student group, dealing with real patients, provides the appropriate setting for all educational needs. It is likely to be more comprehensively successful in so doing than the other 'extreme' approaches, but not universally so. We have used the word 'extreme' to describe all three of these: the lecture-focused approach; the virtual campus approach; and the problem-based learning approach, be-cause each of them begins with a singular approach to teaching and learning. Yet, when you examine the required capabilities of graduates, some methods seem more appropriate to help students achieve some of them than others. We would argue that the most appropriate approach should be chosen to meet the particular educational need. This is likely to include a mix of the three ap-proaches described, not just one of them, plus aspects of other approaches as well. For instance, it is not self-evident that any of the approaches necessarily addresses the experienced variation requirement we outlined in Chapter 2.

Tresolini *et al.* (1994) investigated six medical schools considered 'excellent in helping students learn a more comprehensive or integrated approach to patient care'. One of the six had a problem-based curriculum. An aspect strongly focused in each one of these cases was long-term physician–patient relationships. Students and residents were able to develop long-term relationships with patients because their clinical experiences began early in the undergraduate medical curriculum and were in community settings close to where the patients live; also their work placements, from six months to two and a half years in length, were in community health centres. This enhanced a focus on the patient as a person rather than just the disease state within the person. Also Ludvigsen (1997) has pointed out how processes within the patient across time became objects of the interns' focal awareness through the inexperienced doctor's interaction with the patient in many situations which make up the illness progression. The point we make here is that an important aspect of the professional competence that should be developed may or may not be a feature of a particular curriculum arrangement or teaching method. As Tresolina and colleagues found a problem-based approach in itself, for instance, would neither imply nor exclude the development of capabilities of fundamental importance for a particular profession.

In a recent study of problem-based learning in teacher education, Gran (1997) found considerable variation between different programmes (for students becoming teachers in different subjects) in the extent to which organization of the studies seemed conducive to learning. However, even greater was the variation related to the students' competence and background. The label 'problem-based learning' is not a very precise description of what is taking place in diverse educational situations, nor are other labels denoting general teaching methods or educational arrangements.

We should mention that in response to our work Eizenberg (1997) is approaching the development of aspects of the University of Melbourne medical curriculum dealing with anatomy topics from a problem-driven rather than a problem-based perspective. He acknowledges our argument for preparing graduates to be able to both appropriately define and solve any problems they meet in their professional role and that the whole educational process needs to be driven by that objective. However, he now sees the problem-driven perspective as a better representation than the problem-based one because the former focuses on the educational goal while the latter focuses on a particular process. While problem-based learning approaches are likely to meet many of these educational needs, Eizenberg acknowledges that other approaches may also be necessary, although they, too, will be driven by the same intention.

Being good at teaching

The recent build-up of pressure on the university from outside for increased accountability brought with it an increased interest in the quality of undergraduate teaching. As the idea that human beings are marching into 'the knowledge society' has grown stronger and stronger, university staff are being held responsible for a critical function in developing what is now widely regarded as the most important productive factor: knowledge. How good is the staff of the university at teaching? How good are university teachers at developing the knowledge and skills of their students?

There has been an increased interest in staff development and appraisal. In some cases appraisal has even been linked with differentiation of salary. The appraisal of teaching has often been based on not entirely convincing ground, such as the blanket approach to student ratings, to be discussed in detail in Chapter 9. More recently, however, appraisal of teaching has been considered much more in terms of student-learning outcomes than before and academics in many universities have developed teaching portfolios.[1] The purpose of teaching portfolios is to provide documentary evidence of the activities of the particular academic in addressing curriculum, planning of learning environments and assessment and evaluation aspects of their teaching role, including the degree of success with each over time. The teaching portfolio would contain outcomes of evaluations, peer reviews of curriculum materials, research-based arguments for innovative approaches used in teaching and learning, evidence of their success including examples of assessment instruments with samples of student responses at various levels of achievement, statistics about student performance, especially in response to such changes, along with arguments linking all of these data to the purposes of the particular programme, to the intended learning outcomes.

By these processes, the issue of appraisal of teaching becomes more constructive in that it is aligned with the university's quest for improved quality of educational programmes. In a sense if each academic kept an adequate and up-to-date teaching portfolio, and if the activities of each academic as reflected in the portfolio showed improving learning experiences for students and improved learning outcomes, then educational quality assurance for the university would be a routine. Student ratings are an important contribution to such portfolios when students comment on aspects that only they can, but such ratings are only one part of the overall picture of the academic's role in teaching. Appraisal processes should reflect that complexity of role and activities and when it does it will contribute to the university goal of better learning.

Discussion about how good staff are at teaching tends to be phrased in general terms. Efficient teaching is mostly seen as a function of some general characteristics of the teacher: being good at structuring and presenting the message, appealing to the students' interests, lively presentation, skilled use of technical facilities etc. You might arrange courses for staff development, where staff from different disciplines and fields of knowledge come together and are being trained in the exercise of such general capabilities. In addition, staff in their daily work may be rated by their peers or students in relation to the extent to which they are seen as showing those general characteristics which define a good teacher.

In Chapter 8 we will make the point that the relationship between the teacher and the students is a particular form of human relationship – it is object-mediated. The teacher and the students have the object of learning as their shared interest, linking them together. In the above-mentioned and universally adopted way of thinking about what it takes to be good at teaching, the object of learning – or the object of teaching – is missing completely. However, being good at teaching means that you are good at teaching *something*. You cannot teach in general and the way in which you deal with the particular content you are dealing with is what matters. In Chapter 5 we described Richard Feynman teaching about Newton's explanation of planetary motions. It was a very particular way of dealing with that subject. For better or worse, it surely made a difference!

Throughout this book we have described different ways of experiencing and dealing with various situations and phenomena. Imagine that when different university teachers deal with the same topic, they deal with it in different ways, reflecting different ways of understanding that topic. Would it matter at all if this were the case? Would it not be relevant to the question of what it takes to be good at teaching?

Even if you accept the thesis that, if the same topic is taught in qualitatively different ways, it could be relevant to how well the topic is taught, you may think that because agreement between experts on comparatively straightforward matters is the hallmark of professional expertise, it is not reasonable to expect to find qualitative differences in how fairly elementary topics are dealt with by highly qualified academics in undergraduate teaching – at least not in mathematics, science, medicine and technology. As plausible as such a view may seem, we would venture to challenge it.

Teaching physics and history

On close examination we find radical differences in how the very same and well-defined topic is dealt with by highly qualified teachers, not only in undergraduate teaching but throughout the whole educational system. Kate Patrick's recent study (1998) is a good example.

Patrick is concerned with physics and history teachers in the final two years of the Australian school system. She has demonstrated that the ways in which these teachers experience the teaching of physics or history, and the way they experience their disciplines as teaching matter, affect the ways they communicate them and the ways students deal with them.

> In her study of history teachers, Patrick focused on how they speak of their subject and how they teach it – reflecting how they experience it, in our interpretation. She found three groups and one group emphasized the delivery of the material, presentation and technique; the subject matter and their students' relation to it was, to them, unproblematic. When they taught they saw themselves as delivering history – defined by them as the content of the course – to their students, and they spoke of teaching it through words such as 'give', 'show', 'look at', 'see' and 'do'. They wanted their students to get an imaginative grip of the topics they were studying, encouraging excursions to historic sites and seeing films of or about the periods studied. They saw their students' difficulties as arising from laziness or lack of interest in the subject, which they saw as being concrete, perceptible and knowable.
>
> Another group viewed the students' learning in two stages: acquiring and accumulating necessary information and interpreting it to achieve understanding. They expected their students to 'look at', 'recognize', 'come to see', 'understand', 'see the structure of', and 'see points of view in' the history they were studying. Teachers in this group see 'learning history' as problematic and their role as a teacher is to help the student come to see it. However, the way in which they might see it was taken to be rather unproblematic – the students were simply to share the teacher's understanding because teachers in this group did not see historical knowledge as problematic in itself. Rather, in contrast to this view, it was something to be acquired and discussed, recognized and contemplated.
>
> There was a third group of history teachers in Patrick's analysis who saw learning history as a process of developing interpretations from the outset. For them, historical

knowledge was far from unproblematic – the way in which material was approached by the students, the questions they were asking and discussing, and the way they were relating aspects to one another were constantly in these teachers' focus. Particular ways of seeing the ideas being treated might be proposed because they represented some normative way expected by examiners, but they were not treated as privileged. The teacher and students together shared the process of grappling with the content, in an attempt to get them to 'think', 'connect', 'change' and 'grow'. That the knowledge they were coming to terms with was contingent was implicit in the way they engaged with their students' learning.

The students' ways of dealing with the history they were studying corresponded to the different ways teachers conceptualized the history to be taught and their ways of understanding student learning. In Patrick's terms, students were seen to construct (we would say constitute) an object of study in a mould their teachers formed. Two years later students read a historical passage and discussed the content and the arguments it contained. There was a remarkable match between the ways in which the teachers and their students faced it when viewed as a historian's account of some piece of history – whether they saw it as unproblematic or as argumentation, with respect to culture, perspective, argument and the role of the historian.

Patrick also reports that physics takes on different meanings for different teachers; they establish different curricula at the classroom level and teach accordingly. She describes the teachers as constructing objects of study for their students, arguing that 'teachers actually present their students with different objects of study, which embody different conceptions of what is to be studied'. She discusses one group of physics teachers who understand physics as a way of understanding the natural world, and who presented students with objects of study reflecting that, asking their students to observe, formulate hypotheses, and give priority to the meaning of what they are faced with rather than the details such as names and formulae. Students were questioned in ways that led them towards the heart of the object of study, rather than to its periphery – emphasizing, for instance, the observed relationship between change and force in Newtonian mechanics. Teachers in this group did this by getting the students themselves to work things out.

Teachers who see physics as practice, as a set of theories which provide an explanatory system, formed another group in Patrick's study. They focus on enculturating the students into the scientific practices of physics and present an object of study comprised of the models and concepts of physics.

Patrick reports a third group of physics teachers as seeing physics as calculations. These teachers constructed an object of study composed of the not unexpected formulae and equations. As might be expected Patrick found that the students of teachers in these three different groups learned, in the first case, to understand phenomena; in the second case, to solve problems; and, in the third case, to recall and apply formulae. As their objects of study have been constructed, so have their objects of knowledge.

What this study shows is that teachers who are teaching exactly the same formal curriculum actually shape it according to their ways of understanding the subject as a whole. They might have just the same education and length of employment, know exactly the same facts, understand the central concepts in exactly the same way and so on, but they nevertheless form and present their subjects in ways that differ radically. In turn their students gain access to a radically different content of learning.

The teacher is shaping an object of study, and that is what the students direct their awareness towards in their learning. The object of study may vary from teacher to teacher, within the constraints of a single, specified and adhered-to curriculum, and that leads to a variation in what students have the opportunity to learn.

Teaching 'the mole'

Tullberg (1998) has carried out recently an in-depth study of the differing ways in which secondary-school teachers understand and handle a particular topic in chemistry.

The topic in question was the 'mole', that in 1971 was agreed to be considered as a unit of amount of substance, one of the seven physical base quantities in the International System of Units (SI) (other quantities are, for instance, mass with its unit, the kilogram, and length with its unit, the metre)[2]. In accordance with Strömdahl's (1996) results originating from the work that Lybeck, Strömdahl and Tullberg carried out together more than a decade ago (1985), Tullberg found that teachers understood the mole in one of four qualitatively different ways:

F_0 One mole is a defined portion of substance (ie as something highly concrete – a certain amount of matter of some kind).

F_1 One mole is an elementary entity (individual) mass (eg 18 g for water, corresponding to the molecular mass of H_2O (= $2 \times 1 + 16 = 18$)).

F_2 One mole is equivalent to the number (Avogadro's number, ie 6.02214×10^{23}) of elementary particles making up an elementary entity mass (eg 18 g for water).

F_3 The mole is a unit of the physical quantity 'amount of substance'.

So, while the first two ways of understanding the mole represent a macroscopic, continuous perspective, a chunk of matter or a certain mass of a substance, the third way of understanding it represents a microscopic perspective, simply a certain number of elementary entities of which the particular substance consists. The last case represents the scientifically authoritative understanding of the mole, also from a continuous perspective, as a *unit* of amount of substance, the corresponding portion of substance having a certain mass, a certain volume and consisting of a certain number of elementary particles.

Tullberg found that only three of 29 secondary teachers showed a consistent understanding of the mole in accordance with the scientifically argued conception (F_3 above, see Table 6.1).

Table 6.1: *Ways of understanding the 'mole' among 29 secondary school teachers in Chemistry (adapted from Tullberg, 1998)*

Conception	No of cases
F_0	1
F_1	3
$F_1, (F_2)$	2
$F_1, (F_2)$	5
F_2	14
$F_2, (F_3)$	1
F_3	3
All cases	29

Tullberg investigated the teachers' ways of making sense of the mole by interviewing them and having them solve a problem reflecting their understanding of the mole. However, she also studied what they did in the classroom when teaching about it and she found that the teachers taught very much in accordance with the understanding they had expressed when answering the interview questions and solving the problem. In addition, the only student in the study expressing the scientifically authoritative understanding was found in a class taught by a teacher expressing that understanding in the teaching.

Teaching accounting

The first in-depth study of variation in teachers' understanding and their ways of 'angling' the same topic in higher education that we are aware of is being carried out by Airi Rovio-Johansson of Göteborg University. Deliberately she chose topics which can be considered very well defined, three in accounting and three in mathematical statistics. She followed three lecturers teaching in both subjects about the three topics. She video-recorded six two-hour lectures and after each lecture she interviewed five students about the topic dealt with. The students were also asked to attempt to solve a problem related to the actual topic.

After analysing the data for accounting she could detect a pattern running through the three teachers' way of teaching. One of them addressed the topics at a concrete, technical level, aiming at the development of the students' capability to solve certain types of problem, defined in advance. The second teacher tried throughout the lecture to situate each topic into a theoretical framework, aiming at a deep as possible understanding of the concepts and principles used. The third teacher was moving between general formulations and specific instances of the same problems, aiming at developing students' capabilities for making and grounding rational economic decisions.

These differences can be illustrated in relation to the first topic investigated, the limiting factor in production. This refers to the factor in the production process which limits the total capacity (given that there are relatively greater resources available as far as the other factors are concerned). The three teachers planned the lecture together. After an introduction a problem was presented and worked through by the teachers. Discussion, mainly carried through by the teacher, followed and the lecture was concluded. In the problem the delimiting factor, which in this case was machine hours available, was identified. Then a decision had to be made about how to decrease the demands on machine hours by buying something ready-made instead of self-producing it. The choice had to be based on optimal contribution to profit.

There were clear-cut differences found among the three teachers, in spite of the fact that the content of the lecture was extremely well defined; they had planned together and they worked through the very same problem. Furthermore, the content of the lecture could be considered fairly elementary and straightforward. Still, the differences were striking. The first teacher talked about the problem while going about solving it on the blackboard. The teacher moved between the actual production process referred to in the problem and the method for dealing with the problem. The second teacher opened up several dimensions of variation in the introduction and talked about different cost concepts, not only the ones immediately relevant to the actual problem, and about different ways of deciding what costs to allocate to different component parts in the production process. This teacher also pointed out the relativity of the very system for accounting, explaining that different systems will give you different kinds of information; therefore 'opening up' a dimension of variation corresponding to the way in which the system for calculating things was set up. It was implied that this can be done in different ways.

The third teacher gave different examples from different companies (this is certainly a dimension of variation) and opened up a dimension of variation corresponding to the way in which costs are determined. Like the second teacher, he also went through the different cost concepts, not only those which applied to costing in the actual case. Furthermore, he made the point that there are other ways for setting prices in addition to calculus, and that finding the appropriate way may vary from case to case.

So, there were differences in what was taken for granted and what was opened up as a dimension of variation. These differences were reflected in the interviews with the students. While four of the five students who had listened to the first teacher were focused on the specific example given, when discussing the limiting factor (they all talked about 'machine hours'), the other students who had listened to the other two teachers dealt with the question in more general terms. Also, there were distinct differences found with regard to the way in which the students went about solving the problem about the delimiting factor during the interview. Although in order to solve the problem everyone had to discern the effect of the limiting factor on the relationship between profitability and profit, students who had been listening to different lecturers approached the problem differently. Students of the first teacher saw the problem from the point of view of the effect of the limiting factor on the relationship between the process of production and the contribution to profit; students of the second teacher, from the point of view of the effect of the limiting factor on the relationship between costs or expenses (such as variable and incremental expenses) and on contribution to profit; and students of the third teacher, from the point of view of the effect of the limiting factor on the relationship between costs and pricing and on contribution to profit (Rovio-Johansson, 1998).

Principles of learning rather than a theory of instruction

Returning to the previous line of argument we can say that each of the general teaching methods commented on earlier in this chapter has an implicit theory that suggests that the particular way of teaching will produce better learning. While we have suggested that the traditional lecture approach has been reshaped largely by social and economic rather than pedagogical factors, there is an assumption that students will be helped to learn if an expert sets out in detail the content to be learned. Presumably the framework provided in the lecture is expected to be up to date, relevant and linked directly to curriculum goals. There is some form of belief that coverage of the syllabus by the lecturer will result in student learning. The use of technology for teaching and learning is a general method which has also been shaped by social and economic factors. There is also an assumption that if students are able to access information in a flexible way, in their chosen time and place, then learning will be enhanced. It is also assumed that students will benefit by being able to progress at their own pace. The problem-based approach is a teaching method whose design has drawn most on pedagogical principles. Quite explicitly, its proponents argue for the integration of underlying theory with practical experience. The assumption is made that if students deal with theory in relation to a particular professional problem situation, then their learning will be more meaningful, longer-lasting and more powerful.

The problem with beginning with the teaching method, the theory of instruction, and then arranging learning within that framework is that it leads to the problem we have outlined, the almost exclusive adoption of one particular teaching method, whether or not it is appropriate in the particular circumstances. Better, we would argue, to begin with student learning, to analyse the principles of learning and then to draw conclusions about what kind of learning environment and what kinds of learning experience will assist students to learn in the way intended. Only then should we design what we call teaching methods so as to provide those environments and experiences. In addition, it is unlikely that by using that approach we will come up with just one particular teaching method. We are likely to conclude that a flexible mixture of learning opportunities is essential. We will explore some of those learning principles in the next section where we illustrate our argument with some examples from university curricula and teaching.

In the section 'Curriculum and variation' in the previous chapter we gave a lengthy example of this kind. As we pointed out, once we take our point of departure in the aims of learning, ie in what capabilities the students should develop, questions of curriculum and questions of teaching coincide. The example in the previous chapter (on learning about force and acceleration) could just as well have been placed in the present chapter – as it originally was – and the following two examples in this chapter could just as well have been placed in the previous chapter – as they originally were. This is because all three examples are about curriculum, and they are about teaching as well. How learning is brought about follows from what learning should be brought about.

Learning through drama

Objectives and curriculum structure

This example is from Colleen Johnson, a teacher educator at Brunel University (Johnson, 1997). It is concerned with the performing arts within the school curriculum and provides a compelling example of what we are arguing for.

The Arts Council of Great Britain in its 1992 document 'Guidance on Drama Education' indicates that the three activities which constitute the subject of drama in education are 'making, performing and responding'. Making drama is the ability to generate and shape dramatic forms in order to express ideas. Performing drama is the ability to engage and communicate with an audience in a dramatic production. Responding to drama is the ability to express understanding, discernment and appreciation of drama in all of its forms.

Johnson's students had read *The Diary of Anne Frank* and used drama to explore relevant issues that emerged from their readings. They were involved in a process of selecting, editing and refining because the performance element was not simply in the classroom, but would ultimately be in the form of a dramatic presentation to others in the school, parents and other visitors. Discussion during the work was about meaning and how to convey the meaning to an audience not involved in the day-to-day process of the drama.

According to Johnson, the intended learning outcomes are that students will:

- learn in and through drama
- gain a perspective about a historical issue
- identify with characters and actions through role playing
- take moral decisions in character
- be able to examine, out of character, why a decision was made and its consequences
- develop an understanding of cause and effect
- be able to use ritual, mime, silence, simple props etc to convey meaning to an audience.

This is quite a complex set of objectives which, for the purposes of this example, will be narrowed. There are two nested sets, the first comprising an understanding of historical events, the issue of moral decision making and the relation between cause and effect. These are all enveloped within another set of objectives concerned with preparation for and use of dramatic forms to communicate these ideas. For the purposes of this exercise, the dramatic form will be set aside and our attention will be focused on the more fundamental human understandings. That is not to say that the communication issues are unimportant, but we are not focusing on them here.

Fundamentally, this inner set can be summarized as being about understanding human behaviour in the context of occupation of one country by the people of another and the ill-treatment of one section of the community. It happens that Johnson focuses on Anne Frank and therefore it is about German occupation of The Netherlands and persecution of Jewish citizens during the Second World War. It could have been about Pol Pot in Cambodia, or it could have been about many other conflicts and incidents we have witnessed over the decades including Bosnia, My Lai or Ruanda, in each of which certain groups of non-combatants were systematically killed. Indeed, Johnson does use reference to some of those other conflicts to illuminate some of the issues that emerge from Anne Frank's account.

From the curriculum perspective, a question we ask is 'What are the key aspects of understanding human behaviour in such circumstances?' Our interpretation of Johnson's work is that the key aspects include an understanding of the nature of historical evidence, the influence of feelings of self-preservation on behaviour, the influence of concern for the welfare of others, the impact of an established belief system on moral decision making, and the nature of fear and power, both individual and group.

A second question is 'What range of contexts will differentiate among those aspects with some being the figure and others the ground in one context, and with variation in figure–ground relations across other contexts?' The contexts identified by Johnson include:

(a) a reading of *The Diary of Anne Frank* as some kind of historical evidence. Questions that are raised include:

- What does the book reveal about the feelings of people whose lives are threatened in this way?
- Do the descriptions, in whole or in part, match those described in other publications about occupation of The Netherlands during the Second World War?
- Do the descriptions match other accounts of German occupation of other countries in the same period?
- Are there any similarities in the nature of the experiences described with contemporary events like the conflict in Bosnia?

(b) a role-play of the situation of a German soldier ordered to carry out the execution of non-combatant Jewish citizens. Questions raised include:

- Would such a soldier be likely to see a moral difference between killing the enemy in battle and executing non-combatants?
- If not, how might this have happened?
- If the soldier believes the executions are morally wrong, but goes ahead because the fact that he received orders to do so relieves him of guilt, is he justified?
- How could a concern for self-preservation overcome any moral concerns or concerns for the welfare of other human beings?
- What is the nature of fear and its impact on the behaviour of all those involved?

(c) a role-play of a discussion of employees with Otto Frank's secretary in which they are told that the Franks are considering trying to leave The Netherlands. Questions raised here include:

- Would they see themselves as already in danger because they are working for a Jew?
- If they were concerned about how were they going to be affected if the business closed, how might they react and why?
- If they were concerned to help the Franks escape, what feelings would they need to overcome and what must be driving their actions?

In context (a), the key aspect – understanding the nature of historical evidence – is in the foreground with the other aspects providing the background. In context (b), this issue of historical record is present but in the background as other aspects, such as beliefs and morals, fear and self-preservation, become figural. In context (c), fear and self-preservation come to the fore as key aspects, along with concern for the welfare of others. The key aspect – the nature of power – has the potential to be figural in all of the contexts but whether it does or not has been found by Johnson to be dependent on the nature of the teaching and learning experiences.

Hopefully, this kind of curriculum design will enable students to understand how historical events can be considered from a range of perspectives and that resolution of inconsistencies that arise from simultaneous consideration of more than one perspective can be difficult, but has relevance to analysis and understanding of contemporary events with which they are familiar.

Learning experiences

The objectives described above were pursued in a variety of ways:

1. Prior reading: students had read *The Diary of Anne Frank*. There was classroom discussion of the details.
2. Teacher and students engage in role-improvization – the teacher as Otto Frank's secretary, telling employees that the Franks are considering trying to leave The Netherlands, and the students as Otto Frank's employees. The questions this experience raises were detailed above.
3. Students come out of the role-improvization and engage in discussion concerning the matter of differences in perspective. Did it make a difference if particular employees were young or older, whether they had worked for the Franks for a long time or not, whether they liked their job or not, whether they were also Jewish but had escaped detection so far or whether they actually knew anything about what happened to Jews once they were taken away by soldiers?
4. Further role-play by the students alone about a proposition by one of the senior managers that the employees should help keep the Frank family hidden until the end of the war.
5. Conscience alley: students form two teams, the first of which has to present arguments for a course of action to help the Franks and the other, arguments against helping. They role-play variously as Franks' employees, soldiers or politicians.
6. In groups of four, the students role-play a family or other group of people living together. Two members of each group role-play as Frank's employees. The other two members of the group role-play people who had been informed at work (elsewhere) that day that if they report any Jews evading capture, and the Jews are eventually caught, there will be a financial reward. All four are asked to improvise a discussion at home that night.
7. Discussion of experiences of (1) to (6).

Johnson (1997) reports that the final discussion becomes focused on the complexity of issues on which peoples' decision making is based. Students became more aware through the role-playing of the difficult issues facing everyone in the kind of context they had been dealing with. When discussions shift to the issue of power, some speak about enjoying the power of being a soldier and intimidating citizens by taking their identity cards and throwing them on the ground, then watching them pick them up. There were discussions about the way that individuals in contemporary society, in families at home, in educational institutions and at work, use power over others. The discussion sometimes moved to the significance of the context of war in changing individuals' status and the role that friendship, family ties, religious faith, national history and identity, feelings of racism, economic conditions and fear play in decisions to exercise or succumb to power of one kind or another.

What are the important features of these learning experiences? Clearly a key feature is for students to place themselves in various role situations so that they can experience the same issues from a number of perspectives. The idea of experience is fundamental but we have argued that the mere variation in experience is not sufficient. The variation itself has to be experienced and therefore the discussion sessions during which the various individual experiences are compared and analysed are also significant. Of course, all of this would be less effective if the students participating had not read the text but it should be said that students do not come to such a situation as *tabula rasa*. They come already with some understanding of the issues that are being addressed. It would be hoped that these experiences would help them develop more complex and powerful understandings – indeed that is the intention. A set of experiences of this kind would also be unlikely to be effective if the role-playing were limited to a narrow choice. The development of an understanding of perspective presumes dealing with a range of different perspectives, therefore some of the scenarios students are asked to participate in are contrived by teaching staff to ensure an appropriate range of experiences.

Firstly, it should be noted that the emphasis here has been on the kinds of experience students have in relation to the intended learning outcomes. Secondly, that the objectives are about development of more complex and more powerful understandings of both specific (related to the example) and general concepts (such as the issue of perspective). The focus is not on details such as dates, places and names, although being inaccurate about those would be an impediment to the other activities. They are important but are not figural in this kind of situation.

Learning about acoustic design

Objectives and curriculum structure
This example is from Robyn Lines at the Royal Melbourne Institute of Technology (Lines, 1997). In 1993, members of the course team for the

Bachelor of Arts in Interior Design were concerned with the absence in the curriculum of any aspect dealing with acoustic design, despite its importance in the professional activities of interior designers. There had been some aspects of acoustics dealt with in the course some years before but it had been dropped out. Acoustics had been taught previously as a technology-based subject and in a way that many designers had found was irrelevant to their design functions. Most reported that while they could remember studying the acoustics subject they could recall little about it, and those who did remember showed many misconceptions about its content.

The starting point for Lines' course team was to research how professional designers integrate acoustics knowledge into their design process. They found six categories of acoustic design knowledge and three overall approaches (or shapes) to working in acoustic design. The three shapes were linear sequential (technical acoustics and then design), parallel interactive (still two processes but at the same time) and simultaneous (ie an integration – acoustic design rather than acoustics and design). They also found that project-based experience was a prerequisite for professional designers to display higher level understanding of acoustic design.

The team designed three subjects and a design studio around these findings. The purposes for these subjects were for students to become aware of aural input (to learn to listen), to develop the skills to operate within spaces (create and control sound) and to think of sound in a design perspective (relating to the context and the intended use).

The first of these relates to the fact that all of us are exposed to the physical stimuli around us that cause vibrations of our eardrums, which are in turn interpreted by the brain, through our nervous system, as sound. Sometimes we do not 'hear' sounds despite the physical effect and this is often idiosyncratic. Some workers in an open-plan office do not hear the telephone conversations of a colleague at the next desk, some people sitting reading in a lounge chair do not hear their partner's or their children's conversation even when it is directed at them. So it is not just a matter of the physical effect. At a more technical level, some people can hear a particular key on a piano during a recital giving an unusual sound while others merely hear the tune being played. This requires some technical understanding, the skill to differentiate sounds and the capability to integrate the two. Carrying forward all the way to the acoustic design level, there is a need to be able to listen in this way but also to hear various kinds of sound across a range of variables and to relate those to the complex physical environment in which they are being heard.

The second purpose is more straightforward and is of a more technical nature although the way it is carried out relies heavily on the capabilities related to the first purpose. We will say no more about this purpose.

The third purpose is of fundamental importance. In a way, the focus of the first two purposes is on the way in which sound is heard and managed. This third purpose is important even when the primary design criterion is not explicitly sound-related; this probably applies to the majority of design contexts. Designing a school classroom, theatre, library and recreation spaces all have a particular purpose, and the overall design needs to take these into account. One of the aspects that needs to be accounted for in all cases is the acoustics but from a different perspective in each case.

The key aspects here appear to be as follows:

- developing technical skills
- hearing sound
- relating what is heard to spatial characteristics
- appreciating the multiple perspectives in the aural–spatial relationships;
- relating the acoustic characteristics to the functions of the space
- resolving conflicting acoustic–functional needs
- integrating the acoustic design requirements with other design imperatives accommodating other contextual and cultural needs of users.

The kinds of experience that students in this programme actually have are:

- experiential discussion sessions in which, say, sounds with varying characteristics are listened to and students indicate what they think those characteristics are and how the sounds they experienced vary on those characteristics. Only then do the teachers introduce the terminology used to refer to loudness of sound (decibels) and other characteristics and these are then related to the students' earlier experiences and interpretations. The relevant aspects here appear to be the first two above
- preparation of a sound space for a festival or other design context with particular characteristics. The additional relevant aspects here appear to be the third and fourth key aspects above
- an evaluation project of the acoustic design of a site. Pre-school centres, a café, bookshops and nightclubs have been used. The additional relevant aspects here appear to be the fifth and eighth key aspects listed.

We will not analyse this further because, at this level of analysis, that is, of a whole programme, it is too general, but the analysis we have done illustrates that different experiences can make different aspects (of acoustic design in this case) more relevant. In particular, the involvement of students in acoustic design evaluation and a design project of classrooms in Arnhem Land being used by the local aboriginal community, in addition to the similar experience in the pre-school centre in a Victorian country town, would have made students aware of the importance of the eighth relevant aspect if they had not been aware before. This variation in experience would have caused every student to develop their understanding of this aspect at least in some way.

The focus here has been on detailing the purposes of the acoustic design subjects and how they relate to the work graduates will undertake as professionals. In Chapter 9 (pages 242–3) we will discuss how the development of these acoustic design subjects was dealt with in the context of educational quality assurance processes.

Learning experiences

To talk about the learning experiences in this case, we need to focus on one area, although similar approaches are used in all of the subjects. In the 'Sound of Space' subject, several contexts are created in key ways. First of all the teaching room is used as a laboratory for understanding acoustic phenomena in rooms. Students use the same experience in the same space and look at multiple ways of understanding and recording that phenomenon. For example, a sound source (usually a pure tone) is set up and students are asked to describe it. As this is early in the students' experience, they usually use quite personal and affective language to describe the sound but there are some words which are also used in technical descriptions of sound. They then attempt to disentangle the descriptions into language that describes their response to the sound and language, which more precisely denotes the characteristics of the sound.

When, later, they are dealing with the concept of loudness and factors which affect the perception of loudness, another sound source is set up and students are asked to describe their experience of the sound at various points in the room. Using sound-level meters they then measure the sound at 2, 4 and 6 metres from the source. They record the measurements and compare them with theoretical free-field results using the inverse square law. They then look at the characteristics of the room and consider how the surfaces are acting to reflect sound and contribute to the higher than free-field values in the more distant measurements. They use a wave tank to do this with a small Lego model of the room so they can see what the sound is doing. They then use absorbent panels, specially constructed as a teaching resource, on the wall surfaces considered to be points of first reflection (they can only do this to a certain extent) and remeasure at the original points. Obviously, these results are different from before and the experiment leads to discussion of the concepts of sound intensity and distance and absorption in interior spaces.

As the programme progresses students are asked to calculate and measure the reverberation time in the room. For design purposes, this is one of the key concepts. They are first asked to estimate the reverberation time by clapping, listening and counting. They then, as a group, measure the space, allocate absorption coefficients to the constructions and calculate the reverberation time using Sabine's equation. They also measure the reverberation time using a starter pistol. They then discuss the numbers in relation to the intentions of the space aesthetically and functionally and their lived experience of its success or failure (mostly failure, Lines' reports, and they discuss this, too, in terms of the dominant visualism in Western discourse generally and design discourse in particular).

In the next exercise, the group suppresses consideration of the aesthetic or intentional aspects of design and students are asked to calculate the reverberation time in the toilets on the same level of the building. Here the students have to measure and assess the construction and assign the absorption coefficients to complete the calculation. Students often make mistakes which show a misunderstanding of the performance of sound and this exercise allows teachers to check this and draw out any problems. Often students assign absorption coefficients on the basis of the surface material alone. For example they treat mirrors which are directly fixed to concrete walls as the same as window glass, not realizing that the low-frequency sound which passes through window glass into the external environment will be reflected back into the space by the concrete behind the mirror. This exercise is used to focus on the technicalities and to ensure the students have a full grasp of these.

The next exercise asks students to use this understanding in a 'real' space, that is one outside the university where they are making a full acoustic design analysis of the space. They choose spaces which are significant in terms of Melbourne's design culture but not necessarily architecturally designed ones. Here they are required to work out the reverberation time, not as an end in itself but as information to inform their critique of the space. This critique has to include an understanding and assessment of the space in terms of its social and commercial function and its design aesthetics. These then have to be related to the established reverberation time and ambient sound levels and an assessment made of the overall quality of the acoustic design and its relationship to the visual and functional working out of the space.

When the students move on to their own design projects they have a kind of 'lived' familiarity with what reverberation times mean as everything is related to spaces they are directly experiencing. They have also begun, at least, to establish an understanding of factors which must influence their formation of acoustic design intentions for their own work.

In other subjects the same kinds of approach to learning are used. When students begin to use a computer modelling program, they model spaces which are accessible and can be listened to and recorded etc. They are always looking for multiple ways of describing an experience and multiple experiences as ways of deepening understanding of an idea. The students, typically, are fearful of equations and numbers and any attempt to teach them in a conventional physics way is doomed to fail. They only use equations by relating them to an experience of what they codify. This may seem limiting but as graduates they will not need to use many equations; they will need to understand the experience of sound in space in a way that can be used when designing. Lines' research (1997) shows that drawing on personal and archetypical sound experiences and attempting to visualize the behaviour of sound are three of the major ways designers do this.

Empowering the learners

We have tried to bring about an axial turn in this chapter. In teaching there is always an object of learning (and of teaching as well, of course) dealt with somehow under a particular arrangement for doing so. The particular arrangements are usually referred to as a teaching method. Discussion about teaching is, as a rule, phrased in terms of teaching methods. We wanted to suggest that we should rather focus on the way in which the object of learning is dealt with. We believe that we should take our point of departure in the kind of capabilities we are trying to contribute to bringing about in the learners. The object of learning should be dealt with in accordance with that. In addition, and the teaching method adopted should allow for that particular way of dealing with the object of learning.

To be more precise, we have argued that we want to develop students' capabilities for engaging in effective action in situations in the future. Furthermore, effective action springs from effective ways of seeing. We should therefore aim at developing students' capabilities of seeing certain situations in certain ways . Being capable of seeing something in a certain way amounts to being capable of discerning certain critical aspects and focusing on them simultaneously. The capability to discern and focus simultaneously originates from the variation experienced. In order to achieve such aims a certain pattern of dimensions of variation corresponding to the critical aspects of the set of situations in question will be present in the learning situation (which is in this case a teaching situation as seen from the point of view of the teacher). This is what matters in our view and this is what must be realized, whatever teaching method we make use of.

Endnotes

1. Teaching portfolios in many respects resemble the quality logs we will discuss in Chapter 9 when we describe the RMIT educational quality-assurance process; they are often developed by individual academics as a subset of the educational programme's quality log (see page 240).

2. According to Fensham (1997) the relevance of the mole is not so much to be seen as a unit of just a quantity in itself but as a unit of a quantity in chemical reactions in that there is always a certain amount of a certain substance that reacts with a certain amount of another substance.

Chapter 7

Finding out what has been learned

This chapter is about the assessment of learning in universities, a topic which makes us think immediately of the examination system, the means by which the university makes judgements about whether students have met the requirements for passing subjects or gaining honours or distinctions. However, while this is a key aspect, assessment of learning in a university includes more than this. Boyle *et al.* (1995) argues that the three broad purposes of assessment can be expressed as providing information to enable judgements to be made in relation to the particular student, focusing and enhancing student learning while learning is taking place, and providing information to enable judgements and plans for improvement of educational programmes *per se*. We have suggested that most people think of the first of these purposes when they talk about what assessment is about. The other two purposes, as an aid to students during their learning and as a means for staff to make improvements to the educational programme as a whole are also important, and they are not unrelated to the first. This chapter is structured around the first purpose, but we will also discuss how appropriate assessment for that judgemental purpose can assist individual student learning and lead to quality improvement in the whole educational programme.

We believe that there is another potential use of assessment, not unrelated to the three purposes above. It can be rarely found but still it is probably the pedagogically most powerful way of using assessment.

We made the point above and in most of the previous chapters that what students learn when they learn something is in fact very hard to know. One of the most useful things we can do is to find out what they learn and assessment – if carried out in certain ways – can enable us to do so. We have then to focus on finding out the ways in which students understand and handle the object of learning and we have to find out about qualitative aspects of their learning (ie what qualities it has), instead of only passing judgements about what they got right and what they got wrong. The kind of assessment we will illustrate in this chapter is that which lends itself to be used for finding out what has been learned.

The uses of assessment

Defining what should be learned

Most readers who felt comfortable with our views on teaching and learning in Chapter 6 and in earlier chapters of this book would be likely to agree with another assertion we make now, namely that assessment should be such that students are motivated to undertake the kind of learning we espouse, ie, assessment should reflect what is to be learned.

We are aware of the important part assessment plays in the way students go about their learning and this is reinforced by findings reported by such researchers as Ramsden (1984). In earlier chapters we discussed the research findings which show that the nature of the assessment system experienced by students has a marked effect on how students approach their learning. The research shows that if the assessment instruments can be negotiated successfully simply by rote learning of information, just before the examination period for instance, then students are demotivated from learning with higher-level objectives in mind throughout the programme. What can we conclude from that research? It seems obvious that any assessment system developed to test student performance should reflect the full range of purposes for which the learning programme was developed. If students have achieved outcomes in line with the intentions of the programme, such as those elaborated in Chapters 5 and 6, then they should have no difficulty in dealing with such assessment. If students have not achieved those learning outcomes, then their assessment performance surely should reflect that. It does not seem reasonable to defend an assessment system that does not discriminate in that way.

Probably it is not difficult to agree with what we have said in the previous paragraph. Of course we should assess across the full range of intentions for the educational programme, but the more contentious issue concerns what we actually mean by that last phrase. Take the force and acceleration example we described in Chapter 5. One reading of 'full range', which would be wrong in our view, is for students to be assessed merely on their understanding of and their capacity to apply the ideas of force and acceleration in each of the contexts described: vehicle on a straight, level road, vehicle on a curved ramp etc. From the perspective outlined in Chapter 5, the full range in this example includes being able to articulate why a different approach is taken in different contexts, knowing how and being able to decide which aspects of the concepts are relevant to the particular context, as well as being able to handle all the relevant aspects simultaneously in formulating and solving a problem in a previously unseen context. So this is the core of the assessment issue for us. It represents what we would call an integrative approach to assessment rather than the additive approach which is so common. We will return to this idea throughout the chapter.

Norm-referenced versus criterion-referenced assessment

Another way of looking at why some assessment practices are poor is to reflect on the differences between what is called norm-referenced and criterion-referenced assessment. The kind of assessment practices we argued for earlier, assessment which discriminates between those who can show evidence of having achieved the intended learning in the subject or programme and those who cannot, would fit into the category of criterion-referenced assessment. The judgements made in such an assessment process use criteria associated with the intended learning outcomes. Norm-referenced assessment, on the other hand, aims to discriminate between students and is designed so that student performance in the assessment is distributed across a range, so that those who do better on the assessment task receive higher grades than those who do less well.

While criterion-referenced assessment also can discriminate between students who have attained the intended learning outcomes and those who have not or who have achieved them less well or less comprehensively, it is not designed with distribution of performance among the students as an intention. Criterion-referenced assessment allows for the outcome where all students have achieved all of the intended learning outcomes perfectly, in which case there is no distinction to be made between them. In contrast, norm-referenced assessment assumes that there will be a distribution of performance among students and, indeed, if all students performed equally well, it would be assumed that the assessment instrument was flawed. The examination, for instance, would be changed for the next occasion to ensure a distribution of performance. In norm-referenced assessment, items are selected as Taylor (1994) puts it 'first and foremost for their discriminating power'.

By such practices the things actually assessed by the examination, say, may be chosen not because they were the primary objectives of the subject but rather because they discriminate between students. In this way, assessment instruments can drift away from the objectives so that they assess things other than the actual purposes for which the subject was designed. That they still provide, say, a normal distribution of student performance, is often used as an argument in their favour. However the validity of such assessment is in doubt. One could just as easily get a distribution among students on the basis of height or weight but that would not be a valid measure of learning in the subject. Only if what is assessed is what was supposed to be learned can an assessment instrument be considered valid. That is why criterion-referenced assessment is to be preferred.

Ramsden's (1984) research, referred to in Chapter 3, shows something that most academics suspect, that students are very aware of the assessment system. They learn with that assessment system in mind and often use past examination papers, for instance, to guide their learning. If the assessment instruments do not actually assess the learning goals, it is no surprise that students learn for the assessment rather than for the goals. If the assessment instruments and the subject or programme objectives (ie the learning goals) are in harmony, the evidence is that students will learn for the goals. If we examine our own behaviour in almost any circumstance, we can see this as a very reasonable response by students. So all universities have to do is to make sure that they assess what students are intended to learn. That is the assertion we began with in the previous section and we believe we have shown why it is a reasonable proposition.

We will now examine a form of assessment which demonstrates what was said in the previous paragraph. The wholesale use of multiple-choice questions (MCQs) in examinations is one approach to assessment that can markedly affect student learning. Even when the deficiencies are acknowledged, the efficiency of the exclusive use of MCQs is seductive. This is demonstrated by, for instance, the examination systems in the USA for licensing medical practitioners. Case and Bowmer (1994) report on the recent developments in testing of graduates for entry into the medical profession. They describe the new licensing examinations in the USA which include a three-step examination, each step of which must be passed. The first two steps consist of 700 multiple-choice questions (MCQs) each and the third step is also comprised totally of MCQs (on such topics as managing patients, including health maintenance, clinical interventions, clinical therapeutics, and legal/ethical and health-care systems). While it is acknowledged that this sort of assessment is less valid than other forms for clinical assessment, the ease of using MCQs takes precedence. Case and Bowmer comment: '[other more valid assessment methods] appear to provide significant advantages over MCQ tests for assessment of clinical competence. However, there are psychometric and practical problems that require better solutions before these methods can be used for licensure in the USA'.

In an allied field, in a book about competency assessment for nursing assistants (Sorrentino and Owoc, 1996), students are given advice about taking MCQ exams. They are told that each question will have four answer choices, only one answer will be correct and, although questions may appear to have more than one possible answer, 'there is only *one best answer* [*sic*]' . Among the guidelines, students are urged not to read into a question, take it as it is asked, not to add their own thoughts or ideas and not to consider 'what if?'. They are also advised not to change any answers (unless they become absolutely sure any one is incorrect) because their first reaction is probably the best. All of this advice may in fact help students to maximize their scores in MCQs. Given such an assessment system, Sorrentino and Owoc may be giving students the best advice. The problem we have with such a system is the negative effects it must have on student learning.

Separation of assessment and teaching

Perhaps every academic has anecdotal evidence, if not direct experience, of the examination question which invites students to tell 'all they know' about concept A or issue B or topic C. Academics who write such questions commonly defend them on the grounds (this is from an actual case known to the authors) that all the students know that 'in the lecture on topic C, I also dealt with issues D, E and F and concepts G, H and I. Their answers should have dealt with all those issues'. Of course the form of the question is a problem in that a student who answers 'nothing' may well be 100 per cent correct but the thinking of the academic is also problematic, beyond that technical wording issue. What particular capability is being tested apart from the capacity to remember a particular lecture and regurgitate the material that was presented on that occasion? This kind of assessment is entirely dependent on the specific nature of the learning experience and of only limited relationship to the capabilities that we have argued must be developed by students if they are to become competent graduates in an unknown future. One necessary conclusion from our view of teaching and learning is that we should have a way of assessing student learning outcomes that are independent of the specific learning experiences students have. In that regard, we share a perspective with the competency movement.

This argument is contingent on an assessment system that is criterion-referenced. It is similar to the 'credit by examination' movement of some decades ago (Marton, 1967). The argument is as follows: if we are able to state clearly the intended learning outcomes of an educational programme or the criteria we require for certification of attainment, and if the assessment process properly measures those outcomes, then we would be confident that anyone passing that assessment has the capabilities required. If that is so, it should not concern us how a person has developed those capabilities. The 'credit by examination' movement of the past and the 'recognition of prior learning' movement of recent decades would argue that universities should allow anyone to be assessed at whatever level they feel confident and, if they perform adequately, then they should be given the appropriate credit. An example often quoted is the assessment of the capability to drive a motor vehicle. In most communities, this assessment involves a test of knowledge of laws and procedures, as well as a practical test. In order to be licensed to drive a car you have to drive a car. It would be highly unusual for the licensing authority to ask questions about how many lessons the applicant has had, where the applicant has practised driving, who has been teaching the applicant or about any similar issues. So it is argued that summative assessment, that is, assessment that a particular standard has been attained (the first of Boyle *et al.*'s (1995) three purposes of assessment), normally for some form of certification, should not be designed so that it is contingent on specific learning experiences. The absurdity of some situations in universities where that principle is breached was elaborated above, hence our heading for this section 'Separation of assessment and teaching'.

However, formative assessment is a crucial aspect of any teaching and learning process. This is Boyle *et al.*'s (1995) second purpose of assessment – to focus and enhance student learning while learning is taking place. As we argued in Chapter 6, students ought to be exposed to many assessment experiences which call on their capability to use discernment and simultaneity to deal with unknown situations. These experiences should be reflected on, discussed and integrated into the teaching and learning processes. They provide an opportunity for students to become aware of how they are addressing such situations and to develop better ways of doing so. From this point of view, teaching and assessment should not be separated at all, quite the contrary – making judgements is an integral part of the teaching–learning process.

Authentic or performance assessment

A recent movement with the aim of developing better ways of assessing learning lives up to the idea of separating teaching and assessment, in its general orientation. It makes use of criterion-referred assessment, and it offers a dramatic solution to the problem of students learning for the tests. Taylor (1994) argues: students should learn for the tests! The trick is that the tests have to be such that the learner cannot pass them without having developed exactly the capabilities that are intended. The learner should demonstrate the expected performance under authentic conditions. The idea corresponds to what we said about driving tests: in order to pass them you have to drive. The same applies to sports: a high-jump competition can be considered a test and you cannot win without jumping high. Such assessment is called authentic or performance assessment. You can easily use them in sports or in arts (for opera singers, for instance) and many other fields where a particular kind of performance is what the learners are supposed to be capable of demonstrating under reasonably well-defined conditions, such as carrying out a comparatively routine surgical operation or a car repair, for instance). However, the argument is that we can also identify complex performances which are central to different fields of study in schools and universities and we can define the educational standards aimed for in terms of those performances. Assessment can then be turned into '... evaluations of student works that are authentic to subject-area disciplines and that reflect the kinds of processes seen as central to each (eg investigating a mathematical concept; writing an essay; conducting, evaluating and generalising from a science experiment; writing a position paper on an environmental issue)' (Taylor, 1994).

Taylor contrasts the model on which such authentic assessment is based (which she calls a standards model) with the measurement model on which norm-referenced assessment is based. Taylor (1994) argues that the standards model suggests a very different set of assumptions. These assumptions are that:

- we can set public educational standards and strive toward them
- most students can internalise and achieve the standards
- very different student performances and exhibitions can and will reflect the same standards
- educators can be trained to internalise the standards and be fair and consistent judges of diverse student performances.

Taylor further suggests that there is a different emphasis which '... is now on standards for what students can do (student performances) rather than simply for what students know (a defined domain of content). (Educators)... are also challenged to identify and define the complex performances and processes that are 'authentic' to (the discipline)'.

It should be noted that these ideas about performance assessment, performance standards and other matters that Taylor discusses such as exemplars, performance criteria, assessment of whether or not the performance standard has been achieved, repeat testing until the standard is reached and benchmark performances are the very principles from which competency-based approaches to education draw.

However, there has been considerable criticism of the authentic assessment movement. A study by Erickson and Meyer (in press) of the Student Performance Component of the 1991 British Columbia Science Assessment system raises questions about what is actually being assessed. He argues that the authentic assessment tasks he analysed (involving, for example, magnetic properties and properties of strings and sound boards) were not assessing well-defined capabilities, or rather, most required students to use prior knowledge from a number of knowledge domains. They quote Selley's (1989) caution '... to avoid the assumption that there are broad, transferable, context-free processes or skills'. Indeed Erickson and Meyer found 'very low to non-existent correlations' between different 'authentic' assessment tasks undertaken by the same students in different contexts. Terwilliger (1997) has recently launched a more general criticism of performance tests. He argues that their advocates make strong validity claims without any evidence whatsoever.

The underlying problem appears to be the same problem that affects traditional university assessment practices. There is the doubtful assumption in traditional assessment that knowing about some aspect of the world is sufficient for a person to deal with new situations in the future that involve that aspect. The authentic assessment movement, on the other hand, recognizes the complexity of real-world situations and argues that the assessment of knowledge in the traditional sense is artificial. What should be assessed, they would claim, is the ability to perform properly some task or process which is or is like the sort of task that graduates will be called on to perform in the future.

However, the criticism (eg Selly, 1989; Erickson and Meyer (in press); Terwilliger, 1997) that there is no solid evidence that such instances of assessment actually measure capacities '... truly representative of performance in the field' (Wiggins, 1989), as claimed by the authentic assessment movement, raises an important question. How can we assess students in a way that addresses their capacity to handle situations in the future that they have not previously encountered? We suggest that the answer to this question is to assess the capabilities which we have shown in previous chapters to be central to dealing with the unknown future, viz. discernment and simultaneity.

Assessing discernment and simultaneity

In line with our view of learning and the kinds of learning outcome desirable for graduates facing an increasingly unknowable future, we argue that assessment in universities must, at least in part, test students' capabilities of discerning the relevant aspects of various situations in their field of study and of handling those aspects simultaneously in order to define and solve problems in previously unseen contexts.

If we want to test whether students can discern and handle simultaneously the relevant aspects of various situations, then the assessment tasks they are faced with must require them to discern what is relevant and deal with the situation accordingly. In many current assessment systems, the form of the question is such that the relevant aspects are given and the capability of the student to discern them is not tested. In the two main sections to follow we will illustrate how this can be done, first with a focus on finding out about the outcomes of learning in individual cases and in the section thereafter on the group level. Finally, we will discuss some of the principles of this kind of assessment.

Describing outcomes of learning

Exploring understandings in physics through research and through examination

If we want to use examinations not only for making judgements about pass or fail, or about different 'degrees of excellence', but to find out what students have actually learned, ie about the qualities of their learning, then we should be able to draw on research driven by this kind of interest.

Bowden *et al.* (1992) investigated physics students' understandings of some basic concepts and principles in kinematics. They addressed 14 questions with 90 students of physics at first-year university level and final-year high school (Australian Year 12). One of the problems used in the interviews with students was as follows: 'A ball inside a train is rolled towards the back of the train. It travels two metres along the floor in three seconds while the train travels forwards at a constant speed of 10 m/s. Discuss the displacement of the ball.'

Some students (Group A) considered the motion only from inside the train and took no account of the motion of the train, therefore they saw the ball as being displaced two metres towards the back of the train after three seconds.

There were a few students (Group B) who saw the motion in two successive stages: first the train and the ball move forward together 30 metres and then the ball moves two metres in the opposite direction. During the interviews, these students were asked to clarify what they meant and in each case it was clear that they saw it as two separate movements. For instance, one student talked about the ball travelling through 32 metres but finishing up being displaced from the starting point only 28 metres.

A number of students (Group C) explicitly addressed the problem using two frames of reference. They saw that the train was travelling relative to the ground in one direction (30 metres in three seconds) and that the ball was travelling relative to the train in the opposite direction (two metres in three seconds). They defined the problem as one of finding out the displacement of the ball relative to the ground. They took the position of an observer standing outside the train. What would the motion look like to the observer if the train walls were transparent? As the train passes, the observer can see both the ball and the train moving forward but the train is travelling away faster than the ball is. Therefore after three seconds, the train has moved further away than the ball has (30 metres as compared with 28 metres).

The quantitative answer for Group C is the same as that obtained by the Group B students. However the explanation is quite different. The Group B students discerned the relevant aspects, viz. the motion of the train relative to the ground and the motion of the ball relative to the train but they dealt with them separately. The Group C students also discerned the relevant aspects but in framing and solving the problem they dealt with the relevant aspects simultaneously. The motion of the ball relative to the ground can be seen as the resultant of the motion of the ball relative to the train and the train relative to the ground. The students in Group C could simultaneously see the motion of the ball both in terms of this resultant and of its composite parts. In contrast, those in Group B dealt with this by suggesting that the ball is making two successive movements.

There were many other students (Group D) who on the surface dealt with the problem in the same way as Group C by subtracting one vector (ball relative to the train) from another vector (train relative to the ground) to obtain the overall displacement of 28 metres. However these students gave no evidence that they were focally aware of any alternative frames of reference or even that they were aware of the concept of frame of reference at all. They merely carried out an algorithmic vector subtraction. There was no evidence for instance that they saw the motion of the ball relative to some observer on the ground.

The variation among these four different ways of responding to this question can therefore be seen as a variation in the extent to which the aspects of the problem that are relevant to a full understanding are discerned by the students and simultaneously present in their focal awareness. As we indicated in Chapter 6, questions which merely ask students to provide a numerical answer do not test these capabilities. In this case, most students reached a quantitative answer of 28 metres. However, their capability to discern the relevant aspects of the situation and to deal with them simultaneously varied considerably and in different ways from one group to another. Given that these capabilities are the very ones necessary to equip graduates for the unknown future, it is essential that questions like this one are part of university assessment systems. In fact this question, and two others from among the 14 used in this research study, have been used in this very way in a course in mechanics at the University of Lund in Sweden recently. These questions are not simply research artefacts but are being used actively by academics at Lund. The teachers of the course have found that such questions enable them to discriminate among students' capabilities in ways that other, quantitative questions had been unable to do. Furthermore, this kind of information about students' ways of seeing such situations provides a valuable guide for curriculum planning and the planning of student learning experiences. You will recall that this was the second of the three purposes of assessment that we noted at the beginning of this chapter.

Another of the three research questions (Walsh *et al.*, 1993) which have been used at the University of Lund to assess students in mechanics, is as follows: 'Martha and Arthur are running along a straight, level road at constant speed. Arthur is ahead of Martha. Arthur's speed is less than Martha's speed. How far must Martha run before she catches up with Arthur, and how long will she take to do this?'

A large number of students addressed this problem by considering the two runners separately. For instance, one way some students tried to deal with the problem was to think of what happened by the time Martha had travelled the distance that initially separated her from Arthur. By that time Arthur would have travelled further forward although now the separation between them would be less. By the time Martha had travelled that new separation distance (in less time than before) then Arthur would still have travelled further although not quite so far as before and so on. As the distance of the segment travelled and the time taken both diminish, Arthur has always travelled ahead, albeit in the end only by a very small distance, by this analysis, Martha can never catch Arthur. This way of addressing such a problem is known as Zeno's paradox after the Greek philosopher Zeno of Elea (in about 450 BC, however, Zeno referred to Achilles and the tortoise rather than to Arthur and Martha).

Many other students also dealt with each runner separately and, from the physicist's perspective, in relation to the ground as frame of reference. However, as in the ball-in-train example discussed earlier, such students generally showed no evidence that they were thinking of frame of reference at all and, generally, these students failed to come up with a strategy for solving the problem.

There were some students however who considered the problem in terms of relative speed. They did not deal with the motion of Arthur and Martha separately but rather they considered the two motions simultaneously. They treated the two runners as a system and so the motion of Martha was considered not relative to the ground but relative to Arthur. One student referred to this relative speed as the 'catching speed'. Another focused on the relative distance between them, which was seen to diminish with time. How much time was a simple relation between the relative speed and the initial distance of separation.

As we mentioned earlier, this research-based problem is now being used successfully at the University of Lund to discriminate between students on the basis of their capability to discern the relevant aspects of the situation and to deal with them simultaneously. A quantitative problem which could be solved without this simultaneity would not assess these capabilities. Neither would it have the diagnostic feature which could feed back into helping students learn better.

Revealing and developing the understanding of pricing

Thomas and Wood (1997) have reported on the impact of research on the way the concept of 'price' is taught. They comment on studies by Swedish researchers (Dahlgren, 1978; Marton and Dahlgren, 1978) and by UK researchers (Thomas, 1985) which showed that many students, including some who had already successfully completed university subjects in economics, understood the concept of price in a limited way. The Swedish research focused on students responses to the question 'Why does a bun cost 50 öre?' The UK researchers asked students 'what happens to the price of ice-cream if it's a hot day and more people want to buy?' Certainly, in both cases, some students saw price as a function of supply and demand. However, the majority of students saw price as the cost of production or inherent value.

The conclusion drawn by Thomas and Wood was that 'normal, everyday experience of transactions within the economic system teaches that price and costs are the same'. This was reinforced by a later study (Thomas, 1996; Parsons, 1997) of a group of students varying from postgraduate economics students through to seven-year-old primary-school pupils. They were asked questions about two stamps, one of which cost 18 p and was supposed to be placed on second-class mail in the UK and the other which cost 24 p and was intended for first-class mail. The students were shown the two stamps, asked if they knew how much they had to pay for each, why there was a difference in price and 'if you were posting a letter, which one would you buy?' The answers were of three different kinds:

- Price reflects the difference in the service – its speed, value or cost.
- Price reflects these same differences in service but this is seen in terms of the creation of different services by the Post Office.
- Price is a market phenomenon with the different services and prices existing only because of differences in supply and demand.

Thomas and Wood (1997) report the striking finding that all but one of the 33 respondents (including the economics postgraduate students) answered in the first or second ways and equated the price of the stamps with speed, value or cost. They ask what is it about conventional teaching of supply and demand analysis, which the economics postgraduates would have experienced, that is not as helpful as might have been expected.

What should teachers of economics and business students do to improve their students' learning? This question was addressed by groups of teachers of economics across the UK and they concluded that students who were understanding price in terms of costs were focusing on the object (the good or service) and its price while those who understood it in terms of supply and demand were focusing on the market and price. They planned curriculum materials with that latter emphasis such as the students being told that they would be expected 'to deal with information about economic events which made newspaper headlines'.

Thomas and Wood suggest that the understanding of price as determined by costs is linked with experience of variation in the costs of commodities: 'In other words, different prices and different costs are what is experienced and cost (rather than the market) is discerned as the feature which varies with price'. The understanding of price as a function of supply and demand is linked with experience of variation in the markets for commodities: 'Different prices are experienced in relation to differences in the characteristics of the markets involved and the markets (in which costs, through supply, are integrated) are discerned as the source of variation in price'.

Thomas and Wood argue that if students are to develop this latter understanding, they need to experience variation in the markets for goods and services since this does not come naturally in everyday experience. Further, in keeping with our theory, they suggest that if the understanding is to be useful in dealing with new problems, then students must have already experienced that usefulness in learning the concept. They need to have experienced variation in the type of situations to which it applies and to have learned to discern the relevant aspects of each situation. The sorts of question asked of students in this example assists teachers to arrange student learning experiences in ways that help them learn better. Of course, in addition, this series of questions tried out by teachers with different groups of students has also contributed significantly to improvements in teaching about these concepts. This particular use of assessment will be further discussed later in this chapter.

Using examination to understand students' understanding in mathematics

Martinsson (1996) used a series of related questions in an examination in order to understand how students understand a topic dealt with in teaching. The topic was computation in different modulos. Within an algebraic structure in which the operations addition and multiplication are modulo, an integer can be represented on a circular number line. Take our system of hours, which is modulo 24, as an example. If the time is 1 pm, for instance, and you add one hour, your arrive at 2 pm, but you will get the same result if you add $1 + 24$ or $1 + 48$ or $1 + 72$ ie. if you add any multiple of 24 $(1 + 24n)$. Similarly, the week is modulo 7. If it is Monday today and you add one day you arrive at Tuesday, but adding 8 days $(1 + 7)$ will yield the same result, as will adding any multiple of 7 to 1 $(1 + 7n)$.

Here is the statement and the first one of the questions the students were exposed to:

In a ring with 1 (ie, with a multiplicative unit usually designated by the symbol 1) you can always multiply an element x with itself. Then you obtain $x \cdot x$ written as x^2. We can then consider the equation $x^2 = 1$. We are now going to investigate the question of how many roots this equation has. The ring is referred to as R.

(A) Address first a question which you are most used to, viz. when R = the real numbers (written as **R**). How many roots does the equation have then? Give an explanation for your answer. State the roots.

The first part of the question is simple enough. The equation $x^2 = 1$ has two roots, $+1$ and -1. All but four of the students knew that. The second question is more difficult. Five students showed that the equation has those and only those two roots, another nine students showed that the equation has those two roots, but they did not show that the equation has only those roots.

The second question was:

(B) Solve the equation **R** = **Z** $_{24}$ (ie in the ring of integers modulo 24 where addition and multiplication are done modulo 24).

So, let us consider this question. We can imagine a ring of integers modulo 24 as a circle with 24 points on it equally spaced. Certainly, with modulo 24, $x = 1$ is a root of the equation $x^2 = 1$. The reasoning is the same as that given in question (A). But also $x = 5$ is a root in modulo 12. Why? Well, 5 multiplied by 5 is 25. And in modulo 24, 25 is 1 just as in modulo 12, if January is 1 and December is 12, then 13 is January again. So now we have 1 and 5 as roots of the equation in modulo 24.

What about 7? Well 7 multiplied by 7 is 49. In modulo 24, 49 is also 1 (going around the circle twice this time). So seven is also a root.

What about 11? Well 11 multiplied by 11 is 121 and in modulo 24, 121 is also 1 (going around the circle five times in this case because 5 x 24 = 120). So 11 is also a root of the equation. In the same way, it can also be shown that 13, 17, 19 and 23 are also roots of the equation.

So the equation has eight roots in modulo 24, namely 1, 5, 7, 11, 13, 17 and 19.

The students have had teaching about computing in modulos. Thirty-eight of them indicated that the equation has more than two roots. We have to skip the following two questions due to the complexity of this case and go to the last question:

(E) Look at Appendix B about quadratic equations (in a given textbook). In the text it is said that a quadratic equation has two solutions. Is it true? Always? When? In what situations? It is also said: 'there is a positive and a negative number, the square of which is 36'. Describe under what conditions this is true. Explain why it should be true.

Here we find the most surprising result. Of the 38 students who to question B declared that a quadratic equation such as $x^2 = 1$ has more than two roots in modulo, only seven tried to point out the conditions for the statement to be true, ie that the equation is solved for real numbers and not in modulo. The other 31 students who to question B declared that the equation $x^2 = 1$ has more than two roots argue now why the equation $x^2 = 36$ has two roots only. It is as though what they said earlier was completely erased from their consciousness when answering question E.

How is it possible? It is not an isolated finding. Of 38 students who gave a counter-example in B, only seven make use of that experience in answering question E. From our view of learning, it is clear that the former students have difficulty in discerning relevant aspects and certainly they have difficulty with simultaneity. What is necessary is for this kind of assessment to be used as part of teaching so that students learn that they need to reflect on knowledge in context and not to allow aspects to be taken for granted.

Martinsson (1994) made a detailed analysis of the students' differing understandings. Here we just wanted to point to the most striking features, with the most straightforward implications. As in our example about force and acceleration in Chapter 5, where we pointed to the need for the different contexts of those concepts being dealt with in relation to each other (as variations on a single theme), computation in modulos has to be dealt with in relation to real numbers in order to develop students' awareness of the taken-for-granted assumptions when dealing with one of the systems only.

The following is another example used in an examination for trainee teachers in mathematics. In this case they brought a particular research report to the examination, *Qualities in Pupils' Thinking*, which was an account of 10-year-old children's struggles with the problem of how to represent fractions as infinite decimal numbers, such as 0.33 (the question was how to divide a piece of wood in three equal parts and represent the operation with decimal numbers). The children had discussions in groups of four and the report is a description and analysis of what happened in the different groups. Students were expected to use the report to address the following question:

On page 72 in *Qualities in Pupils' Thinking* we could read:

The depth of intention in students' understanding

We can conclude that the students reach a considerable depth in their understanding of the problem that they are trying to solve. Even if Ida and Maria do not reach insightful resignation they succeed in maintaining their curiosity and formulating the problem in a clearer way at the end of the working session than in the beginning.

In the above quote there are three statements:

1. The students reach a considerable depth in their understanding of the problem.

2. The students manage handling the uncertainty in the solution process.

3. The students formulate the problem more clearly at the end of the working session.

Choose one of these statements. Show how that which is stated is expressed through what the students say or do, by selecting an example in chapter 2 [of the report students were given].

In this case the mathematics students are really facing a situation they have not faced previously. Furthermore, they are expected to focus on children's ways of dealing with mathematics and not on mathematics proper.

When the answers to the question were analysed Martinsson (1996) found a number of qualitatively different ways in which this problem was handled. Some students simply came up with some quote, others tried to develop a line of argument, others again related the question to educational theory or to mathematics or to their practical experiences. Occasionally the question is related to educational theory and mathematics and practical experiences. The last alternative represents discernment and simultaneity, corresponding to aims we are arguing for in our book.

As a third mathematics example we will show a problem given to engineering students in a mathematics examination. This is a problem which differs from prototypical problems at university level. And it is open to different formulations and therefore different ways of solving it.

Emil has a one-litre bottle (A) filled with orange juice and an empty one-litre bottle (B). He pours some of the juice from the full bottle A into the empty bottle B. He then fills up bottle B with water and thoroughly mixes the juice and water together. Then he fills up bottle A again with the mixture from bottle B. Show that bottle A now contains at least 75 per cent of the original juice.

The problem can be solved geometrically by using a synthetic approach originating from ancient Greece. Or analytically, the equation $y = x^2 - x + 1$ can be formed, where x is the proportion of juice poured from the first glass to the second in the beginning and y is the proportion of juice in the end. Again, there are two different ways of proceeding.

We can derive the function y and solve y' for 0, which gives

$y' = 2x - 1 \Rightarrow 2x - 1 = 0 \Rightarrow x = \frac{1}{2}$

ie pouring over half of the juice gives lowest concentration in the end (75%, when substituting $x = \frac{1}{2}$ in the original equation).

The other way (and probably the most elegant) is solving the problem through quadratic completion). Rewriting x as

$2.\frac{1}{2}x$ and adding $(\frac{1}{2})^2 - (\frac{1}{2})^2 (= 0)$ to the equation $y = x^2 - x + 1$

we obtain $y = x^2 - 2.\frac{1}{2}x + (\frac{1}{2})^2 + 1 - (\frac{1}{2})^2$ and $y = (x - \frac{1}{2})^2 + \frac{3}{4}$

Now, y has obviously its lowest value

$(y = \frac{3}{4})$ when $x - \frac{1}{2} = 0$ for $x = \frac{1}{2}$,

which is naturally the same result as above.

This problem has been used in mathematics competitions for younger students. If they have not studied calculus and have not come across the principle necessary for the geometric solution (that for a given circumference of rectangle you get a maximum volume when the rectangle is a square), the only solution available for them is the third one with quadratic completion, which can be considered the most elegant solution. We can say that it is the easiest way for them to solve it (actually the only way). All of the engineering students solved the problem using calculus – just as they have solved so many other problems. We can say that quadratic completion is actually the most difficult way for them to solve it in spite of the fact that many of them probably belonged earlier to the same group of mathematically able young students who might have used that solution. For the engineering students it turned out to be the most difficult way – very much because through their studies they have learned to see such problems as calculus problems.

Describing effects of educational experiences

In this chapter we are arguing for using assessment to define learning aims, for revealing students' capability for discerning critical aspects of certain classes of situations and to find out what students have learned in general. We have to use certain kinds of questions to achieve these aims. The questions have to be open, 'naked' (ie non-technical) and novel to students. Above all else, they have to deal with things central to the field of study as well as to the fields of applications. Finding out what has been learned is of vital interest not only on the individual but on the group level as well. We need to gain insights about the effects of our subjects, courses and programmes in order to find out how they work and how they can be improved.

Evaluating courses in physics and engineering

In the first example we used in Chapter 2 to illustrate qualitative differences in learning, the point of departure was a question from an investigation of engineering students taking a course in mechanics: 'A car is driven at a high, constant speed straight forward on a motorway. What forces act on the car?'

We described two ways in which this question was made sense of by the students, one of which is the Newtonian way of thinking (as the car is travelling at a constant speed, the forces acting on it are in balance) – a fundamental idea in mechanics. The other is a common everyday understanding (as the car is moving, there must be an excess 'pushing' force acting on it). Because much of what you learn in mechanics builds on the Newtonian principles, you would expect the students to exhibit more of a Newtonian way of reasoning as a function of their studying mechanics, also in relation to this deceptively simple question.

However, this is not what happened. According to Johansson, Marton and Svensson (1985) studying mechanics at university level does not have any effect on how students deal with this type of question. In Chapter 3 (page 65) we referred to Prosser and Millar's (1989) study in which the effects of participation in a six-week course in mechanics, specially designed to develop students' understanding of force and motion, for instance, was investigated. Effects on the learners were measured by using questions like the one discussed here, before and after the course. Other questions were in accordance with what we said in Chapter 3 (page 65):

> A golfer hits a ball and it lands on a completely level green – what kind of path will it follow and why?
> A puck leaves an ice-hockey stick and glides straight ahead on smooth ice – what happens to the puck and why?

As we can see in Table 3.5 (on page 66) students mainly adopting a deep approach to learning developed their understanding of the phenomena dealt with in this specially designed course, while students mainly adopting a surface approach did not do so.

Dahlgren (1978) demonstrated that studying economics at university level has marginal effects only on how students deal with questions of the kind discussed above in this chapter (pages 170–71), such as:

- What is the meaning of the statement 'too high wage increments will cause inflation'?
- What would be the consequences for the Swedish labour market if England devalued the pound in relation to the Swedish Krona?
- Why does a bun cost 50 öre?

In spite of discouraging results, if we believe that university studies should develop students' understanding of the phenomena dealt with in their studies, the types of question we are advocating here lend themselves well to finding out about the possible impact participation in a particular course may have on students' understanding. As the questions are non-technical and focus on central aspects of the phenomena students are supposed to learn about, it makes sense to use them at the beginning, as well as at the end, of the course. In the studies referred to above they were used on both occasions in order to find out about the effects of courses. As should be obvious from what was said above the effects were not very impressive – they were basically non-existent.

Similar questions were used in the evaluation of a range of courses at the Technical University of Denmark in Copenhagen. This was part of a quality improvement process similar to those we will discuss in Chapter 9. Questions were used at the beginning of courses in order to reveal the students' pre-understanding, during courses to identify conceptual difficulties and at the end of courses to explain the effects on the students' understanding. In some cases courses were revised on the basis of the observations and the effects of the revision were evaluated. The following is an example of the questions used:

Consider a horizontal pipe with a contraction as shown on the figure. The fluid flow from cross section 1 to 2 is considered frictionless. The pressure at the two cross sections are called P_1 and P_2 respectively. Indicate whether you expect (and state your reasons): (*a*) $P_1 > P_2$ or (*b*) $P_1 = P_2$ or (*c*) $P_1 < P_2$

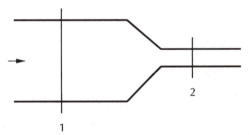

Horizontal pipe with a contraction (May, 1997)

Many students who chose the right answer to this question were unable to explain why it was correct. The answer concerns the Bernouilli equation which, qualitatively, is about the relative contributions of pressure, kinetic energy and potential energy. The slow-moving water (in the wide pipe) has a higher pressure than the fast-moving water (in the narrow pipe). One of the difficulties many students appeared to have was that while the Bernouilli equation assumes incompressible fluids, such students thought in terms of molecules squeezed together, much like a crowd passing through a contraction – leaving a smoke-filled building in panic, for instance. They were unable to maintain the incompressibility condition in their thinking and failed to take a global view of the system. May (1997) believes that questions like this are making 'the conflicting intuitions about pressure, force and impact (momentum) explicit'.

Data originating from this project is still being analysed, but May states that the findings appear very similar to those above; they are reminiscent of those found by Bowden *et al.* (1992) as discussed in Chapter 5 (pages 116–17).

> ... because of the priority given to computational skills in solving simple problems at examinations as well as during the year (in special 'group exercise' classes where students are trained in recognizing and solving the type of problems posed at earlier examinations), almost all engineering students tend to focus on physical and chemical laws as something of a purely formal nature. Laws are remembered for the purpose of identifying their context of use in typical exercises and substituting numbers in the general expressions of the formulae for the purpose of calculating the results.

May also reports on a finding by Nakhleh and Mitchell (1993) who tested the belief of fellow teachers in chemistry at Purdue University that '... the computational skills demonstrated at traditional examinations in chemistry would also be an indication of an understanding of the underlying concepts of chemistry'. They found that this was not so for at least half the students.

There was one disheartening finding (in complete agreement with the results reported by Nakhleh and Mitchell) running through all of the courses. By using the tests consisting of the kinds of question discussed here, staff involved in running each course could determine the level of acceptable understanding. By and large 25 per cent of the students participating in the different courses achieved that level of understanding. They all passed their examinations as well. Twenty-five per cent of the students failed the examinations and none of them had reached the acceptable level of understanding but 50 per cent of the students passed the examination without having an acceptable understanding of material assessed (see Figure 7.1) (Jacobsen, 1998).

As we mentioned earlier, the observations have been used to improve learning and we still do not know how successful those attempts turned out to be. We would argue that the observations on the relationship between understanding and examinations are universally typical. So it is exactly here that we find a formidable potential for improving the quality of learning and therefore the quality of universities.

Assessing effects of attempts to improve learning

We mentioned above that questions used to assess learning should be independent of specific learning experiences. This is of course necessary when we are to compare the effects of two different educational experiences as was the case with Inglis, Dall'Alba and Broadbent's (1993) study of a teaching innovation for which they were responsible. A first-year subject in accountancy was offered to some students in an undergraduate business degree course as an intensive programme over summer. The report compares students – so far as learning experiences and outcomes of learning are concerned – in this 12 × 3.25 hour seminar course over summer with a control group of students in the traditional 20 hours of lectures and 20 hours of tutorials during the normal semester. Among the measures used to compare the two programmes was an assessment of student understanding of a key concept, production cost, at both the beginning and end of the programme.

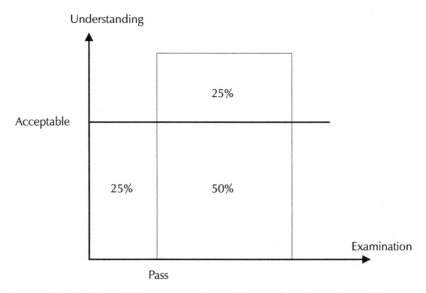

Figure 7.1: *Relationship between understanding and examination result (adapted from Jacobsen, 1998)*

Our focus here is on the nature of the assessment used. Several questions were asked of which the following is typical:

> In discussing the performance of IBM with the production team, the manager reports that an IBM PC costs $1,000 to produce.
>
> (a) What does the production cost of $1,000 mean?
> (b) How could IBM management make use of this figure? [Inglis, Dall'Alba and Broadbent, 1994.]

The authors indicate that students' understandings of production cost could be categorized in one of three ways:

- costs incurred in producing a particular PC

- costs apportioned to producing one PC
- costs varying according to context.

The first way of understanding production cost relates each component cost to the overall cost of a particular PC, including the costs of parts, labour and overheads. The second incorporates this understanding but extends it by recognizing that while some costs, such as those of materials, can be directly attributed to a particular PC, others, such as electricity charges, have to be apportioned across all the PCs produced. The third way of understanding production cost incorporates the previous two but is more complete. It recognizes that different ways of costing could be involved, such as direct costing or absorption costing, for instance, and that the meaning of production cost would depend on what approach was used in this particular context.

These three ways of responding show variations in the relevant aspects of the problem discerned by different students. In addition, the third response involves seeing the individual aspects and their relation to each other simultaneously. Again we stress the importance of assessing these capabilities in students and that this kind of question makes that possible. Note again that, since the more complex understanding of production cost was a primary objective of the subject, the assessment was in harmony with the subject objectives, gave students a clear indication of what they were trying to learn and provided direct evidence of the success or otherwise of the teaching in the subject.

We have listed in Table 7.1 the distribution of student responses across these three categories both at the beginning and end of the period of study for both the summer-school and the regular semester subjects.

Table 7.1: *Summer-school and regular pre- and post-test results (adopted from Inglis, Broadbent and Dall'Alba, 1993)*

Category	Summer School		Regular Semester	
	Pre-test % (n=37)	Post-test % (n=37)	Pre-test % (n=32)	Post-test % (n=32)
1 (costs incurred)	73	32	72	53
2 (costs apportioned)	27	38	25	22
3 (costs varying)	0	30	3	25

Nearly three-quarters of the students in both the summer intensive and the traditional semester groups exhibited the first understanding before the programme began. Only one of nearly 70 students showed an understanding before the course equivalent to the more complete type 3. After the course, over 50 per cent of the students who experienced the traditional semester course still showed the first understanding of production cost while 25 per cent showed a type 3 understanding. Those who experienced the summer intensive programme were evenly divided among the three different ways of understanding production cost.

Our argument is that the important function of the assessment process is to find out about the way in which students' understandings of production cost have developed. The assessment instrument should not be of such a kind that only those students who have had a particular experience (and are aware of it) can successfully negotiate the assessment. Indeed, it needs to be recognized that even when students do share particular formal learning experiences, their learning proceeds in quite different ways from one to the other and the assessment should measure the outcome, not chart the process of learning. This calls for much clearer statements of purpose for educational programmes and more purposeful assessment systems. It should be noted that these two courses that were compared took place at different times, with the normal semester course taking place some months after the summer intensive. Assessment of this kind can be used for such evaluative purposes at different times.

Making comparisons across time

One of the greatest obstacles to progress in education is that we are usually ignorant of the effects of our efforts. In particular we cannot keep track of the effects of changes in curriculum, teaching methods, examination etc. We may introduce changes, innovations, in one respect or in another, but we do not know whether it has been a change for the better or the other way around. It is very hard – not to say impossible to improve any kind of activity without such feedback. In Chapter 9 we will discuss the importance of being able to make comparisons across time in any efficient educational quality assurance system.

The question is, what is to be compared? Again we would like to argue that the focus should be on the students' understanding of critical aspects of the phenomena they are dealing with in their studies. Such understanding can be explored by using the kinds of question discussed in the present chapter. As an example we are using Beaty's (1987) study of the effects of a social science course on the students' understanding of some societal phenomena, as compared with the effects of a new course revised on the basis of what was found out about the students' understanding of the phenomena dealt with in the first course.

At the Open University in the UK during the 1980s, all undergraduate students were required to take a foundation course as their first unit of study. One of these was in the social sciences and over a period of years the course was regularly upgraded. At one particular stage, Beaty (1987) engaged in a research project which focused on the content of learning in the course as a quality rather than as a quantity. She had several aims: to find out what the students' under-standings of some key concepts were, to use such assessment at the beginning and end of the course to evaluate their learning in the course and to use this information as formative evaluation in the production of new course materials.

A number of topics or phenomena considered central to the course were selected. Beaty gives five examples: capitalism, division of labour, power, price control and class. Questions were formulated and they were used as points of departures for discussions of the topics with the students in individually run interviews, in which their first answers were followed up in detail. This was done both before and after the course. The interviews were transcribed word by word and the transcripts were subject to qualitative analysis. Distinctly different ways of understanding the phenomena were identified. Beaty elabo-rates the question aimed at revealing the students' understanding of capitalism. The question used as the point of departure was simply: 'Is Britain capitalist?'

The students' first reactions were followed up by questions such as 'Why do you say that?' and 'What do you mean by...?'

Some of the students declared their ignorance; among the others three qualitatively different ways of understanding capitalism were found:

A. Describing the role of profit motive as the defining feature of a capitalist system. The answer suggests that where there is a production to cater for interests uneconomically this is not capitalist.
B. Distinguishing between private and state ownership and control of production, without discussing the profit motive. These answers include reference to the workings of a market economy contrasted with a planned economy.
C. Discussing consequences of capitalism, eg inequalities of wealth, class system, people working for a wage, without drawing out the features described in (A) or (B).

As interviews were carried out both before and after the course and as the differing understandings were put in a hierarchical order for each topic, the number of students showing a 'better' or a 'weaker' or the same understanding could be determined (see Table 7.2). So far as the above question about capitalism is concerned, for instance, category A was seen as being more in line with the understanding the course set out to promote than category B, which in its turn was seen as reflecting a better understanding than category C.

Changes for the better on the group level could be observed in relation to two of the topics only but all of the analysis was used to try to make improvements. As the investigation was carried out at the Open University in Britain, an institution for distance learning, the course team producing the study material holds the key to any improvements. They were informed about this first part of the study and in rewriting the study package they tried to draw on what had been found out about the differing ways in which the students understood and made sense of what the course was about. They learned about the students' conceptual difficulties and probably also about what they erroneously had taken for granted in their presentation and explanation.

Table 7.2: *Changes in understanding (adopted from Beaty, 1987)*

Topic	Understanding		
	Better	Weaker	Same
Capitalism	8	3	5
Class	1	2	12
Division of labour	9	1	6
Power	2	4	6
Price control	3	3	10

In the research study a new group of students using the new course package was followed in the same way as the first group mentioned above. The understanding of the different topics by the students who completed the new course could now be compared with the understanding of these same topics by the students who completed the old course. For the question about 'capitalism' the results are shown in Table 7.3.

Table 7.3: *Frequencies of different ways of understanding 'Capitalism' after the course (adopted from Beaty, 1987)*

Category*	Old course	New course
A	5	14
B	7	1
C	0	1
'Don't know'	3	0
Total	15	16

* For explanation of categories, see text.

The pattern was similar – although not as pronounced as for the other questions. The revision of the course was found to be successful. It seems as if we can improve students' understanding by finding out what their understanding is like.

If we now go back to the problem we raised at the beginning of this section, namely how we can compare outcomes of learning across time, the answer was pretty straightforward: by using the same questions. This is, however, hardly a general solution. It is not only that the content of courses is changing, but if we want to use examination data to keep track of changes in learning outcomes, it would not be a very clever recommendation to use the same questions year after year. There are, in fact, techniques for linking different tests, which allow for comparisons to be made between them; a statistical method known as the Rasch model does exactly this (see Stephanou, 1997a, b).

Finding out what is learned

Formulating questions

First of all, if the learning we are interested in means of developing capabilities for seeing, experiencing and making sense of certain situations in certain ways, then finding out what has been learned (which we see as one of the main points of assessment) amounts to finding out in what ways the students are capable of seeing, experiencing and, making sense of those situations. Accordingly, this implies finding out what aspects of the situations in question that the students discern and attend to simultaneously. Doing that takes situations and problems where the students have to do the discerning themselves (in contrast with standard problems where the relevant aspects are defined in advance and what the students are supposed to do is to make use of more or less obvious relations between them). Therefore we have to use questions, problems and situations that are *open* to different perspectives, from which different aspects can be seen.

Secondly, the questions should preferably be *non-technical*. They should not focus on specific facts or procedures, because specific facts or procedures usually rest on taken-for-granted ways of seeing, which are not put to the test. This does not imply that the knowledge of specific facts or the capability of using specific procedures should not be tested. Our point is they should not be the only things that are tested.

Thirdly, the questions that are open and non-technical should focus on phenomena, concepts and principles that are central to the field of knowledge studied and which are vital to the students' capabilities for handling situations in the future which we are trying to prepare them for.

Analysing answers

If we want to use assessment questions to find out what the students actually learn and how they understand what they have been taught, using particular kinds of question is not sufficient. This information must be found out from their answers and this is by no means a trivial undertaking.

In most of our examples we have described what was learned in that particular instance, in terms of variation between different ways of understanding and what the learning task was about. In each case a limited number of qualitatively different ways of understanding the task, problem and topic were identified and characterized in terms of appropriate categories of description. The different understandings reflect what the students have discerned and are focusing on due to their differing prior experiences of a pattern of variation (at least according to the theory presented in Chapter 2). However, in order to reveal the variation in the students' understanding the teacher has to discern and focus on critical aspects of the students' understandings and these can be discerned precisely due to the variation in the answers. The teacher has to read each answer through an awareness of all of the other answers. It is through the contrast with other ways of understanding the object of learning that a particular answer can be made sense of as expressing a particular way of understanding the very same object of learning. This is an iterative process and time consuming but is worth while in the end. A hidden world of varying ways of thinking about the phenomena dealt with in teaching is revealed. The teacher learns from and about the students (see Marton and Booth, 1997).

Part Four

A Learning University

Chapter 8

Collective consciousness and the ethics of learning

Collective consciousness in learning

In Chapters 2 and 3, we referred to a view of learning as mainly being a by-product of participation in social practices and of becoming a participant in social contexts. However, common forms of institutional learning, normally not depicted as authentic practices from the point of view of the social practice perspective of learning, are fundamentally social. A solitary student, sitting reading a textbook, is trying to find a way into and around a landscape of ideas, concepts, terms and facts shared by others. Scientific knowledge – scientific in a wide sense of the word – is public knowledge. It is in the open and in principle available to everyone. When it comes to teaching – or to being taught – a central idea in our view is that the student should become aware of the teacher's way of seeing the object of teaching and appropriate it and go beyond it, of course, as we argued in Chapter 6. Nevertheless, seeing something that someone else sees and seeing it as someone else sees it is the baseline of a shared awareness. If we are in the same material and social context, we usually take for granted such a shared nature of the perceived world around us. Such an assumption may turn out to be unjustified – in fact it is quite often unjustified. Frequently, we see a context, a situation or a phenomenon, which 'objectively' is the same in qualitatively different ways. If we become aware of others' ways of seeing this, then we have a certain degree of *collective consciousness*. We are simply aware of some of the ways in which something appears to others and if we are, we have an interpretative framework for making greater sense of whatever the others may say about the shared object of attention.

As mentioned above, an important idea with teaching is to help the student see what the teacher sees. Preferably the student should recognize the teacher's way of seeing just as a way of seeing, in contrast, or in agreement, with the student's own way of seeing the same thing. It is important for both teachers and students to acknowledge that explicitly, as part of their relationships.

The kind of teaching we are talking about, in Chapter 6 for instance, must necessarily build on the teachers' understanding of the qualitatively different ways in which students make sense of the object of teaching. This is even more true for the activity we would prefer to talk about, rather than talking about teaching, namely designing learning environments. Teachers therefore have to learn from students and when they do so, collective consciousness is being built mutually. Moreover, students should learn from other students and teachers from other teachers. By becoming aware of other people's ways of seeing various phenomena one's understanding is enriched and therefore becomes more powerful; one can see one's own way of seeing exactly as a way of seeing (rather than 'seeing what something is like') and individual awarenesses are linked to each other, forming a *collective consciousness*.

In the section on 'Object of learning' below we argue that independently of human beings we cannot define the object of learning. On the contrary, we suggest that learners contribute to defining this by learning about it and by doing so the object of learning is set in new human contexts and its meaning is enriched in the process. It might be difficult to see how a phenomenon of natural science can be enriched by some undergraduate students' thinking. Their thinking is most probably partly right, partly wrong (from the point of view of science), partly the same as others' and partly different. What individual students may add to the core meaning of the phenomenon may not be very useful in the laboratory, but meaning it is. In fact the idea that students not only learn from teachers and the textbook, but actually contribute to the joint constitution of knowledge about the world is much easier to accept in social sciences (or at least in some of them) such as in the case below.

Forsén (1995) describes a training programme for social workers at Göteborg University. The programme is three-and-a-half years' long, one term being community-based studies. During that term the students, supervised by their teachers, are involved in studies and projects in the community, working with professionals and clients. This term is included in the first basic block of studies making up the first three terms.[1]

The idea of the programme is to make as much use of students' previous experiences as possible, to make use of personal experiences for developing professional knowledge and to make professional knowledge personal. Students are invited to reflect on their previous and new experiences, to share their experiences with the teachers and each other. A quote from Gerdman (1989) is used to formulate the main aim of the programme:

> The aims of the education can be summarized in the following way: during her education the qualified social worker should have built up a personal theory of social work, that is she should be able to consciously and concisely formulate and précis the personal system of knowledge, experiences and values which form the foundations for her or his professional action. This personal professional theory

is of course dynamic and under constant change. It is practical in the sense that the holder has a personal relationship to it. The personal professional theories of different people have large similarities but are never identical.

An important part of the training is letting students formulate their own personal practical professional theory. They have to work on it during each one of the first three terms and present and discuss it with their peers and teachers by the end of every term. In fact this is the central way for them to demonstrate their development. The theories the students develop are about professional issues and practices common to them all, but still they are personal and therefore different. Students make use of their own personal experiences and commitments for developing them. So, by putting together the different accounts, we arrive at a theory (or at least material for a theory) of the professional practice of social work which is potentially much richer and more powerful than any of its constituent parts, the different personal theories.

Having developed something personal and genuine was deeply felt by the students. One of them said after the third term:

> Professional journal writing has really given me a lot. It has given me a more stable ground to stand on. I know how I think now (how I look at things) and I have formulated a personal theory of social work. A theory which I believe in and which I stand for. Of course, my opinions will still change over time, because you are always developing and constantly meet new situations which provide new experiences and so on. But at least I have some ground to stand on now and to depart from (Gerdman, 1989).

Another example comes from a study by Åkerlind (1997) who has investigated some Australian university academics' perceptions of their role as teachers, as part of a broader research study. One of the academics she interviewed is a teacher in cultural studies, who saw his teaching role being as much about learning (for him) as it was about teaching. A large proportion of the students enrolled in his classes were from a diverse range of countries other than Australia. This academic spoke excitedly and enthusiastically about the pleasure he got from going to each class. He talked about the fact that at every stage in his teaching, he was getting new insights into what he was teaching about from the inputs made by all of these students from the perspectives of their varied cultures, from the way they address the issues from perspectives he could not have. He saw his acts of teaching as opportunities for learning, opportunities which became reality nearly all the time. This is a wonderful example of the kind of collective consciousness that develops in teaching and learning situations, with students making real contributions to forming the collective. The following are some selected quotes from the interview (Åkerlind, 1997):

I think of myself primarily as a learner. I don't see a one way flow of learning or teaching; it is a two way flow. And that is very important for me because it helps me not to stagnate, I want to keep developing. And the classroom is a very propitious environment for engaging others in that two way learning. You get to be alerted to some weaknesses in your thinking, to learn from a variety of students... You not only learn in an intellectual way, you learn about human relationships as well because an intellectual environment is also an actively social environment. So you get to really tap into all of these human resources. And we are lucky in Australia where there are lots of overseas students from non-English speaking backgrounds present in lots of the classrooms. You get to learn about... approaches to knowledge and human relations.

So this area of knowledge you've been wrestling with and cultivating, and you too are being cultivated by it, and you become entangled in it; the classroom becomes the area where you disentangle it, where you share whatever you've been learning with others. And I think the greatest thing about that is... and you go there to the classroom and once you tell or disseminate it suddenly it becomes something else that everyone else owns or shares or appropriates... That is your approach or your methodology or your angle, and it is beneficial that learning is shared in the classroom situation. Because I think I've crafted the view that research feeds into teaching and teaching feeds into research. So as you adjust your research your teaching will be adjusted accordingly and vice versa.

... and that knowledge necessitates the humility, the humility to learn and to listen and to be aware of other viewpoints and other cultural perspectives, a very valid thing. People talk about making the world a better place – to actually translate that into action more than any other profession.

So indirectly my research helps me to make my students think, you know, that there are always a wide range of viewpoints, and no matter what I say or what anybody else says, there is another view, another perspective. So for me that is really the best thing you could teach students – to think. Because information is no longer a problem – you can always go to the internet. But to really instil in them that particular ethos – because then you are really creating thinking citizens and thinking human beings.

Collective consciousness in research

A fundamental aspect of pedagogical relationships, of which teaching is by far the most common, is that people are supposed to have a shared object that they are oriented towards. It is this object that connects them in the first place. Pedagogical relationships are object-mediated relationships (note that 'object' is used in a very wide sense, as a synonym to 'topic', 'theme' or even 'capability'). Also the relationship between doctoral students and their supervisors are (or should be) object-mediated. The same principle applies to relationships between members of research groups, as is shown in the next section.

The inner life of university departments

Bennich-Björkman (in press) has recently presented an interesting study of creative and less creative research environments in the social sciences in Sweden. She found, according to our reading of her results, that in creative research environments researchers and doctoral students have the object of research in common; the object links them to each other. This does not imply, of course, that they all are dealing with the same problem, but that the problems are closely connected such that they can be seen as different, but related, parts of the same whole, or different aspects of it, or different perspectives on it, or slightly differing ways of seeing it. If this is the case the members of the research group are dependent on each other; they are drawing on each other's research and therefore everybody keeps supporting everybody else. Such a state of affairs has far-reaching implications for departmental life. In contrast, in departments that lack a shared object of research, senior people are not likely to go to seminars, and if they do, they do it to boost spirits. In departments with a shared object of research both senior and junior members of staff attend seminars because it is in their own interest to go there and hear what is being said, simply because what is being said is to a certain extent about their own research object. Similarly, when it comes to commenting on each other's manuscripts for instance, if there is a shared object of research, one's colleagues will do it because it is in their own interest. Otherwise, they may do it merely to be kind, friendly or polite. The reading and the comments will in all likelihood be more helpful in the former case. Whether or not a supervisor and PhD student are linked to each other through a shared research object will show in their discussions. If there is a shared object the supervisor will probably have the expertise necessary to support the student's work. Discussions will revolve around the object of research. If the supervisor and the student do not share the object of research the supervisor will probably lack the expertise necessary to support the student and the discussions will likely be of a more general nature, frequently with a methodological focus and a flavour of moral support.

So members of successful research groups making up creative environments were found to be linked to each other by means of shared objects of research. Another vital aspect of the relatedness of members of research departments is the difference between horizontal and vertical patterns of collaboration. The former refers to co-operation between equals and between members within a generational group that is proceeding towards occupying a dominant position within the organization. The latter refers to co-operation between members of the group separated by their positions, such as in the case of co-operation between supervisor and doctoral student. Such a relationship is likely to change when positions change, its nature becoming more transitional. Due to the positionally superior partner's awareness of its transitional nature, that person '... may not invest as much emotional capital in the relationship as anyone who is aware of the relationship being a lasting one (which is much more probable with the horizontal pattern). The vertical collaboration pattern is more likely to present traits of a more impersonal kind (Bennich-Björkman, in press)'.

From the point of view of the likelihood of survival of the research environment, a distinction between open and closed patterns of collaboration is superordinate to the distinction between vertical and horizontal partnerships. In the case of open collaboration there are bonds established between many different partners, creating temporary partnerships between many in the organization. In the case of closed co-operation there are only permanent partnerships between few. The research environment is more stable when the pattern of collaboration is open, as it is less vulnerable to partnership breakdowns. These conclusions resemble Granovetter's (1973) discussion of 'the strength of weak ties'.

Bennich-Björkman points to Edge and Mulkay's (1976) account of how radio astronomy as a field of study was established in Britain by two research groups: one at Cambridge and one at Jodrell Bank. The former was more successful, having two of its leading figures, Anthony Hewish and Martin Ryle, receiving a Nobel prize in 1973 and could be characterized by an open pattern of collaboration with each other; the leader, Ryle, had co-authored articles with everybody else. At Jodrell Bank the pattern of collaboration was more distinct and more closed, with stronger ties, but fewer of them: '... at Cambridge, stable supervisor/student relations are difficult to see, but at Jodrell Bank the ties are much more obvious' (Edge and Mulkay, 1976).

Shared objects of research

Bennich-Björkman (in press) suggests the rise of 'The Chicago School of Sociology' as an example of the decisive importance of turning research into a collective enterprise instead of seeing it primarily as an individual activity. Advancing sociology at the University of Chicago to an internationally leading position within just seven or eight years was a highly calculated undertaking. Our own understanding is that a necessary condition for bringing about collaborative working practices is a shared object of research. The Local Community Programme seemed to make all the difference. The city of Chicago itself became the shared object of research!

The collective consciousness of the research community

We now turn to quite a different problem and envisage a research community scattered at different places, not working together but having an object of research in common. In all likelihood members of such a community have partly overlapping and complementary ways of seeing their shared object of research. So if someone, sufficiently knowledgeable of the field, could explore the insights

– some common and some different – that the members of the research community have arrived at, our understanding of the object of research and of the problem to be solved, could possibly be enhanced to a considerable extent. In a way, this would amount to simulating what the collective consciousness of a research community would be like if it were really collective. We might this way even take a decisive step towards obtaining an answer we are looking for. There are actually such attempts on the way as we can see from the following example.

Caroline Baillie of Imperial College, London, in her plans for a research undertaking with the above orientation, writes as follows:

In composite materials the interface between fibre and matrix is crucially important in determining the ultimate mechanical properties. Stress is applied to the composite and is transferred through the matrix to the fibre, which reinforces it. If the composite is used to provide toughness, as in the case of a crash helmet, when an impact occurs the fibres will pull away from the matrix thus absorbing energy which would otherwise be transmitted through to the head. Hence a weak interface is required. In contrast, if fatigue strength is required as in an aircraft wing, then a strong interface under cyclic loading is needed. Trying to optimize the interface for strength and toughness for each particular fibre/matrix combination, at different processing conditions and at different service conditions, has been the subject of research for more than forty five years (for reviews see Baillie, 1991, Buxton, 1997). Particularly in the last ten years or so, it has become evident that little progress has been made.

In order to gain from the experience of the research and thinking within all the related engineering and science disciplines studying composite interfaces and within biology and medicine, we need to take a step back and immerse ourselves in the way people think within a research field. Hence a series of interviews would be conducted with chemists, biochemists, materials scientists and engineers about the way they conceive of interfaces within their object of study. I am presently commencing a pilot of such research with fellow materials scientists.

Marton and Booth (1997) suggest that experience is constituted between person and world, reflecting both, an internal relation that cannot exist without both its constituent parts. Being good at something is to be capable of experiencing or understanding it in a certain way. If we refer to the object of learning on the collective level as the complex of different ways of experiencing the phenomenon to be learned about, then we can construct an object of knowledge or build knowledge in this way. By interviewing a range of scientists and engineers from different disciplines, it is hoped that an understanding of what the interface issues are and how they might be solved might be created by developing a combined awareness of the concept of stress transfer across some kind of interface. These may then be tested experimentally (Baillie, 1997).

Collective consciousness in learning and in research

In the previous sections we dealt with 'Collective consciousness in learning' and 'Collective consciousness in research' one at a time. The former refers to the degree of awareness among teachers and students of the others' ways of seeing the shared object of knowledge; the latter refers to the degree of awareness among researchers' and graduate students of the others' ways of seeing the shared object of knowledge, the shared object of research. Do we have to deal with two distinctly different and separate entities? Are they separate in principle? Are they and should they be separate in practice? Objects of knowledge are obviously more narrowly defined and extend more in depth in research than in undergraduate studies. However, does this make the collective consciousness of each inevitably irreconcilable?

We have to address two questions in our search for an answer. First, are more and less advanced forms of thinking continuous or discontinuous? Second, if they are continuous, how distant are they from each other? Although we obviously cannot go very far with our generalizations (the concrete answers are contingent on the different domains of knowledge) we consider these two questions.

The first question concerns the issue whether more advanced (later) forms of thought build on earlier forms, or if thinking within highly specialized fields of scientific research is entirely unique for those fields and therefore does not have to do with thinking outside those fields. We have in fact already taken a stance on this question. The view of learning presented in Chapter 2 implies that whatever phenomenon we encounter, we make sense of it in terms of all that we have encountered earlier. We always see the world through our previous experiences and therefore without the previous experiences the world does not make any sense at all. This applies, we believe, also to highly specialized forms of human thinking such as research in natural science. In Chapters 1 and 4 we argued that the most fundamental thing about great scientific discoveries is that they introduce new ways of seeing something. We characterized a way of seeing something in terms of what aspects of the phenomenon are discerned and are objects of focal awareness at the same time. If learners manage to discern and focus simultaneously on the same aspects that were discerned and focused on simultaneously the first time it was done, they will basically see the phenomenon in the same way as it was seen at the time when the discovery was made.

The argument for the continuity of human thought is implicit in this line of reasoning. A more explicit position can also be derived from one of the most basic ideas underlying the phenomenological school of thought, according to its founder Edmund Husserl, which posits that all scientific knowledge develops from our experience of the life-world. Reflection originates in the pre-reflective experience, the sophisticated grows from the mundane and the world as experienced spontaneously is the soil from which the most advanced forms of scientific thinking spring (see, for instance, Husserl, 1970).

Piaget's genetic epistemology, which rests on the assumed parallelism between ontogenesis and phylogenesis, ie on the conjecture that individual (intellectual) development resembles collective historical development, offers a less explicit, but still pretty straightforward support of the idea of continuity (between different forms of thinking). The changing ideas the child develops about the physical world for instance, more or less follow the order of the appearance of those ideas in the history of humankind. Aristotelian ways of thinking are followed by Galilean ways of thinking, which are followed by Newtonian ways of thinking, just to take one example (see Piaget and Garcia, 1989).

Further arguments can be found in case stories of major figures in the history of the development of human knowledge; in a great number of instances we find that the full-blown scientific achievements were foreshadowed by ideas and ways of understanding appearing early in the individual's life. The life and work of Robert Burns Woodward (1917–74), one of the greatest chemists of this century who was awarded a Nobel prize in 1965 for his 'meritorious contributions to the art of organic synthesis', illustrates this excellently. As his daughter, Crystal Woodward, points out, his major achievement, the synthesis of various organic substances, was made possible by his remarkable ability '... for visualising three-dimensional molecular structures. It was as though he could move, in his mind, among these structures, viewing them from all angles, even foreseeing their transformations, as he effected, step-by-step, their pathways toward new possibilities and eventual targets' (Woodward, 1989).

Woodward began thinking about and trying to 'dream up' syntheses as early as the age of 12, when he worked out a synthesis for quinine, an outstanding scientific achievement. In this instance we find a perfect case of continuity within the individual, ranging from the very young boy's first ideas about chemical compounds to his finding of his orientation and idiosyncratic style as a researcher in his early teens and stunning scientific career. However, in Woodward's case we can find the link between learning and research not only in the individual but also in the social or pedagogical sense. In 1948 Woodward, who was American, visited Europe for the first time and gave one of his electrifying lectures at Imperial College in London. Derek Barton, who received a Nobel prize for his work on conformational analysis in 1969, was there and commented on it later:

> It was a brilliant demonstration of how you could take facts in the literature which seemed obvious and just by thinking about them, as he so ably did, interpret them and obtain the results and then go into the laboratory and *prove* it was the right result. That we thought was the work of genius... Ten years later (at Imperial College) our second year undergraduate students could do that problem, and... about 25% of them could get it right. Now, does that mean that in 1958 we had 25% mini-Woodwards in the second year class? No, of course it didn't. What it meant was that Woodward *had taught us organic chemists how to think* (Barton, 1981).

We do not think that collective consciousness in learning and collective consciousness in research have to be separate because of some so-called discontinuity between the forms of thought that constitute them. We think that there are continuities all the way in the world of human thought. Still, it could be the case that the two spheres are just so far apart that it is practically impossible to link them to each other. This is typically a question for which there cannot be a general answer. It has to be examined in relation to every domain of knowledge. Our impression is, however, that the distance between the research specialists' more advanced ways of thinking about their own field and the students' less advanced ways of thinking about the same field may be overestimated.

James D Watson was surely not an average science undergraduate when, as a 23-year-old, he came to Europe in 1951. He was no undergraduate at all; he was a microbiologist from Indiana University on a post-doctoral fellowship, the aim of which was to learn some biochemistry in Copenhagen. Nurturing a deep interest in DNA he was very impressed by an X-ray diffraction picture of DNA that Maurice Wilkens from King's College in London presented during a conference in Naples in April 1952. Watson decided to go to the Cavendish Laboratory in Cambridge to study crystallography in order to become able to use the X-ray diffraction technique for exploring the structure of the DNA molecule. In August 1952 he wrote to the Fellowship Board for permission to transfer his fellowship from Copenhagen to Cambridge. His proposal was turned down because the Board did not believe that he, without any qualifications in crystallography, could profit from being at Cavendish. Using the $1000 that he had saved during his stay in Copenhagen for another year in Cambridge, he decided to go there nevertheless. By early March, 1953, ie just about six months after his arrival in Cambridge, Watson, at the age of 25 and together with Francis Crick, had solved the structure of DNA and by doing so made one of the greatest scientific discoveries of this century.

We find in Watson's classic account of the discovery, *The Double Helix*, an excellent example of closeness to the frontiers of knowledge almost by definition being necessary for great discoveries in science (Watson, 1968). This closeness can be personal, as was in the case of Watson – he was basically in touch with all the important figures in the field all the time – or it can be gained by making use of scientific reporting as was the case with Einstein. We should remember that Einstein developed the special theory of relativity and his theoretical account of the Brownian movements and the law of photoelectric effect for which he was awarded a Nobel prize in 1922, among other things, as a not too successful graduate of a teachers' college in Zurich, working at the patent office in Bern, in his mid-20s. The conditions did not turn out to be too bad after all: 'On the one hand thanks to intensive reading in the middle of the ongoing discussion, on the other hand in an institutional periphery so he could find his central problems and contemplate them, without being absorbed by day to day research and being fixated with conventional approaches' (Fölsing, 1996, our translation).

There may very well be fields so highly specialized that it is difficult to discuss them in a meaningful way with undergraduates. We have, however, some difficulties with envisaging such a case. Trying to develop students' awareness of what is going on in the research field or what is happening at the frontiers of knowledge, must force researchers to focus on a more fundamental and less technical level. Students' reactions may bring out taken-for-granted aspects of the problems they are dealing with and therefore trigger their own reflections, an exercise probably very useful for both parties.

In other words, we find it both possible and meaningful to alert students to what their field of study may look like, from the point of view of highly specialized research about some of its aspects or parts, and to alert researchers to what their specialization may look like from the point of view of a more general interest in the field to which their specialization belongs. This may awake interest among some students and activate some of the vast potential that exists among people for solving urgent problems of science and human-kind. Not only may this enlighten students' minds but it may enlighten researchers' minds as well. The collective consciousness in learning should expand into the collective consciousness in research and vice versa.

Collective consciousness in organizations

Commonalities

In *The Division of Labour in Society* Emile Durkheim points out that the law is about consequences of actions contrary to rules never stated. The law does not command respect for the life of another (the rule) but it says that the assassin will be punished. The reason for this is that the rule is supposed to be known by everyone. Durkheim says: 'The totality of beliefs and sentiments common to average citizens of the same society forms a determinate system which has its own life; one may call it the *collective* or *common conscience* (Durkheim, 1964)'.

As Lukes (1973) points out, the French word 'conscience' (used by Durk-heim in the original) is ambiguous in that it embraces the two English words 'conscience' and 'consciousness'. To the extent that we can argue that Durkheim actually talks about collective consciousness (also) – and it seems, indeed, we can – it refers to that which is common in society.

The same expression has also been used with reference to certain groups within society, again denoting what is common to them:

... a specific emphasis, an emphasis on the collective consciousness and ... the forms of communications that carry it. Thus, culture includes shared knowledge, values, experiences and connected patterns of thought. But it does not only exist inside people's heads. The consciousness becomes shared only by communicating, sharing a language, understanding codes and messages, seeing the whole environment as loaded by meaning in a way that is reasonably similar for all – or at least for most – people (Hannerz, Liljeström and Löfgren, 1982, quoted and translated by Sandberg, 1997).

In a similar way, Bennich-Björkman (in press), drawing on the study discussed above, talks about 'a shared awareness of common goals' that characterize more successful and creative research environments and make them collective rather than merely individual establishments. As Sandberg (1997) points out, in management circles there are widespread beliefs about the importance of shared symbols, beliefs and visions unifying companies. To this Sandberg adds the importance of a shared understanding of the work carried out.

What is common and shared is surely fundamental to the collective consciousness of an organization. Most importantly we believe there have to be shared values and as far as learning and research are concerned there have to be shared objects of learning and research. However, as much as we acknowledge the importance of what is common, we want to emphasize complementarities as an equally vital component of collective consciousness, at least in the specific context of the university, where we use the concept.

So to begin with in a particular research environment, in addition to having a shared object of research and awareness of the goals, there are important and, in our understanding, most fruitful differences as well. Even if the object of research is shared, people are, as a rule, not dealing with identical problems; there are a number of different but complementary questions asked, relating to different aspects or parts of the shared object of research. The different contributions relate to each other and lend each other more meaning and greater power. Even the very same problem or component part of the shared object of research is understood somewhat differently, even in a group of highly specialized researchers. Such differences may be more or less subtle and more or less significant. When it comes to novel or unsolved problems it seems reasonable to us to consider the variation as a potential resource to draw on.

Regarding variation as an asset is more obvious when the variation itself is more obvious. Or when arrangements are made to constitute variation (in perspectives, insights and methodologies) around a shared object of research, as is the case with research undertakings that are set up to transcend narrow specializations, or even disciplinary boundaries. The carefully planned rise of the Chicago School of Sociology was a result of exactly such a cross-disciplinary undertaking with a shared object of research as the hub (the city of Chicago), skilfully orchestrated by the sociologist Albion W. Small, the economist Leon Marshall and the political scientist Charles Merriam.

Complementarities

As mentioned earlier, we find it very reasonable to see shared ideas, values and goals being fundamental components of the collective consciousness of an organization. They may not be explicit; they are often taken for granted and different members of the organization may have acquired them independently from each other, simply by being socialized into the same society, profession and discipline or the same research community. We are emphasizing more the differences and complementarities and in order to profit from the differences and the complementarities they must be brought out into the open; they must become visible. Only then will they enrich collective consciousness, which we defined earlier in terms of the extent members of a certain group, a certain organization are conscious of the ways in which phenomena of common concern appear to other members of the group or organization.

This does not necessarily imply that every individual thought should become known to everyone else. If certain members of the group become conscious of a certain variation in insights and in ways of seeing, and other members become conscious of the variation in other respects, given that there are substantial overlappings between members sharing insights about and perspectives on different things, then every insight, perspective and way of seeing will be linked with all the others through those overlappings. So, if A and B both are aware of certain things and B and C both are aware of some other things, we can say that A's and C's awarenesses are linked through B, and therefore A, B and C have a certain degree of collective consciousness. This accords very much with the Wittgensteinian notion of family relations that, like a thread, run through all members of a group without anything necessarily being common to them all. There are two ideas with collective consciousness: first, when we become aware of someone else's understanding of a certain phenomenon our own understanding of the phenomenon is likely to be enriched, a point we have made several times already. Second, when we become aware of someone else's understanding of a certain phenomenon this understanding gets related to what we know about the world (which is more or less different from what the other person knows about the world), therefore the very insight we became conscious of becomes enriched. Enrichment works in both directions.

Constituting, developing and making use of the collective consciousness requires things to be said and made visible; it takes interaction and communication that goes on and on across the place. An organization characterized by chains of interactions and communication is likely to foster trust in its members. Trust can be regarded as a result of co-operation and not necessarily as a precondition for it. Bennich-Björkman (in press) says when referring to the studies carried out by Axelrod (1984) and Gambetter (1988): 'And trust is conducive to scientific work by making it easier for people to launch bold ideas in a collective context. It lowers the perceived risk with exposing unfinished ideas. At the same time such exposure appears vital to the necessary critical examination and refinement of those ideas'.

Shared objects of research – again

So, how are frequent interactions and communication brought about? Drawing on our interpretation of Bennich-Björkman's research (in press), we have already answered this question: by having a shared object (or related objects) of research (or research problems). If this is the case,

> ... communication regarding research matters seems... almost inevitable. The choice of problems closely related to one or several of the others' problems further leads to a higher intensity of communication and, if the problems are close enough, in favourable cases to a mutual dependence where sharing and discussion of ideas can no longer be avoided since it is necessary in order to make progress with your own research. In a way it is possible to say that such an institutional setting as just outlined forces the individuals to interact. Interaction and communication *regarding research matters* are thus a consequence of crucial importance...[2]

If the advancement is a function of a comparatively high degree of collective consciousness, and if the degree of collective consciousness is a function of the extent of interaction and communication, and if interaction and communication are a function of the presence of a shared object of research, then we end up with a structural explanation of things that are often dealt with in psychological terms. This is exactly Bennich-Björkman's point. Where members of a research environment do not have a shared object of research it is very difficult, not to say impossible, to maintain an enduring high level of interaction, communication and co-operation (so far as research matters are concerned) even if there is a sincere intention among the members of the group to do so. If the research problems are too far apart, the costs of investments of time and interest in other people's research just grow too high in relation to the returns gained.

This structural explanation, neat in our view and supported by empirical findings, creates a paradox however. Even if the object of research can be defined more or less widely (in the case the Chicago School of Sociology the object of research was very widely defined, for instance), the focus on one shared object of research may work at the level of a particular research environment and it may work well for a smallish kind of department, but as a rule not for larger units such as schools, faculties and even less for an entire university. The paradox is that what unites at one level separates on a higher level. The shared object of research keeps together those who share it but separates them from those who do not.

This paradox prevails while the objects of knowledge are stratified only in one way, for instance along disciplinary lines. In that case there cannot be much of a collective consciousness at the university level.[3] If we want to link people to each other we have to define objects of research or at least objects of scholarly attention, in more than one way. If staff are connected to more than one object of research and if the combinations are sufficiently diverse, then all staff in the university could in principle be linked to each other through the above-mentioned, Wittgensteinian family relations. In the next chapter we will discuss two dominating ways of organizing knowledge: disciplinary and professional. We could therefore think of people having a professionally defined object of research or scholarly interest in common, while having different disciplinary defined objects of research and vice versa

Collective competence

At the end of Chapter 5 we gave our view of individual competence formulated mainly as a capability for dealing with novel and varying situations within certain specified spheres. We could in a similar way speak of the competence on the collective level, as the capability of an organization for dealing with novel and varying situations within certain specified spheres. 'Dealing with novel and varying situations' refers simply to the situations which the individual or the organization has to deal with in the future. We just wanted to underline that we believe that the situations that individuals or organizations will have to deal with are becoming increasingly novel and varying. We could as well have said that competence in our view is the capability for engaging in effective action within certain spheres.

As should be obvious from the previous section, we do not see the capability of an organization for handling its problems only as a function of individual capabilities present in the organization. 'Collective consciousness' actually reflects the extent to which the organization manages to draw on specific combinations of individual capabilities.

Collective consciousness, in the context of the university, presupposes shared objects of knowledge. It embraces both what is common – we talk about insights, perspectives and ways of seeing – and that which is different and therefore complementary.

In each particular case there is an optimal balance between the two. We believe that so far as research is concerned there is a need for much greater coherence, in terms of shared objects of research, but also for greater variation related to those objects.

Objects of research do not last forever, or at least are not dealt with forever. New objects of research emerge and have to be taken care of. The competence of the organization for doing so is a function of the individual competences available and the capability of the organization for making use of them. From the point of view of the varying demands the university is facing, varying individual competences that can be brought together are needed. If the stratification of objects of research is unidimensional, ie if each researcher is linked to one shared object of research only, efficiency may increase within the given specialization, while the competence for addressing problems outside that specialization may decrease. In the previous section we suggested that objects of research should be defined in more than one way and that staff should in general be grouped in more than one way. The collective consciousness feeds on individual competences, but it is also true that individual competences feed on the collective consciousness. The richer and more interconnected the collective consciousness is in the organization the more likely it is that the variation both between and within individual competences increases.

Again, the collective competence is a function of the level and mix of individual competences within the organization and of the extent to which the organization manages to draw on and further develop individual competences by organizing itself in such a way as to enhance the development of collective consciousness.

Collective competence on the national level

We now turn to the national level. If, within different disciplinary and professionally defined fields of knowledge, groups of researchers and graduate students take on shared objects of research, not only at a single university but within all universities throughout an entire country, the objects of research are likely to be chosen and defined differently at different universities. Each one is then likely to become leading in its own specialization within the country and probably quite competitive internationally as well. Somewhat paradoxically such specialization at the local level and differentiation on the national level is bound to yield greater diversity from the perspective of the system within the country. It will reach higher levels in more fields. In addition, by being more varied and more diversified it will be better off when it comes to handling the varying and unpredictable demands of the future. This line of reasoning is also relevant in relation to the training of doctoral students discussed briefly in the previous section. We indicated there our agreement with the point made by Bennich-Björkman (in press) that unbounded options for a choice of topic for PhD theses may not always be an advantage and this may sound a bit off-putting. Should doctoral students not be driven by their interests and inclinations? Is not an independent mind something important for someone who wants to become a researcher? The objection might not sound completely unreasonable in the context of one single department. However, on the national level, where different departments of different universities and possibly different research groups within them focus on different specializations, there should be a fair chance for every doctoral student to find the right place, given that doctoral students are prepared to move. In countries like Sweden and Australia, for instance, the problem is that they do not seem to be too keen on that and, of course, this works in both ways. Applicants for doctoral studies with heterogeneous interests restrict the departments' possibility and eagerness to specialize. Conversely, the departments will fail to satisfy those prospective doctoral students seeking a specialized environment matching their particular interests.

We have discussed the collective competence of the university system at the national level from the point of view of research and doctoral studies. A more differentiated system would be one where groups of researchers and doctoral students focus on shared objects that differ from university to university within the same disciplinary and professionally defined field of knowledge. This would probably yield a system which is internationally more competitive within each specialization and taken together represents a more varied and therefore wider collective competence on the national level. It would be better equipped to handle novel and unpredictable challenges.

We mentioned earlier the need for multiple stratification of knowledge; the need for the same staff to share different objects of knowledge in different combinations of people. We argued that this is how a collective consciousness can be formed. This principle applies at the national level as well. There must be ways in which staff and doctoral students from different universities come together in contexts grounded on principles other than the various specializations. The ideal is a highly differentiated and integrated system both on the level of single universities and on the national level as well. Such a system would be ideal, not only from the point of view of research and training of doctoral students, but also from the point of view of undergraduate studies.

Before concluding this section we would comment briefly on the collective competence of the national system as reflected in the individual competences of the graduates – as seen from a collective (organizational, national) perspective.

We are tempted to believe that more competent individuals within a nation imply a more competent nation. This is not necessarily true, however. Once again, the whole is more than the sum of its parts. The competence of a collective is not only – or perhaps not even mainly – a function of the competence of the individual members of the collective, but of the particular pattern or mix of competences represented by them.

As pointed out above, not only individuals, but also collectives, are facing an increasingly unpredictable future. How can a nation prepare for dynamic changes, diversity and variation in circumstances, conditions and demands? The fact is that, just as is the case with organizations, greater variation in the competences of the workforce enhances the likelihood of the match between individual competences and the varying demands on the nation. In times of dynamic change, stability can only be achieved through variation (Marton and Marton, 1997). Taken seriously, this line of reasoning implies that it can be a good idea to let the students choose and combine different subjects as freely as possible as we suggest in Chapter 10.

Objects of knowledge

As should be obvious from the above, when we talk about collective consciousness we refer to the consciousness of *something*. Collective consciousness emerges when different people are conscious of the same phenomenon – or object of knowledge – and are conscious to a greater or lesser extent, of each other's ways of seeing, experiencing and thinking about that phenomenon. In what sense can we talk about the same phenomenon? The most obvious is in the sense of stating that it is the same phenomenon, regardless of who is seeing, experiencing or thinking about it. It is independent of these human beings who may not be able to capture (see, experience and understand) the phenomenon as such, but they may form an idea of it. The relationship between 'the phenomenon as such' and 'the phenomenon as understood' is then a relationship between 'the real thing' and a more or less distorted image of it. This is how most people would think about the relationship between subject and object, the experience and the experienced or 'a dualistic ontological commitment'. 'Dualistic' because subject and object are seen as separate; they are two (obvious as this may seem), 'ontological' because it is about the nature of reality (ontology has to do with what we consider to be real) and commitment, because we can hardly prove our view of reality. Such an assumption or way of seeing has certain implications.

Our own starting point, as stated earlier, is different in that everything we experience, we experience in a number of qualitatively different ways. Accordingly, also the nature of reality can be seen in different ways. Dualistic ontology is just one way of thinking, although admittedly by far the most frequent in Western thinking, about the relationship between person and world (or between subject and object). Instead we adopt a relational position. We do not see subject and object, person and world, and experience and experienced as separate. We see them intertwined and argue that neither of the two in each pair could be the way they are without the other. The idea that human beings would not be the kind of beings they are without the world in which they live may be fairly easy to accept. It is probably a bit harder with the idea that the world we live in would not be the same world without us, especially if we think of the material world. The Moon, the Milky Way and the platypus must surely be the same with or without human beings. The fact is that the Moon, the Milky Way and the platypus are talked about, thought about and conceptualized in one way or another. We cannot describe anything without a describer being present in the description. Our position is not that the reality we experience is just our construction (this would be the thesis advocated by the constructivists). Reality is, in our view, *constituted* through the mutual and intertwined emergence of humans and their world. We believe that our reality reflects the world as much as it reflects ourselves. Could we then imagine a world beyond human experience and human thoughts? We cannot. As soon as we try to capture what such a world is like we have already invaded it with our thoughts and our words. The only Moon available to us is a humanly experienced, conceptualized and computed Moon; we cannot grasp the Milky Way, nor the platypus in other than humans' ways. What they are is what they are for us. There could be other beings, from other parts of the universe, who could describe the world beyond human ways of describing it. However, that would be their ways and indeed they could not go beyond what *they* are capable of experiencing. Nobody can, in fact.

Does this imply that the world is exactly what we see, that no distinction can be made between our way of seeing the world and the world in another and more inclusive sense? No, it does not. As we see the world differently, our way of seeing it cannot be identical with what it is. A phenomenon could be understood as the complex of all the conceivable ways in which it can be experienced, made sense of and thought about – now and in the future. This is a rather abstract concept, implying that every phenomenon is inexhaustible, in the sense that there can always be new things seen and discovered about it. The relationship between our way of seeing a phenomenon and the phenomenon (as a complex of all the possible ways of seeing it) is a part–whole relationship. In the dualistic ontology this relationship is a relationship between the phenomenon as seen (distorted) and the phenomenon as such (as it really is).

As stated above, an ontological commitment is exactly a commitment. It cannot be proved true, or false for that matter but we can examine its implications and the implications of a relational view are far-reaching.

First, acts of knowing and objects of knowing are not separate. Our knowledge reflects both in spite of the fact that the acts of knowing are usually not seen; they are tacit.

Second, our knowing is a collective enterprise. Other ways of seeing a phenomenon than the one representing current received wisdom are also parts of our way of knowing the phenomenon. This does not imply that anything can be a part of a phenomenon. In spite of its inexhaustibility, there are constraints on how a particular phenomenon can be experienced.

Third, continuity within individuals, dealt with above, can be made sense of in terms of this framework. Learning is then not so much replacing one view of a phenomenon with another, more correct one, but a widening of the space of different views available to the individual.

Fourth, the continuity between individuals, also dealt with above, can be interpreted in terms of the idea of phenomena seen as complexes of the different ways in which they can possibly be viewed. Different people's differing thoughts about the same phenomenon reside within the same space of ideas (ways of seeing the phenomenon in question).

Fifth, if accounts of the world, held provisionally true, reside in and derive their meaning from complexes of different ways of seeing the world, then knowing the world is to a considerable extent knowing people's ways of thinking about it. (This may, in fact, sound stranger than it is – a scientific theory, for instance, is very much understood through knowing what accounts it is an alternative to.) So when assisting other people to develop new insights about the world, the best thing we can do is to learn about their way of thinking partly because this probably is the most efficient pedagogy (see Chapter 6) and partly because by doing so we enrich our own understanding of the world.

Sixth, if for each phenomenon we envisage a complex of conceivable ways in which it can be seen and if we consider all the various phenomena in the world to be connected to each other, those different complexes of ways of seeing must be considered in relation to each other. Such a complex of complexes is in fact the world as experienced, or rather all the possible ways in which the world can be experienced. This is a shared world, a collective world, the joint capability of humankind to experience the world. As our shared world comprises all the ways in which we can think about reality, we are all contributing to it. Each single individual makes it into a richer world; without each single individual it would be a more impoverished world. Our particular view of learning, resting on a particular ontological commitment, has ethical implications as a consequence. It cannot be separated from respect for other people's ways of seeing the world. Even if certain ways of seeing certain phenomena are indeed more powerful than others in certain contexts, all the different ways of conceiving the world have to have bestowed upon them equally genuine interest and respect.[4]

The ethics of learning

The last point in the previous section relates to the classical question of the relation between what is good and what is right or, if we narrow it down just slightly, does a powerful way of learning have to rest on sincere ethical commitments? We are not too keen on addressing this question in general. We would argue, however, that the particular view of learning we subscribe to is a powerful one and that it has important ethical implications (or that it builds on important ethical commitments). This is not to say that the good and the right are universally intertwined, but to say that under certain circumstances good ethical principles go with the right (yielding powerful learning).

What follows from our line of reasoning above is that we grasp the world more fully by taking part in each other's differing ways of seeing it. This means that not only students are supposed to learn from their teachers but also teachers from their students and in research we are supposed to learn from each other, too. By linking different ways of viewing the object of research we gain a fuller understanding of it. So in studying, as well as in research, we should strive for increasing *collective consciousness*, by pooling our ideas, thoughts and ways of experiencing phenomena of shared interest and doing so, implies – or rather rests on – respect for other people's ways of seeing the world.

As we briefly implied in Chapter 4 (page 85), Björklund (1990) argues that the research connection (ie the connection between teaching and research) means above all '... opening the scholarly discourse to the student, inducing her to see as her own arguments, the arguments for and against standpoints constituting the scientific exchange of opinion' . 'Scholarly discourse' implies that if we want to convince you about something (above all having an impact on your way of looking at reality) we want to convince you exactly on the same grounds that convince us. This is sharply different from persuasion through the exercise of power: 'Unless the teacher conveys the impression that the (students) are (her) equals in the sense of being capable of grasping the grounds which (she) presents for the opinions to be learned, an incentive will be lost and searching will degenerate into persuasion'.

The scholarly discourse is discourse between equals. The most fundamental thing about the systematic search for knowledge, which we call research, is the realization of the fact that 'I can be wrong'. Without such an insight research becomes meaningless and 'scholarly discourse' impossible.

Jacob Bronowski's TV series *The Ascent of Man*, broadcast by the BBC in 1972 and later published as a book (Bronowski, 1973), dealt with the history of science in its broadest sense. In a moving scene he relates the principle of uncertainty or, as he prefers to call it, the principle of tolerance, suggesting that all knowledge is limited, including the evil deeds of those who did not think that their knowledge was limited. Bronowski is at the pond of the Auschwitz prison camp; squatting down, he dips his hand into the water to take up a handful of mud, perhaps containing remains of his relatives flushed out with the smoke from the crematorium, and says:

> It is said that science will dehumanize people and turn them into numbers. That is false, tragically false. Look for yourself. This is the concentration camp and crematorium at Auschwitz. This is where people were turned into numbers. Into this pond were flushed the ashes of some four million people. And that was not done by gas. It was done by arrogance. It was done by dogma. It was done by ignorance. When people believe that they have absolute knowledge, with no test in reality, this is how they behave. This is what men do when they aspire to the knowledge of gods.
>
> Science is a very human form of knowledge. We are always at the brink of the known, we always feel forward for what is to be hoped. Every judgment in science stands on the edge of error, and is personal. Science is a tribute to what we can know although we are fallible. In the end the words were said by Oliver Cromwell: 'I beseech you, in the bowels of Christ, think it possible you may be mistaken' (Bronowski, 1973).

Endnotes

1. The Swedish academic year runs from about 1 September to 20 January (autumn term) and from about 20 January to mid-June (spring term)

2. In passing we might mention that Bennich-Björkman stresses the relevance of this line of reasoning for the teaching and supervision of doctoral students. She is comparing what she calls the American and the German models. While the former, very much characterized in the above quote and emphasizing the collective nature of research, creates a frame around the individual, the latter, emphasizing the radically individual nature of research through students' unbounded choices of topics for doctoral work '... provides a platform, a horizontal line, from which the individuals "take off" in parallel courses'. While 'the chosen few' will survive in the German model, many will never complete their work. The American model is much more likely to draw on the contributions of most students and to support them in completing their degress.

3. This applies so far as staff are concerned. Students cross these boundaries simply by studying different things. One could argue that they keep the university together.

4. The tricky issue is, of course, what counts as different ways of seeing the same phenomenon. We have to establish criteria in terms of the interconnectedness of different ideas (of the same phenomenon).

Chapter 9

Quality and qualities

The search for 'quality'

There has been a significant interest in most Western democracies in the past decade or so in matters concerned with quality assurance and this has included quality assurance in universities. The meaning of this term will be discussed below but what has emerged is that many organizations are demanding assurance from others that the quality of the processes and the outcomes related to their interaction will be of an appropriate standard. They have sought that assurance either by demanding that the quality of the outcomes be demonstrated directly or by requiring the other entity to show that there are appropriate quality maintenance processes in place so that the quality of outcome is assured.

The interest in quality assurance, especially at a government level, is linked to the growing concern in recent decades that government should get value for money from the institutions it funds. Governments had a particular question in mind: is quality going to suffer if resource levels reduce or is quality independent of resources beyond a certain level? As a background to this development we can mention, as an example, that in the period from 1989 to 1996 the student population in higher education in England grew from 761,000 to 1,270,000, an 87 per cent increase. At the same time government funding per student allocated to universities dropped from £6,672 to £4,479, a 33 per cent decrease, with the inflationary effect disregarded (Clark, 1997). The trend is very similar in the 1990s in Sweden both as increase in student numbers and as reduction in funding per student are concerned (Bauer, Marton, Askling and Marton, in press).

Currently in the USA, where quite disparate educational streams are seen as parts of the system of higher education, more than 85 per cent of an age cohort have a high-school diploma and about half of them are enrolled in college. In other countries such as Australia and England, for instance, there has been a recent fusion of such disparate streams into a single system of higher education.

In Sweden a major reform of higher education was undertaken in 1993 with the view of developing the country's intellectual resources for the new knowledge society. Generally, knowledge is increasingly considered as the most important productive factor both at the company and the national level when it comes to international competitiveness.

While the felt importance of higher education both on the national and the individual level keeps growing, confidence in those institutions is falling. In the USA, whites with college degrees earn 41 per cent more than whites with only high-school diplomas; for blacks the differential is even greater. Nevertheless, while 61 per cent of a representative sample of US adults expressed a great deal of confidence in the institutions of higher education in 1966, the corresponding figure was 36 per cent in 1981 and 27 per cent in 1995 (Graham, Lyman and Trow, 1995).

Against such a background, the recent pressure for information about how well institutions of higher education are doing makes a great deal of sense. The pressure is coming from politicians, business and industry, students, prospective students, the parents of students and prospective students as well as the general public, especially taxpayers.

So the recent urge for accountability, quality control and quality assurance can be understood against the background of increasing student numbers (the proportion of an age group probably going up to 50 per cent in many countries in the not too distant future), decreasing funding per student, increasing heterogeneity among university systems, increasing importance of higher education and decreasing trust in it, and a general concern that there is value being provided by universities for the taxpayer dollar.

In addition, the demands for accountability, quality control, quality assurance and the like relate to the question that has always been a burning issue in the history of universities, the balance between public (or external) regulation and self-regulation.

National and regional governments, whose major interaction with universities has been through funding of agreed programmes of research, and the teaching and community service, are among those who first began discussing quality assurance with universities. In addition, industry and business as potential employers of university graduates have increased their status as university stakeholders. At one time the quality of university student learning might have seemed to be an internal matter for the university, but it has now become a topic of more general community interest and a focus of government attention during the late 1980s and the 1990s.

This begs the question as to whether any of the quality demands referred to and the quality assurance processes they instigate relate to the qualities of the universities *per se* or to the qualities developed by graduates. This chapter is concerned centrally with that relationship. It is examined from a number of perspectives: a definition of terms, a historical perspective on the way universities and academics have dealt with their internal and external relations in the past and ways they have addressed the quality of teaching and learning, and a discussion of the principles underlying educational quality assurance and which underpin 'the university of learning'.

Defining 'quality'

No author of a document describing any substantial organization in the 1990s would feel able to omit the word 'quality' from the text. During the last decade, the word quality has been used almost as a slogan by many individuals and organizations to indicate that the politically correct approach is being taken and, as a consequence, the frequency of use of this word has increased exponentially. In the process, with the word 'quality' being used in an increasing range of contexts and with a multiplicity of purposes, its meaning has become confused. The way it is used often seems to imply that its meaning is self-evident, but unfortunately that is often not so.

The different ways the word 'quality' is being used include the following:

- the quality of X in this organization is of a high standard.
- X is of high (or low) quality in this organization.
- This is a quality organization ('it provides quality services').
- This organization has quality ('Quality is considered vital to [this organization]').

The first two ways use quality as a noun and there is an implication of some comparative judgement about quality being made. The third usage may have a similar element but it is more ambiguous in its meaning. The fourth is a nonsense usage. As Sachs and Ramsden (1995) indicate, it leaves the question 'quality of what?' unanswered.

Dictionary definitions

The *Oxford Dictionary* focuses on two kinds of meaning for the noun 'quality'. They are concerned either with excellence or with attributes; that is, we can speak of some object being of high quality, meaning that it has a high degree of excellence, or we can speak about the object having a particular quality or qualities, such as durability, brightness or usefulness.

These definitions are not without complexity. At first glance, it might be thought that the quality movement of the past decade has been using the word only in the former sense, that is, in terms of excellence. However, we have to ask what it is that allows a judgement to be made that an object is of high quality. It must be that the perceived qualities of the object contribute to that judgement. This means that certain characteristics of the object contribute to the judgement about its quality, as does the capacity of the judge to perceive those characteristics. The latter introduces a contextual element to the process.

Secondly, the outcome of that judgement must depend on the value placed by the judge, or by those who devised the criteria for judgement, on particular qualities compared with others. This is a second contextual element.

Thirdly, any simple statement that an object is of high quality begs the question: high relative to what? There is therefore a third contextual element to be dealt with.

Qualities of universities

So, for any statement that something is of high quality to be meaningful, a range of contextual detail is necessary, including detail about its qualities. This has not always been the case in discussions of quality in university education. Governments, vice-chancellors, members of the community and academics have talked about quality universities, world-class universities and the like, as if such statements are unambiguous. Yet each university will have a variety of qualities: a specific university may:

- be well or badly managed
- produce graduates who easily find employment or graduates who have difficulty using their education for work, or both, either generally or in specific areas
- enjoy good morale among staff or have problems with staff who are frustrated and angry with management
- help students develop an interest in lifelong learning or focus students' attention on learning for their first job on graduation
- encourage students to use their time at university for personal growth, beyond vocational or intellectual goals, or it may not
- be financially profitable or in financial difficulties
- provide a pleasant physical environment for students or a cluttered, unpleasant environment
- have a strong or a weak research profile
- have strong connections with business and industry, or not
- have a good or a poor equal opportunity record, and so on.

Not all of these qualities are correlated. A profitable university is not necessarily one which produces the best graduates. A university which has the highest graduate employment rate is not necessarily the one with the most pleasant campus. It is not enough to say that a specific university is of high quality or is a world-class university. The contextual aspects need to be spelt out for any such statement to have meaning. What qualities are being referred to, what criteria for judgement are being employed and what are the value systems of those applying the judgement?

In much of the discussion of quality with respect to universities in recent decades, the external focus has predominantly been on the existence of quality assurance mechanisms, the financial management of the university and its research record. However, inside universities and among academics, there has been a strong scepticism about such a focus on quality assurance mechanisms, which are sometimes seen to be at the expense of a focus on the quality of student learning *per se*.

The meanings of various 'quality' terms

Reference has already been made to the plethora of terminology containing the word 'quality'. These include:

- quality control
- quality assessment
- quality audit
- quality assurance
- quality improvement
- quality improvement cycle
- quality management
- quality development Total Quality Management (TQM).

In a university context, where there has been a historical interest and contemporary focus on continual improvement in the quality of student learning, these terms need to be reinterpreted from their original context – industrial manufacturing – to the educational context. Figure 9.1 gives some order to the terminology and relationship among the various terms.

The idea of quality improvement has been a quest of universities since their beginning; it is the cornerstone of what a university is about when it talks of advancing knowledge. To make improvement, it is necessary to be aware of the current status of the knowledge, process or outcome that is being improved. This implies evaluation of some kind, either implicit or explicit. It also implies some follow-up which makes use of the outcomes of evaluation in undertaking research and modifying existing practices, with the expectation that this will lead to improvement. It makes sense then to engage in follow-up evaluation of what the effects of the changes have been, including as a check as to whether the expected improvement has occurred in response to the changes made. This is an iterative process because the follow-up evaluation is likely to lead to further potential improvement processes.

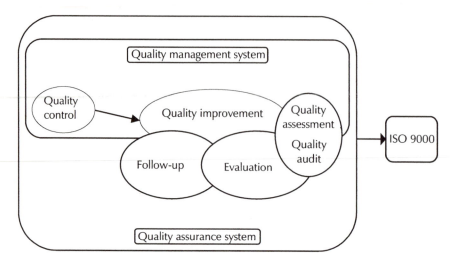

Figure 9.1: *Relationship between 'quality terms'*

This overall process is commonly referred to as a quality improvement cycle or quality circle and demonstrates that 'quality' is dynamic. Processes are never perfect; the circumstances at any one time differ from those previously and demand different outcomes, however subtle those differences might be.

> The idea of 'quality' as a goal that, once attained, remains unchanged and unquestioned into the future, does not fit reality. The quest for quality in any activity is a constant struggle to maximize the extent to which goals have been achieved despite constantly changing contexts: contexts which not only affect both process and outcome but also catalyse changes in goals. Quality is never attained in an absolute sense; it is constantly being sought. The notion of improvement in such a system is necessarily goal-directed, but not in a narrow, static sense; it is a dynamic process, with the goals also constantly under review (Bowden, 1997).

Given the external accountability of universities, made more explicit in recent decades as those who provide resources to universities have demanded an accounting of how well the resources have been used, the quality improvement cycles described above have had to be formalized. As a consequence, the evaluative elements referred to have been differentiated and two aspects that have been delineated are quality assessment and quality audit. While in recent years, the use of such terms has not been uniform, there has generally been a distinction made between activities designed to measure the quality of some aspect of the university (eg assessment of the worthwhileness of the research that goes on in the university or the employability of its graduates) and those designed to demonstrate the existence of appropriate internal processes likely to lead to high quality outcomes. The former, which is a detailed summative process, is referred to as 'quality assessment'. The latter is termed 'quality audit'.

Most of what has been described has assumed that the active participants in a particular area are engaged in quality improvement cycles and that the assessment or audit processes are some kind of check on the efficacy of those cycles. There is another way of operating and that is for some central authority to prescribe certain requirements and for outputs to be continually checked against the stated criteria. This is a quality control process which may be in addition to or in place of the more distributed process already described. The idea of quality control originated from the manufacturing industry (although not all manufacturers adopt it as we will report later in this chapter). It is normally based on the assumption that if a process is carried out in exactly the same way each time, then the quality of the product will be consistent, that is, its quality will be controlled.

The idea of quality control is not easily applied to learning in universities; quality assurance for teaching and courses are complex, not least because the activities with which they are concerned are not simple ones. The notions of product, manufacturer, supplier, customer and other terms, which are the common parlance of TQM systems outside educational contexts, do not readily translate into university functions, even though attempts are made to use them in higher education. The TQM approach assumes that the product is a given and that quality management is merely a question of controlling the process: we will argue that a fundamental aspect of quality management at universities is the process of finding out what we want to produce, that we cannot take the product as given.

> Would the term 'product' be best applied to the degree programme (as a syllabus and set of experiences in which someone can enrol) or to the actual degree conferred following successful participation in such a programme, or to the person who has graduated? Who is the 'supplier'? Is it the government which subsidizes many of the programmes, the university which endorses and runs them, academics who devise and teach within them, or students themselves who are in fact the only ones capable of producing the final outcome? Certainly, only the student could reasonably be assigned the role of 'manufacturer'; everyone else has a supporting, facilitating role (Bowden, 1997).

All of the quality-oriented processes, to whatever degree and in whatever mix they exist, need to be managed; the structure established for that activity is termed the quality management system. An example of a quality management system is the TQM approach referred to above. This is a particular system based on detailed specification of procedures which, in some respects, make the assumption that if the process is undertaken as prescribed then the outcomes will be of high quality.

All of the activities and procedures described above, encompassing the activities defined by the terms 'quality improvement', 'evaluation', 'follow-up', 'quality assessment', 'quality audit', 'quality control' and 'quality management', contribute to the characteristics of the organization's quality assurance (QA) system. It is by these mechanisms that the organization tries to assure its stakeholders, to greater and lesser extents depending on the nature of the QA system in place, that the quality (of processes, outcomes, products) is adequate. That is not to say that the mere existence of such elements provides outcomes of adequate quality. The way they are used and their relationship to each other and to organizational planning and development processes are crucial; they need to be consistent and applied in an integrated fashion (Boyle and Bowden 1997).

Finally, there is an international system of standards such as ISO 9000 which certifies that the QA system of a particular organization is adequate. In many cases for instance, without ISO certification, an organization is barred from tendering for, say, government contracts. Whether ISO certification serves more than a political purpose is a question that each person and organization need to consider for themselves. Some organizations have found difficulty in integrating ISO processes with a developmental improvement approach to quality of products and services. Others have developed a balanced approach in which the primary focus of the quality system is on improvement of the quality of products and services but ISO 9000 certification and the underlying processes associated with ISO have been incorporated whenever they support the primary goal.

One such company is the Swedish-based, international manufacturer, SCA Mölnlycke, which has a quality management system that is not designed around ISO 9000. Rather the company has established team processes, all of which are focused on quality improvement directed towards locally established missions. These local mission statements, which vary with area, market and time, fit within a company vision statement which, while fairly stable, is also subject to review. Its major features are a concern to manufacture continually improving products and to have increasingly satisfied customers. As a consequence, the company's processes will have to be continually reviewed and modified, if the vision for the company is to be realized. This involves cross-functional, international teams which try to integrate the ways of operation of the various working areas of the company with the perspective of customers and other clients. In this way, the manufacturing processes and the activities of company employees reflect both the company framework and the framework of the changing client base. ISO 9000 certification is sought where and when appropriate but it is certification of the quality processes developed by the company within the framework described above, rather than design of the company's quality processes directly using the ISO 9000 standard clauses as a base. We will return to the SCA Mölnlycke example later when we discuss other aspects of quality management processes.

A practical definition of 'quality'

Boyle and Bowden (1997) suggest that:

> ... most progressive thinkers and those who are motivated by positive practical outcomes, have moved on from the endless esoteric debates on conceptions of 'quality'... There is strong support for conceiving of quality and quality improvement in terms of expressed values, purpose and goals. Such a definition is built on the now widely accepted fundamental definition of quality offered by Ball (1985) as 'fitness for purpose'. In the context of purposeful organizations and enterprises, quality can only be defined in relation to articulated values, purposes, and desired processes, experiences and outcomes.

Formal education has to become a normative, purposeful activity based on values and goals shaped by the interests of a range of stakeholders. Its dynamic nature derives from the variation in such influences across stakeholders and time. This means that, within this definition, the purposes are also subject to review at all times. We underline the idea in the last sentence of the quote above and emphasize the importance of adequate and appropriate determination of purposes as an integral aspect of quality processes.

As mentioned earlier, finding out our aims in terms of the nature of the capabilities is probably the most profound contribution to the improvement of learning. In higher education we have to find out again and again what our products are and what they should be. In Chapter 2 we argued that students should develop the capability to engage in effective action in novel situations within their field of expertise. So this is one sense of 'purpose' in 'fitness for purpose'. Furthermore, we argued that effective action in a situation springs from seeing that situation in an effective way. The capability of engaging in effective action amounts therefore to the capability of seeing certain situations in certain ways. 'Quality' in the university context has a lot to do with the quality of learning and the quality of learning has a lot to do with the qualities of different ways of seeing.

Institutional autonomy and academic freedom

Two fundamental issues need to be addressed if quality management of teaching and learning in universities is to be discussed adequately; they are academic freedom and university autonomy. These two concepts are always raised for debate whenever government agencies are commissioned to investigate the quality of academic functions of universities or whenever university management introduces any evaluative system directed at the functions of its academics. What are the cluster of ideas that these terms represent, where do they come from, in what way are they different in the 1990s from their meanings decades or even centuries ago and what is their relevance for quality management in the twenty-first century university?

Academic freedom

The origin of the term 'academic freedom' is the medieval intellectual tradition associated with universities as quasi-ecclesiastical institutions (Russell, 1993) and its latter-day expression can be found in the 1988 UK Education Bill which suggested that academics should be free within the law '... to question and test received wisdom, and to put forward new ideas and controversial or unpopular opinions without placing themselves in jeopardy of losing their jobs or privileges they may have at their institutions'.

This proposition is usually represented in terms of its contribution to the good of the community rather than as a benefit to the individual academic *per se*. Indeed, without public good flowing from it, society would be reluctant to embrace the concept at all. Russell (1993) suggests that '... to argue a claim for academic freedom in the national interest imposes on university champions an intellectual discipline for which they will be none the worse. It will at least force them to attempt, in their own minds, a distinction between academic freedom and their own self-interest'.

In many respects, Western society does embrace the difficult to justify idea that university work is somehow independent (of sectional and commercial interests), free from bias, and true. The number of advertising agencies that rely on slogans like 'university tests prove' is evidence that they at least believe that the community perceives universities in that way.

The 1988 UK Education Bill does capture the essence of the concept of academic freedom, in our view; other concepts such as academic tenure and autonomy of academics are associated with the principles of academic freedom, but not identical with it. However, the distinction Russell makes between academic freedom and academic self-interest is a crucial one because the way that the term 'academic freedom' is sometimes used in industrial processes, such as enterprise-bargaining negotiations, seems to relate more to the interests of the individual than the community. This raises some questions. In what ways do the more personal issues of tenure and autonomy link to the public good nature of academic freedom? Can academic freedom be preserved in a context of diminishing tenure and increasing scrutiny of the work of individual academics, especially in regard to teaching and learning activities?

More central to the purposes of this chapter is the relation between academic freedom as defined above and academic autonomy. Do academics require an open licence to do whatever they wish, without sanction, in order for academic freedom to be preserved for the public good? The way that question has been expressed invites a negative response and a more useful question is: when a government or a university introduces a quality assurance and/or quality improvement system, which necessarily places some limitations on individual academic autonomy, what is the nature of the effects on academic freedom and its public benefits? Is there a way to maximize the public good through the benefits of such quality systems while preserving essential academic freedom and thereby maintaining its continuing benefits for the community? This chapter will draw out principles which maximize the complementarity of quality systems and academic freedom.

University autonomy

The concept of university autonomy has common origins with that of academic freedom. They are related ideas but different in their application. Arblaster (1974) deals with their relationship and makes an important addition by including students within the concept of academic freedom:

> ... the social function of education is critical, questioning, experimental and innovatory. It is at the same time geared primarily not to economic needs, nor to the employment prospects of young people, but to their needs as complete human beings, as individuals and as citizens. If these are, or ought to be, the principal commitments of education, then clearly both the freedom of the individual teacher and student,[1] and the autonomy of the educational system as a whole, are of the greatest importance – not only to educationalists, but society as a whole.

Arblaster argues that high levels of state control or financial dependence on private industry are inconsistent with that view. He suggests that both the control and dependence are increasing and that both are inspired, or reinforced, by the belief that the chief social function of education is to serve the immediate or future needs of the economy.

> Instead of allowing individual educational institutions to spend public money according to their own self-chosen educational priorities, governments are increasingly allocating money for development in particular areas and subjects which they deem to be of 'national' importance and, conversely, withholding money from subjects which, in their eyes, serve no obviously useful purpose... The overall effect... is to diminish the independence of tertiary education (Arblaster, 1974).

This is linked to the notion that people (the taxpayers and the government) provide money 'for a purpose'. This is taken up by Stephens and Roderick (1975) who relate the increasing interest of government in university affairs to increasing financial costs and to doubts about the quality of universities' contribution to society: 'The escalating costs which governments have to bear have already led to a demand for public accountability... It is seriously being questioned whether society is getting value for money and it is suggested that universities be subjected to cost-benefit analysis'.

In the decades following these quoted comments, there has been no alteration of the trends described but there have been arguments, then and now, that they are appropriate actions. Russell (1993) sees the problem as:

> ... a clash between two valid principles. The case for free academic enquiry must be unanswerable, for without it, what is the value in having academics at all? Yet, at the same time, the principle that public money ought to be accounted for is at the heart of democratic principles. Taxes are voted by consent, and that consent must rest on some understanding about how they are to be used... Any right to receive public money must carry with it a reciprocal duty, and where there is a duty, there must be accountability for its performance... Yet there is a point where the demand for accountability becomes, in the literal and not the legal sense, ultra vires; it is beyond their powers. Accountability must not be extended to the point where it interferes with the proper discharge of the service for which the money was granted.

Russell uses the example of fighter pilots who, he suggests, are quite properly held accountable for the use of the planes they fly; they cannot use them for private purposes for instance. Yet if they are to be held accountable for the detailed use of the controls, for choice of speed, altitude and angle of approach to landing, for example, this must be done, if at all, only by another pilot. Government certainly lacks the competence to do it. If, for example, the government instructs pilots to fly at a particular speed in order to save fuel, it may unwittingly place the pilots and their planes at risk, and the order may well be disobeyed. This is particularly relevant to recent quality review processes in universities, instituted by government.

Russell's argument and example are uncannily close to the mark for those who have experienced the debates about the various national quality assurance systems over the past few years. The aptness of Russell's comments can be seen from several perspectives – with public servants in educational bureaucracies seeing their practice conforming to Russell's implicit demands of academics for accountability and academics identifying with his implicit criticisms of governments which try to control university activities beyond the limits of their competence. That these contrary perspectives exist is not surprising and the debates between universities and the state have ebbed and flowed for more than half the current millennium.

Russell goes on to argue that progress can be made on both fronts if both parties accept that each principle, albeit firmly held, cannot be held 'in splendid isolation'. He draws the analogy of the principles of racial equality and appointment by merit; in university appointments, Russell claims, 'the principle of affirmative action has made a steady and controlled progress, normally... without significant erosion of academic standards'. He goes on to ask:

> Are... academics, facing the principle of 'efficiency', able to achieve the same feat? Are we able to invoke a principle, generally accepted in our national life, which

is able to provide a check and balance to the principle so vigorously invoked by the government? It is [suggested] that we are and that the principle on which we should fall back is that decisions should be made by those whose professional training, expertise and knowledge qualifies them to make an informed decision.

By using health service and other analogies, Russell argues that it is possible to justify a principle that the government should not make academic judgements. Academics must be left to resolve arguments for themselves but remain accountable. This principle forms the basis of the approach to educational quality assurance argued for later in this chapter.

Aspects of governance

In his interpretation of Max Weber's ideas, Gustavsson (1971) argues that there are two forms of rationality: rationality in relation to a value on the one hand and rationality in relation to a goal, on the other hand. There are two forms of ethics as well: the ethics of ultimate ends and the ethics of responsibility.

Politicians are in roles which demand that they act in ways which appear rational in relation to the goals they have set up to achieve and that they bear responsibility for their actions. Scientists on the other hand are supposed to act in ways which appear rational in relation to a value ('widening and deepening knowledge') and they have to be driven by ultimate ends (the betterment of conditions of humankind). This leads to a seemingly paradoxical principle. 'In order that science may be able to contribute to rationality in relation to a goal and to an ethic of responsibility, scientists must be guided by rationality in relation to a value and by an ethic of ultimate ends' (Gustavsson, 1971).

This implies that in order to be useful, science (or more generally: the university) has to be free. Sverker Gustavsson presented his plea for institutional autonomy in his PhD thesis in political science in 1971. Twenty- six years later, after having been deputy secretary of higher education while the Social Democrats were in power in Sweden during the period 1986–91, he wrote a paper with the provocative title 'Why not eliminate the universities?' The point he is making – as the devil's advocate – is that during the 1990s the threat to autonomy originates mainly from market-oriented models of organization. Why not lay off those employed by the universities and let them form their own private companies, the services of which can be hired by the state, business or industry, when necessary (Gustavsson, 1997)?[2]

Such an arrangement would, however, put the academics in a very weak position indeed; their acts could not be driven by 'ultimate ends'. They could hardly afford that, nor could they act rationally in relation to their values. Not even in relation to the customer's goals would such a mode of organization be rational. In Chapter 10 (page 274) we refer to Dill and Sporn's (1995) study in which they argue for the efficiency of the network model (which is close to the university's traditional mode of operating) as compared to the hierarchical or market model of organization. We also make the point that the network model enhances the collective consciousness of the university, ie the awareness of others' ways of thinking among the employees and students within the university. We make the assumption that setting one's own field of expertise in the context of others is a powerful means for dealing with problems both in research and outside it.

Alternative models of organization within the university reflect its relation to the surrounding world. Susan Marton suggests that we should separate two different aspects of this relationship. She distinguishes between the dimension of centralized versus decentralized governance on the one hand and the dimension of cultural versus utilitarian (internally versus externally oriented) governance, on the other hand (see Figure 9.2). The first dimension refers to the role of the state and the second to the immediate purposes the system of higher education is used for (S Marton, 1997).

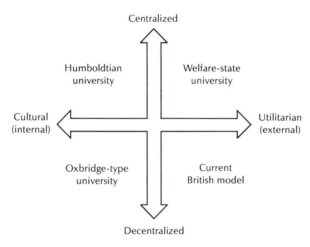

Figure 9.2: *Typologies of governance models (adapted from S Marton, 1997)*

In the upper left-hand corner of the figure we find the autonomous Humboldtian university protected by the state from external influences. The university is supposed to be driven by noble aims: search for the truth and the cultivation of minds and personalities. In the upper right-hand corner, there is the welfare-state university, the state itself being the external influence, using the university as a tool for social purposes – equity, regional politics, economic development and so on. Swedish universities have been of this kind – at least up to the 1990s. In the lower left-hand corner there is the autonomous British university, the classical Oxbridge model. Teaching and research are very much in the hands of the academics themselves and are driven by questions originating from within the system. The lower right-hand corner represents where British universities could be heading today. They are becoming increasingly dependent on market demands.

In the next chapter, we refer to Johnson's (1992) argument against trying to decide whether individual initiatives or a team approach should be the preferred mode of operating within an organization. Such differences should be dealt with instead as a polarity so the positive aspects of both poles are maximized at every point in time. In accordance with this line of reasoning and with Figure 9.2, we do not consider internal and external or centralized and decentralized governance as two dichotomies. They are dimensions in which universities are located. The meanings of the different positions and which are the preferred ones have to be negotiated continuously.

Gustavsson (1997) reminds us that the distinction between centralized and decentralized governance is not such a straightforward matter. While there was a serious political will for the devolution of power from state to universities during the 1990s in Sweden, power could easily end up being centralized at the level of university leadership. In other cases again, power was devolved from vice-chancellors to deans where it stayed, yielding a centralization at the faculty level (Bauer *et al.*, in press). Our own interpretation is that this is what is likely to happen in a hierarchical organization. Although power is devolved hierarchically, it stays focused, at one level or the other. Again, the network university described in Chapter 10 (pages 273–4) appears as a model to aim for.

The changing role of university education

Perhaps another historical perspective that is worthy of consideration relates to the increasing proportion of the community undertaking university education. In times past, when university education was more élitist, those who enrolled expected immediate tangible advantage from completing their university programmes and they got it. At that time, a university degree was a licence to participate in a range of relatively lucrative professional roles and most of the university's clients would have been satisfied; irrespective of the quality of the university processes, tangible outcomes were available to graduates.

As a new millennium dawns, there is a decreasing level of guarantee that completion of a university degree will bestow a material advantage on graduates. With an increasing proportion of the community undertaking university education, the competition for tangible rewards is related not merely to the possession of a university degree but also to more subtle distinctions between graduates competing for employment. At least in part, and perhaps a large part in the perception of students, the perceived quality of teaching and learning and the perceived quality of the university in general play some role in such competitive circumstances. Add to that the increasing level of payment by students in many countries, either through direct fees or through government loan schemes, and it is no surprise that the community is demanding more explicit accountability from universities and academics.

The advent of quality assurance systems has coincided with a shift in the way management is viewed (Dunkin, 1997), but not necessarily in the way that governments have tried to manage the university system. A style of management of the past which has in many business contexts been supplanted has been labelled as scientific. There has been a focus on tasks, structures and processes, with everything specified and little interpersonal trust. Narrow quality assurance processes have been linked to this style of management. This has generally given way in business and some public service contexts to a management style better described as human relational, participative and incremental. There has been a shift from quality control to quality improvement as the focus for action. A shift in focus too from the task at hand to the relation between the participants and the task, with people trusting each other as they engage in quality circles. This shift in management styles parallels the shift in thinking about teaching and learning which modern learning theories embrace (see Marton and Booth, 1997 and our accounts in Chapters 2 and 6).

Principles underlying educational quality assurance

It can be inferred from the introductory sections of this chapter that quality assurance can be seen as having two aspects: improvement and accountability. Indeed, both are essential elements of a successful quality assurance system.

Accountability for the proper conduct of a set of responsibilities is a normal part of everyday life, whether it concerns expenditure of public funds or not. In universities, which attract large sums of money from government sources, there is a reasonable expectation that the quality of university activities is being attended to properly and there is a need for quality assurance to be transparent. In addition, to the extent that the involvement of government bureaucracies in university processes represents taxpayers' concerns, a broader understanding of the role of universities emerges if we deal adequately with this dimension of variation. This is a public good.

All university activities contribute to the outcomes by which universities are judged. These include research as well as teaching and learning activities. Traditionally, research outcomes have been assessed by judgements about research communications of various forms, primarily books and journal articles, but also other outcomes such as patents and commercial applications. Those judgements have implicitly been linked to peer review so that publications in refereed journals, especially those with a reputation for rigorous standards, are rated most highly. Similarly, the work of new researchers is normally judged by detailed appraisal of the PhD thesis by international experts in the field. Such a system has served the research community well in the past in terms of quality assurance and has provided an incentive to researchers to improve the quality of their work. However, given the massive increase in the number of researchers over recent decades and in turn their attempts to publish, there has been an explosive increase in the number of journal titles worldwide so judgements about quality have been more difficult to make. It is less likely that the quantitative measures (numbers of publications of various kinds) correlates as well with the quality of the research as it once did. Even in the past, such correlations carried weight only within a field and not across fields. Recent government reviews in many Western countries have generated heated debate about appropriate performance indicators for research and these matters have yet to be resolved.

Given the difficulty of actually addressing the quality of the research undertaken in universities, there has been a tendency to use input indicators such as the number, size and prestige of research grants awarded and the number of postgraduate research students enrolled, as well as the quantitative output variables associated with publication referred to above. There is little evidence that the primary purpose of such quality assurance systems in the research area has been other than to make comparison between organizations or between individuals. There are few signs that such systems have been concerned with producing better research, except by placement of funding. As Dunkin (1997) suggests: 'this is precisely because of the difficulty of defining ahead of time the outcomes of the research process or even whether there will be any; it can't be mandated'.

What we want to concentrate on here are quality assurance issues associated with the university's teaching and learning activities. However, we do see research as learning too and will make specific reference to aspects of research as appropriate. In our view, there are three underlying principles which should guide the creation of an educational quality assurance system. Below we will develop a line of argument around these:

- The focus should be on quality improvement with accountability being a consequence, not the focus, of the educational quality assurance system because this is the way to produce better outcomes across the board.
- Educational quality improvement is concerned with quality of student learning.
- Educational quality assurance requires some basis in evidence for claims made, whether for accountability purposes or for improvement.

Focus on quality improvement rather than accountability

While quality assurance in education necessarily comprises both the improvement and accountability aspects, we suggest that for successful quality assurance of teaching and learning in university educational activities, the focus needs to be on improvement. If improvement is addressed properly, evidence for accountability will be developed automatically.

The reverse is not necessarily the case. Focus on accountability in quality assurance for university programmes is less likely and, in practice, often does not result in quality improvements in teaching and learning or research. Accountability is an important and necessary feature of an educational quality assurance system but having accountability as the focus is counter-productive as is argued in the next section.

Experience in Australia and the UK of activities undertaken by universities in preparation for external audit visits leads to the conclusion that universities usually focus on providing whatever evidence can be uncovered to show the university in a good light. Sometimes a flurry of activity quickly produces the kinds of evidence that had not been collected before but in a way and for a purpose that leaves most academics feeling cynical about what are, supposedly, quality processes. This kind of action may be a rational response to the external stimulus but nevertheless has a lower probability of quality outcomes than an improvement-focused system. This applies to research when academics or postgraduate research students are encouraged to steer their research towards areas that will result in rapid and frequent publication rather than to take more time to concentrate on potentially more important but more difficult research questions. A focus on accountability can result in a lowering of quality of outcomes, including research outcomes.

In turn, within the university, if certain goals are aimed at a particular level in the university, these aims can be experienced as demands on the next level down in the hierarchy of power and transformed there to other aims. As shown in Figure 9.3, these aims may again be experienced as demands on the next level, transformed to other aims again, and so on.

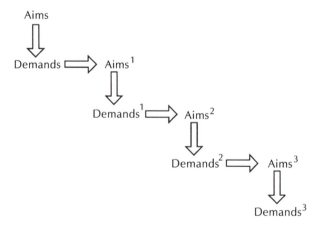

Figure 9.3: *Relationship between aims and demands*

This may apply to the different hierarchical levels within a university: board or council, vice-chancellor, faculties, departments and staff. Most typically it applies to what is taking place between teacher and students in a single class. The teacher may, for instance, aim at having students develop a thorough understanding of the content studied, while students may experience a demand to be able to recall 'what is in the book' and make this their aim. The object of learning and the object of teaching are then split into two. Similarly, the leadership of the university may aim at raising the quality of teaching and research, while staff are experiencing a demand to boost some indices, which are supposed to measure quality. They may try to increase student participation in lectures or increase the frequency of citation of their work, by more or less opportunistic and artificial means.

If an organization, or a part of it, is to move in a certain direction then what is intended has to be shared. Goals cannot be achieved except by becoming aims (and not demands) for those in the organization, by becoming driving forces for their actions. There must be a reasonably high degree of collective consciousness in the organization, ie understanding and awareness of other members' aims, thoughts and attitudes (see Chapter 8). The more people know about what other people know and how they feel, the better from the point of view of the potential for action in relation to the goals. This applies equally to interactions of the universities with government.

Any educational quality assurance approach needs to recognize this complexity and the need to balance a quality improvement orientation with accountability. A quality assurance system is also constrained in any organization by the attitudes and values of its staff on these matters. Such constraints have to be dealt with and the attitudes of staff will have been formed significantly on the basis of both internal and external, and local and national level developments and experiences. There will always be a range of historical, political and cultural issues or factors which need to be considered when change or development is being sought. In universities these include:

- individualism in universities, identification of academics with their international discipline and the relative lack of corporate commitment. This is consistent with the individual competitiveness encouraged in the past by such factors as the emphasis in promotion systems on research product characteristics. Many quality systems in industrial or business contexts either build up or build upon a sense of corporate loyalty and commitment. The corresponding focus in universities has been on individual autonomy and the sanctity of the classroom. As Dunkin (1998) suggests: 'this is changing, not just because of accountability requirements but because the emergence of new technologies are causing new approaches to be developed'.
- academics' responses that, like those of other professions such as lawyers and doctors, often reflect feelings of having been insulted when confronted by

expectations that they need to be involved in organized quality assurance processes. Their perspective is that quality assurance has been something which has always been taken care of by individuals as a matter of course and that the system is dependent on each academic as the individual expert. So corporate team-based systems are seen as devaluing, inappropriate and time-wasting. This extreme position takes Russell's (1993) notion of 'peer' to another level because it implies that there may be no appropriate peers in the university who can assess the quality of an individual academic's work

- a drift in resource allocation away from the primary role of teaching and learning, as university budgets have relied increasingly on external earnings and as more and more tertiary institutions have sought improved status through research, with a consequential shift in the balance of academic work
- lack of integration of strategic planning, performance planning, performance evaluation and staff development.

If a university is to adopt a focus on quality improvement, then it needs to deal with the whole range of impediments described in this section.

Evidential base

The primary intention of evaluation activities undertaken for many quality assurance exercises, with accountability as the focus, has been to gather positive evidence to demonstrate how well the university is performing. In contrast, the purpose of evaluation for quality improvement is to find evidence of both strengths and deficiencies so that changes can be made to deal with the problems, in addition to learning from the experience of those things shown to be working well. Improvement is produced only by looking comprehensively at the status quo, including both pros and cons; a focus on accountability mitigates against that. An evidence-based approach to quality improvement is required if a university is going to attend to both the improvement and accountability aspects of quality assurance.

Using student feedback well (or badly)

A number of universities have developed or supported the development of student evaluation questionnaires which are used to get feedback from students about the teaching and learning they have experienced. There are important questions that students can answer which no one else can. It is the student who has experienced the physical environment of the classroom, who has used links to the university's computers to participate in various chat sessions from home or who has interacted with teaching staff, both in the classroom and away from it. So students are able to comment on the effects of those experiences on their learning and to give some form of judgement about their value.

It seems to be a reasonable assumption that the purpose of getting this kind of feedback from students is to find out what is working well and what is not working well so the teacher can learn from the feedback by building on strengths and dealing with deficiencies. We discussed the Course Experience Questionnaire (CEQ) in Chapter 3; the feedback obtained from the CEQ provides useful indicators of areas to be focused on in quality improvement activities.

Presumably as well, in line with any well-designed evaluation system, feedback from students would form one part of an array of mechanisms, which together would provide a more coherent picture than any one piece of evaluation data alone. Other mechanisms might include feedback from employers, graduates, academics in the same field in other institutions and reflection and discussion among staff of the teaching team itself, perhaps following readings of relevant educational research material.

Finally, it would be valuable if the findings of such an evaluation system were to be shared, certainly within the teaching team but also between teaching teams in other parts of the university. It is only by this kind of process that a collective development can take place in which the standard of teaching and learning in the university improves across the board, the development of a collective competence (see Chapter 8). In turn, the development of the individual teacher can be enhanced.

Some universities have responded to national government pressures regarding quality assurance, not by developing systems that reflect the above thinking, but by introducing standardized student rating forms which, given the way they have been implemented, can serve no other purpose than to provide just an appearance of accountability. A common approach is to use a university-wide standard student feedback questionnaire comprising a single set of about six questions, administered to all classes in all subjects at the end of every semester. So students fill out this same questionnaire many times each semester, rating each teacher whose classes they have attended. The data from all these questionnaires are analysed and scores produced for each teacher for each class, therefore a particular academic may have a score of, say 3.6 on a five-point scale for one class and a score of 4.2 for another class. Another academic may have scores of 2.5, 4.4 and 4.5 for three different classes.

What can be done with these scores? It would seem that very little could be done with them, even if they were fully valid and reliable. It would be difficult to advise the first academic mentioned in the previous paragraph about the differences between the two scores. Do they indicate better or worse teaching? Even if they do, and that is arguable, do they give any indication as to what improvements are needed?

Readers might like to compare the scenario described above with the description in Chapter 3 of the way the modified CEQ is used to get feedback every two years from recent graduates from Australian universities. First, it is based on graduates' response to a whole programme, second, it has a number of different scales which can be used as indicators for further investigation, third, it is based on an articulated theory of learning and, fourth, it or other versions of it have been evaluated and validated in many countries. This is in contrast to the unsophisticated approaches described above.

Consider another alternative based on the following case: an academic sought advice about compiling just such a questionnaire, but particularly concerning whether the objectives of the subject were being clearly understood by students. So questions like 'Does the lecturer make the objectives clear?' were in mind (a question of this kind is often on standardized questionnaires). The advice we gave was to prepare a list of the major objectives the lecturer considered central to the subject, ask students at the beginning of the next lecture to individually write down what they thought the key objectives were, brainstorm the students' ideas on to the board, compare the students' list with the teacher's, note the similarities and differences and resolve any misunderstandings.

This procedure takes about 20 minutes of lecture time and it certainly lets the teacher know whether or not the objectives have been made clear previously. Moreover, it highlights for both the teacher and students what has been made clear and what has not and, of most importance, it enables any discrepancies to be dealt with on the spot. Provided this is done early in the semester and not at the end, such an exercise assists students to learn better. In this way, evaluation involving feedback from students is made part of the learning process.

The standard end of semester questionnaire can only tell you that, say, 70 per cent of students believe that the objectives were made clear (if that is one of the questions). Now the classroom brainstorming procedure that we have described often demonstrates to students that even though they thought they understood what the key objectives were, they are sometimes wrong (almost always they find they have misinterpreted at least some aspect of the course objectives). In the end of semester survey approach, how many students think the objectives were made clear (therefore giving higher ratings to the teacher) but are in fact mistaken? We will never know because this kind of survey does not provide the data that can be used to answer the question and given that it is at the end of semester, it does not help improve learning by those students either.

We would therefore encourage academics to seek feedback from students informally and during the teaching so that the evaluation process is a learning experience for everyone and appropriate adjustments can be made. Further, if a comprehensive set of indicators needs to be collected at the end of the teaching period, then academics should use well-validated, research-based instruments such as the various versions of the CEQ, but even then such instruments should be used sparingly and appropriately as we discussed in Chapter 3.

Focus on student learning

When educational quality improvement is embarked on by academics, there is an understandable tendency for the focus to be on their teaching activities *per se*. Teachers commonly become concerned to improve the way they lecture, or how they handle small group discussions, or with the reliability of their marking, for example. These are important matters to be concerned about but it is the criteria that are applied that are more important. Making changes to lecturing style so that the teacher feels more satisfied is certainly helpful but the central issue is whether the changes make any difference to student learning. It is difficult to support a claim that quality has been improved if the change is simply in the teacher's behaviour, with no influence on what or how well students are learning. So the purpose of any quality improvement in teaching and courses must include the effects on students' experience of the changes that are introduced and the effects on their learning.

Take, for example, the interest shown by external audit agencies in the use of computers in teaching. Often there seems to be greater interest in how many courses use computers than in the nature of the effects of such usage on student learning. A similar, simplistic focus on whether or not the university has in place a system of student evaluation, which embraces all courses, often ignores the question of whether student evaluation outcomes actually influence changes in teaching designed to aid student learning.

Any educational quality assurance system concerned with improvement in teaching and courses must place the students and their learning at the centre. Improvements have therefore to be judged in terms of the outcomes of learning in the first place.

As mentioned above, the kind of learning we are focusing on means that students develop capabilities for seeing certain ways of seeing certain classes of situations (which enable them to engage in effective action in these situations). In Chapters 2 and 3 we presented a theoretical line of argument as support for our stance. In addition, we have illustrated qualitatively different ways of seeing different kinds of situations and different phenomena. We have shown how learning can be conceptualized in terms of developing ways of seeing, how ways of seeing can be considered learning goals, how ways of seeing can be brought about by teaching and how judgements about educational arrangements can be made in terms of the extent to which certain ways of seeing have been brought about.

Some implications of those principles

There are a number of implications that we think follow from these principles:

- There is a need for a theoretical base that drives the improvement process.
- Evaluation is an integral component.
- The improvement process should be at the level of student experience – at least in part at the level of the degree programme and there is a need for teaching teams to work collaboratively.

Need for a theoretical base

The kind of quality improvement system referred to above is a purposeful one. Difficulties are identified and changes made to deal with them. Implicit in such a statement is the expectation that the most appropriate changes will be made, ie those most likely to lead to improvement.

But how is the choice made? Such choices should be informed by educational theory of some kind. Any educational adviser who merely offers a strategy, with an invitation to a teacher to come back for something else to try if the first strategy does not work, would not stay in that role for very long (see Bowden and Martin, 1991). Neither should an academic working alone or in a teaching team try some teaching approach simply because it is available. The implications of using the approach would normally be reflected on in the light of educational research literature and personal experience, because any changes need to be purposeful and should be expected (but of course not guaranteed) to lead to improvement; hence the need for a basis in some form of educational theory, no matter how informal.

Evaluation

The discussion of underlying principles above leads to the inevitable conclusion that evaluation must be an integral part of any educational quality assurance system. It is self-evident that some form of knowledge about the status quo is needed to inform the purposeful improvement process. Similarly, to know if the intended improvements have been effective, further evaluation in some form is necessary. While evaluation outcomes will not constitute the whole of the evidence, they are an integral component.

Level of change and the need for teaching teams

There is a tendency for educational development activities to be pitched at a fairly specific level, usually the teaching by a particular academic or of a particular subject. The normal, organizational structure of universities also tends to focus such activities at best at the department level but often at an even more localized level than the department. However, most educational programmes involve the student in studying an array of content in a variety of ways in many different contexts, almost always across departmental and often faculty boundaries.

How can the university ensure that the relationships between the parts of a degree programme can be addressed by students so that the whole is greater than the mere sum of the parts? How can the university avoid having students merely collecting a series of unconnected educational experiences, however fine each might be in its own way, and graduating with a Bachelor of Bits and Pieces? Since the graduate's educational and personal attainments relate to the whole programme that has been experienced, there is a responsibility to ensure that the improvement process is not just at the subject level. Attention needs to be paid to how the parts relate to each other, how they fit the whole and how they contribute to the kinds of outcomes we expect for our graduates.

One way to deal with this is to appoint one academic for each programme who has the responsibility to plan the overall programme and ensure coherence. The problem with that approach is that it is additive and not integrative. This approach may ensure that the whole programme is comprised of the appropriate parts in the most effective relationship but it does not address the need for each individual teacher of a particular part to relate that part to the whole.

It can be argued that it is necessary for all academics, who teach in a particular educational programme, to communicate with each other, plan the programme together and collectively address the quality improvement process – hence the need for teaching teams. The expectation that teaching teams will address the linkages and take a holistic approach to the student's entire programme seems to be an essential characteristic of an educational quality assurance system.

Dill (1997) argues that it is crucial, for this reason, that educational coherence be used 'as a basis for choice among potential candidates for academic curricula'. He suggests the following rule of coherence: 'For an academic curriculum to be offered by the university, it must seek to provide a coherent academic experience for its students. To meet the rule of coherence, an academic curriculum must be able to provide ongoing, summative evidence that its students have had a coherent learning experience'.

Quality assurance systems

National quality audits

It is within a context of greater community awareness of, and interest in, what universities are doing and because of changing relationships between government and universities that many countries have established quality audit systems for universities as well as for other public institutions. The quality audit systems and processes vary from one country to another but there are some recurring themes, such as self-evaluation documents by the university, a brief visit of a small team to the university to meet and interview selected members of the university, usually including students, a draft report fed back to the vice-chancellor for comment, public announcement of the outcomes usually presented as a rank-order or in a form from which a rank-order could be derived and, finally, a written report to the university, normally fairly brief. These are the kinds of procedure, more or less, which have operated in Australia, The Netherlands and Scotland for example, with many of these aspects also to be found in quality audit systems for universities in England, Hong Kong and Sweden as well.

England

Probably the most well-known quality system on the national level is the system for Quality Assessment in England. Its purposes were described by its architect Paul M Clark as:

- to secure value for public investment and to demonstrate public account-ability for this investment
- to encourage improvements in higher education
- to provide effective and accessible public information on the quality of the education for which the Higher Education Funding Council for England (HEFCE) provides funding.

The method for quality assessment (on the level of subjects) used from April 1993 to April 1995 was somewhat modified on the ground of the experiences from using it. The current practice of assessing the quality on a subject basis comprises:

- requirements for a clear statement of subject-specific aims and objectives
- self assessment
- three day assessment visit by a team of academic or professional peers
- a profile of judgements of six major aspects of academic provision, each one rated on a 4-point scale and a summative judgement on a 2-point scale
- one public report, containing a verbatim reproduction of the provider's statement of aims and objectives. Under specific circumstances, an appeals procedure would be involved (Clark, 1997).

Australia

We are also going to describe the Australian approach, because we know it well and because it has combined most of the elements found in the other systems with an additional element, the attachment of a significant level of funding to the outcome. In Australia, the origins were political, with members of government questioning whether universities were being run efficiently and then focusing attention on the quality of university teaching and research. Value for money was the central theme.

In sequence there was a national sampling of opinion through discussion meetings involving the chair and members of the Higher Education Council which resulted in a report titled Higher Education: Achieving Quality (1992) (Chubb Report). Eventually a national committee was formed – the Committee for Quality Assurance in Higher Education. The Committee was given the task of reviewing the quality of university functioning with respect to teaching and learning, research and community service. All three aspects were examined in a composite evaluation in 1993, the teaching and learning function was the primary focus in 1994 and research and community services were evaluated in 1995.

The review process in Australia was undertaken by just a few evaluators in a short space of time, with a lot of money at stake. Up to 78 million dollars was potentially available for distribution to the 36 universities on the basis of the quality review each year. In the event a sum of about 200 million dollars was distributed in this way over three years. Participation was not compulsory but with such financial incentives, none of the 36 universities in the Australian Unified National System declined to participate in any of the three years.

Government–university relations

In terms of Russell's 'clash between two valid principles', the issues here are whether universities should be accountable for the way they spend their resources on teaching and learning, research and community services and the quality of those functions; whether those who undertook the evaluations in each country were competent to do so; and whether the process infringed institutional autonomy of the universities in a way that undermined their functions?

It would be difficult to argue that universities should not be accountable for the quality of their functions. We would not mount such an argument. As to the competence of the evaluators, there is certainly substantial face validity as the majority of the visiting team members were academics and academic managers from other universities. It is in most countries a 'peer review' system and in that regard meets Russell's criteria. The third issue is debatable. The process itself is certainly questionable. What has to be distinguished is the following: the quality and rigour of the review process itself; the quality and rigour of the classification of the universities according to the categories devised for each criterion; the allocation of the 'quality money' on performance with universities given the highest grades receiving the most money, in contrast with an alternative – allocating the money on a needs basis with the poorest rated universities receiving the most money; and the possibility that the existence of such a quality review system with its cash rewards, irrespective of the rigour of its processes, has had a beneficial effect by motivating universities to pay attention to the quality of their functions in ways they would not have done otherwise.

The first two of these, the quality and rigour of the review process itself and the classification process, have been the subject of vigorous criticism over the last few years. Attempting to do too much in too little time with too little expertise summarizes the criticism of such review processes themselves. In Australia, a visit by an audit team for one day, during which time about eight interviews with groups of eight people were undertaken, is perhaps an extreme case. However, similar processes for three half days in Hong Kong and three days in The Netherlands or in England, even though the latter were on a subject basis, compared with the Australian and Hong Kong reviews of whole universities, still raise questions about what such a team can assess in that period of time. Even discounting the inadequacy of the review processes, the use of many different teams to review different universities, as happened in the Australian system, raises questions about the reliability of the outcomes.

So there are questions about the processes themselves but are there other consequences independent of the process? First, in the Australian system the rich got richer and this approach of having some areas judged to be of higher quality receiving money at the expense of other, supposedly lower quality areas is common across the countries mentioned. Is this a case of quality improvement or simply widening the existing gap? If a government truly wanted to improve quality might it not choose to put more money into areas that needed fixing? From the perspective of students at a university which receives a low rating on teaching and learning, with no extra and possibly reduced funding, it must seem strange that, at the same time, their friends who are studying at another highly rated university would find that university having even more money to spend on making it better still. How does this improve the quality of the learning experience for students already receiving relatively poor quality education?

It should be said however that, irrespective of the ratings and the money distributed, these kinds of process certainly have had a catalytic effect on most universities, which in the 1990s are operating internally in ways that make outcomes themselves (including student learning outcomes) and the relation of process to outcome more explicit criteria in planning and review processes. The quality of student learning is now something which universities are interested in and are monitoring, far more than was so in the past.

Graham, Lyman and Trow, three major figures in American Higher Education, focused on the balance between internal and external accountability, corresponding to self-regulation and public regulation. They argued that internal accountability should be handled in terms of self-evaluation focusing on teaching and learning, on identifying weaknesses and on the effectiveness of actions taken to address those weaknesses. External accountability is supposed to provide evidence, mainly to audiences outside the university, about the extent to which the mission of the university is being accomplished. Such processes should not focus on the assessment of quality of an institution, but rather on the internal quality control mechanisms of the institution (Graham, Lyman and Trow, 1995). This conclusion is very much in accordance with our discussion above of institutional autonomy.

Sweden

The Swedish model for Quality Assurance and Enhancement comes comparatively close to Graham *et al.*'s ideas. All institutions of higher education are expected to develop their own quality assurance systems and to account for quality measures in triennial reports to government in connection with the appropriation proposal for the next three-year cycle.

At the national level there is a requirement for the Higher Education Agency (Bauer, 1996):

- to make triennial audits of the local quality assurance systems and programs for quality development
- to carry through evaluations of system and other aspects which are the responsibility of the central level
- to accredit for the right to examination of courses at advanced levels new to an institution or for institutions applying for higher education statements.

The national system for quality assurance was part of a reform in 1993 which was driven by the ambition to contribute to the development of Sweden as 'a knowledge society' of good international repute (Askling and Almén, 1997)[3]. The reform was aimed at decentralizing to the academics in the different fields, power over curriculum decisions, the content of teaching and the outcomes aimed for. Instead of allocating resources entirely on the grounds of the number of student places '... each institution was individually contracted for a period of three years to produce a certain number of undergraduate exams for a fixed lump sum, of which 60 per cent was allocated on the basis of the students' performance'. The input model was thus replaced by an output model (Bauer *et al.*, in press)and the idea of assuring quality through planning was replaced by the idea of assuring quality by means of internal control. There was the ambition '... to design a flexible and loosely organized system, which allows for fluctuations and an interplay with external – and international – forces' (Askling and Almén, 1997).[4]

This reform opened up 'the space of action' in several dimensions. Questions about content, learning and knowledge became topics of lively discussions. The system made the institutions fully responsible for the study opportunities they offered. Making decisions about those offers promoted interaction within and between faculties (the recipients of the lump sums), and within and between departments.

In Chapter 2 we dealt with dimensions of variation, in terms of which people experience the world around them, discern and are aware of patterns of critical aspects. We could talk of the complex of dimensions of variation as 'the space of variation'. In this particular case 'the space of variation' is the experiential correlate of 'the space of action'. If people can make – and actually do make – choices between different options, the dimensions comprising those options – or rather aspects of them – define variation: in action and in experience.

This filtering down of the power, freedom and responsibility calls paradoxically for more local planning, accountability, control and responsibility. It calls for stronger and more pronounced institutional management (Bauer *et al.*, in press).

Universities and the individual academic

There are issues arising from these changes in the distribution of power and responsibility, and from the increasing quality assurance activities in universities, issues that influence the relation between universities and their staff. What can be handed down from above as a given and what must be developed from below, in both sets of relationships? How do these two aspects of authority/autonomy interact? An academic may perceive as acceptable some top-down action from senior management internally if it is seen as a reasonable balance of power within the university but may resent it if an outside government agency is seen to have triggered it. Yet the government agency influence may be seen by university management as a legitimate aspect of the division of powers between university and government. This is part of the aims and demands problem highlighted in Figure 9.3.

University level quality assurance systems

In this section, we discuss the characteristics of a university quality assurance system which fits the educational principles we embrace in this book. We describe here the Royal Melbourne Institute of Technology (RMIT) educational quality assurance system as an example and, as much as possible, we will draw out more general conclusions. The key elements of the RMIT system are:

- The focus is on teaching teams working together to continually improve the quality of teaching and learning and taking responsibility for that quality and its evaluation.
- Teaching teams are expected to engage in continual improvement of students' learning experiences and of the learning outcomes through attention to teaching, curriculum, assessment and course management issues. (The term 'course' in the RMIT context refers to an educational programme such as a Bachelor of Engineering or a Graduate Diploma in Finance.)
- The continual improvement processes and their outcomes are fully documented for each course. Teams are encouraged to keep records not by creating special 'quality documents' but through normal processes such as minutes of team meetings, filing of working papers, copies of submissions to curriculum committees and so on. This is increasingly occurring electronically using intranets.
- Development support is provided through an academic development group to ensure that such improvements are soundly based in terms of pedagogical theory and evaluation practice.
- Annual summaries of the quality improvement processes and documentation are provided to a central committee; these report achievements against past quality improvement targets as well as plans and targets for the coming year.
- Each course is audited once every five years and the audit uses the documentation collected continually across the five years. No special audit document is required from course teams.

- The course quality assurance processes are intended to be linked to the University's Teaching and Learning Strategy and other strategic planning, performance planning and academic promotion procedures, to minimize duplication of effort by academic staff.

So, this educational quality assurance system is an evidence-based and improvement-focused quality assurance system. It includes processes whereby teaching teams establish quality improvement cycles of evaluation or design, reflection, change and evaluation. Evidence for strengths and weaknesses of existing processes, with learning outcomes as the central criterion, is gathered and reflected on. Appropriate change processes are developed, justified and implemented. Subsequently, evaluation of learning outcomes and processes is undertaken to produce evidence of the success, or otherwise, of the changes put in place.

Interestingly, the approach of the Mölnlycke AB, a middle-sized Swedish company in the manufacturing industry sector, which we have mentioned already, is very similar to the approach to quality management of RMIT, despite its business being manufacturing and not university education. Mölnlycke staff work in teams to determine whether their mission and objectives need adjustment, how the various processes are working in terms of meeting the agreed objectives, and how the processes could be changed to better meet the agreed objectives or to meet new objectives being developed. Significant changes are recorded and filed locally and when audits are undertaken, no special documentation created for the audit is expected; the documentation filed on a continuing basis forms the paper trail. It is often suggested that quality assurance in industry must be more prescriptive than the RMIT system which we suggest is most appropriate for universities. But the Mölnlycke example shows that the same improvement-focused approach to quality assurance can work in international manufacturing industry too.

The emphasis on the evidential basis of quality improvement cycles, fundamental to the RMIT system, ensures that the quality improvement process automatically provides much of the evidence on which accountability is dependent. It is in this way that Russell's challenge of handling 'two things in splendid isolation' is met. For the RMIT educational quality assurance system is not merely a means to address accountability responsibilities. It would have taken on a different form if it had only that limited objective. In the next section, we show that the RMIT educational quality assurance system is solidly based on a philosophy of quality improvement in teaching and learning. That word 'improvement' is used not to indicate that the University's staff are performing below standard. That is likely to be true of everyone some of the time but, beyond that, it is necessary to recognize that in a constantly changing world, maintenance of quality implies continual adjustment therefore improvement.

Furthermore, the RMIT educational quality assurance system is in the form of a framework, with the majority of the activities undertaken being at the discretion of the academics who teach the courses. The system has been designed and attempts have been made to ensure that, at all stages, there is an appropriate balance between individual professional autonomy and responsible organizational control as discussed earlier in this chapter. This is reminiscent of the loose-tight model described by Hallett (1997): '... [it] acknowledges the integration of "top-down" [management] processes with "bottom-up" initiatives generated by practitioners. Emphasis is on capturing up as much activity as possible in policy structures and processes, whilst simultaneously developing proactive policy initiatives from the top'.

One important way of understanding an educational quality assurance system, which is focused on quality improvement, is to examine the record of an academic team who are working within that system in their pursuit of improvements within the programme they teach. To do so we describe the activities of the academic team at RMIT responsible for Bachelor of Arts in Interior Design who sought to add appropriate acoustic design subjects to the programme.

An educational quality assurance example: acoustic design subjects

In Chapter 6, we discussed this acoustic design example from the curriculum and teaching perspective. The course team were concerned to re-introduce acoustics into the Interior Design and Architecture courses at RMIT but they wanted to make it more effective than it had been before. The fundamental shift has been from seeing learning acoustics as the acquisition of a set of technical skills, which designers can use, to the development of the capability to think about sound from a design perspective. Our focus here is on detailing the way this acoustic design example illustrates the educational quality assurance system.

In 1993, members of the course team for the Bachelor of Arts in Interior Design at RMIT were concerned with the absence in the curriculum of any aspect dealing with acoustic design, despite its importance in the professional activities of interior designers. There had been some aspects of acoustics dealt with in the course some years before but it had been dropped. It had been taught previously as a technology-based subject and in a way many designers reported was irrelevant to their design functions. Several members of the course team took an interest in exploring this issue on behalf of the whole team.

Over a period of several years, as reported by Lines (1997), investigations were made into the ways this subject has been taught elsewhere, the ways professional designers undertake acoustic design, what the central purposes of an acoustic design subject would be, how an acoustic design subject would fit into the faculty's largely studio-based learning approach and how the learning outcomes could be assessed.

While the main effort came from the small group led by Lines, there was significant involvement from others in the faculty (the subject became part of the Bachelor of Architecture course curriculum as well), from professional designers and from academics in other faculties such as physicists in the Faculty of Applied Science and music educators in the Faculty of Education.

The approach was developed incrementally with each step open to public scrutiny and with considerable effort to obtain evaluative feedback. All activities and feedback were documented and contributed to the next phase. An acoustic design seminar was undertaken in 1994, the development of an acoustic design minor study, the teaching of a Soundwaves design studio in conjunction with the Next Wave Festival and a community project on internal acoustics in a pre-school centre in 1995. In 1996 came the first teaching of the Constructing Sound subject in the acoustic design minor, as well as the Perfect Form studio in conjunction with the Next Wave Festival, and the Yirrkala studio in Arnhem Land in collaboration with a Yolngnu (aboriginal) community to address acoustic design in classrooms that were to be both thermally and culturally appropriate (this studio involved both staff and students working with the aboriginal community in Arnhem Land for several weeks). In 1997, the second subject in the acoustic design minor was taught in both the Interior Design and the Architecture degree programmes.

The developments summarized above were punctuated by reflection, writing, staff development activities, informal discussions and formal meetings involving interior designers and architects both from within the faculty and from outside the university. The documentation includes papers both collected and written by course team members, memos distributed within the faculty, minutes of (or notes from) formal meetings, course planning documents, formal faculty course change documents, student feedback reports, research reports on the ways professional designers acquire acoustic design knowledge, a report on the development by the course team of a new sound mapping technique involving visual images which has now been made available to professional designers, curriculum materials, project planning (eg Yirrkala) documents, project reports and project evaluations (including outcomes from exhibitions to the public).

These documents have been available to all members of the faculty and all involved in the project to provide both a means of communication and a base for coherent development. They were not collected separately for educational quality assurance purposes, rather they were the means by which the various teams, committees and individual participants remained aware of the whole change process while making their particular contributions. The educational quality assurance system required only one extra step so far as documentation was concerned and that was to lodge indexed copies of each document in a single file. The file is an impressive record of a substantial educational change process. From the perspective of the course team, that change process has not ended. The same developmental approach, with the same attention to public exposure and feedback, will continue as the acoustic design minor grows and reshapes according to the changing environment. The existence of documented evidence of the changes so far and the reasons for them, provide both a historical base and a framework for future development. That is the essence of this aspect of a good educational quality assurance system.

Doing what you do – better

The system for Quality Assurance at Göteborg University for instance states simply that each unit (department, faculty etc) at all levels has the responsibility to evaluate and document its own actions and performance continuously and at least once in each six years carry out self-evaluation in combination with an external reviewer. It is further stated that the student's view should be taken into consideration as one kind of evidence, that every teacher should have the opportunity to engage in research, that all newly appointed staff have to participate in basic pedagogical training and that they also should be offered follow-up development opportunities regularly. Although there are obvious differences, the Göteborg University system comprises all the functions of the university. From the particular point of view discussed in this section, it is no different from the system at RMIT discussed above.

The 'quality movement' has not always been happily embraced at universities. Most academics felt that more things were being added to their already heavy workload of teaching, research and administration. However, the point is that the 'quality' being referred to is the quality of what you are doing, or rather the quality of what you are achieving; of the learning brought about and of the research carried out. So improving the 'quality' is simply doing better what you are doing anyway.

Endnotes

1. We should remember that 'Lehrfreiheit, the right to teach one's competence, [and] Lernfreiheit, the right of the students to have access to knowledge' (Rothblatt, 1997), are defining features of the Humboldt university (see Chapter 1, page 5) (Note added by the authors of this book).

2. This could have been Gustavsson's own defence for universities, but he is emphasizing the universities' critical role, of vital importance for a democratic society. He argues that we need institutions which provide a sufficiently independent, competent and strong counterbalance to the power of the state and the market, by adopting a critical stance. Science (or rather, the universities) and art can and should have such a role, Gustavsson believes. In another country the Law, the judicial system, would probably have been referred to as an independent force. It might be the case that the separation of the state and the Law is less clear-cut in Sweden.

3. Askling and Almén's (1997) interpretation is that the liberal-conservative government of 1993 was driven by aims internal to higher education, such as academic quality, as compared with the previous social democratic government's ambition to use higher education to advance greater equality among individuals. Sverker Gustavsson, who actually was the deputy-secretary of higher education during the social-democratic rule, 1986–91, argues otherwise as we pointed out above (Gustavsson, 1997). He would probably agree with Sture Åström – deputy secretary of agriculture when the social democrats returned to power in 1994 – who claims that there are differences within all parties in the externalistic versus internalistic governance of higher education dimension (see Figure 9.1 page 216). The ideological difference between the two governments is to be found (Åström, 1997) along the dimension centralized (social democrats) and decentralized (liberals and conserva-

tives). At a closer look it seems in fact that the reform introduced by the liberal-conservative government was partly grounded by social democrats of the preceding government who, like Gustavsson himself, were in favour of greater institutional autonomy (see Bauer *et al.*, in press).

4. The 1993 reform of higher education was part of reforms common to the entire Swedish public sector. This is reflected in the strong role that the Finance Department played at this time, as well as global trends to 'new public management' (S. Marton, 1998).

Chapter 10

Organizing learning

In this chapter we look at the organization in which the learning takes place. We know that in any organization, those who are committed to change and innovation are not always successful no matter how well argued their goals and strategies may be or how much energy they expend. In addition, we know that unless there is some kind of cultural change in an organization, which affects the existing structural or functional arrangements, or both, then it is unlikely that efforts by a few to change the goals and outcomes will be successful. So we faced a decision on what we should say about the university as an organization. There are many books about organizational change, some about universities in particular, and we did not feel we could or should try to emulate them. What we decided to do was to follow the theme of this whole book and look at the organization from the point of view of learning. Hence our title for this chapter, 'Organizing learning'.

We want to say at the outset, however, that while we are focusing on student learning as our point of departure for discussing the university as an organization, we are well aware that we are writing this book at a time of substantial change for universities throughout the world. Already there are global communications networks whose owners and managers have shown an interest in engaging in the education industry. There are global networks of universities emerging which raise questions about the viability of autonomous, self-contained, local universities. The debate about the pros and cons of these changes is not the subject of this book but throughout this chapter we will at every stage consider the implications of our conclusions about organizing learning, not just as it applies to traditional university arrangements but in the globally networked context as well.

Those who have read our chapters so far will have concluded that what we advocate for student learning in universities is not what commonly occurs. It certainly takes place in some universities and in some parts of most universities, but it does not seem to be the norm. If the kind of learning we advocate were to become routine, then what changes would necessarily follow in the way the university manages the learning that takes place there?

A vital element in our line of reasoning is a shift in the way the university is organized from a focus on teaching to a focus on learning. This idea is a key implication of our theory of learning, which we have advocated for several decades. Such a shift has also been argued for by Barr and Tagg (1995) who have called for a change from what they call an instruction paradigm to a learning paradigm although they say little about what that learning paradigm is.

Within that ethos of a focus on learning, there are two, apparently contradictory changes in the way educational programmes are organized that follow, if learning for the unknown future is to be successfully implemented. They are the need to develop integrated curricula, which include a range of prescribed learning experiences which all students must have and the need to develop a flexible approach to teaching and learning so that student choice is maximized. In this chapter we will elaborate these two themes and their organizational consequences, and solve the apparent contradiction. However, before doing so we want to look at a learning example which illustrates some of the major themes outlined above. In particular it illustrates the development of an integrated curriculum which brings together two forms of knowledge, the disciplinary and the professional.

Disciplinary and professional forms of knowledge

The example in this section illustrates one aspect of an integrated curriculum and is from a medical education programme at the University of Melbourne in Australia. We include this example for two reasons which build on each other. The first reason is that this example illustrates a shift from a focus on teaching to a focus on learning and also builds in a high level of collaborative effort by a range of staff in the university. The second reason is that it illustrates one aspect of the integrated curriculum which we want to develop in this chapter as a sub-theme, the importance of striking a balance between two legitimate ways of organizing knowledge, from a disciplinary and professional perspective. There are other forms of knowledge besides those two. Universities tend to focus on the disciplinary framework and we argue that it is important that in educational programmes the professional framework also plays a part. However, it could be argued that a more thematic, transdisciplinary framework, the third possible form of knowledge in our analysis, could be developed and used to structure knowledge. One example of that is the development of educational programmes on social policy which run across a range of traditional disciplines like planning, sociology, psychology and so on. The fourth framework could result from a strongly felt need in society which shapes the way knowledge is structured and which is not related to any particular profession. An example is the way that the field of health care is developing into a team process, with the need of the community for integrated health care filtering through to the way that individual programmes like medicine, nursing, physiotherapy and social work are organized. While we acknowledge that these third and fourth forms of knowledge are legitimate and could be developed, we have chosen to focus on the relation between the disciplinary and professional frameworks, which are central to a large number but, of course, not all educational programmes.

Example: anatomy in an undergraduate medical programme

New approaches to teaching anatomy have been pioneered over the past decade by Norm Eizenberg (1988, 1991, 1997). He has noted that anatomy is a subject commonly perceived to be a vast array of facts which have to be learned by rote. The kinds of traditional approaches to teaching that we discussed in Chapter 6, which dominate large first-year classes in subjects like anatomy, reinforce that view of learning anatomy. It has tended to typify the 'information transmission' mode of teaching. Eizenberg has developed curriculum materials (Eizenberg, Murphy and Briggs, 1993) and new approaches to the teaching and learning process, and to assessment, which challenge that traditional view of teaching anatomy.

Learning anatomy the Eizenberg way involves focusing on the learning outcomes necessary if medical or other health sciences graduates are to make effective use of what they have learned when confronted with real cases in professional practice. Then the curriculum, the teaching and learning and the assessment are organized with these purposes always in view. So, the curriculum focuses on learning of principles of anatomy, learning about normal variation and learning about the links between the principles and details of disciplinary anatomy and their clinical manifestation in the professional work of doctors, physiotherapists and other health professionals. Being assessed on what you have learned in anatomy becomes a process whereby, in responding to open-ended questions, you have to give explanations about the anatomical basis of clinical phenomena rather than simply regurgitate facts in an unreflective response to closed questions about disciplinary anatomy. Learning for such assessment becomes equivalent to learning for the programme goals.

Evaluations throughout the development of this new programme have generally shown a shift in student approaches to learning from a surface to a deep approach, an integration of the disciplinary and clinical perspectives as students learn anatomy and a generally positive response from students meeting this approach as their first experience of learning anatomy. Positive responses also came from later-year students who compared the new textbook and the innovative learning and assessment processes with those they had experienced in the early years of their own medical studies and, in addition, from tutors who were making similar comparisons with their own past experience both as learners and teachers (Driver and Eizenberg, 1989, 1993).

Disciplinary and professional perspectives

To give readers an idea of what the disciplinary and professional perspectives on anatomy mean in practice, we describe the way the knowledge is structured for one particular part of the curriculum, namely 'ligaments'. Many readers will have a similar knowledge of ligaments to us. We are aware of injuries to well-known sports stars whose 'cruciate' ligament in the knee becomes strained or ruptured in some way and they are unable to play their sport for many months, perhaps a year, following an operation. Indeed, we have now found (Eizenberg *et al*. 1993) that ligaments are fibrous bands that bind bones together and that the 'famous' cruciate ligament in the knee is just one of many ligaments in the body but that it is a particularly vulnerable one under the stress of professional sport.

From the disciplinary perspective, ligaments can be considered in terms of their *composition* – collagen (dense connective tissue which resists stretching) except for special ligaments of elastin (which allow stretch). They can also be considered in terms of their *classification* (accessory capsular, extracapsular and intracapsular), *location*, *attachments*, *form*, *function*, *blood supply* (relatively poor – hence their slow healing), *relations* to other body structures and systems and their *variations* with age, sex and build.

From the clinical (professional) perspective, ligaments are considered in terms of *ligament injuries* and the *pathological condition* involved; the *type* of injury, varying from a sprain to a partial rupture to a complete rupture; the *predisposing factors*; the *mechanism* of injury; the *effects* of injury; the *associated injury to related structures* such as dislocation or bone fracture; the *signs* and *symptoms*; the kinds of *investigation* warranted; *diagnosis*; *treatment*; *complications* such as lengthening of the ligament and weakness due to inadequate repair; *prognosis*; and *prevention* through strengthening, training or strapping.

Both of these ways of organizing knowledge about ligaments are legitimate, they have a different focus and they are complementary. In the past, the organizing principles drawn from the professional perspective, the clinical perspective, did not play a significant part in the design of the anatomy curriculum. The disciplinary perspective was the prevailing one and still is in many anatomy programmes. In the new approach developed at the University of Melbourne, the curriculum, the teaching and learning activities and the assessment in the anatomy subject have students continually moving from one perspective to the other in explaining clinical phenomena and their own observations during dissection. The disciplinary and professional perspectives are genuinely integrated in this curriculum.

Concurrent changes in the Medical Faculty at the University of Melbourne

The development of the anatomy curriculum over the past decade has involved Eizenberg in a series of collaborative activities with other anatomists, clinicians, surgeons and education professionals. This subject is now part of a more broadly based medical curriculum, beginning in 1998, which is premised on the same organizing principle – a team approach across disciplines and between the disciplinary and clinical perspectives. It has necessitated a shift from departmental 'ownership' of subjects to a collective ownership model involving teaching teams. It has produced a change across the whole programme – the curriculum, the nature of student learning experiences and the way students are assessed. It applies not just to the anatomy subject but to all subjects in the undergraduate medical programme.

The anatomy example above shows some of the implications for the way universities need to organize learning if students are to develop a capability to deal with the unknown future. In the following sections we will elaborate those ideas in a more complete way.

Shift from a teaching focus to a learning focus

The shift for universities from organizing their policies and activities with teaching as the focus towards policies and activities centred around learning is not just a semantic shift because it will result in quite different policies and activities from those in place at the moment. The way academics work would be different and the policies and processes of the university that support academic work would also change from the way they are now. Academics would necessarily work more collaboratively; teaching and learning would be undertaken in a less ordered way than now; assessment of student learning outcomes would be more complex but more valid, and decisions about the distribution of money and other resources in the university would pay much more attention to the quality of student learning as a determining criterion than they currently do. Barr and Tagg's (1995) representation of the need to change from an instruction paradigm to a learning paradigm addresses some aspects of what is needed, although we would go further.

Barr and Tagg talk of the shift in mission and purposes from a knowledge-transfer goal to one of eliciting student discovery and construction of knowledge. They argue that universities should not see themselves simply as offering courses and programmes but as creating powerful learning environments for students. They see the criteria for success of universities shifting from inputs like quality of entering students, enrolment numbers and quality of staff towards learning and student-success outcomes, quality of exiting students and aggregate learning growth. They argue that teaching and learning structures should consider the whole programme prior to the parts, rather than vice versa. They envision flexible learning environments organized around learning needs rather than inflexible teaching arrangements organized around the needs of the organization or its staff. They see a curriculum focus on specified learning outcomes rather than mere coverage of the field. Finally, they celebrate the notion of a degree qualification as representing the achievement of demonstrated knowledge and skills rather than accumulated credit hours. However, Barr and Tagg are effectively silent on the kind of learning focus which should replace the instruction paradigm. We have articulated throughout this book the particular learning focus that we believe should guide university policy and practice.

This shift from a teaching focus to the kind of learning focus argued for represents a very significant challenge for the organization of the university. As indicated by Barr and Tagg (1995), the kinds of change implied by their argument for a shift from an instruction paradigm to a learning paradigm are just what various educational developers and other change agents in universities have advocated over recent decades and have achieved to varying degrees. However, what is required is full systemic change, not just change by a small number of dedicated teaching staff, because their isolated efforts and achievements will be washed away by the predominant culture. A number of innovatory projects in universities in the UK failed to achieve their potential because the students studying in the innovative subjects were still enrolled in a large number of other subjects whose characteristics were less supportive of a deep approach to, or meaning orientation in, learning (Gibbs, 1992). It was only a problem-based course in engineering that had a pervasive effect on students' approaches to learning and this was because 'it involved comprehensive changes in students' entire learning time for two terms rather than modifications to only one of several parallel courses students were taking' (Gibbs, 1992).

The nature of the regressive culture referred to above and implied by Gibbs is illustrated by Barr and Tagg (1995) when they describe the action of a dean who came to evaluate his junior colleague's teaching. He found him in the midst of his students, who were spread out across the room in a range of small groups and enthusiastically discussing various issues, with occasional inputs from time to time by the roving academic. The dean, after a few minutes, told his colleague he would come back some other time 'when he was teaching'. It is necessary for deans of the future and everyone in the university, to recognize that many different arrangements for learning represent what teaching is about.

This same attitude has affected some academic staff we have worked with who are reluctant to introduce what they are convinced are more effective learning experiences for students, for reasons related to the attitudes of their academic colleagues. They have refrained from replacing lectures with other more interactive learning experiences for students, which is what they believe they should do, for example. They have said that their colleagues would see them as reducing their teaching effort and would pressure them to take on extra responsibilities in other areas to make up for the apparent workload reduction. This kind of thinking is reinforced by institutional resource distribution based on the number of lectures given, sometimes directly but often indirectly through the funding of teaching modules, which themselves are defined by the number of lectures. Both Dill (1997) and Barr and Tagg (1995) argue against such practices on the grounds that they inhibit innovation and encourage poor learning practices among students.

The integrated curriculum

We now focus on two aspects of the kind of learning we have previously discussed. The first aspect is that students need to learn to be able to deal with the unknown future they will confront after graduation and to do so the curriculum needs to go beyond the specific content. This means that it will include integrating, holistic goals, making the whole greater than the sum of the parts, and will address as well the development in students of a capability to deal with that content in professional contexts. Secondly, the development of that capability is dependent on the ability to discern the relevant aspects of the professional phenomenon, to relate the disciplinary and professional perspectives and to deal with the relevant aspects simultaneously in identifying the problem and designing the solution.

There are several conclusions that can be drawn from the above about the way learning in the university would need to be organized. We have already discussed the general shift from a teaching to a learning focus but we now mention some other, more specific conclusions. First, the university's adoption of a student learning outcomes focus will result in integrated academic programmes rather than differentiated, fragmented curricula and the planning of such integrated curricula will involve academic teams working together rather than individuals working solely in parallel. Second, the university will have developed processes which involve members of the community, including professionals and graduates, in the design of curricula. Third, there are structural implications for the university, arising from these changes. Fourth, academic policy will need to be realigned to ensure that students experience coherent academic curricula and, fifth, these changes need to be effectively communicated.

Academic teams for curriculum design

In Chapters 5 and 6 we discussed the kind of curriculum design necessary for graduates to be prepared for an unknown future. The conclusion was drawn that it is important that students learn in an integrated way if they are to develop the discernment necessary to make judgements about what aspects of their knowledge are relevant to a particular situation. The learning of large numbers of different pockets of information, which both Dill (1997) and Barr and Tagg (1995) show are common in today's universities, seems to be unlikely to prepare graduates adequately. This implies that the goals of university education would need to be redefined and there would be a need to get consensus on that issue within the university. That will not be easy and will need solutions fashioned for each particular institutional context.

In addition, it is difficult to see how integrated curricula would be produced unless the university has teams of academics working on curriculum development rather than leaving it to individual academics to work out on their own, as many universities currently do. The kinds of learning outcomes desired require integration across what are currently isolated parts of the curriculum. That integration has to be planned and this can only occur through co-operative processes.

For many academics this will not be an easy transition. They have become used to acting autonomously and often prefer to do so despite the fact that assumptions made by an academic about what is happening elsewhere in the programme can be completely mistaken. We have had the experience of getting a very reluctant engineering academic team together to discuss the various aspects of the programme taught by each academic. Their attitudes largely were that, because each subject had only one expert, no one else could make any comments on the curriculum that could be of value to that person, who in turn could not comment on others' curricula. Fairly early in the meeting one academic, responsible for a second-year systems subject based on computer modelling, complained about the fall in the quality of students in recent years; students now found difficulty in completing the computer-based tasks he asked of them. Later in the meeting, the academic teaching computer programming in the first year remarked that two years earlier, he had reduced the number of computer languages he taught so that he could focus on programming principles. When the first academic asked which programming language had been dropped two years before, the answer he was given provided a far more obvious explanation for his students' recent performances than he had earlier assumed. Of course, why he had not detected the real problem before that moment is a reasonable question to ask. However, the fact that there had been no process which would have brought these two academics together to discuss the curriculum in terms of student learning is at the heart of the matter. There should have been a mechanism for the relation between the various aspects of the programme to be constantly under joint review by those teaching in it. Our argument for integrated learning is more subtle than this example but the issue is the same – unless academics plan curricula together, they cannot possibly co-ordinate their activities to the benefit of their students – and our approach requires even more co-ordination than academics have in general been so far used to, if learning is to be the focus.

Johnson (1992) has written about the ways in which attempts of the kind argued for here to bring about a shift from an individual approach to a team approach can fail. He suggests that, irrespective of whether the existing paradigm is for an individual or team approach, the tendency is for the status quo to continue until the disadvantages outweigh the advantages and then a shift to the other approach will take place. He illustrates this process diagrammatically as shown in Figure 10.1. He suggests that members of the organization end up in never-ending cycles of change from working alone to working in a team to working alone, *ad infinitum*.

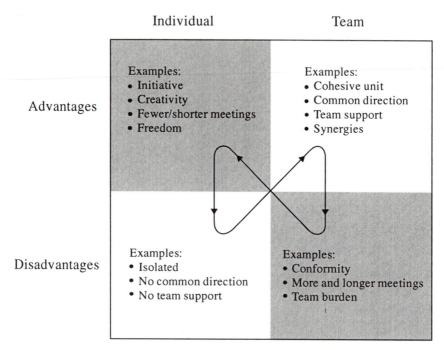

Figure 10.1: *Individual–team polarity map (adapted from Johnson, 1992)*

Johnson suggests that the failure arises from treating either development of individual initiative or team building as problems to be solved. It generates unnecessary and costly resistance and causes staff to spend needless time focusing on the downside of one or both of the poles. He advocates a polarity management perspective by which resistance is anticipated and worked with so that the positive aspects of both poles are maximized. The loose–tight process for quality assurance discussed in Chapter 9 is of this kind. Currently it is coincidental that the economic market encourages a team-oriented approach, which is what we are arguing for as well, but on pedagogical grounds.

When discussing transitions, from working individually to working in teams or vice versa, we should remember that 'working in teams' might mean radically different things to different people, as Joan Benjamin's (1997) study shows. She found five distinctively different ways in which academic staff working together (in teams) thought about it and handled their shared tasks. Working in teams meant:

A. sharing the workload among the teaching team members – divide up the parts of the curriculum between the teachers (this means not having very much shared discussion; the teachers are all specialized on some unit and one follows after the other)

B. sharing the workload among the teaching team members – to ensure the stability of delivery and regularity of the curriculum (this is the opposite of A; each teacher can teach everything within the programme; hence they can easily replace each other)

C. sharing the workload among the teaching team members – to give breadth to the curriculum (in contrast to A and B, the whole is seen as greater than the sum of the parts; different teachers are pooling what they can contribute)

D. involving the teaching team – to improve the teaching and the curriculum (doing what they do in C but with the explicit purpose of improving the way they work)

E. involving the teaching team – to improve learning (doing the same as in D but with a point of departure in a theoretically grounded understanding of how it may contribute to improving student learning).

Obviously we would not only wish that teachers worked together but also that they were driven by motives of the kind depicted in category E.

Given that these transitions are not easy for academics, it is important that there are staff development opportunities provided to assist them to deal with rapid change. It is important also that the reward systems of the university are not at odds with the changes the university expects staff to undertake. The shift from a focus on teaching to a focus on learning implies the need for academics to think differently about their work, to develop new skills and to carry out their work differently. They will need time, opportunity and support to make those transitions and when they do, when their focus on different work activities shifts and a new balance is reached that is different from before, the reward systems of the university need to be in harmony with those new directions, not just formally but in practical ways.

Disciplinary socialization

Another example, which graphically illustrates the need for changed practices if learning is to be a focus, comes from a research study on assessment of a cross-disciplinary student project reported by Wistedt (1997). The project concerned the construction of an electrical circuit and part of the assessment was by a group report; there were three examiners – a physicist, a mathematician and a statistician. Two of Wistedt's findings are relevant to the issue we are discussing. The first is that the different examiners' judgements on the reports varied enormously in a way that reflected different expectations and different norms of behaviour in the different disciplines. These norms and conventions are often taken for granted within the discipline but can pose a problem for students. In this case, the convention in mathematics not to have large numbers of references to the literature is in contrast with what is usual in physics and statistics. This is related to the greater level of discourse in the latter. Another, seemingly insignificant difference in conventions, which caused different judgements from the examiners about the student reports, is the practice in mathematics of numbering only a few significant formulae/equations whereas all are numbered in running order in physics.

In a differentiated curriculum, this is not seen as an issue because in such a system, as Wistedt suggests for example, 'you do not learn mathematics, you just get used to it'. The student learns not only the content of the discipline but also the stylistic demands and conventions of that discipline as one thing. It is when the student is confronted with an interdisciplinary project that this idea of knowledge being culturally defined and influenced by social and individual factors becomes relevant. In addition, of course, the real experiences of the student after graduation will be interdisciplinary so this is an important aspect of their learning overlooked in a differentiated curriculum. These conventions are taken for granted by people in the various fields but can be seen by students as lots of different local rules without much structure. Often students cannot quite understand what is required in a particular case; they cannot see the examiner's intention, and the natural response is to resort to regurgitation of memorized material – a surface approach which is contrary to what most educators desire in their students. In the case reported by Wistedt, these differences were made explicit and became a source of learning for students. By experiencing variation in these norms and conventions among the different examiners, the very existence of such norms and conventions became visible to the students and could be dealt with.

There was a further report from that project, which is worth discussing, because there was learning by the examiners themselves as well. As they discussed with the students their various responses to the student group reports they had read, and as differences in their views became apparent, they shared the underlying reasons for their particular perspectives. In this way, the varying norms and conventions came to be discussed. This was in part a revelation for the three examiners as well as for the students but, moreover, each examiner began to question whether what appeared to be a convention in their discipline really was consistent with their own normal behaviour and that of their colleagues. They not only learned more about the existence of different conventions among disciplines, they also began through this collaborative process to question their taken-for-granted assumptions about their own discipline's conventions. The experience of variation caused a revision of taken-for-granted knowledge. This raises the question of whether what was in this case a chance event should instead be planned, with this kind of learning becoming the norm in all of our university educational programmes. It may be too valuable an opportunity to lose and it seems it can only be attained by the commitment of academic teams to curriculum development.

This is not to argue that the departmental structure of most universities, which is largely based on discipline, should be changed. We discuss this point further below when we examine structural implications. There are many reasons related to research specializations and the need to provide a social context for students, which make such a departmental structure valuable, although this is not the only contextual arrangement possible or needed by students. However, it is the lack of co-operative processes across and within departments which leads to the difficulties we have outlined. The fact that the debilitating fragmentation occurs not only across departments but also within them indicates that the problem is also a cultural and not simply a structural one. We will argue later in this chapter that educational programmes and organizational structures together need to reflect the interdisciplinary reality outside the university. Already, current educational programmes more closely reflect the structure of knowledge in the professions in which graduates will be working than does the university's organizational structure. The discipline-based departmental structure is transcended as students experience learning in a range of departments and in workplace settings. However, we argue that more needs to be done to facilitate this integration. The professions provide an alternative way of organizing knowledge and the curriculum process needs to respond to both the disciplinary and professional frameworks.

Pusey (1992) suggests that it is not easy for graduates to leave behind the specialization culture they became used to during their education. This applies equally to academics as to anyone else. Pusey uses the Australian Government's Senior Executive Service as an example. He compares the attitudes of those who had been trained as economists and those who had been trained in the humanities or social sciences. He asked them to respond to four policy questions about distribution of gross national product (is it biased to wage and salary earners, balanced or biased to capital?), deregulation of the labour market (approve or disapprove?), trade unions (less power than business? both balanced? more power with business? no answer?) and relations between capital and labour (complementary and equal rather than unequal? unequal and exploitative rather than complementary and equal? categories no longer relevant?). He found that the educational qualification is a more powerful predictor of orientations to policy and management than other variables such as age, socio-economic status, seniority and so on. Those with economics degrees were more likely to respond that there is bias to wage and salary earners, approve deregulation, respond that trade unions have more power and that capital and labour are complementary and equal.

Pusey's study supports Dahlgren's (1989) earlier finding. He was able to demonstrate that even if studies in economics may have a limited effect on students' use of powerful conceptual tools – as was shown in Chapter 7 in the examples of the understanding of price, for instance – they strongly influence students' general orientation. Dahlgren found that four years of studies in economics and business administration were correlated with a shift from an initial focus on the uneven distribution of economic resources, either from an international or from a national perspective, to a focus on the more efficient utilization of resources or on the necessity for more incentives for individual or collective initiatives.

The perspective of the professions and employers

Concerns about fragmented, content-focused curricula often produce a reaction as if the choice were between a content-focused curriculum and a generic skills-focused curriculum. Many argue for a shift to a generalized focus on generic skills. However, we would assert that it is not the focus on content that is problematic. It is the differentiation of that content into isolated and unrelated pieces. Employers acknowledge that graduates know a lot of these bits and pieces but argue that graduates simply do not know what to do when faced with novel situations (see Chapter 5). The capability to deal with unknown situations is not content-free. It has very much to do with knowing something, having knowledge about certain phenomena, about a content, including also the knowledge of bits and pieces but, in addition, understanding the relations among the bits and pieces, and between that knowledge and the context in which it is being considered. As well, it is necessary to understand how that knowledge links to knowledge in related areas; knowing the limitations of the usefulness of a concept is as important as knowing the concept itself. In fact it is part of really knowing the concept as was seen in the force and acceleration example in Chapter 5. So rather than react by moving away from content, it is necessary to focus on the relations within the content fields and between content and context. Again disciplinary and professional frameworks need to be complementary contributors to that process.

Employers, members of professions, other members of the community and graduates who are in the workforce, are well aware of the contexts in which graduates will find themselves. Often they are more aware than are the academics themselves. Some way of including people such as these in the curriculum-development process would be valuable so as to establish a balance between the professional and disciplinary frameworks. Some universities require each educational programme or each department to have a programme advisory committee on which representatives of the named groups sit. Such universities often have a policy of not approving any academic curriculum that does not have the support of such an advisory committee. Some process of this kind would be valuable for any university interested in preparing graduates for their future roles. This is taken up in the next section.

Structural implication: planned coincidence of authority and capability

We now consider some structural issues concerning the organization and management of learning in the university. We are focusing on the curriculum question. The locus of operation can be at one or a combination of three levels in the university:

1. at the level of the department
2. at the level of the educational programme
3. at the level of the university itself.

Consideration of the kind of learning argued for here leads to the conclusion that the optimal arrangement would involve a series of different responsibilities at each of these levels rather than the current focus on level (1) in most universities, with variable impact of level (3) influences. The organizing principle would be that, with maximized quality of student learning outcomes as the central criterion, responsibility for any aspect of the programme should be placed where the expertise exists to ensure the aspect is effectively implemented, that is, a planned coincidence of authority and capability.

Proposed structural model

We show in Figure 10.2 the kind of organizational structure we have in mind. We have already outlined an argument for the curriculum-development function to be at the level of the educational programme, ie undertaken by a team of academics who teach in the programme (which we will refer to as the programme team). There are other issues to be addressed about programme-team membership including involvement of library and other learning-support staff and the way of managing both large teams and dispersed teams. There are examples of the former in the RMIT EQA system (see Chapter 9) where 50 or more staff teach in a particular programme and matrix models are used to manage the interactions. The dispersed situation will inevitably arise with networked and global universities and the functional management of such international programme teams is an issue yet to be addressed. Again our belief would be that the processes to be used should be chosen on the basis of their effectiveness in promoting the intended learning outcomes for students. Clearly the very technology which has made such networked universities possible would also contribute to these management solutions.

There is the issue of the links between programme teams and academic departments in this model. The academics in the programme team would be members of the departments many of whose subjects would constitute the educational programme and the programme team acts as a natural bridge between the integrated programme and the separate departments. We have reported that in some universities a programme advisory committee is also established for each educational programme and that such a committee usually comprises professionals in the field, employers and past graduates of the programme currently working in the relevant profession. This kind of organizational arrangement is consistent with the requirements for the kind of learning we have discussed.

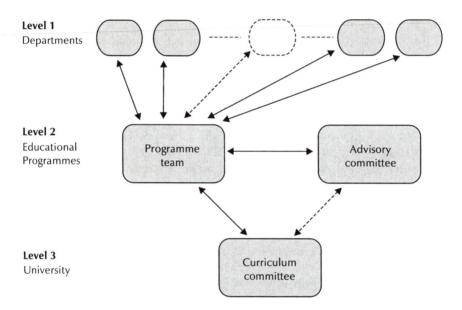

Level 1
Departments

Level 2
Educational
Programmes

Level 3
University

Figure 10.2: *Approval structure for educational programme and curriculum development*

The existence of departments at level (1), of a programme team and an advisory committee at level (2) and a university curriculum committee at level (3) would facilitate the kind of integrated curricula shown to be needed by students and would meet the test of placing authority where there is expertise to deliver. It could work as follows:

1. The programme team could develop the general themes for a new curriculum and would submit an outline to the university's curriculum committee for approval to go ahead with the next phase. The criteria could be related to traditional issues such as the wider university educational programme profile, the state of the market for a programme of that kind and the availability or accessibility of appropriate human and other resources. Because the detail would not have been developed at this stage, pedagogical criteria *per se* would play a more minor role in the decision to sanction what is effectively a comprehensive development of

the educational plan.

2. What would follow then could be iterative processes between the programme team and the advisory committee, especially regarding the interface between the disciplinary and professional perspectives. Naturally much of the teaching would be actually undertaken in departments in some contractual arrangements with the programme team but since each relevant department would have members on that team who would also, by necessity, be teaching in the programme, there is a natural relationship between the two structural entities and the functions they share. The department is the guardian of the disciplinary perspectives, the members of the advisory committee the most effective spokespersons for the professional perspective and the programme team would have the responsibility to articulate the relation between these, and express them in terms of student learning needs and the nature of the learning experiences and assessment necessary to achieve the integrated objectives.

3. The programme team would submit a final, complete proposal to the curriculum committee, which would also receive comments from the advisory committee.

4. The curriculum committee, which would consider those documents, would not be an expert committee in terms of each specific curriculum proposal because it would be a central committee with membership across the full range of the university's fields of study. The curriculum committee could analyse the coherence of the programme, its adherence to assessment policy and other relevant policies, and to the advice of the expert advisory committee who would have commented on the adequacy of the curriculum design and implementation plans in terms of the links between the disciplinary and professional frameworks.

The status quo in many universities has curriculum development largely as a departmental function undertaken by the academics in the department with some more or less perfunctory central committee input. The consequence is a fragmented curriculum which cannot prepare students to cope with the unknown future as professionals. In such a system there is no one with both the expertise and authority to address the integrated whole and the aspects of the curriculum that go beyond the content. There is normally little involvement of stakeholders or experts outside the university and this would be an anachronism in the era of the networked university.

Resource distribution

There is a resource-distribution issue associated with this kind of process. A decision that the university would have to make, if it were to adopt the kind of arrangement we have outlined, is whether to retain the current resource-distribution model (which is usually linked to departmental or faculty structures) or whether to include in the model a more indirect distribution focused around the educational programmes, with the programme teams having a say in the final distribution, with students' learning needs as the major criterion.

We would argue in favour of the programme team having the responsibility to negotiate with departments for the provision of their services to the educational programme. This would be likely to encourage greater compliance with the programme team's requests for more integrated, learning-centred curriculum and teaching, especially if the programme team had the authority to outsource some aspects of the teaching should one or more departments fail to provide high-quality outcomes. We believe that this kind of arrangement is necessary if we are to truly have resource distribution determined by the quality of learning outcomes as Barr and Tagg (1995) have argued.

There are some questions raised by this proposal, which has been framed in response to an assumption that the status quo in universities is generally for departments to be the most powerful entities. What is the role of the faculty? Will the resource-distribution power for the programme team interfere with the efficient distribution of resources from the university management to the departments, often through a faculty? What about universities in which departments have little power and the faculties are the bodies with authority? What about educational programmes that are not organized by the university around a particular theme, ie programmes in which students can choose any combination of subjects or units that they like? We will address each of these questions in turn.

There are many different organizational structures in universities and the power-sharing also varies among the various academic entities such as super-faculties, faculties, schools, departments, centres and units. We have discussed the role of departments already, but what is the role of the faculty? In the structural model shown in Figure 10.2, we anticipate that many educational programme teams will have significant membership of a particular faculty. For example, the majority of members of programme teams for medicine, engineering, accountancy, art or chemistry are likely to be members of departments in faculties of medicine (or health sciences), engineering (or technology), business, arts or science, respectively. Significantly some members of each team will be from different faculties and the process proposed will focus the interaction between constituent faculties in ways that relate to the learning needs of students. This will not prevent faculties, where they exist, from going about their normal business but it will limit the extent to which faculty business distorts students' learning experiences and that is the intention.

Will the resource-distribution power for the programme team interfere with the efficient distribution of resources from the university management to the departments, often through a faculty? In our experience, departments already receive funds from a variety of sources. Certainly, considerable resources do come either directly from university management or indirectly through a faculty as intermediary. However, most university departments also earn external grants of various kinds, run short courses for profit, negotiate consultancy projects with private enterprise, make agreements about resource transfer to and from other departments in relation to collaborative or service activities and so on. Our proposal would merely represent another aspect of an already varied array of funding avenues.

What about universities in which departments have little power and the faculties are the bodies with authority? Our proposal would necessarily result in a shift of power from such faculties towards the departments and the programme teams. We would argue that the detailed curriculum integration necessary, if the form of learning we argue for is to be achieved, must be taking place at the department level, in addition to the need for action at the collective level. The development of a capability to deal with unknown situations is related both to the understanding of particular content relevant to such situations and experiences of variation which enable discernment of the relevant aspects of that knowledge in the situation. This will necessarily involve work both at the department levels and across faculty boundaries. Our model is one in which the matrix of authority is coincidental with the matrix of competence to deliver. This necessarily implies a spread, a balance of authority; a university which has entities at just one level maintaining all power is unlikely to be successful in fostering the kind of learning outcomes we espouse.

What about universities in which departments already wield most power with respect to curriculum and teaching? Our proposal again would tend to develop a balanced power distribution, with various entities such as departments retaining control over functions at which they alone are expert but yielding power to others when a broader or different expertise is needed in order to maximize the quality of student learning.

What about educational programmes that are not organized by the university around a particular theme, ie programmes in which students can choose any combination of subjects or units that they like? Such programmes, which we would refer to as 'smorgasbord degrees', may result in a coherent outcome but is unlikely to in many cases. It relies on one of two things being true. First, the enrolled student has the experience to judge how the various pieces can be integrated and the capacity to ensure that the university provides appropriate opportunities for this to occur. Second, the university provides an advisory service which helps such students with those tasks. One example of the latter is the Bachelor of Art and Design degree at RMIT. The Faculty of Art and Design boasts of providing as many different educational programmes as there are students enrolled. Each student takes a unique programme. However, this is not without considerable effort by academic staff, who provide an advisory service for students choosing their combination of subjects and learning experiences and then jointly monitoring them across the period of study. Again, such activities need to be planned and co-ordinated, and in fact they become just one *modus operandi* for a particular programme team. So this model is in fact a subset of our model in Figure 10.2. We argue that the university has a responsibility to provide support and advice to maximize the learning experiences and outcomes for all students and our model facilitates this, even for students with a completely free choice of subjects within the educational programme. It is apparent that the student–adviser role envisaged in this model is not one which all staff would be experienced with and, as with other things we have discussed, the staff development and university rewards systems need to recognize these roles and provide support for staff if they are to be undertaken as seriously as is warranted.

Quality assurance

The model in Figure 10.2, which places responsibility for any aspect of learning in the place where the expertise lies, provides an ideal opportunity, as discussed in Chapter 9, for educational quality assurance to be focused on student learning. The programme team is responsible for ensuring both that the content detail and the broader capabilities associated with it in an integrated curriculum are planned appropriately and that students' learning experiences result in the learning outcomes desired. The team is in an ideal position from which to keep records of these processes, collect evidence about the outcomes and take action as necessary to make improvements. This is the essence of quality assurance, and further checks and balances are provided through the programme team's dealings with the university's curriculum committee, the departments themselves and the advisory committee of professionals and employers.

Staff workload

We emphasize that our argument for academic teams to be responsible for curriculum development does not imply that there should be substantially more work for academics. Our emphasis is on working differently, perhaps working smarter. Currently, academics spend varying amounts of time developing curricula in the subjects they teach. They contribute to some kind of documentary process when the curriculum is first approved by some central university committee. We envisage that a more collaborative process such as that outlined above may be more efficient and certainly more productive and satisfying. The overall process could also be more rational. The issue would not be for academic staff to do more (in workload terms) but to do what they need to do differently and with more appropriate application of expertise, so that the intended student learning outcomes remain the focus.

In addition, the new economics for universities entering the new millennium and associated changes to intellectual property principles and practice mean that the processes for development of curriculum and course materials need to be reconceptualized. These same issues of economies of scale apply both to networking and use of information technology to broaden the student base and to make the cost of producing high-quality curricula and course materials financially beneficial. The same argument applies to the number of weeks a year that the university uses its facilities for undergraduate teaching. One of the examples we discussed in Chapter 7 involved using student assessment outcomes as an evaluation measure in comparing the teaching of an accountancy subject in a summer-school intensive mode compared with the traditional teaching during semester. How long will it be before students will no longer see first enrolment in a university programme as normally taking place at the beginning of the academic year? How long will our current idea of an academic year remain? How will the university organize learning under more flexible arrangements like these so that quality in student learning is not a casualty? It seems obvious that all staff in the university, not just academics, need to feel part of the education process so that their decisions about their own functions, whether they appear to be educationally linked or not, take as their point of departure the need to provide a quality learning environment.

Ensuring implementation through policy change

Of course, there must be some way to ensure that the integrated curriculum is a reality. As we have already argued, there is a need for some measure of agreement in the university community that this is a good idea. There is a need for appropriate curriculum policies and processes and we have talked about those. However, they are not sufficient in themselves. Academics are subject to many pressures on their time in their increasingly busy life at university. As a consequence, there is likely to be slippage in practice unless there is some kind of pay off for academics to continue to devote time to designing the complex curricula we are arguing for and maintaining them. It would be easier just to list the various topics from the textbook or from recent research publications and give a lecture on each. It is much more difficult to plan, in a collaborative way with colleagues, for students to experience this same content in ways that lead to more powerful learning outcomes. We referred in Chapter 9 to Dill (1997) who argues that '... it is crucial educational coherence be used to choose among potential candidates for academic curricula'. He suggests that academic curricula should provide a coherent academic experience for students and that there must be evidence that students have had a coherent learning experience. We would add 'and have developed the capability to discern relevant aspects of professional situations and to deal with them simultaneously'.

Obviously in such circumstances the university needs to have a clear and adequate assessment policy. Given the new focus for university policy on learning for the unknown, there needs to be an assessment policy which requires summative assessment across the full range of objectives, including those associated with the capability to deal with novel contexts. Even when assessing technical aspects, assessment should be required to address underlying meaning and the university needs ways to ensure that the assessment conforms to these expectations. Also, if students are to develop the capabilities expected, they need to have practice in, for instance, dealing with unknown contexts. The use of formative assessment for experience and feedback as a part of learning is an essential feature of any university's assessment policy and it should be explicitly stated and monitored.

Communication of the changed curriculum purposes

Even if all staff agree with the kind of curriculum and the teaching, learning and assessment experiences we suggest are necessary for graduates to cope with the unknown future, how will potential students who are choosing a university, deciding on which educational programme to enrol in or selecting which subjects or modules to take, know what their choices are? For statements of educational purposes (education goals and objectives) to be adequate, they need to be more completely elaborated than is commonly the case now. Often statements of purposes of, say, a particular subject do little more than indicate that students will develop knowledge and understanding of a range of listed topics. Little is said about the way the learner will change, either with respect to the specific content or in more general ways associated with the links between that particular content and the overall focus of the educational programme. In general, a prose format would be better than a list format because it facilitates the expression of what are relatively complex intentions in ways that a listing process generally fails to communicate. It is in the interest of student learning and development of their professional competence that such statements of purpose be more explicit; but it is essential for assessment purposes.

It is difficult to believe that the assessment of student learning outcomes according to the criteria we have embraced could be undertaken properly without explicit statements of purposes. We know that assessment practices affect students' approaches to learning and if the purposes, the learning and the assessment are to be in harmony, the details of each need to be explicit and unambiguous. In Chapter 5 we suggested that the writing of a syllabus for a physics subject in a list format provides a protective barrier for academic teachers and that almost any kind of teaching could be undertaken within such a syllabus. We suggested further that a more informative statement, of which we gave a sample, would make academics and the university more accountable. Such explicit statements may be a disincentive for some potential students but they are also likely to be a strong incentive for many. Any university, which adopts this kind of approach, is likely to attract motivated students and will be able to justify its educational practices with reference to those statements of purpose. Furthermore, it is likely to have its students 'learning for the assessment' but because the clear expression of purposes will enable valid assessment, student learning will be directed towards acquisition of the capabilities intended.

Flexible learning environments

In Chapter 3, on student approaches to learning, we described Ramsden's (1984) research which showed that students are more likely to adopt a deep approach to learning and are more likely to seek meaning and understanding if they are able to exercise a degree of choice about what and how they learn. It is important that, as much as possible, the learning environment is flexible so that students can exercise such choice and develop as the kind of independent learners we seek.

In addition, in our discussion of the development of collective competence in Chapter 8, implying respect for the perspectives of others, we discussed the need to recognize that students are part of the collective and that as they learn so does the whole university. Most of us would be able to recall many occasions when we have had sudden insights into some aspect of our field through contributions by our students. The university of learning will value this and will avoid introducing inflexibility into the learning environment that is likely to curb such student contributions.

Finally, there is a much greater level of community influence on what students do and universities cannot ignore the community expectation of greater flexibility in universities and their functions in these times of mass education. This expectation includes the provision of flexible learning environments. These issues will be discussed below.

Current learning environments

The degree of flexibility in opportunities provided to learners varies from one university to another and from time to time. In many universities, students do choose what course to undertake, albeit in a competitive environment. They have a varied mix of compulsory and optional subjects to study within that course and they usually have a limited choice of planned learning experiences, some of which they must attend if they are to successfully complete the course (such as laboratory or clinical work) with others being optional (such as lectures or tutorials). Students still normally (but not universally) have to attend a university campus regularly to complete the learning programme, with the alternatives at a distance often being difficult to manage. Sometimes, but not often, students are given choices about the way they undertake certain aspects of the programme, eg a lecture series over a semester, or a week-long intensive, or a set of computer-based activities. They are rarely offered a choice of forms of assessment even when the intended outcomes are clearly spelt out and could reasonably be equally tested by a variety of means. In addition, students have only limited access to assessment opportunities which are planned primarily as part of the learning process rather than for grading. Finally, while students are increasingly being provided with access to technologically based learning opportunities, they have limited access to training programmes to teach them to use the new systems and they have to grapple with technological infrastructures that are often inadequate.

While this is a common picture, it is not universal and many programmes or parts of them could be characterized quite differently, however we consider that the list above represents the general situation. The matter of limited learner choice is the theme that runs through that list, a lack of flexibility on the part of many universities in the educational opportunities they provide to learners. A university that intends to survive into the new century must be different.

From a teaching to a learning environment

The kind of learning experiences we argued for in Chapter 6 will not be as well ordered and tightly managed as, say, a traditional lecture programme. Barr and Tagg (1995) criticize the traditional lecture approach on several grounds but primarily on the basis that the one-teacher, one-classroom, 50-minute lecture as the cornerstone of teaching creates limitations on the physical architecture, the administrative structure and the daily schedules of staff and students. These limitations are 'antithetical to creating almost any other kind of learning experience'. Difficulties arise in such an environment in dealing with varying student experience and attainment prior to entry to the university or in addressing such aspects as ethics, communications skills and learning skill within the content learning to which they apply. Barr and Tagg deplore the usual solution of setting up remedial, study-skills or communication courses taught by other academics, probably also in the 50-minute lecture blocks that are the source of the problem. They argue that those capabilities, which are often called generic skills, need to be seen in the context of the subject content, and we concur. What Barr and Tagg are criticizing is what we have argued represents differentiation without integration, a fragmenting of the curriculum which is to the detriment of learning. Staff at the moment endure substantial resistance if they try to overcome these barriers to flexible approaches to learning. To achieve the kind of learning we have embraced, the organization of teaching and learning experiences in the university needs to change.

Resolving the apparent conflict

While the status quo is represented as being less than adequate, what is the ideal situation? Should universities organize themselves so learners can choose to do whatever they want, whenever they want and however they want? It is easy to dismiss this as fanciful but questions about how much flexibility and what kind of flexibility in educational provision are optimal must be answered. We have argued for some aspects of curricula and learning experiences to be prescribed for students and that the flexibility in their learning experiences should be maximized. These views appear to be in conflict and we will deal with that apparent conflict in this section. To do so, it is necessary to consider who or what else besides the learner should have an influence on what learners do in universities.

One primary influence is pedagogical which, as we discussed in Chapters 5 and 6, is a crucial one. We have argued that there are some particular experiences that students may need if they are to achieve the desired learning outcomes. When this is so, student choice should necessarily be limited. There are other influences which place limits on student choice and these include government policies, the state of the economy, the needs of industry and employers, the resource levels in the universities, the requirements of professional organizations, the skill profile and cultural preferences of university staff, the adequacy of various systems (eg information technology) to provide viable alternatives and the characteristics of the learners (eg where they live, work and prefer to study). We have already argued the case for some influence by some of these, including the professions and employers. Necessarily, the degree of student choice is limited by the licensing requirements of professions or government agencies, expectations by the community of universities as shown through financial support of programmes deemed important to the nation and lack of support for others, and the way the university uses the resources it has available.

The last of these three provides the key to the creation of a flexible learning environment. The basic principle is that, within the financial, community and pedagogical framework described, student choice should be optimized. This is in keeping with the findings by Ramsden (1984) that development of independence in students through choice of how and what to learn encourages a deep rather than a surface approach to learning. In addition, it is also in accordance with the argument put forward in the previous chapter that collective competence and preparedness for an unpredictable future is enhanced through greater variation in the nature of competence developed on the individual level. Some limits may need to be placed on student choice where the government and community require it or when relevant learning theory indicates it is more effective to do so, but otherwise the university should create a flexible environment in which student choice is maximized, within the limits of its resources – human, financial and physical. This qualified notion of optimizing of student choice is in contrast with the fanciful notion dismissed earlier of anything, anyhow and anytime. In practice, the optimization for an individual learner will be through negotiation between the learner and teaching staff, an interaction which in itself is a central part of the learning process.

It should be emphasized that there are two kinds of choice included here. One relates to the subjects enrolled in and the other to the sorts of learning experiences students engage in, in order to achieve the outcomes intended. Our argument for qualified choice applies to both. In varying ways from one programme to another, there are likely to be some compulsory subjects because they are pedagogically crucial to students achieving the intended outcomes for the programme. Outside of that qualification we would argue for maximized student choice according to relevance and interest.

Secondly, within any particular subject the need for students to be able to exercise choice of what and how they learn can be facilitated by provision of alternative ways in which students might undertake various aspects of their learning. It might be regarded as essential that students understand certain disciplinary concepts but whether they interact with such content, through attending a lecture series, accessing material on the Internet, reading in the library or by using a multimedia program on their computer at home, could be a choice they have. It might be thought essential that they engage in some interaction with staff and other students in developing their understanding but whether that is through conventional tutorials, chat sessions on the Internet or through electronic bulletin boards might be left to individual students. They may also be expected to solve a number of problems of various kinds related to those issues, which they may choose to do by attendance at problem classes on campus or by using problem sheets at home and keeping in touch with academic teachers and other students through email and a bulletin board on the Internet. They are also likely to have to learn to deal with the unknown, to develop discernment and a capacity to deal with relevant aspects of a new situation simultaneously. The university may decide that this can only be done effectively face to face over an extended period of time and may require all students to attend a series of compulsory one-day workshops. It is this combination of stipulated types of experience, with choice where possible but not where that would be counter-productive, that we believe is likely to be optimal for student learning. In this notion of a flexible learning environment, the flexibility for some parts of the environment to be compulsory is included. Whether it is likely to contribute to student learning remains the criterion for decision making.

In summary, we can say with some certainty that if the university is to do an effective job of arranging a more flexible environment for learning, it needs to be clear about the following aspects of its educational programmes:

- the kinds of outcomes intended for and by learners
- what aspects of the particular programme are essential (prescribed aspects) and what aspects can be chosen without restriction (ie within the constraints of the university's commitment to its graduates having a specified set of attributes, and within the context of external expectations from industry, the professions, government and the community)
- similar consideration of what kinds of learning experiences are essential (prescribed aspects), again often mandated by the need to develop professional competence

- negotiation of the previous two points between teaching staff and learners as an integral part of teaching and learning (student choice)
- the range of options the university is able to offer, eg for students to choose to use a learning package rather than attend a lecture series, or to learn through a problem-based project rather than a conventional class contact and examination (student choice).

The organization of the university as the embodiment of its collective consciousness

Differentiation and integration

In this section we look at differentiation and integration. The university is probably the most differentiated institution we have, with extensively special-ized parts, each with a high degree of autonomy. In fact, its differentiated nature and its loose organization have been referred to as the main explanation for its adaptability to changing conditions and therefore its power to survive (Kerr, 1982):

> About 85 institutions in the Western world established by 1520 still exist in recognisable forms, with similar functions and unbroken histories, including the Catholic Church, the parliaments of the Isle of Man, Iceland and Great Britain, several Swiss cantons, and 70 universities. Kings that rule, feudal lords with vassals and guilds with monopolies are gone. These 70 universities, however, are still in the same locations with some of the same buildings, with professors and students doing much the same things, with governance carried on much the same way.

In Chapter 8 we argued that having a variety of people dealing with the same object of knowledge is central to research and also to studying. This means differentiation in terms of objects of knowledge. At the same time, it means integration of the differing views of different people having the same object of knowledge in common. We also made the point in Chapter 8 that there should be multiple stratification of the objects of knowledge. A particular person would have a certain object of knowledge in common with some people and another object (or other objects) in common with other people. In this way we can potentially come up with a network to which all members of the organization belong and through which they are linked to each other in multiple ways. This is how the collective consciousness of the organization might evolve. We should observe that this is integration through differentiation. Individuals are connected to each other (inte-gration) through multiple objects of knowledge (differentiation).

In addition, of course, in accordance with our comment on Johnson's (1992) study earlier in this chapter, differentiation and integration define a dimension, the very dimension being a critical feature of the university as an organization, just as the dimension defined by the distinction between working individually and working with others is. Discussions are often mistakenly framed in terms of being for or against the independent individual with a critical-mind type of research, on the one hand, and working in teams on the other. As Johnson (1992) says, instead of seeking to come up with conclusive evidence in favour of or against one or the other, we have to realize that working individually versus working in teams constitute a critical dimension of the university structure, a prominent feature, which we have to deal with to the best of our powers, and certainly allow for movement and dynamics in it. We cannot fixate a unique point in this dimension at which we should stand, but have to examine the different cases from the point of view of which style of working is preferable. The same applies to differentiation and integration as well. The balance between them cannot be settled once and for all. It has to be found – again and again.

In Chapter 8 we dealt with differentiation and integration in terms of shared focus, absence of shared focus, awareness of others' ways of seeing, absence of such awareness and so on, ie in terms of what is going on in people's minds, in their thoughts and in their awareness. In the present chapter, we are dealing with differentiation and integration in terms of organizational structures and the two are not independent. People's ways of seeing the world are partly a function of the institutional context in which they are situated and the institutional context derives its meaning very much from the people for whom it is a context. We will return to this issue below.

There is therefore a dialectical relationship between the institutional context on the one hand and the people in the institutional context, on the other hand. As we pointed out in Chapter 9 Askling and Almén (1997) argue that institutional context provides the participants with a certain space of action. Some options for acting are available to them, while others are constrained. If the participants make full use of those options, and they do so by undertaking considered choices, then we can expect a certain correspondence between the structure of the space of action defined by the system, and the structure of variation in what is focused, discussed, reflected on and in consequence the structure of variation in the participants' awareness. In this case we can say that individual awarenesses are framed, formed or moulded by the institutional context.

However, it is rarely the case that the participants adapt completely to the system. They may not make full use of the options available to them and to the extent they do they may not make considered choices, springing from reflection, but act by routine, tacitly taking for granted the course of action. In such a case the institutional context providing a potential space of action will differ from the institutional context providing a space of action actually used. The latter is defined by those making use of it, the participants: teachers and students.

According to the contingency model of organization the form and management is contingent upon the technology utilized and the pattern of competition (Lawrence and Lorsch, 1986). In an early application of this theory, Burns and Stalker (1961) demonstrated that a stable external environment and relatively certain technology (such as the paper goods industry, for instance) were matched by a well-defined, hierarchical, industrial organization with clearly specified rules and procedures, while a rapidly changing, external environment and uncertain technology (such as in the electronics industry, for instance) were matched by adaptive, free-flowing 'organic' organizations (a flat structure allows for adaptation to rapidly changing markets) with strong emphasis both on intense, multidimensional interactions among employees and also professional autonomy.

Uncertainty must be addressed through differentiation. We made the point above that we can only prepare for the unpredictably varying conditions of the future through heterogeneity and variation here and now. We made this point on the individual level in Chapter 2 and in relation to the idea of collective competence in Chapter 8. Darwin, in fact, made the same point in relation to how species can survive under widely changing conditions.

We have argued that you do not know what the university is producing or what it has to produce. You must find out and this is true both for studying and for research. In this sense, the university probably has the most uncertain technology ever thought of. The external environment is not stable, in fact, the labour market the graduates are going to face is becoming less and less predictable. This certainly calls for differentiation and variation.

However, when it comes to the graduates, they are going to have to handle situations in which they will have to draw on different kinds of specialized knowledge in accordance with the situations in which they are used rather than knowledge structured in terms of specializations from which they originate. Many research questions cannot be neatly sorted into those pigeon holes either but in order to structure knowledge differently you have to structure the university differently. In order to integrate knowledge you have to integrate the university.

The network university

As we pointed out above, a hierarchical organization with a one-dimensional stratification of knowledge does not bring people or minds or ideas in touch with each other. Recently there has been a move towards more market-oriented forms of organization with patterns of exchange and with reliance on prices and specified contracts between operating units. As Dill and Sporn (1995) point out, both the hierarchical and the market model of organization are likely to fail in circumstances of high competition and complexity, circumstances calling for 'frequent, rapid, reliable and rich information' . These two models of organizations are sparse in meaning (focusing mainly on assigning values to exchanges: individual compensation in the hierarchical model and money in the market model) or expressed, as we say, they are not good at bringing collective consciousness about.

In the hierarchical model communication takes place mainly between different levels; entities located on the same level are isolated from each other in terms of the formally defined pattern of communication. Few links exist in the system on the whole, and the communication that takes place through those is power-rather than context-oriented.

In the market model of organization there are specialized units with little communication between them. The extreme form is called *outsourcing,* which refers to reliance on units which are not even parts of the organization (in this case the organization is handing over certain tasks to external agencies). Links exist mainly between sellers and buyers and units may appear in both roles, but in relation to the external world mainly as sellers (providers of services). Few links exist between different units in such an organization, and the communication that takes place through those is oriented towards (commercial) transactions rather than towards content.[1] So, neither of these two models is conducive to the ascent and growth of a collective consciousness in the organization.

In a network organization, on the other hand, there are many links between units in the organization and the communication is content-related, ie it is about work that people carry out together with mutual support. Such contacts are likely to enrich the shared understanding of the object of communication.

Dill and Sporn (1995) argue that universities should aim at a network organization, something which is not very far from the way in which universities traditionally operated: 'A network implies a structural process for relations among individuals or groups, a lateral pattern of exchange with reciprocal lines of communications' (Powell, 1990).

'A network university' might mean an organization with multiple grounds and multiple sites for gathering. As the people of the university represent different fields of knowledge, when they come together in different kinds of groups, knowledge itself is stratified in different ways. This is how collective consciousness comes about.

In this chapter, we have already dealt with two forms of stratification: disciplinary and professional. The departments represent the former and the educational programme teams primarily the latter. We mentioned two other grounds on which people may come together: research questions of a cross-disciplinary nature or research and development questions originating outside the university. There could be many others. We could say that each one of these different grounds on which staff and students might work and study together represents different kinds of objects of research; some lasting, some temporary.

We described above a model where resources go to the programme teams. We also mentioned that other resources go in various ways to the faculties and departments. As far as learning and research are concerned, resources should always be allocated to identifiable objects of knowledge and by doing so the organization will become the embodiment of its collective consciousness.

Again, we return to Askling and Almén's (1997) concept of the space of action denoting the boundaries for the participants' options for action. If staff are free (within certain limits) to choose what to teach, it is more likely to become a topic of discussion than is the case when what to teach is decided on a level above. If you are free to choose what to do research about, what you are going to do research about is more likely to be discussed with colleagues than it would be if the research topic were decided by someone else. In accordance with what we said in Chapter 2, whatever varies is likely to come to the fore in people's awareness. So to the extent that there are different options as to the choice of the topic of research and different views expressed on those options, the question of the research topic will be focused on by those involved. When the object of research is given, all that can become prominent in people's awareness are their views on that topic. If both the object of research and the perspective from which it is seen are given, then all that can be focused on are different facts about that perspective on that particular topic. The more that is given, the less likelihood there is of discussion of options and the more that creativity is stifled; the more options, then the more discussion and the more potential for new ideas. The same principle underlies the RMIT EQA system: programme teams are expected to develop their own ways of improving the quality of student learning and establish the evidence for such improvements. The intention is to make the very processes of quality improvement an object of discussion in the programme team.

As we have pointed out several times, options have to be used in order to turn the space of action into an experienced reality. However, the principle still holds: if you want people to focus on a particular aspect of the world around them, you must allow for variation and you must give them options. This is the organizational counterpart of Gustavsson's (1971) paradox of university politics mentioned in Chapter 9 (page 223): in order to be useful universities have to be free.

When you are a member of a programme team, and you integrate different disciplinary perspectives into a professional framework, you might find that different patterns of perspectives, or differently focused perspectives, are applicable under different circumstances. The programme-team model very much embodies the idea of 'the network university' and is an important vehicle for the enhancement of collective consciousness. There is a comparatively wide space of action and a corresponding comparatively wide space of (experienced) variation. It is in this sense that we can claim that in the model described above and illustrated in Figure 10.2, the matrix of authority matches the matrix of competence. People are free to act and have the authority to act in certain respects or in certain dimensions. These respects or dimensions constitute the space of action and to the extent that they make use of this (potential) space of action, they become focally aware of the corresponding dimensions of (experienced) variation constituting the space of variation. This is the way in which power and meaning are related.

We could argue that what matters is not only that there are options available, but, above all, the basis on which the options are chosen. This is true especially when priorities have to be made, for instance, concerning how resources should be allocated to which objects of knowledge (programmes, projects and subjects), how much and on what grounds.

Shared values

In Chapter 8 we were arguing that the collective consciousness comprises what is common and what is complementary. The network structure of organization represents interconnected diversity, that is, the complementary part but in addition to that a university needs vision-shared ideals, a common direction or a path to follow. We have argued for a particular kind of knowledge and for a particular kind of university, committed to development of that kind of knowledge but above all a university must have a moral commitment. We pointed to the ethical implications of the view of knowledge underlying the argument. We will develop this theme further in the next chapter.

In addition to the requirement that the knowledge produced – through studying or research – serves noble purposes (the ethical aspects) and has certain qualities (the epistemological aspect), there has to be a demand for it (the economic aspect). We have therefore to use our resources to produce knowledge of a certain kind about objects of knowledge, which humanity needs to know more about – as we see it and as others see it.

We set our priorities in accordance with the dynamic interplay among the three aspects of our value system (the ethical, the epistemological and the economic). We think the ordering should be the one just used but even if everybody accepts this, it will not turn out to be self-evident how to decide in each situation; different time perspectives might imply different conclusions, for instance. So even if there are values shared by all, priorities have to be based on an ongoing discussion and because of this it will alert us all the time to what is important about the university.

Endnote

1. Interestingly, the two forms of institutional organization resemble the two externalistic forms of governance depicted in Figure 9.1 (page 216): the hierarchical organization seems to correspond to the externalistic-centralized form of governance, while the market model seems to correspond to the externalistic-decentralized government (which is in fact a market model).

Chapter 11

The University of Learning

Summing up

Quality is concerned with doing what we do well. Consequently, improving quality is concerned with doing better what we are doing anyway. The best way to achieve such an aim is to reconsider what the university is about. Any improvement in what the university is doing must originate from a better understanding of what it is supposed to do.

We argued that the three main missions of the university – teaching, research and services – can be rewritten in the form of one function only: it is all about knowledge formation and forming knowledge is learning, so it is in fact all about learning, although of different kinds. Teaching is supposed to contribute to student learning. Students are widening the world which they know about by finding out things which are new to them, but not necessarily new to others. This is learning on the individual level. In research, people are trying to find out things which are new in an absolute sense and by doing so humanity learns. We can call it learning on the collective level. 'Services' refer to services to the community or to society. This has to do with the formation of knowledge as a response to specific, often local, demands, or the making of knowledge available for specific purposes or the involvement of people outside the university in finding out things of vital interest to those involved. We can call this learning on the local level.[1]

Our main focus in this book has been student learning, ie learning on the individual level, and to the extent that we have gone outside this topic and dealt with other issues, such as research, organization and government policies, we have always done it from the point of view of the learning that the students are – or should be – engaged in. We will maintain this as the main focus of this concluding chapter as well.

Our suggested approach to the question of quality improvement and 'quality maintenance' relates to the internal aspects of quality – we believe they should be in the hands of the universities. There is an external aspect too, however, and it relates to the way in which universities prove their accountability to the outside world. This should be done by showing what the universities are doing in order to find out about the quality of their achievements, in order to make improvements, to observe the outcomes and to learn from the observations.

The most fundamental step a university can take in order to improve the quality of learning is to try to find out what quality of learning should refer to. We addressed this very question from the point of view of another question. Universities are supposed to enable their students to engage in effective action in situations they are going to encounter but as the future is increasingly unknown, these situations are impossible to define in advance. What universities have to offer is knowledge and therefore you must prepare for the unknown by means of the known.

As we always act in relation to situations as we see them, effective actions spring from effective ways of seeing. Preparing students for situations in the future amounts to developing their capabilities for seeing in effective ways and developing the eyes through which these situations are going to be seen.

Seeing a situation in a certain way amounts to discerning certain aspects of the situation and focusing on them simultaneously. Seeing a situation in an effective way amounts to discerning those aspects which are critical for engaging in effective action and taking all of them into consideration (focusing on them) at the same time. In order to discern certain aspects, one must have experienced variation in those aspects. There is no discernment without variation. The only way we can prepare for the undefinable variation in the future is by experiencing variation in the present and by having experienced variation in the past.

Developing new ways of seeing (situations, phenomena) is, of course, not the only form of learning, but it is the most fundamental and neglected form of learning. The reason is that once we have developed certain ways of seeing, they become taken for granted: we believe that what we see is the world as it is, and not the world as it is seen by us. We all take our ways of seeing the world for granted and we see it differently from each other, mostly without being aware of these differences. This is perhaps the most serious dilemma of the university when it comes to developing knowledge, which is new for the individuals – through teaching and studying – or knowledge, which is new in an absolute sense – through research. Knowledge rests always on particular ways of seeing the world and usually we are not even aware of them. When the different ways of seeing are not shared, by teachers and students or by researchers representing somewhat different specializations, it is a most serious and often unseen problem. It is serious precisely because it is unseen.

The relationship between learning and research is to be found here in its most profound sense: through the most important form of learning learners develop new ways of seeing and through the most important form of research new ways of seeing are introduced in our collective understanding of the world.

As we implied above, before quality can be managed or assured it has to be found. What capabilities the students should develop, what should be learned, how the goals, aims or expected outcomes of learning should be characterized is by no means a trivial matter. The so-called competency movement suggests a particular kind of answer: well-defined, observable capabilities, described in workplace terms. We believe that we need deeper and more holistic goal statements, in terms of capabilities for seeing certain phenomena and situations in certain ways and, accordingly, capabilities for dealing with these phenomena and situations in certain ways.

So, in order to develop certain ways of seeing, the learner must experience a certain pattern of variation. If the aim of learning is to develop a certain way of seeing, a corresponding pattern of variation must be present in the teaching or, in more general terms, in the learning environment, regardless of the method of instruction or of studying that is being made use of. We suggest therefore that we should think in terms of patterns of variation in the learning experience rather than in terms of teaching methods. Of course the former can be – and should be – embodied in the latter.

Consequently, when it comes to assessing learning we have to make use of novel, open, non-technical, and in a way simple, questions to explore students' capabilities for discerning and simultaneously focusing on relevant aspects of the problems or situations presented. By using such questions the teacher can learn from the students. The answers will not only reveal whether the students got it right or not but they will show the qualitatively different ways in which students make sense of what is presented. Finding out what these different ways are is not that straightforward, in fact it is a bit like doing research about your students' understanding of what you have taught. What is gained then is that grasping the variation among the students alerts the teacher to what should be attended to in teaching and it also informs the teacher about setting the learning targets. The point is that, whenever you have failed to assist someone to understand something, you have taken something for granted that should not be taken for granted. In addition, what has mistakenly been taken for granted will show in the students' understanding of the open-ended, simple and novel problems posed to them, revealed through the analysis of their answers.

The teacher–student relationship is of a particular kind; it is object-mediated. The object of learning is what the teacher and the students have in common above all. This applies to research as well. Having a shared object of research is essential not only for work in teams but for graduate supervision. To the extent we become aware of each other's way of seeing the same object in studying or in research, our understanding grows richer and more complex. Again, this applies to teachers and students as well as to researchers. By having the landscape of knowledge stratified in several ways, ie teachers, students and researchers having several different objects of knowledge in common, and having them in common in different combinations, a network may be created within the university where virtually everyone is in principle connected to everyone else – through others. Again, through awareness of each other's differing ways of seeing various things, a collective consciousness evolves within the university.

Such a collective consciousness, a potentially formidable power, has to be embodied in the organization of the university. It is by tradition structured around certain kinds of objects of knowledge or, rather, domains of knowledge. These are the academic subjects holding departments together. We can also define knowledge domains from the point of view of the professions. There are many other ways: thematic structuring, fields of study or research of transdisciplinary nature, originating from previous research or from societal needs. Allowing for the formation of groups of teachers, researchers and students on different grounds (for the sake of simplicity we will call these grounds 'different kinds of object of knowledge') means further differentiation, but it is exactly through such differentiation that the university can be truly integrated with the network being the organizing principle. Such a university is organized in terms of objects of knowledge, to which resources are allocated to produce new knowledge about those objects and for developing capabilities for seeing those objects in certain ways. There is a shift in focus from teaching to learning and resources are linked to learning aims. The organization embodies the collective consciousness of the university and because of the integration of knowledge through multiple stratifications its structure can match the intended competence structure of the students (eg knowledge integrated in terms of professions).

Structuring in terms of objects of knowledge cannot be permanent: certain objects of knowledge will be dropped, others will be taken up. The university must be a flexible and dynamic organization as is necessary for matching an increasingly changing environment. On one level, there are continual decisions to be made about the constituent parts of the organization, the objects of knowledge and about the resources allocated to them. On another level, there are continual decisions to be made (by the teams held together by the objects of knowledge) about how to deal with the objects of knowledge. What is to be aimed for? What do we want to find out? What capabilities do we want to develop? How are we going to do that? How do we find out what has been achieved? How can we learn from what has happened? The decisions to be made and the options available define the space of action corresponding to the space of variation in the awareness of those having the responsibility for the decisions. To the extent that there are degrees of freedom for action, to the extent that there are options and there are the power and responsibility to decide, and above all to the extent that the options available and the power to decide will be made use of, there will be variation experienced. What varies is discerned and the organizational structure is likely to affect the structure of the awareness of the staff in powerful ways.

What is to be done

The university is a knowledge organization. Everything is about how to produce knowledge and capabilities – how to bring about learning. Everything is about how to deal with knowledge and what knowledge to deal with. Who can have informed views about such matters?

Finding out what is to be done in every field of knowledge anew

We now look at issues of learning that students are supposed to engage in. We argue that the point of departure has to be the question of what kind of capabilities we would like to contribute to developing. Chapter 5 mentioned that discussions on this topic are frequently phrased in terms of general capabilities such as expressing oneself clearly in written or spoken language, the capability to learn, to solve problems, to be innovative or to be flexible on the one hand, and subject specific knowledge, on the other. We get the impression that those general capabilities are so general that students with any study orientation can take the same course in communication, learning skills, problem-solving or creativity. It implies that what students would need are more and more general courses. We disagree with these views. Such courses, we believe, are of little use and in fact there is a considerable risk of students ending up being weaker in areas they were supposed to become better at. Why? One of the most fundamental aspects of the acts of knowing is that they are intentional. When we communicate, we communicate about *something to someone*, when we learn we learn *something*, when we solve problems – exactly – we solve some *problem*. The acts of knowing point always beyond themselves, they are always directed towards something. When students are being trained in learning skills in general, without relation to any particular object of learning, attention will be focused on the act of learning itself, instead of on its object. This means that the learner is pushed away from what is most fundamental in learning: the oneness with its object (see Chapter 2, pages 39–40). General capabilities such as being good at learning, expressing oneself clearly in speech and in writing, solving problems and acting in flexible and effective ways, are aspects of our ways of handling what we are talking or writing about (ie the object of learning) and such capabilities can be best developed by reflecting on, discussing, analysing and practising how we express ourselves and learn or solve problems in relation to the objects of learning: in the context of studies in specific domains of knowledge.

The capabilities we have been focusing on are capabilities for engaging in effective action in certain kinds of situations. As effective actions spring from effective ways of seeing, the capabilities for seeing certain situations in certain ways are our favoured aims for learning.

As previously mentioned, discussions about learning goals are frequently phrased in terms of general capabilities, which are so general that they are basically the same regardless of the different domains of disciplinary or professional knowledge. The implication seems to be that they can be learned by everyone in the same form and applied to the different fields, and facts and technical skills, which are specific to the different fields, would be learned separately. Almost all thinking about education is framed in terms of such a general–specific dichotomy. We strongly disagree with such a view. Ways of seeing, which we keep talking about, are inherent and crucial for the different domains of knowledge. The general capabilities originate very much from the capabilities for seeing certain things in certain ways and from the awareness of the alternative ways of seeing. The specific facts and technical skills derive their meaning from the ways of seeing which are essential for their origination.

So, without neglecting more general or more specific capabilities, we should aim at what we believe to be the key capabilities, which are to be found between the very general and the very specific. In accordance with this, the learning goals should be defined in the first place, but not only in terms of *capabilities* for seeing certain things (situations, phenomena) in certain ways. This is by no means a trivial undertaking. Ways of seeing have to be found, revealed, discovered, and doing so is well on a par with any research achievement. It is, in fact, a major research achievement and also the key to better learning.

Once we know what particular capabilities that learning (in a specific course, subject or programme) should result in, we should find out how to assess them, ie find out in what context, under what circumstances and how students are supposed to show those capabilities, regardless of the way in which they have achieved them. This has been the topic of Chapter 7.

Furthermore, we have to offer opportunities for learning that aims at the capabilities stated. We should develop learning environments conducive to such aims. We have argued that we should aim at developing effective ways of seeing and this has many times been characterized in terms of the aspects discerned and focused on simultaneously. Not only does this suggest necessary conditions for finding out to what extent students have developed these capabilities – the assessment must allow for and require the discernment and simultaneous focusing on the critical aspects – but it also implies what necessary characteristics the learning environment must have. As simultaneity is a function of discernment (you cannot experience two things simultaneously if they are not discerned) and as discernment is a function of variation, the learners must have experienced a certain pattern of dimensions of variation in order to develop the capability of seeing a certain kind of situation in a certain way. The nature of the capability implies the necessary conditions for detecting it and for bringing it about as well.

Assessment still has to have some form and the pattern of variation has to be embodied in some kind of learning environment or teaching method, but finding out what we are aiming for (in terms of capabilities) brings us very close to achieving them.

Seen from this perspective and at this level of detail (or rather lack of detail), questions of setting the goals, working for them, and making judgements about the extent to which they have been achieved collapse into each other. In addition so do questions of learning, teaching and evaluation. It is all about the nature of capabilities, the question of what is learned and the question of what should be learned. We consider that the dividing lines are not so much between learning, teaching, research, goal setting, assessment and evaluation but rather between different objects of learning. It is all about what students are going to learn. So discerning critical aspects and focusing on them simultaneously, experiencing particular patterns of variation and developing certain ways of seeing, mean as many things as there are objects of learning. We have to find out the specific meanings of critical aspects, dimensions of variation and ways of seeing in each case anew, in every domain of knowledge, defined in disciplinary, professional, transdisciplinary or communal terms. This is what has to be done but the question is who is going to do it?

Insights into how knowledge is formed

While formulating our conclusions about 'what is to be done?' we keep interspersing the question 'who is going to do it?' which is in fact the main additional focus of this chapter. Before addressing this 'who?' question, we will once more deal with the nature of the issues underlying the question 'what is to be done?', but from a somewhat wider perspective, from the point of view of all three forms of learning: collective, individual and local.

For this we turn to research. In research it is the object of research that is in the focus and so it must be. It can be an idea, however, to stand back now and then and to raise questions about what tacit assumptions are underlying our way of acting, what alternative approaches might be conceivable, what invisible constraints we have imposed upon our search, why we are dealing with the very question we are dealing with, what development within the field has led to the situation we are in, why the problem is seen in different ways by different researchers and why we have to do what we are doing. These seem very useful questions but who should ask them?

We have argued that individual learning and research are two forms of knowledge formation. The above questions about learning and research are questions about knowledge formation. So those who have the interest in and insights into how knowledge is formed within different domains should ask those questions.

What do we mean by 'insights into how knowledge is formed in a certain domain?' Knowledge derives its meaning always through other things known to us. It presupposes that we ask certain questions and that we do not ask some other questions – there are always things taken for granted. Knowledge serves certain purposes and it springs from certain conditions. It has constituent parts and it is a constituent part of greater wholes. Knowledge of a certain kind exists because we see the world in a certain way and it gains meaning when we see it through our previous experiences. New knowledge is formed by searching for it in certain ways and it is new only in relation to what is not. Knowledge can appear in different forms; some forms presuppose other forms, just as wholes presuppose parts and parts presuppose wholes.

The expression 'insights into how knowledge is formed' refers therefore to insights into perspectives, meanings, questions asked, questions not asked, purposes, conditions, ways of seeing, ways of searching and, parts and wholes within various domains of knowledge. A domain of knowledge is not necessarily a discipline; it can be defined in terms of a profession or on other grounds (thematic, for instance).

So we believe that such insights would be of greatest importance for enhancing learning and research. However let us elaborate a bit further on the nature of such insights, specifically in this case in relation to what has been described as 'the third task of the university': service to the community.

Focus on how knowledge is formed, how it appears in different guises and how it gets differentiated and integrated from the point of view of more elementary forms, makes us aware of the continuities in human knowledge, that there are links between highly specialized knowledge and everyday knowledge, that knowledge of the adult grows from the knowledge of the child and that the knowledge of the scholar grows from the knowledge of the student. This makes us more sensitive to other forms of expression than those we are used to. We will handle questions formulated in other terms than ours with greater ease and we will be better off when it comes to expressing what we know in other ways than the ones we are used to. Focus on how knowledge is formed is a focus on the human aspects of scientific knowledge and a focus on people within the university as well as outside it. From such a point of departure it should be easier to explain what the university has to offer people outside it and to understand what those people have to offer the university.

So all of this was about the meaning of 'insights into how knowledge is formed in various domains of knowledge'. All of the examples discussed are examples of insights into how knowledge is formed within various domains of knowledge. After having explained what we mean by these particular kinds of insights and after having vigorously argued that it is exactly these kinds of insight the university needs in order to dramatically raise its level of excellence, the hard questions still remain: where are these insights to be found? how do they show? and the answer to this last question is 'unfortunately, very sparsely!'

Separating knowledge from how it is formed

Through the course of history, questions relating to how knowledge is formed have become separated from different domains of knowledge – of whatever kind. What we find within these domains are insights into the various objects of knowledge which define the domains. Then we have some specializations on how knowledge is formed, where you find insights into the acts and processes through which knowledge comes into being – in a general sense though and not so much into how certain kinds of knowledge come into being (other than examples). Such specializations are, for instance, history of ideas, philosophy of science, theory of knowledge, education, sociology of knowledge, psychology etc.

The acts of knowledge have been separated from their objects. This implies that questions concerning perspectives, meanings and taken-for-granted parts and wholes within a certain domain of knowledge are left mainly unanswered. It is exactly these kinds of question that are of decisive importance when it comes to advancing the formation of knowledge within a certain domain (by means of teaching or research, for instance). The questions and the answers have fallen between specializations representing interests for particular kinds of object of knowledge and specializations representing general interests for the acts and processes of knowledge formation. Therefore the insights we would need are extremely scarce commodities, because insights into how knowledge is formed in various domains of knowledge are not parts of those domains of knowledge.

What is missing?

What are those questions that have fallen between the different specializations? The whole matter is a bit paradoxical. We have given many examples of the kinds of insight which we argue do not exist. In Chapter 4, for instance, we referred to analyses of a series of scientific discoveries and in Chapter 8 we referred to a very thorough study of organizational aspects of research in social sciences; in most chapters we gave examples of in-depth investigations of how students make sense of and handle the objects of their studies in different domains of knowledge. In fact, we give many examples of the exact kinds of insight which we claim do not exist. We should say that the insights that exist are scarce and cover little of what is dealt with at the university. We are actually arguing for more insights of the kind that can be found in the examples we are making use of, but, in fact, we believe there is more to our concerns.

Even if such insights exist they are not necessarily used to enhance the formation of knowledge within the different domains. This is the case not only because many of the studies yielding those insights have been carried out by people who are outsiders to the fields (frequently, however, with a substantial background in the field although often no longer being members of it) – people such as educationalists, psychologists, philosophers or historians. The lack of impact is more because the relevance of those insights to knowledge formation within a particular domain may not at all be obvious to those inside the domain. In order to see them as relevant one must have gained an understanding of the interrelatedness of knowledge on the one hand and the acts and processes through which knowledge comes into being, on the other.

This is therefore the evil of the separation of knowledge from the acts and processes through which knowledge is born and is growing. However, there is another kind of separation as well. In Chapter 4 we commented on the continuity of human thought. We made the point that even the highest scientific achievements build on, and therefore are extensions of, very ordinary forms of knowledge. Not everybody believes so. Even if a teacher thinks that studies of how students understand the theory of evolution is highly relevant to the question of how to teach about evolution, the same teacher may not think at all that an analysis of Darwin's discovery is relevant in the same educational context. The continuity between what we have referred to as learning on the individual level and learning on the collective level may not be seen at all.

Reorganizing knowledge

Because the lack of insights of the kind we would need and the lack of specializations which would have given birth to those insights is due to the organization of human knowledge within the universities, it is nothing less than a partial reorganization of knowledge that is called for.

There are two things to be done. First, we have to establish relationships between specializations on different processes of knowledge formation, such as social, historical, psychological and educational; between those dealing with learning on the individual and on the collective level; between those dealing with studying and those dealing with discoveries. By doing so we establish a new field of inquiry. We will refer to it as 'studies of knowledge formation'.[2]

The second thing that has to be done is to project the general interest for knowledge formation into different specific fields. The idea is that questions about knowledge formation will be developed into legitimate specializations within those fields. This would mean that studies of knowledge formation in physics would become a part of physics proper, for instance, and studies of knowledge formation in social work would become a part of social work as a field of study, and so on.

When we are suggesting that studies of the acts of knowing should be integrated with studies of the objects of knowing we are suggesting a partial restructuring of the institutional organization of knowledge. It is not our intention to claim, however, that these two aspects of human knowledge have always been kept separate. On the contrary, we have many examples of brilliant and profound studies of how knowledge is formed within different fields, such as analyses of how decisive steps in the history of science were taken, investigations of how children or adults master some part of human knowledge or studies of how knowledge comes into being socially in the interaction among people and between people and the societal or physical world that surrounds them. In addition, there are teachers within the universities who nurture a passionate interest for how students are trying to find structure and meaning in what they are studying. They are – as a rule – excellent teachers and often they have received their original inspiration from the work of staff development or educational development units in universities.[3]

Improving quality

As previously mentioned in Chapter 9, quality issues should not be something separate from, or added to, the work that is carried out at the university. What we are suggesting is that improving learning in the different senses of the word and on the different levels mentioned (individual, collective and local) should take place by developing the insights of the staff (all staff) and the students (all students) into the acts and processes of the different kinds of knowledge formation within the various domains of knowledge. This should come about primarily by allowing and working towards the development of a focus on knowledge formation within the various domains as one of their legitimate specializations. These specializations would partly feed on a 'centre', focusing on the general theoretical and methodological questions about knowledge formation, combining different perspectives, such as developmental, historical, organizational, educational, sociological or psychological perspectives.

A university, where interest in and insights into questions concerning knowledge formation have a place in its heart and are distributed across its entire body (through the different domains of knowledge), would be a different and in many senses better university than a university without those attributes.[4]

Who is going to do this?

We have now discussed the kind of specific insights which would need to be developed; we have discussed how they could be used and we have even talked about necessary structural changes. However, to achieve the aims stated we would need people, people having the expertise within different domains of knowledge as well as the expertise in how knowledge is formed within those domains (this is exactly the 'who?' question we have kept referring to throughout this chapter). There are such people, in fact most of our examples have been provided by them. However, they are few and far between and there are no legitimate specializations and therefore no epistemological infrastructure necessary for building networks and for building research communities. What we are arguing for is that such legitimate specializations should be established with different domains of knowledge and they should be linked to each other.

A bold undertaking

Here is an idea:

1. Draft a declaration of intent, circulate it around the university and raise funds (preferably from external sources) amounting to, say; 1 per cent of the annual budget of the university for each of the coming six years.
2. Invite people having interest in and insights into general questions concerning knowledge formation (in educational development, philosophy, history of ideas, education, psychology, sociology etc) to constitute a centre for studies of knowledge formation.
3. Invite all departments to open up their doctoral studies for specialization on knowledge formation in the discipline or domain.
4. Advertise a number of doctoral positions within those disciplines or domains that are willing to open their doctoral studies for specialization of the kind proposed (the number may correspond to about 1 per cent of the total number of doctoral students at the university). The objects of the doctoral research should be relevant to the intention of developing competence of staff and students in relation to knowledge formation within their domain of knowledge. Each doctoral student will have a group of supervisors representing general as well as specific interests in knowledge formation.
5. Make arrangements for developing insights into questions of knowledge formation within their own domain of knowledge among all staff.
6. Establish introductory courses for all students focusing on knowledge formation in studying and research, at both the undergraduate and postgraduate levels. Arrange for tutorials throughout the studies, following up the introductory courses and focusing on the act aspect of studying, ie on questions concerning how students are going about their studies or research work. Also focus on the more general aspects of the competence to be developed, such as the capability to learn, express oneself and solve problems; all should be dealt with in relation to the content of the studies.

By using money, amounting to about 1 per cent of its annual budget, for developing the university's understanding of itself, the university could take a most decisive step towards realizing the ideals described in this book. The doctoral projects should focus on issues of concern for the university itself. As mentioned in Chapter 8, the university itself should be transformed into a shared object of research. The doctoral students together with their supervisors, staff and students at a centre for studies of knowledge formation, staff engaged in teacher education, student teachers spread across the university in accordance with the model suggested, would constitute a formidable power, keeping the university together and making it focus on how its main mission, the formation of knowledge, is carried out.

What we are talking about should not be an alien idea to the university. We urge it to understand itself better: more effective ways of acting originate from more effective ways of seeing.

In relation to the grandiose project we are suggesting, you will recall that in Chapter 9 (page 238) we referred to three of the people who know higher education in the US best: Patricia Albjerg Graham, Richard W Lyman and Martin Trow. In the paper we cited, they also raise the issue asking why questions about the university, of the kind we are dealing with here, have not been an object of a really ambitious research undertaking and they make a comparison with the Manhattan and the Genome project (Graham, Lyman andTrow, 1995) and it is something of that sort that we have in mind.

A new kind of PhD

The key element in our suggestion for improving the quality of learning (in all the three senses used in this book) is in addressing the problem of scarce supply of competence among staff for dealing with the knowledge-formation aspects of different domains of knowledge and the problem of creating a 'critical mass' of people with such expertise and inclination. The solution we proposed, in what we called a daring project in the previous section, is to introduce a new kind of PhD. The idea is – as we said above – that different departments open up their doctoral programmes for specialization on knowledge formation in the different domains of knowledge. The students enrolling would do all the course work which is common for doctoral students in the subject. As a specialization – as far as course work is concerned – they could take courses in studies of knowledge formation and they would write theses with focus on knowledge formation in their fields of knowledge. We have shown many examples of theses in this book and in fact most of them would qualify when it comes to conveying the flavour of the orientation argued for. Some of the work would even qualify as examples of potential PhD studies – or part of it – with such an orientation. This is certainly true as regards, for instance, Tullberg's (1998) study of different ways of understanding and different ways of teaching 'the mole' (pages 146–7), Rovio-Johansson's (1998) investigation of how certain topics in accounting are dealt with by the teachers and are understood by students (pages 147–9), Martinsson's (1996) exploration of qualities in students' thinking about certain problems in mathematics as revealed by their examination responses (pages 172–5) and Baillie's (1997) project on the use of the interface between fibre and matrix in determining the mechanical properties of composite materials by interviewing members of the relevant research community and by exploring their understanding (page 195).

We made the point above that work with a focus on how knowledge is formed in various fields should contribute to improving the university's understanding of itself. We have also repeatedly made the point that gaining better insights into the nature of the capabilities that studies in different fields are supposed to develop in students is the most critical step towards enhancing the likelihood of those capabilities being developed. Such insights make the students' conceptual difficulties and the teachers' taken-for-granted assumptions inherent in their teaching visible. By focusing on what is difficult and by making what is taken for granted explicit we are very likely to facilitate better learning. Analyses of the nature of the capabilities that the university is trying to bring about in the students in different domains are highly challenging and fundamentally important tasks and the set of potential research problems is basically inexhaustible. What might they be like? Whelan's (1988) study of clinical problem solving (pages 109–112) and Booth's (1992a) study of learning to program (pages 54–6) are excellent examples, insofar as they illuminate the nature of the capability to come up with correct diagnoses and with effective programs respectively. These studies illuminate as well the difficulties with developing those capabilities.

Other kinds of problem, potential PhD topics, are about how the conceptual difficulties, once they are identified, can be dealt with. It is not so much general teaching methods we have in mind (working in groups, discovery learning etc) but taking the nature of conceptual difficulties as the point of departure for dealing with them. The study by Ueno *et al.* (1990), mentioned on pages 127–8, is a good example. As we described, the researchers identified the taken-for-granted nature of the ground (rest) as the frame of reference in students' thinking about bodies in movement as the major source of difficulty in their understanding of Newtonian mechanics. In order to bring about a change the researcher introduced variation in the frame of reference. The experiment was successful: by means of experiencing variation in this respect students developed a more Newtonian understanding of bodies in motion.

When it comes to research, there are possibilities to follow ongoing research projects, or to trace research projects, discoveries in the past and explore the conceptual spaces in which these projects are, or have been, situated and how the conceptual spaces are transformed through the very research undertakings investigated.

In order to illustrate the nature of the kind of PhD we are arguing for, we want to give some further examples of possible topics. They have been suggested by our colleagues in other disciplines or invented by ourselves. They vary in precision, from pointing to a field of inquiry to presenting a possible subject for a PhD thesis.

Learning tonal discrimination in adult age

In some languages tonal discriminations are made. In Cantonese, for instance, there are nine different tones, in Mandarin four and in Swedish two. For a non-native, adult learner, those discriminations are extremely hard to master.

We do not even know whether – or rather to what extent – adult learners possibly succeed in mastering them. Further, is there a way to develop full mastery in adult age (for instance, by experiencing systematic variation in accordance with the principles outlined in Chapter 2)?

Meanings, metaphors and modelling in chemistry

Models are commonly used in science to illustrate processes, structures and concepts. These models may be in a physical form (eg representing the structure of molecules), in a mathematical form (eg Ohm's law) or in conceptual form (eg potential and kinetic energy). Do these models represent the phenomenon itself, or the current theory, or something else? Are the models metaphors, shorthand representations or, possibly, replacements for the phenomenon itself? Do they take on a different role among learners, scientists or researchers? What is happening when scientists personalize the models by making statements, for example, that electrons 'want' to move towards positively charged entities? This research project would investigate the way in which models such as these provide a bridge between the observed phenomenon and the developed theory which explains the observations. It could focus on one discipline such as chemistry and some possible areas of investigation could include (1) the focus in chemistry on physical models of molecular systems and the relatively weak teaching of intellectual models, (2) the different ways in which energy is represented in various areas such as organic, inorganic and physical chemistry, or (3) the different ways in which oxidation is represented in various areas.

The relation between the characteristics of medical practitioners and their learning experiences

There are a range of ways in which medical curricula are devised and taught. The traditional approach is to build curricula around discipline knowledge and to progress to clinical problem solving from the disciplinary perspective. The problem-based approach focuses on the clinical setting and allows for the knowledge aspect to be determined by the needs of the clinical situation. A third approach integrates the disciplinary and clinical frameworks in the formation of the curriculum so that medical students are constantly relating one framework to the other. A fourth approach would add a community framework. A study of medical practitioners and their attributes in their first and fifth year after graduation, in relation to the nature of their learning experiences as undergraduates, would address questions of the influence and durability of those learning experiences with their professional competence.

A comparison of the scientific world view of histologists and anatomists

Histology and anatomy are both concerned with aspects of the human body but in different ways, from a micro- and a macro-perspective respectively. There is evidence from the writings of each that the alternative perspective is often not seen – to the detriment of scientific advancement. This project would explore the reality of histologists' and anatomists' scientific world views and seek to describe what an integrated perspective is like.

Exploring the nature of the professional competence of the medical practitioner in the emergency ward

During the past decade, the fields of anatomy and clinical practice have come together to form the new field of clinical anatomy. This integration is spawning new medical curricula and this research study would investigate whether individual integration takes place anyway in the emergency ward. One could surmise that a disciplinary focus alone could lead to an inability to act, a clinical focus to a possibility of acting rashly while an integrated perspective might promote an ability to act wisely. The nature of the professional competence of medical practitioners in such a context would be explored with that question as a focus.

The post-modern emergence of sound in design from the ocular-centric preoccupations of modernity

This project would explore the re-emergence of sound in design, the conditions of post-modernity which have allowed this and the ways sound can be explored in actual designs. This involves looking at the dominance of visual regimes in modernity, the challenges to the dominance of these regimes in contemporary critical thinking and architectural theorizing and the ways in which this has and can be manifested through design.

Design as artistry or design as social function – or both

A historical study which examines the social, political and economic influences, which have contributed to the dominance of each view at different times.

How universal are 'literary studies'?

Is 'literary studies' a reasonably universal field of knowledge? What does it take to study 'Chinese literature' in China as compared to studying 'French literature' in France? Such a comparison could involve examining curricula and textbooks, but also an empirical investigation of the ways in which students in different countries make sense of their studies.

Does the study of economics pay off?

Do investors make use of any theoretical knowledge at all? Are there any principles or techniques taught at business schools that can be useful for investors in the share market? Are there successful investors at all? What makes them successful?

People's understanding of democracy

What do people living in a parliamentary democracy refer to when they talk about 'democracy'? What are the defining features used? To what extent are they shared? What values are attached to the differing aspects? Do people with varying political sympathies have varying understandings of democracy?

What is evident and what is obvious?
What qualifies as mathematical proof? Are there differences between mathematics and computer science? How has the idea of mathematical proof developed historically? What are students' understandings of what counts as mathematical proof?

Can everyone compose music?
By using a synthesizer linked to a computer storing the traces of people's musical acts the following questions can be investigated: Can anybody compose music? Is musical composition a general human capability which basically everybody has – to differing extents, of different kinds – much like drawing or singing? Are there any criteria we might apply to musical compositions, distinguishing them from noise? What are the characteristics of musical compositions and are there any interesting differences in the way in which people go about composing?[5]

Doing the right thing

The argument for a focus on knowledge formation is an argument for taking variation into account – variation between different ways of seeing among students and variation between different ways of seeing dominating different periods in history. One argument is that one way of seeing something derives its meaning from other ways of seeing it. Therefore the ways of seeing we want our students to appropriate very much derive their meaning from ways of seeing to which there are alternatives. Another argument is that ways of seeing differing from the received wisdom are not just plainly wrong – even if judged against the received wisdom as the criterion – they are partial. Understanding other ways of seeing things is understanding each other and understanding each other is a highly efficient way of assisting each other in understanding things better.

Becoming aware of one's way of seeing in research opens up other options. Contrasting different ways of seeing the same research object frequently enriches our understanding of it. Taking other perspectives than one's own is vital in the university's dealings with the community.

On the individual level we argued that only by experiencing variation can we prepare ourselves and others for a future varying in unknown ways.

The point we have been trying to make throughout is that an unprecedentedly powerful university can be built by taking variation in critical aspects fully into account.

However, there is more to variation. As we pointed out in Chapter 8, if the different ways of seeing the world constitute our world, we must have respect for different views. Taking the students' ways of seeing as the point of departure for trying to contribute to developing their understanding implies a sincere approach to the meanings inherent in them. The same applies always when we try to make sense of other people's ways of seeing: people outside the university, our colleagues or our predecessors. Trying to find out the meaning something has for someone amounts to trying to see what the other person is seeing or has seen.

At the end of Chapter 8 we used a quote from Bronowski to point out what we believe to be a most fundamental principle within the university: you must assume that you can be wrong. If you assume that you can be wrong, and if you are wrong, then you can be right.

If you assume that you can be wrong, you are more likely to listen to counter-arguments. And so you should at the university. Ideally, the force of argument does not have anything to do with who is making the argument. We all have the right of having our statements judged only in terms of the power and the qualities of the statements, regardless of our wealth, religion, gender or colour. In terms of its ideals, the university is our most egalitarian institution.

The university capitalizes on thoughts, ideas, observations and labour of people regardless of where they live and what they look like. And the university capitalizes on what previous generations have done. The university is the most collective undertaking of humanity. It embraces humanity across boundaries in time and space. It is free to make use of anyone's thoughts and anyone is free to make use of the thoughts it has embraced. The university has a moral obligation. It has to serve humanity and it has to pay equal respect to everyone. Doing so is doing the right thing. And the University of Learning is supposed to do the right thing because without a soul its power will be gone.

Endnotes

1. This is about developing knowledge mainly within the university and dispersing it to the world outside. It goes without saying that human knowledge is formed mostly outside the university.

2. The corresponding Swedish term *kunskapsbildning* sounds more self-evident for the purpose. It also carries the meaning of the German term *Bildung* denoting the process through which humans and humanity create themselves, forming something new, impossible to define in advance.

3. Internationally, educational development units have a somewhat unclear status in their universities. Are they academic departments (they rarely are) or service groups dispensing teaching tips (they are normally more than this)? Do they deal with information technology in learning or is there a separate unit for that? While we

acknowledge that all kinds of services are important, a main theme of this book is that questions about ways of learning, teaching, doing research, serving the community and how knowledge is formed in various fields are no less important than and are just as challenging and scientific as questions about the objects of learning, teaching, research and community services in each field. So the support needed is of a theoretical, methodological, research-based kind, rather than useful commonsense tips and advice. Educational development should be upgraded and widened and grow into centres for studies of knowledge formation. They should be academic departments with staff equal to other staff at the university with regard to academic standing.

4. A transformation of this kind would surely have significant implications for teacher education, for instance. A university with well-developed interests in, and insights into, the acts and processes through which knowledge is formed within different domains, would be a very natural home for teacher education. It could be projected into the different parts of the university. So philosophy of education should be dealt with in philosophy, history of education in history, problems of learning and teaching chemistry in chemistry and so on. Above all we would have a centre for studies of knowledge formation as a very vital resource for teacher education to draw on. Therefore teacher education would be present all over the university and the focus on knowledge formation would transform the different parts of the university into fertile ground for teacher education, which in its turn would work as a powerful driving force when it comes to developing interest for and insights into questions of knowledge formation within different fields. Teacher education is at the same time 'the interface' through which the university could reach out to the new generations.

5. This thesis is actually written already (Folkestad, 1996). We wanted to include the topic as an interesting example of research in the intersection between musicology and education. The investigation in which eight young people (15 years old) participated, yielded an answer to the first question in the affirmative: yes, everybody can compose!

References

Åkerlind, G (1997) PhD thesis in progress.

Åström, S (1997) Personal communication.

Ahlberg, A (1992) *Att möta matematiska problem: en belysning av barns lärande* (Meeting Mathematical Problems: An Illumination of Children's Learning), Acta Universitatis Gothoburgensis, Göteborg.

Alexandersson, M (1994) Focusing teacher consciousness: what do teachers direct their consciousness towards during their teaching?, in I Carlgren, G Handal and S Vaage (eds.), *Teachers' Minds and Actions: Research on Teachers' Thinking and Practice* (pp. 139–49), Falmer Press, London.

Arblaster, A (1974) *Academic Freedom*, Penguin Education, Harmondsworth Middlesex.

The Arts Council (1992) 'Drama in Schools, Guidance on Drama Education', Arts Council, London.

Ashton-Warner, S (1963) *Teacher*, Simon and Schuster, New York.

Askling, B and Almén, E (1997) From participation to competition: changes in the motion of decentralisation in Swedish higher education policy, *Tertiary Education and Management*, 3, 199–210.

Australian Government Department of Employment, Education and Training (1987) *Policy Discussion Paper on Higher Education,* Australian Government Printing Service, Canberra.

Axelrod, R (1984) *The Evolution of Cooperation*, Basic Books, New York.

Baillie, C A (1991) The effect of an oxidative surface treatment on the adhesion of carbon fibres in an epoxy resin matrix, PhD thesis, University of Surrey.

Baillie, C A (1997) Research on research in material science, unpublished manuscript.

Ball, C (1985) What the hell is quality?, in D Urwin (ed.), *Fitness for Purpose: Essays in Higher Education*, SRHE and NFER-Nelson, Guildford.

Barr, R and Tagg, J (1995) From teaching to learning: a new paradigm for undergraduate education, *Change*, November/December, pp 3–14.

Bartlett, R (1992) The Feynman effect and the boon docs, *Physics Today*, 45 (1), 67.

Barton, Sir D R (1981) Some recent progress in natural products chemistry, paper presented at the 182nd Annual Meeting of the American Chemical Society, Woodward Memorial Symposium, New York.

Bauer, M (1996) The Swedish approach to quality in higher education, paper for the Institutional Management of Higher Education project on Institutional Responses to Quality Assessment, October.

Bauer, M, Marton, S, Askling, B and Marton, F (1999) *Transforming Universities: Governance, Structure and Learning in Swedish Higher Education at the Millennial Turn*, Jessica Kingsley, London.

Beaty, E (1987) Understanding concepts in social science: towards an effective strategy, *Instructional Science*, 15, 341–59.

Benjamin, J (1997) Academic staff conceptions of and approaches to collaboration in the teaching of large first year university courses, paper presented at the HERDSA Annual Conference, Adelaide.

Bennich-Björkman, L (1998) *The Inner Life of University Departments*, Elsevier, Oxford.

Biggs, J (1987a) *Student approaches to learning and studying*, Australian Council for Educational Research, Hawthorn, Victoria.

Biggs, J (1987b) *The Learning Process Questionnaire (LPQ): Manual*, Australian Council for Educational Research, Hawthorn, Victoria.

Björklund, S (1990) The research connection, *Studies of Higher Education and Research*, National Board of Universities and Colleges, Stockholm.

Bloom, B S (1974) An instruction to mastery learning theory, in J Block (ed.), *Schools, Society and Mastery Learning*, Holt, Rinehart and Winston, New York.

Bloom, B S, Hastings, J T and Madaus, G F (1971) *Handbook on Formative and Summative Evaluation of Student Learning*, McGraw-Hill, New York.

Bond, C (1996) Conceptions of learning, manuscript.

Booth, S A (1992a) *Learning to Program: A Phenomenographic Perspective*, Acta Universitatis Gothoburgensis, Göteborg.

Booth, S A (1992b) The experience of learning to program. Example: recursion, in F Détienne (ed.), *5 ème Workshop sur la Psychologie de la Programmation*, INRIA, Paris (pp. 122–45) (the fifth workshop of the Psychology of Progamming Interest Group).

Bowden, J A (1986) Educational development and phenomenography, in J Bowden (ed.), *Student Learning: Research into Practice*, CSHE, University of Melbourne, Melbourne.

Bowden, J A (1988) Achieving change in teaching practices, in P Ramsden (ed.), *Improving Learning: New Perspectives*, Kogan Page, London.

Bowden, J A (1989) Curriculum Development for Conceptual Change Learning: A Phenomenographic Pedagogy, paper presented at the 6th Annual (International) Conference of the Hong Kong Educational Research Association, November (also available as RMIT EQARD, occasional paper no. 90.3).

Bowden, J A (1990) Deep and surface approaches to learning, in M Akbar Hessami and J Sillitoe (eds.), *Deep vs Surface Teaching and Learning in Engineering and Applied Sciences*, Victoria University of Technology, Footscray.

Bowden, J A (1997) Competency-based education: neither a panacea nor a pariah, paper presented to TEND 97, Abu Dhabi, April 6–8.

Bowden, J A (1997a) Theoretical and practical aspects of a development-based, educational quality assurance system, in J Bowden and J Sachs (eds.), *Quality Management of University Teaching and Learning*, DEETYA, Internet address – http://www.deetya.gov.au/divisions/hed/operations/Bowden.htm.

Bowden, J, Dall'Alba, G, Martin, E, Masters, G, Laurillard, D, Marton, F, Ramsden, P and Stephanou, A (1992) Displacement, velocity, and frames of reference: phenomenographic studies of students' understanding and some implications for teaching and assessment, *American Journal of Physics*, 60, 262–68.

Bowden, J and Martin, E (1990) *Report on Validation Study of Course Experience Questionnaire*, Centre for Technology and Social Change, Wollongong.

Bowden, J A and Martin, E (1991) The role of an academic staff development unit after the White Paper and the Second Tier Agreement, *Research and Development in Higher Education*, 13, 293–97.

Bowden, J A and Masters, G N (1993) *Implications for Higher Education of a Competency-Based Approach to Education and Training*, AGPS, Canberra.

Bowden, J A and Sachs, J (1997) Top-down and bottom-up symbiosis: both an external and an internal educational quality management issue for university survival into the 21st century, manuscript.

Boyer, E L (1990) *Scholarship Reconsidered*, The Carnegie Foundation for the Advancement of Teaching, Princeton, NJ.

Boyle, P and Bowden, J A (1997) Educational quality assurance in universities: an enhanced model, *Assessment and Evaluation in Higher Education*, 22 (2), 111–21.

Boyle, P, Dall, J, Dlanksby, V, Marshall, H, and Smith, P (1995) *Assessment: Guidelines for Good Practice*, RMIT, Melbourne.

Bronowski, J (1973) *The Ascent of Man*, BBC, London.

Brown, J S, Collins, A and Duguid, P (1989) Situated cognition and the culture of learning, *Educational Researcher*, 18, 32–42.

Brumby, M N (1979) Students perceptions and learning styles associated with the concept of evolution by natural selection, unpublished PhD thesis, University of Surrey, England.

Burke, J B, Hansen, J H, Houston, W R and Johnson, C (1975) *Criteria for Describing and Assessing Competency Programs*, National Consortium of Competency-based Education Centers, Syracuse.

Burns, T and Stalker, G M (1961) *The Management of Innovation*, Tavistock, London.

Burrows, A, Harvey, L and Green, D (1993) Is anybody listening? Employers views on quality in higher education, in L Harvey (ed.), *Quality Assessment in Higher Education: Collected Papers of the QHE Project*, QHE, Birmingham.

Buxton, A (1997) Interfacial failure phenomena in carbon/epoxy composites, University of Sydney, manuscript.

Case, S and Bowmer, I (1994) Licensure and specialty board certification in North America: background information and issues, in D Newble, B Jolly and R Wakeford (eds.), *The Certification and Recertification of Doctors: Issues in the Assessment of Clinical Competence*, Cambridge University Press, Cambridge.

Christie, M J (1985) *Aboriginal Perspectives on Experience and Learning: The Role of Language in Aboriginal Education*, Deakin University Press, Malvern.

Clark, P (1997) Reflections on quality assessment in England: 1993–1996, *Quality Assurance in Education*, 5 (4).

Colaizzi, P (1973) *Reflection and Research in Psychology: A Phenomenological Study of Learning*, Kendall/Hunt, Duquesne.

Dahlgren, L O (1975) *Qualitative Differences in Learning as a Function of Content-oriented Guidance*, Acta Universitatis Gothoburgensis, Göteborg.

Dahlgren, L O (1978) Effects of university education on the conception of reality, Reports from the Institute of Education, University of Göteborg, 65.

Dahlgren, L O (1948) Outcomes of learning, in F Marton, D Hounsell and N Entwistle (eds.), *The Experience of Learning*, Scottish Academic Press, Edinburgh.

Dahlgren, G and Olsson, L-E (1985) *Läsning i Barnperspektiv* (The Child's Conception of Reading), Acta Universitatis Gothoburgensis, Göteborg.

Dall'Alba, G and Sandberg, J (1992) A competency-based approach to education and training: will it improve competence?, occasional paper 92.4, RMIT Educational Research and Development Unit, Melbourne.

Dall'Alba, G, Walsh, E, Bowden, J A, Martin, E, Masters, G, Ramsden, P and Stephanou, A (1993) Textbook treatments and students' understanding of acceleration, *Journal of Research in Science Teaching*, 30, 621–35.

Debling, G (1989) The Employment Department/Training Agency standards programme and NVQs: implications for education, in J W Burke (ed.), *Competency-based Education and Training*, Falmer Press, London.

Dewey, J (1929) *The Quest for Certainty*, Minton, Balch and Co, New York.

Dill, D (1997) Student learning and academic choice: the rule of coherence, paper presented at 'What kind of university?', an international conference, London, June.

Dill, D D and Sporn, B (1995) University 2001: What will the University of the twenty-first century look like?, in D D Dill and B Sporn (eds.), *Emerging Patterns of Social Demand and University Reform Through a Glass Darkly*, Pergamon, London, pp. 212–36.

Driver, S C and Eizenberg, N (1989) How is a medical textbook chosen?, Australian and New Zealand Association for Medical Education, *Bulletin*, 16 (4), 36–44.

Driver, S C and Eizenberg, N (1993) How do textbooks influence learning?, Australian and New Zealand Association for Mecical Education, *Bulletin*, 20 (4), 2–16.

Dunkin (1997) PhD Thesis in preparation.

Dunkin (1998) Personal communication.

Durkheim, E (1964) *The Division of Labor in Society*, Free Press, New York.

Edge, D and Mulkay, M (1976) *Astronomy Transformed: The Emergency of Radio Astronomy in Britain*, Wiley, London.

Einstein, A (1933) *The Method of Theoretical Physics*, Oxford University Press, Oxford.

Eizenberg, N (1988) Approaches to learning anatomy: developing a programme for preclinical medical students, in P Ramsden (ed.), *Improving Learning: New Perspectives*, Kogan Page, London, pp. 179–98.

Eizenberg, N (1991) Action research in medical education: improving teaching via investigating learning, in O Zuber-Skerrit (ed.), *Action Research for Change and Development*, Avebury, Aldershot, pp. 179–206.

Eizenberg, N (1997) Personal communication.

Eizenberg, N, Murphy, M and Briggs, C (1993) *Practical Anatomy: Guide and Dissector*, Pilot Textbook, Anatomy Department, University of Melbourne.

Ekeblad, E (1996) *Children. Learning. Numbers: A Phenomenographic Excursion into First-grade Childrens Arithmetic*, Acta Universitatis Gothoburgensis, Göteborg.

Entwistle, A and Entwistle, N (1992) Experiences of understanding in revising for degree examinations, *Learning and Instruction*, 2, 1–22.

Entwistle, N and Marton, F (1994) Knowledge objects: understandings constituted through intensive academic study, *British Journal of Educational Psychology*, 64, 161–78.

Entwistle, N and Ramsden, P (1983) *Understanding Student Learning*, Croom Helm, London.

Erickson, G and Meyer, K (1998) Performance assessment tasks in science: what are they assessing?, in K Tobin and B Fraser (eds.), *International Handbook of Science Education*, Kluwer Publishing Co.

Fairbank, J K (1992) *China – A New History*, Harvard University Press, Cambridge, Mass.

Fazey, J A and Marton, F (2002) Understanding the space of experiential variation, *Active Learning in Higher Education*, 3, 234–50.

Fensham, P (1997) Personal communication.

Fleming, W and Rutherford, R (1984) Recommendations for learning: rhetoric and reaction, *Studies in Higher Education*, 9, 17–26.

Fölsing, A (1996) *Albert Einstein: En biografi* (Albert Einstein: A Biography), Nora, Nya Doxa.

Forsén, B (1995) Från plattform till personlig praktisk yrkesteori. Göteborgs universitet, Institutionen för socialt arbete (From platform to personal practical professional theory.), Göteborg University, Göteborg.

Fransson, A (1977) On qualitative differences in learning: IV – effects of intrinsic and extrinsic motivation and test anxiety on process and outcome, *British Journal of Educational Psychology*, 47, 244–57.

Gambetter, D (1988) Can we trust?, in D Gambetter (ed.), *Trust, Making and Breaking and Relations*, Basil Blackwell, New York.

Gardner, H (1987) *The Mind's New Science*, Basic Books, New York.

Gerdman, A (1989) *Klient-paraktikant-handledare* (Client-intern-supervisor), Wahlström and Widstrand, Stockholm.

Gibbs, G (1992) *Improving the Quality of Student Learning*, Technical and Educational Services Ltd, Bristol.

Gibbs, G, Morgan, A and Taylor, E (1984) The world of the learner, in F Marton, D Hounsell and N Entwistle (eds.), *The Experience of Learning*, Scottish Academic Press, Edinburgh, pp. 165–88.

Giorgi, A (1986) A phenomenological analysis of descriptions of concepts of learning obtained from a phenomenographic perspective, *Publikationer från institutionen för pedagogik, Göteborgs universitet*, 18.

Gonczi, A, Hager, P and Oliver, L (1990) *Establishing Competency-Based Standards in the Professions*, NOOSR Research Paper No. 1. Department of Employment, Education and Training, Canberra.

Goodstein, D and Goodstein, J (1996) *Feynman's lost lecture: The motion of planets around the sun*, Jonathan Cape, London.

Graham, P A, Lyman, R W and Trow, M (1995) Accountability of colleges and universities, an essay.

Gran, B (1997) *Problem-baserad inlärning inom grundskollärarutbildningen. Pedagogisk-psykologiska problem: G34* (Problem based learning in teacher education), Lunds Universitet, Lärarhögskolan.

Granovetter, M (1973) The strength of weak ties, *The American Journal of Sociology*, 78 (6), 583–602.

Gruber, H E (1974) *Darwin on Man*, Wildwood House, London.

Gurwitsch, A (1964) *The Field of Consciousness*, Duquesne University Press, Pittsburgh.

Gustavsson, S (1971) *Debatten om forskningen och samhället* (The debate on research and society), Almqvist and Wiksell, Stockholm.

Gustavsson, S (1997) Varför inte lägga ned universiteten?, in S Dahl (ed.), Kunskap så det räcker? (Why Not Do Away with the Universities?), Saco, Stockholm, pp. 103–132.

Hallett (1997) Top-down, bottom-up: developing an educational quality assurance System: the Experience of the Total Quality Improvement Project (TQIP) at Victoria University of Technology, 1993–1995, in J Bowden and J Sachs (eds.), *Quality Management of University Teaching and Learning*, Canberra, DEETYA: Internet address: http://www.deetya.gov.au/divisions/hed/operations/Bowden/Cha.htm.

Hannertz, U, Liljestroöm, R and Löfgren, O (eds.) (1982) *Kultur och medvetande.* (Culture and Consciousness), Stockholm, Akademilitteratur

Hanson, N R (1958) *Patterns of Discovery*, Cambridge Unversity Press, Cambridge.

Harvey, L (1993) Employer satisfaction: interim report, presented to the Quality in Higher Education 24-hour Seminar, University of Warwick, December.

Harvey, L, Burrows, A and Green, D (1993) Someone who can made an impression: report of the QHE employers' survey of qualities of higher education graduates, in L Harvey (ed.), *Quality Assessment in Higher Education: Collected Pepers of the QHE Project*, QHE, Birmingham.

Harvey, L and Green, D (1993) Defining quality, *Assessment and Evaluation in Higher Education*, 18, 9–34.

Hattie, J and March, H W (1996) The relationship between research and teaching, Paper presented at the AERA Annual Conference, New York, April.

Hempel, C (1996) Vetenskapsteori, Lund, Studentditteratur (Philosophy of Science).

Higher Education Council (1992) *Higher Education: Achieving Quality*, AGPS, Canberra.

Hofstadter, D R (1979) *Gödel, Escher, Bach: An eternal golden braid*, The Harvester Press, London.

Hounsell, D (1997) Learning and essay-writing, in F Marton, D Hounsell and N Entwistle (eds.), *The Experience of Learning,* 3rd edn., pp. 106–25, Scottish Academic Press, Edinburgh.

Houston, W R (1985) Competency-based teacher education, in T Husen and T Postlethwaite (eds.), *The International Encyclopedia of Education: Research and Studies*, Pergamon Press, Oxford.

Humphrey, S (1992) A national skills recognition system – setting standards and establishing credentials, *In Education in the 1990s: Competencies, Credentialism, Competitiveness?*, Australian Government Publishing Service, Canberra.

Husserl, E (1970) *The Crisis of European Sciences and Transcendental Phenomenology*, Northwestern University Press, Evanston.

Inglis, R, Dall'Alba, G and Broadbent, A (1993) Comparative evaluation of a teaching innovation in accounting education: intensive learning in a seminar format, *Accounting Education*, 2 (3), 181–99.

Jacobsen, A (1998) Kvalitetsutviklingsprojektet Faglig Sammenhang (The quality development project 'Professional contexts'), Institute of Technology and Social Sciences, Technical University of Denmark, manuscript.

Jaeger, R M and Tittle, C K (1980) *Minimum Competency Achievement Testing: Motives, Models, Measures and Consequences*, McCutchan, Berkeley.

Jessup, G (1989) The emerging model of vocational education and training, in J Burke (ed.), *Competency-based Education and Training*, Falmer Press, London.

Jessup, G (1991) *Outcomes: NVQs and the Emerging Model of Education and Training*, Falmer Press, London.

Johansson, B, Marton, F and Svensson, L (1985) An approach to describing learning as a change between qualitatively different conceptions, in A L Pines and T H West (eds.), *Cognitive Structure and Conceptual Change*, Academic Press, New York, pp. 233–57.

Johnson, B (1992) *Polarity Management*, HRD Press Inc. Amherst, Massachusetts.

Johnson, C (1997) Personal communication, Seminar, at Brunel University, School of Education, Twickenham, June.

Johnston, H N (1992) The universities and competency-based standards, in D Anderson (ed.), *Higher Education and the Competency Movement*, Centre for Continuing Education at the Australian National University, Canberra.

Keller, E G (1983) *A Feeling for the Organism: The Life and Work of Barbara McClintock*, Freeman, New York.

Kerr, C (1982) *The Uses of the University*, 3rd edn., Harvard University Press, Cambridge, Mass.

Kerr, R and Booth, B (1977) Skill acquisition in elementary school children and schema theory, in D M Landers and R W Christina (eds.), *Psychology of Behaviour and Sport* vol. 2, Human Kinetic, Champaign, Ill, pp. 243–47.

Kinsman, M (1992) Competency-based education in TAFE, in D Anderson (ed.), *Higher Education and the Competency Movement*, Centre for Continuing Education at the Australian National University, Canberra, pp. 25–49.

Kjellgren, K. Ahlner, J, Dahlgren, L O and Haglund, L (eds.) (1993) *Problembaserad inlärning – erfarenheter från Hälsouniversitetet* (Problem based learning), Lund, Studentlitteratur.

Kuhn, T S (1970) *The Structure of Scientific Revolutions*, 2nd edn., The University of Chicago Press, Chicago.

Laurillard, D (1993) *Rethinking University Teaching: A Framework for the Effective Use of Educational Technology*, Routledge, London.

Lave, J (1988) *Cognition in Practice*, Cambridge University Press, Cambridge.

Lave, J (1996) Teaching, as learning, in practice, *Mind, Culture and Activity,* 3, 149–64.

Lave, J and Wenger, E (1991) *Situated Learning: Legitimate Peripheral Participation*, Cambridge University Press, New York.

Lawrence, P A and Lorsch, J (1986) *Organization and Environment*, 2nd edn., Harvard Business School Press, Boston, Mass.

Linder, C (1997) Personal communication.

Lines, R (1997) Personal communication.

Ludvigsen, S (1997) The transition from student to doctor – what are the learning implications? Paper presented at the Third International Conference on Learning in Medicine, Oslo, June.

Lukes, S (1973) *Émile Durkheim: His Life and Work*, Penguin Books, London.

Lybeck, L (1981) *Arkimedes i klassen: En ämnespedagogisk berättelse* (Archimedes in the class-room), Acta Universitatis Gothoburgensis, Göteborg.

Mansfield, B (1989) Competence and standards, in J Burke (ed.), *Competency-based Education and Training,* Falmer Press, London.

Martinsson, M (1996) Studier av matematiskt tänkande (Studies in mathematical thinking), manuscript.

Marton, F (1967) *Prov och evaluering inom den akademiska utbildningen (UPIVI)* (Tests and evaluation in higher education), Universitetskanslerämbetet.

Marton, F (1974) Inlärning och studiefärdighet (Study skills and learning), *Rapporter från Pedagogiska institutionen, Göteborgs universitet*, nr 121.

Marton, F (1975) On non-verbatim learning. I: Level of processing and level of outcome, *Scandinavian Journal of Psychology*, 16, 273–79.

Marton, F (1983) Beyond individual differences in learning, *Educational Psychology*, 3, 291–305.

Marton, F (1994a) On the structure of teachers' awareness, in J Bowden and E Walsh (eds.), *Phenomenographic Research: Variation in Method*, EQARD – RMIT, Melbourne, pp. 89–100.

Marton, F (1996) Seminar presentation, RMIT, October.

Marton, F (1998) Towards a theory of quality in higher edication, in B Dart and G Boulton-Lewis (eds.), *Training and Learning in Higher Education: From Theory to Practice*, ACER, Melbourne.

Marton, F, Asplund-Carlsson, M and Halász, L (1992) Differences in understanding and the use of reflective variation in reading, *British Journal of Educational Psychology*, 62, 1–16.

Marton, F, Beaty, E and Dall'Alba, G (1993) Conceptions of learning, *International Journal of Educational Research*, 19, 277–300.

Marton, F and Booth, S (1996) The learner's experience of learning, in D R Olson and N torrance (eds.), *The Handbook of Education and Human Development: New Models of Learning, Teaching and Schooling*, Blackwell, Oxford, pp. 534–64.

Marton, F and Booth, S (1997) *Learning and Awareness*, Mahwah, N J, Lawrence Erlbaum.

Marton, F, Dall'Alba, G and Tse, L K (1992) Solving the paradox of the Asian learner, paper presented at the Fourth Asian Regional Congress of Cross-Cultural Psychology, January 3–7, Kathmandu, Nepal.

Marton, F and Dahlgren, L O (2978) Students' conceptions of subject matter: an aspect of learning and teaching in higher education, *Studies in Higher Education*, 3, 25–35.

Marton, F, Fensham, P and Chaiklin, S (1994) A Nobel's eye view of scientific intuition: discussions with the Nobel prize-winners in Physics, Chemistry, and Medicine (1970–1986), *International Journal of Science Education*, 16, 457–73.

Marton, F, Hounsell, D and Entwistle, N J (1997) *The Experience of Learning*, 2nd edn., Scottish Academic Press, Edinburgh.

Marton, F and Marton, S (1997) The University of Learning or The University of Politics, paper presented at the conference 'What kind of University?', London, June.

Marton, F, Runesson, U, Prosser, M and Trigwell, K (1997) Teaching and Learning Science: Teachers' Perceptions of Problem Solving in University Science Courses, paper presented at the 7th European Conference for Research on Learning and Instruction, Athens, Greece, August.

Marton, F and Säljö, R (1976) Qualitative differences in learning I: outcome and process, *British Journal of Educational Psychology*, 46, 115–27.

Marton, F, Watkins, D, and Tang, C (1997) Discontinuities and continuities in the experience of learning: an interview study of high-school students in Hong Kong, *Learning and Instruction*, 7, 21–48.

Marton, F and Wenestam, C-G (1988) Qualitative differences in retention when a text is read several times, in M M Gruneberg, P E Morris and R N Sykes (eds.), *Practical Aspects of Memory: Current Research and Issues*, vol. 2, Wiley, Chichester, pp. 370–376.

Marton, S (1997) *Changes in Swedish Higher Education Policy*, Norwegian Centre in Organization and Management, Bergen.

Marton, S (1998) Personal communication.

May, M (1997) Conceptual understanding of engineering courses: cognitive and didactic aspects, paper presented at the 7th European Conference for Research on Learning and Instruction, Athens.

Mayer, E (1992) Employment-related key competencies for post-compulsory education and training, A discussion paper, Melbourne Ministry of Education and Training.

Mayr, F (1982) *The Growth of Biological Thought*, Havard University Press, Cambridge, Mass.

Moxley, S E (1979) Schema: The Variability of Practice Hypothesis, *Journal of Motor Behaviour*, 2 (1), 65–70.

Nakhleh, M and Mitchell, R (1993) Concept learning versus problem solving: there is a difference, *Journal of Chemical Education*, 70.

Newble, D I and Clarke, R M (1985) The approaches to learning of students in a traditional and in an innovative problem-based school, *Medical Education*, vol. 20, pp. 267–73.

Newble, D, Jolly, B and Wakeford, R (1994) Background to the conference and issues in certification and recertification, in D Newble, B Jolly and R Wakeford (eds.), *The Certification and Recertification of Doctors: Issues in the Assessment of Clinical Competence*, Cambridge University Press, Cambridge.

Newman, J M (1873) *The Idea of a University*, Doubleday, New York. Papastephanou, M (in press) University on multiversity? What is *left* of German idealism, in T Belghazi (ed.), *The Idea of the University*, Mohammed V University Press, Rabat.

Parsons, C (1997) Young people's conceptions of economic phenomena, unpublished Mphil thesis, University of London.

Patrick, K (1998) Teaching and learning: the construction of th object of study, unpublished PhD thesis, the University of Melbourne.

Pfundt, H and Duit, R (1994) *Bibliography students alternative frameworks and science education*, 3rd edn., Institute for Science Education, Kiel.

Piaget, J and Garcia, R (1989) *Psychogenesis and the history of science*, Columbia University Press, New York.

Pierce, C S (1931) *Collected Papers*, Harvard University Press, Cambridge, Mass.

Polanyi, M (1958) *Personal Knowledge*, Routledge and Kegan Paul, London.

Pong, W Y (1998) The inter-contextual and intra-contextual variation in the understanding of two economic themes – price and trade – among Canadian high-school students, PhD thesis in progress.

Popham, W J (1978) *Criterion-Referenced Measurement*, Prentice-Hall, Englewood Cliffs, New Jersey.

Powell, W W (1990) Neither market nor hierarchy: network forms of organisation, *Research in Organisational Behaviour*, 12, 295–336.

Pramling, I (1986) The origin of the child's idea of learning through practice, *European Journal of Education*, 3, 31–46.

Pramling, I (1990) *Learning to Learn*, Springer Verlag, New York.

Prosser, M (1994) Some experiences of using phenomenographic research methodology in the context of research in teaching and learning, in J A Bowden and E Walsh (eds.), *Phenomenographic Research: Variations in Method: The Warburton Symposium* RMIT, Melbourne, pp. 31–43.

Prosser, M and Millar, R (1989) The 'how' and the 'what' of learning physics, *European Journal of Psychology of Education*, 4, 513–28.

Pusey, M (1992) Canberra changes its mind – the new mandarins, in J Carroll and R Manne (eds.), *Shutdown*, The Text Publishing Company, Melbourne, pp. 38–48.

Ramsden, P (1984) The context of learning, in F Marton *et al*. (eds.), The Experience of Learning, Edinburgh, Scottish Academic Press, pp. 144–64.

Ramsden, P (1991) A performance indicator of teaching quality in higher education: the Course Experience Questionnaire, *Studies in Higher Education*, 16 (2), 129–50.

Ramsden, P (1992) *Learning to Teach in Higher Education*, Routledge, London.

Rothblatt, S (1997) *The Modern University and its Discontents: The Fate of Newman's Legacies in Britain and America*, Cambridge University Press, Cambridge.

Rovio-Johansson, A (1998) On the educational constitution of differing meanings of the content of teaching in higher education, PhD thesis in progress.

Russell, C (1993) *Academic Freedom*, Routledge, London.

Rüegg, W. (1992) Themes, in H de Ridder-Symoens (ed.), *A History of the University in Europe vol. I: Universities in the Middle Ages*, Cambridge University Press, Cambridge, pp. 3–34.

Sachs, L (1983) *Evil Eye or Bacteria: Turkish Migrant Women and Swedish Health Care*, Stockholm Studies in Social Anthropology, Stockholm.

Sachs, J and Ramsden, P (1995) Introduction: the experience of quality in higher education symposium, in J Sachs, P Ramsden and L Phillips (eds.), *The Experience of Quality in Higher Education Symposium*, Griffith University, Brisbane.

Säljö, R (1975) *Qualitative Differences in Learning as a Function of the Learner's Conception of the Task*, Acta Universitatis Gothoburgensis, Göteborg.

Säljö, R (1979) Learning in the learner's perspective, I: some common-sense conceptions, *Reports from the Department of Education, Göteborg University*, 76.

Säljö, R (1982) *Learning and Understanding: A Study of Differences in Constructing Meaning from a Text*, Acta Universitatis Gothoburgensis, Göteborg.

Sandberg, J (1994) *Human Competence at Work: An Interpretative Approach*, BAS, Göteborg.

Sandberg, J (1997) The nature of collective competence and its development, paper presented at the 14th Nordic Conference on Business Studies, Bodo, 14–17 August.

Selley, N (1989) Philosophies of science and their relation to scientific processes and the science curriculum, in J Wellington (ed.), *Skills and Processes in Science Education*, Routledge, London, pp. 83–88.

Skinner, B F (1953) *Science and Human Behaviour*, Macmillan, New York.

Smedslund, J (1953) The problem of 'what is learned?', *Psychological Review*, 60, 157–8.

Sorrentino, S A and Owoc, C S (1996) *Nursing Assistant Review for Competency Evaluation*, Mosby Lifeline, St Louis.

Spady, W G (1977) Competency-based education: a bandwagon in search of a definition, *Educational Researcher*, 6 (1), 9–14.

Spiegelberg, H (1982) *The Phenomenological Movement: A Historical Introduction*, 3rd edn., Martinus Nijhoff, The Hague.

Stephanou, A (1997a) Using the Rasch model to study large scale physics examinations in Australia, paper presented at the 9th International Objective Measurement Workshop, Chicago, March.

Stephanou, A (1997b) The measurement of conceptual understanding in physics, internal report to the Centre for the Study of Higher Education, the University of Melbourne.

Stephens, M D and Roderick, G W (1975) *Universities for a Changing World: The Role of the University in the Late Twentieth Century*, Douglas, David and Charles, Canada.

Stephenson, J (1992) Capability and quality in higher education, in J Stephenson and S Weil (eds.), *Quality in Learning: A Capability Approach in Higher Education*, Kogan Page, London, pp. 1–9.

Stephenson, J and Weil, S (eds.) (1992a) *Quality in Learning: A Capability Approach in Higher Education*, Kogan Page, London, pp. 10–18.

Stephenson, J and Weil, S (1992b) Four themes in educating for capability, in J Stephenson and S Weil (eds.), *Quality in Learning: A Capability Approach in Higher Education*, Kogan Page, London, pp. 10–18.

Stinner, A (1994) The storey of force: from Aristotle to Einstein, *Physics Education*, 29, 77–85.

Strömdahl, H (1996) *On Mole and Amount of Substance: A Study of the Dynamics of Concept Formation and Concept Attainment*, Acta Universitatis Gothoburgensis, Göteborg.

Svensson, L (1976) *Study Skill and Learning*, Göteborg Acta Universitatis, Gothoburgensis.

Svensson, L (1984) Människobilden i INOM-gruppens forskning: den lärande människan (The image of man in the research of the INOM-group: man as learner). *Reports from the Department of Education and Educational Research, Göteborg University*, 3.

Székely, L (1950) Productive processes in learning and thinking, *Acta Psychologica,* 7, 379–407.

Taylor, C (1994) Assessment for measurement or standards: the peril and promise of large-scale assessment reform, *American Educational Research Journal*, 31 (2), 231–62.

Taylor, E and Morgan, A R (1986) Developing skill in learning, paper presented at the AERA Annual Conference, San Francisco.

Terwilliger, J (1997) Semantics, psychometrices, and assessment reform: a close look at 'authentic' assessments, *Educational Researcher*, 26, 24–27.

Thomas, L (1996) Economic experience and young people's awareness of the economic system, in W Walsted (ed.), *Secondary Economics and Business Education: New Developments in the United Kingdom, the United States and other nations*, Economics and Business Education Association, UK.

Thomas, L and Wood, K (1997) How can research help classroom teachers? – an illustration of work on price, in preparation.

Thomas, L (1985) The core of Economics – a Psychological Viewpoint, in G Atkinson (ed.), *Teaching Economics*, Heinemann Educational, London.

Tresolini, C P, Shugers, D A, Storaasli, A G and Lee, L S (1994) Expanding the biomedical model: case studies of five medical schools, paper presented at the annual meeting of the American Educational Research Association, New Orleans, Louisiana.

Trigwell, K and Prosser, M (1996) Congruence between intention and strategy in science teachers' approaches to teaching, *Higher Education*, 32, 77–87.

Trigwell, K, Prosser, M and Waterhouse, F (1999) Relations between teachers' approaches to learning, *Higher Education*, 37, 57–70.

Tullberg, A (1998) *Teaching 'the mole': A Phenomenographic Inquiry into the Didactics of Chemistry*, Acta Universitatis Gothoburgensis, Göteborg.

Tuxworth, E (1989) Competency-based education and training: background and origins, in Burke, J W (ed.), *Competency-based Education and Training*, Falmer Press, London.

Tydén, T (1997) Den tredje uppgiften är två för mycket (The third task is two too much), *Universitetsläraren*, 18, 14–15.

Ueno, N, Arimoto, N and Fujita, G (1990) Conceptual models and points of view: learning via making a new stage, paper presented at the annual meeting of the AERA, Boston, April.

van den Vleuten, C (1998) Towards new paradigms in higher education, keynote address at the 50th Bi-annual Conference of the Association of European Universities, London Guildhall University, May.

van Rossum, E J and Schenk, S M (1984) The relationship between learning conception, study strategy and learning outcome, *British Journal of Educational Psychology*, 54, 73–83.

Velde, C and Svensson, L (1996) The conception of competence in relation to learning processes and change at work, 4th Conference on Learning and Research in Working Life, Steyr, Austria, July.

Walsh, E, Dall'Alba, G, Bowden, J, Martin, E, Marton, F, Masters, G, Ramsden, P and Stephanou, A (1993) Physics students' understanding of relative speed: a phenomenographic study, *Journal of Research in Science Teaching*, 30, 1133–48.

Watson, D J (1968) *The Double Helix*, Weidenfeld and Nicolson, London.

Wenestam, C-G (1980) *Qualitative Differences in Retention*, Acta Universitatis Gothoburgensis, Göteborg.

Werner, H (1948) *Comparative Psychology of Mental Development*, Interantional Universities Press, New York.

Wertheim, M (1996) Heavenly geometry, *The Australian Review of Books*, 31, 9–10, October.

Wertheimer, M (1945) *Productive Thinking*, Harper and Row, New York.

Whelan, G (1988) Improving medical students' clinical problem-solving, in P Ramsden (ed.), *Improving Learning: New Perspectives*, Kogan Page, London, pp. 199–214.

Wiggins, G (1989) Teaching to the (authentic) test, *Educational Leadership*, 46, 41–47.

Wikström, Å (1987) *Functional Progamming Using Standard ML*, Prentice-Hall, Hemel Hempstead.

Wistedt, I (1997) Assessing student learning in gender inclusive tertiary mathematics and physics education, manuscript.

Woods, Donald R (1994) *Problem-based Learning: How to Gain the Most from PBL*, D R Woods, Waterdown O N Canada.

Woodward, C (1989) Art and elegance in the synthesis of organic compounds: Robert Burns Woodward, in D B Wallace and H E Gruber (eds.), *Creative People at Work*, Oxford University Press, New York, pp. 227–53.

Index